WINNING THE WEST WITH WORDS

Winning the West with Words

LANGUAGE AND CONQUEST
IN THE LOWER GREAT LAKES

JAMES JOSEPH BUSS

University of Oklahoma Press : Norman

Chapter 5 of this work appeared earlier, in somewhat different form, in "'They found and left her an Indian': Gender, Race, and the Whitening of Young Bear," *Frontiers: A Journal of Women Studies* 29, nos. 2–3 (2008): 1–30, and is reprinted here with permission of the University of Nebraska Press, Lincoln.

Library of Congress Cataloging-in-Publication Data

Buss, James Joseph.
    Winning the West with words : language and conquest in the lower Great Lakes / James Joseph Buss.
        p.   cm.
    Includes bibliographical references and index.
    ISBN 978-0-8061-4214-2 (hardcover : alk. paper)   1. Pioneers—Great Lakes Region (North America)—History.   2. Frontier and pioneer life—Great Lakes Region (North America)   3. Indians of North America—Great Lakes Region (North America)—History—19th century.   4. Land settlement—Great Lakes Region (North America)—History—19th century.   5. United States—Territorial expansion—Social aspects.   I. Title.
    F551.B87 2011
    977'.02—dc22

                                                                        2011012762

The paper in this book meets the guidelines for permanence and durability of the Committee on Production Guidelines for Book Longevity of the Council on Library Resources, Inc. ∞

1 2 3 4 5 6 7 8 9 10

Contents

Illustrations

Introduction

Clearing the Middle Ground for American Pioneers

The white settler has merely moved into an uninhabited waste; he
does not feel that he is committing a wrong, for he knows perfectly well that the land is really owned by no one. . . . The settler
ousts no one from the land; if he did not chop down the trees,
hew out the logs for a building, and clear the ground for tillage,
no one else would do so. . . . this great continent could not have
been kept as nothing but a game preserve for squalid savages.

—Theodore Roosevelt, *The Winning of the West* (1889)

The middle ground is the place in between: in between cultures,
peoples, and in between empires and the nonstate world of villages. It is a place where many of the North American subjects
and allies of empires lived. It is the area between the historical foreground of European invasion and occupation and the
background of Indian defeat and retreat. . . . The real crisis and
the final dissolution of this world came when Indians ceased to
have the power to force whites onto the middle ground. Then the
desire of whites to dictate the terms of accommodation could be
given its head. As a consequence, the middle ground eroded.

—Richard White, *The Middle Ground* (1991)

In 1916, Hoosiers gathered across Indiana to celebrate their state's centennial. Communities organized fairs, marched in parades, and dramatized the pioneer era by way of elaborate outdoor pageants and parades.
In early October, state leaders invited fellow Hoosiers to join them in

1

Indianapolis to celebrate "Admission's Day." Organizers pronounced the celebration as the "two greatest civic weeks in all Indiana history." The festivities included an Olympiad; a flag drill performed by 30,000 local schoolchildren; speeches from Indiana governor Samuel Ralston, President Woodrow Wilson, and former president and Supreme Court chief justice William Howard Taft; and the much anticipated Pageant of Indiana.[1]

Nearly 3,000 actors and supernumeraries spread across the grassy outdoor stage at Indianapolis's Riverside Park, as the pageant opened with an "introduction" to the early history of the Hoosier state. In the opening scene, American Indians, as played by white actors, and a man representing French explorer Robert Cavelier Sieur de La Salle moved across the large lawn as they re-created the earliest tours by Europeans of the lower Great Lakes. As they exited, another group of Indians appeared as allies to British officers. After that, Indians graced the stage again, this time as friends of Hoosier hero George Rogers Clark. The tempo now quickened, as decades of history unfolded in mere minutes. The portrayal of this early period came to a climax when an actor playing William Henry Harrison accompanied a supporting cast of troops in a dramatization of the Battle of Tippecanoe. Viewing this spectacle was a crowd that numbered in the tens of thousands; not since the days of Buffalo Bill Cody's Wild West show had Americans enjoyed such a large-scale reenactment of Indian and white conflict.

Newspaper reporters observed that although "the savage red man [*sic*] gave their war whoops, encouraged by the Prophet," they inevitably fell to the marksmanship of American soldiers. One writer insisted that the Prophet, encouraged by drunken bravado, initiated the campaign, which sounded the death knell for Indians across the region. He was right, as far as the pageant organizers were concerned; from that moment on, Indians disappeared from the narrative—the pageant moved on to the story of Indiana's white pioneers. The fourth act, "The State of Indiana," focused on the transformation of the region from an ambiguous space filled with scattered settlers to a political entity racing toward development. On the huge outdoor stage, groups of "pioneers, backwoodsmen, Quakers, farmers, and soldiers" assembled to form the outline of the state of Indiana, as Lady Liberty suddenly appeared perched

atop a larger-than-life black stallion and brandishing a giant American
flag. She wore a white robe and a red cloak draped over her shoulders,
so that it whipped behind her as she crossed the stage. Eighteen other
women, also on horseback, followed, each representing one of the other
eighteen states at the time of Indiana's admission.[2]

The cavalcade of horses and riders approached the pioneer men and
women. At precisely that moment, a young girl emerged from the crowd.
"Lady Liberty" rode over to the child and offered her a robe and shield.
The girl took them, donned the robe, mounted a horse of her own, and
galloped about the stage. From seemingly nowhere, two hundred girls
draped in green and blue gowns materialized and sang "The Hymn to
Indiana." Hoosier author Meredith Nicholson pronounced, "No son or
daughter of the Hoosier commonwealth, no one living within the state's
borders, should fail to see this moving, stirring visualization of the history of Indiana."[3]

Indiana had caught centennial fever. In Bloomington, Indiana University students joined the local community to witness a parade "led by
a band of Indian warriors in full paint and riding bareback." Actually,
the "warriors" consisted of local white community leaders "playing Indian." Volunteers "stripped to the waist," "wore long hair," and splashed
themselves with bright hues of face and body paint. One local reporter
mindlessly believed they "would have done justice to the most blood-
thirsty band of redskins that ever roamed the forests" of southern Indiana. Men and women donned pioneer costumes and marched behind
them. Other symbols of American progress followed: a prairie schoo-
ner, a hand-pump fire engine, and a scene meant to dramatize Indiana's
involvement in the abolitionist movement (white men and women in
blackface running from slave masters). The entire spectacle ended with
"Uncle Sam, clad in stripes and carrying a large flag."[4]

The Pageant of Indiana, the Bloomington parade, and hundreds of
other centennial performances across the state shared a common scene
of erasure whereby Native Americans symbolically or physically exited
the stage. Moreover, despite real violence between whites and Native
peoples that characterized the late-eighteenth- and early-nineteenth-
century settlement in the lower Great Lakes, these pageants, parades,
and other forms of civic celebration portrayed the erasure of indigenous

communities as a passive and inevitable consequence of settlement. Even
in the case of the Pageant of Indiana, where Indian warriors and white
soldiers clashed, the battle was merely followed by the absence of Native
people (women, men, and children) from the rest of the drama. In other
words, the stories told by Hoosiers during their centennial celebrations
were narratives of conquest that underplayed the very action of conquest.
Instead, they highlighted the rise of state institutions and valorized the
role of early Americans in establishing "civilized" governments in the
West. This study attempts to deconstruct this well-trodden narrative of
statehood development in order to reveal a history of subjugation and
dispossession that underlies that oft-told history of American progress.[5]

Scholars have long shown how knowledge and narration can be used
as weapons of domination.[6] Nearly every schoolchild has heard, "The
victors tell the story of the vanquished." But narrating conquest has real
consequences for real people. Thus this study views historical interpretation as more than a simple recounting of the past. It examines how
people in the past used historical interpretation as a tool of the colonial
project itself. Scholar Nicholas Thomas has outlined the role of culture
in the process of colonialism. "Colonialism has always, equally importantly and deeply, been a cultural process; its discoveries and trespasses
are imagined and energized through signs, metaphors, and narratives."[7]
This book takes seriously the role of language and the cultural expressions of language—treaty council protocol, settler petitions, letters,
paintings, newspaper articles, captivity narratives, county histories, expositions and exhibits, and centennial pageants and parades—as linguistic forms of domination. It accepts historian Patricia Nelson Limerick's nearly two-decade-old challenge to "study words about the West
as artifacts, products, even symptoms of American culture, not simply
as records of the 'facts' of Western history."[8] Simultaneously, it explores
the ways that cultural conquest provided opportunities for subjugated
peoples to turn what Limerick has termed a "shiftiness of language"—
the "verbal behavior" employed by Americans to "justify, promote, sell,
entice, cover up, evade, defend, deny, congratulate, persuade, and reas-
sure" themselves about their role in western conquest—on its head and
subvert the colonial system.[9] To accomplish these goals, this book has become an amalgam of disciplinary approaches. It borrows from the work

of geographers, literary studies scholars, anthropologists, and historians in order to tease apart the historical role of language in the growth of an American empire in the lower Great Lakes.

A study of this region promises to shed light on the larger process of American colonialism that took place elsewhere. Since the early nineteenth century, the popularized image of the white yeoman pioneer, which first developed east of the Mississippi, has propped up a powerful American narrative about western expansion, an inclusive American democracy, and unlimited national progress while disempowering and dispossessing America's indigenous peoples by historicizing them and writing them out of a narrative of modernization and progress. The image of this process may perhaps best be captured in John Gast's painting *American Progress* (1872), which depicts a half-clad, spectral woman—representing Progress—floating across the landscape, ushering technology, education, civilization, and white people westward. Whites and Indians did not share equally (for Indians, not at all) in this story, as

George A. Crofutt. *American Progress.* Chromolithograph, ca. 1873, after an 1872 painting by John Gast. Courtesy of the Library of Congress.

Gast consigned the latter to a space in the marginalized lower left-hand corner of the canvas. They appear destined to exit the scene entirely, as do a herd of buffalo pictured above them. Gast's painting demonstrates the way that Americans viewed conquest as a passive act. Nowhere in the painting do whites and Indians interact; rather, Native people simply flee in the wake of white advancement.

For *Winning the West with Words*, the myth of the vanished Indian and abandoned landscape was, and continues to be, grounded in the larger belief that Native peoples simply ceased to exist in the lower Great Lakes at the beginning of the nineteenth century. For the lower Great Lakes this moment of Native dispossession and victimless settlement—what I refer to as the clearing of the middle ground—became the region's creation story. Over the past one hundred years, this moment of erasure (a form of literary genocide) has marked a transitional moment from the region's colonial past to one of statehood development. Scholars have spent the last two or three decades rewriting this story, reminding us that Native Americans simply did not vanish after the War of 1812 or even the Indian Removal Act (1830).[10] Hard-and-fast dates from the removal period should indicate as much: soldiers did not usher the Potawatomi along the Trail of Death until 1838, the first major group of Miami families to leave Indiana did not do so until 1839, and the Wyandot Nation of Ohio did not depart from the Buckeye State until 1843. Even more surprising perhaps to those who do not study the region, some American Indians, including a large number of Miami families in central Indiana, never left the lower Great Lakes. Their very presence undermines the validity of the region's creation story. Yet the type of narrative dramatized in the Indiana Pageant persists, as Americans still celebrate the icon of the American pioneer as a figure who marched steadfast into an untamed and *uninhabited* wilderness.

This book begins in the late eighteenth century, as Americans during that time were already trying to imagine a cleared landscape. During the 1820s and 1830s, the story of the vanished Indian and stalwart pioneer gained traction, as new opportunities for telling the story emerged. This period—long exalted as the "age of the common man," the Jacksonian era, the Market Revolution, a transportation revolution, and a period of religious reawakenings—both witnessed the expansion of American democracy and exposed the exclusionary nature of the nineteenth-century democratic movement.[11] In many ways the process of imagining a clean conquest of western lands and its people was simply that, an imagining. The 1820s and 1830s saw the beginnings of a communications revolution, and in this early American version of the information age, words carried greater and greater meaning.[12] Language could be employed at increased speed and with more weight as new means of communication created avenues for employing discursive practices as instruments of conquest. Verbal contests produced a new vocabulary for describing settlement, a new lexicon for describing what settlers were doing, and new meanings for the American enterprise of expanding the nation (birthing the roots of Manifest Destiny). Even literature of the early nineteenth century reflected an acknowledgment of the malleability of language and life on the frontier. In the highly popular 1843 publication *Adventures of Captain Simon Suggs*, the book's namesake declares his life's motto: "It is good to be shifty in a new country."[13]

In the lower Great Lakes, white settlers built their reputations on presenting themselves as honest pioneers living in a stable country, not backwoodsmen scrambling to survive. They also presented the region as empty, which required a creative and imaginary rerendering of what has been described as a middle ground. The idea of a middle ground employed in this study echoes Richard White's *The Middle Ground: Indians, Empires, and Republics in the Great Lakes Region, 1650–1815*.[14] Admittedly, my vision is not the same as that employed by White, who defined it as both a process of "mutual and creative misunderstandings" and a place— the *pays d'en haut* of the Great Lakes. But his description of a middle ground requiring a "rough balance of power, mutual need or a desire for what the other possesses, and an inability by either side to commandeer enough force to compel the other to change" is a valuable concept for this study. More important, White argues that the middle ground eroded following the War of 1812.[15] *Winning the West with Words* essentially chronicles this erosion as the "clearing of the middle ground."

This book differs greatly from White's work because it examines language and storytelling as its central themes. Few historians have taken seriously how the ability to shape the history of place can serve as a tool in extending the reach of a nation. In his groundbreaking study, historian

Coll Thrush examines the place-story of the city of Seattle. Place-stories, he argues, do more than simply recount the past; they constitute a process whereby communities past and present impart meaning on spaces by fashioning their creation stories. These stories have powerful interpretive consequences as they are used to extend colonial projects and verbally marginalize indigenous peoples, casting them as people of the past rather than the present. Thrush studies how this process unfolded in an urban area, but place-storytelling also occurred in the lower Great Lakes and often acted as a means of replacing a messy history of violent and incomplete conquest with a triumphal tale of development on the antebellum frontier.[16]

Although *Winning the West with Words* is essentially a study of language and the process of storytelling, it also is a history grounded in place. This book focuses exclusively on the lower Great Lakes, a region north of the Ohio River and south of the Great Lakes (the present-day states of Ohio, Indiana, and Illinois). But place and storytelling might not be entirely divorced from one another. By erecting what Stephen Aron has labeled "cartographies of colonialism" and periodizing the history of the region as pre- and postcolonial, American agents of empire have been able to shape the way that the past informs the present.[17] By grounding this study in place rather than following a group of people or depending on the elusive concept of the frontier, this approach provides an opportunity to analyze the power of creation narratives in shaping contemporary understandings of place. Anthropologist Keith Basso reminds us, "If place-making is a way of constructing the past, a venerable means of *doing* human history, it is also a way of constructing social traditions and, in the process, personal and social identities. We *are*, in a sense, the place-worlds we imagine."[18]

Some historians of the Midwest have employed the study of place and storytelling to yield insights into the history of the region. Essays in Andrew Cayton and Susan Gray's *The Identity of the American Midwest* demonstrate how "midwesterners had flattened the complicated and contested history of the Great Lakes and Ohio Valley regions into a linear narrative of unimpeded progress."[19] But historians of the Midwest tend to be constrained by the ways in which the discipline periodizes the past, as one group of historians examines the American antebellum era while another explores the Gilded Age and Progressive Era. *Winning the West with Words* seeks to bridge these periods and draw connections between them. In addition, it attempts to connect regional history to the making of a national identity.

The conclusions of historians studying other regions in the United States highlight the connections between local storytelling and national identity. In *Dispossession by Degrees*, Jean O'Brien demonstrates how seventeenth- and eighteenth-century New Englanders erected "narratives of Indian extinction."[20] More recently she has explored how northeasterners tried to excise American Indians from the historical narrative and supplant them with white settlers as the region's first inhabitants. O'Brien's concept of "firsting and lasting"—"that non-Indians were the first people to erect proper institutions of a social order worthy of notice" and that Native people were relegated to the past by denying them modernity—echoes throughout this book.[21]

Instead of dismissing stories like those embodied in the Pageant of Indiana or the Bloomington parade as the quaint yarns of yesteryear, *Winning the West with Words* seeks to examine how they have operated as symbolic moments that still inform our understanding of the region's history. The dispossession acted out in the Pageant of Indiana and chronicled by other historians is one example that reveals the underlying problem with the ways Americans have told and retold stories about the end of the moving frontier. By affixing a date or general period to the moment when American Indians left the lower Great Lakes, writers have historicized the region's indigenous peoples and exiled them to the past. Moreover, this banishment has left no room for the complicated realities of life in the region, where whites and Indians shared a physical space and often relied on one another for their livelihoods. As we will see in this book, when faced with situations in which the tidy story of pioneers moving into an abandoned landscape failed to describe the scene before them, settlers in the lower Great Lakes simply invented alternative fictionalized stories.

In fact, the very title of this book is adapted from a late-nineteenth-century narrative that creatively underplayed the realities of dispossession and conquest: Theodore Roosevelt's three-volume western epic *The Winning of the West* (1889–96). This romantic treatment of western settlement captured the sentiments of nineteenth-century Americans by declaring that great American pioneers simply had "moved into an uninhabited waste."[22] Roosevelt's history exemplifies what scholar Mary Louise Pratt has called a narrative of "anti-conquest." Although Pratt used the term to describe the works of European travel writers who employed "strategies of representation whereby European bourgeois subjects seek to secure their innocence in the same moment they assert European hegemony," such terminology might easily be used to describe the narratives of statehood development that emerged from the lower Great Lakes.[23]

These accounts of passive conquest resonate in Roosevelt's work, which claimed that American pioneers entered an empty landscape. It also can be seen in the slightly later work of historian Frederick Jackson Turner, whose famous essay came to dominate the scholarly debate for more than a century. In 1893, Turner, a young scholar from Wisconsin, articulated his image of western settlement in a paper delivered at the annual meeting of the American Historical Association in which he declared that the true genius of the American people rested in their systematic conquest of the West. Turner challenged the notion that Americans and Europeans shared a common past, common culture, or common experience. A prolonged struggle with the wilderness, he explained, had forged a new people. In other words, the frontier experience had made the United States exceptional. But few Indians appeared in Turner's frontier thesis. Instead, American pioneers toiled in the wilderness or on the frontier—spaces of hardship and real challenges but rarely places inhabited by real people.[24] Turner's thesis, like Roosevelt's multivolume work, acted as national narratives of anti-conquest by dismissing the active role of whites in dispossessing and disempowering Native people.[25]

To capture this elusive story, *Winning the West with Words* is broken into three parts, each of which explores a different stage in the production of conquest narratives that involved the clearing of the middle ground. Instead of presenting a new narrative for the nineteenth-century lower Great Lakes, this book might best be read as a collection of connected essays that attempt to deconstruct old narratives and highlight instances when those narratives were challenged. Part 1 begins with an examination of how Americans came to dictate the language of the middle ground. A decade of conflict included two embarrassing military defeats at the hands of Little Turtle's Indian confederacy and ended with General Anthony Wayne's victory along the banks of the Maumee River at the Battle of Fallen Timbers (1794). Thereafter, Americans stood ready to open the vast American West (at the time, an area extending only to the Mississippi River) for white settlement. But they were not in a position to dictate terms; the nation struggled in its infancy to gain the respect of its European counterparts, and the presence of British military posts scattered throughout the lower Great Lakes required a nuanced approach toward indigenous peoples who had once been British allies. Chapter 1 examines the changing rhetoric in American Indian diplomacy in the years between the Treaty of Greenville (1795) and the end of the War of 1812. This chapter seeks to clarify the argument set forth by Richard White that Americans came to believe that they could forever dictate the language of the middle ground after winning the physical war. Chapter 2 investigates how individuals both before and after the war tried to promote or report on the settlement of the region. From promotional materials to travel journals, individuals from a variety of backgrounds presented the lower Great Lakes as a territory ripe for settlement yet destined to endure clashes between civilization and savagery. This particular narrative held grave consequences for Americans who wanted to settle in the region, as it portrayed the frontier as a corruptible force that might degrade them. Consequently, settlers drafted numerous petitions begging for the government to aid them. A war of words ensued as settlers, land speculators, and politicians attempted to employ a "shiftiness in language" to define proper settlement.

Part 2 examines the rhetorical clearing of the middle ground and the opportunities created by this malleability of language for Native people to subvert removal attempts. Chapter 4 highlights the role of language in allowing the Wyandots of Ohio to elude removal for more than two decades. Although ultimately unsuccessful in preserving their lands in the Buckeye State, the Wyandots still used their knowledge of white verbal practices to thwart numerous removal agents. In chapter 5, we see how even those who opposed removal nevertheless participated in justifying the dispossession of the region's indigenous population. This chapter primarily focuses on the life of George Winter, an artist who traveled west to paint romanticized images of Great Lakes Indians before they could be displaced. An examination of Winter's life, alongside a study of northern Indiana in the 1830s, reveals the role of individuals in constructing and perpetuating narratives of conquest. A final chapter in part 2 seeks to explain how perceptions of race and gender played a role in recording and remembering the region's past. In particular this chapter examines the story of Frances Slocum, a woman who failed to fit the role of either white or Indian prescribed by white narrators.

Part 3, entitled "Remembering and Forgetting," explores the ways that late-nineteenth- and early-twentieth-century Americans commemorated their pioneer ancestors while trying to forget about Native peoples who once inhabited—and in some cases still inhabit—the lower Great Lakes. These chapters explore written histories, public performances, and community celebrations as sites of storytelling in order to demonstrate how the narrative of conquest, or anti-conquest, continued into the twentieth century and informed civic celebrations such as the Pageant of Indiana that opens this introduction. Chapter 6 examines local organizations, from Old Settler societies to state historical associations, to demonstrate the process by which the caricature of the pioneer emerged as a symbol of America's bygone years of innocence and simpler times. By the late nineteenth century these stories became standardized in popular county histories printed by some of the largest publishing houses in the region. Chapter 7 explores the role of this story in erasing an indigenous history of the lower Great Lakes through an examination of fair exhibitions, the printed word, and public speeches. As Americans in the lower Great Lakes sought to venerate their pioneer ancestors, they also struggled to hide stories that indicated both Americans and Indians ever co-inhabited the region after the War of 1812.

The epilogue attempts to connect the history of these narratives to the centennial celebrations of the early twentieth century. As the bicentennials for the two states being studied, Indiana (2016) and Illinois (2018), approach, it seems particularly important that we attempt to understand the consequences for how we commemorate or celebrate them. What does all this mean for historians today? How does our understanding, not of the past, but of how Americans have told the *story* of the past, change our understanding of these events and their meaning? The answers to these questions promise to inform the way we think about our histories and ourselves as active players in creating new place-stories.

The story of American settlement in the lower Great Lakes has been disputed for nearly two centuries. Easterners, westerners, and American Indians fought over the very ability to tell the story. At no point was the narrative of conquest—or anti-conquest—complete or unchangeable. Prophets, seemingly speaking from our present perspective of cultural relativity, existed and, indeed, fought on behalf of American Indians. Such stories provide hope that the stories of the past are still malleable. But we will also see that those who appeared to fight against dispossession helped create the narratives of anti-conquest that justified the very process of displacement that they sought to stop. The war of words is not over: Americans are haunted by ghosts from their past. As I hope this book illustrates, history is never fully written.

PART ONE

The Language of Conquest

The transactions that took place between the Indians and white people at Greenville are yet fresh in our minds. At that place we told each other that we would in the future be friends, doing all the good we could to each other, and raise our children in peace and quietness. These are yet the sentiments of your children, the Miamis.

—Little Turtle, quoted in Indianapolis *Western Speculator* (1811)

We shall push our trading houses, and be glad to see the good and influential individuals among [Great Lakes Indians] run in debt, because we observe that when these debts get beyond what the individuals can pay, they become willing to lop them off by a cession of lands. . . . But in the whole course of this, it is essential to cultivate their love.

—Thomas Jefferson to William Henry Harrison (1803)

The picture that is emerging here, of Indians forcing whites to play by their rules, is a misleading one, though, if it ignores the ability of the whites then to subvert, in a whole number of ways, the meaning the Indians gave to the event.

—David Murray, *Forked Tongues: Speech, Writing, and Representation in North American Indian Texts* (1991)

CHAPTER 1

"A Peace, Sincere and Lasting"

Treaties and the Eroding Language of the Middle Ground

The clearing of the middle ground happened in the American imagination long before it took place in practice. American officials had not always intended on pushing Indians westward; initially they sought to create a boundary between white and Indian spaces. Before the Treaty of Greenville in 1795, American officials and Indian leaders were even willing to compromise and accept each other's customs of diplomacy, but by the end of the War of 1812, American leaders (especially western ones) decided that cooperation ultimately impeded their goal of acquiring land and advancing white settlement. At the second Treaty of Greenville, concluded in 1814, federal agents no longer wished to accommodate Native interpretations of their mutual relationship. While physical violence had come to characterize this period, Native leaders and American diplomats also engaged in a war of words that helped shape the following 150 years of white and Indian history.

Almost two decades ago, the preeminent western historian Patricia Nelson Limerick argued that the "process of invasion, conquest, and colonization was the kind of activity that provoked shiftiness in verbal behavior."[1] For American diplomats and Indian leaders, treaty councils emerged as places where language and history mattered. These councils also provide historians with a place to trace a shiftiness in language that shaped the place-stories written by later Americans. To gauge the role of historical interpretation in shaping this relationship, we must first briefly explore American Indian policy in the years that preceded the 1795 Treaty of Greenville.

When violence erupted between Indians and Kentuckians along the

Ohio River in the 1780s, Secretary of War Henry Knox acknowledged that Indians possessed "the right of the soil," which prevented the United States from taking land without the Indians' "free consent, or by the right of conquest in case of a just war." He demanded that the United States "be influenced by reason" and formulate an Indian policy that adhered to the "fundamental laws of nature." By 1790, Knox had come to believe that the United States must accept the premise of an indigenous right to the soil as outlined by the Treaty of Fort Harmar. The treaty extended additional rights to Indians as it established a policy of punishing settlers who ignored boundaries and crossed onto Indian lands. Knox pushed American politicians to consider Indian policy as a diplomatic issue rather than a domestic problem.[2] Early Americans were unwilling to conduct their national experiment on an unjust acquisition of Indian lands. Instead, they turned toward Enlightenment fundamentals of justice in their push for expansion. These ideas informed the treaty councils that followed.

The council proceedings at Greenville in 1795 provided American officials the opportunity to gain legitimacy by exhibiting magnanimity in partaking in Native council ceremonies and accepting Native practices as equally lawful as their own. Americans also sought to gain the trust of Native leaders by acting in an honorable and benevolent fashion during the proceedings. Federal officials demanded that their western representatives to the councils set a positive example for their soldiers, white settlers, and Indians by stressing the principles of truth and honesty. Secretary of War Timothy Pickering instructed the head American official at Greenville, General Anthony Wayne, to make the Indians feel at "perfect liberty to speak their sentiments" and insisted that "*a rigid adherence to truth*" should govern the proceedings. Thereby, federal authorities hoped that this council would serve as a new model for future Indian relations and legitimize American claims.[3]

Many historians argue that little true negotiating took place at Greenville, but this view of the treaty council underplays the vital role that Native leaders took in shaping a shared historical memory for the region.[4] Stressing the treaty as the beginning of America's lust for Indian lands, too many scholars ignore the subtle moves made by both sides in defining their delicate relationship with one another. Leaders on both sides saw that the treaty offered a new beginning and marked an opportunity for Americans and Indians to construct a shared space where they could both live in peace.[5] In other words, American officials at the negotiations in Greenville were willing to allow Native leaders a voice in crafting a future direction for Indian-white relations.

Indian leaders entered the treaty talks at Greenville with a set of expectations based on their previous experiences with European diplomats. Native people had not always engaged in treaties, and the written compacts certainly had not always served as the basis for their relationship with others—economic systems of trade, intermarriages, and exchanges of gifts in ceremonies of reciprocity guided daily life much more than words inked on parchment. When they wished to befriend their indigenous neighbors in the years before American hegemony, European agents routinely had engaged in practices other than treaty councils. Often these included an incorporation of Native customs and practices into calls for assistance or alliance.[6] For example, when he met Indian leaders in their villages during the American Revolution, British general Henry Hamilton presented each chief with a war belt made of wampum and demonstrated his understanding of Indian culture by dancing for them as he "sung the War Song."[7] In return, Native leaders accommodated Europeans by accepting Euro-American forms of negotiation, such as recognizing an authority for written documents.

If American officials demanded that Indian chiefs acknowledge the power of written texts, they were willing at first to respect the authority of indigenous protocols and ceremonies such as the exchange of wampum and extended oratory. At the same time, Native leaders at Greenville initially voiced concerns about using past treaties as the basis for new ones. Federal officials acknowledged that many of the tribes present at Greenville had not participated in the earlier treaties, and they urged Wayne to base the new treaty on a "full representation of all nations" of the Great Lakes. Nevertheless, Wayne continued to insist that the old treaties be given reverence. He carried several massive volumes with him to Greenville that contained the copies of every previous treaty signed between Indians and the United States (and many of the treaties signed between the tribes and the British government). Native American leaders capitalized on Wayne's willingness to acknowledge the indigenous right to possess land, enumerated in the older treaties, and persuaded him to acknowledge their own right to relinquish more.[8]

Indian leaders clearly understood the obsession of Americans with the authority of texts and tried to use them, when they could, to advance their own agendas. Some Indian chiefs appeared at treaty councils bearing their own copies of older treaties and letters written by American officials. They hoped that if they recognized an American reliance on the written word, American officials would reciprocate by recognizing their customs of diplomacy. Chippewa chief Masass brought his own copy of the Treaty of Fort Harmar with him to Greenville and tried to use it for leverage in gaining Wayne's graces. The Americans had not even invited Masass to the council. But the Chippewa chief insisted on attending; he believed that his presence at the signing of earlier treaties (such as the Treaty of Fort Harmar) gave him personal insights into the history of the documents.[9] Miami chief Little Turtle likewise produced written texts in an attempt to win Wayne's favor. He presented the general with papers given to him by George Washington that guaranteed Indians the "enjoyment" of their hunting grounds and protection from whites who attempted to purchase Indian lands.[10] Wyandot chief Tarhe (or the Crane) quoted a letter that he had received from Washington, in which the president promised to "defend his dutiful children from any injury that may be attempted against them."[11] Tarhe went as far as to suggest that he would notify the president if he suspected the Americans at Greenville of any wrongdoings.

Native leaders also wanted their participation at the treaty council to be preserved in writing for future councils. The day after presenting Wayne with the letter from George Washington, Tarhe produced a written copy of his speech, insisting that the commander attach it to the official treaty proceedings. Conceivably, Tarhe was trying to prevent white translators from manipulating his words, but more likely, the Wyandot chief was working to demonstrate his willingness to participate in American forms of negotiation and recognize the authority of texts.[12] In this way, Indian leaders throughout the negotiations used their knowledge of American diplomatic practices to advance their positions and demand respect.

Claiming too much knowledge of the past, however, could get one in trouble. Masass perhaps too closely tied himself to the Treaty of Fort Harmar. Wayne praised the Chippewa chief's "open and generous manner" and "honest, open, and manly heart" in front of the other chiefs, but such accolades drew the ire of chiefs who competed for Wayne's attention.[13] Native leaders squabbled among themselves over who had the authority to claim ownership of the lower Great Lakes and sign the new treaty. Little Turtle, leader of the Indian confederation that crushed armies under Colonel Josiah Harmar and territorial governor Arthur St. Clair, said that, although he was "ignorant" of the proceedings at Fort Harmar, he believed the new commitment should not be based on the previous one.[14]

As Indian chiefs supported Little Turtle and cursed the old treaty as unjust and illegal, indigenous leaders who had so adamantly linked themselves to the agreement found themselves at odds with neighboring tribal leaders. Masass, who twenty-four hours earlier boasted about his attendance at the previous council, quickly made an about-face and claimed that his Wyandot uncles had ordered him to sign the treaty, even though he did not fully understand what it had said. He blamed bad American interpreters for misleading him, which, he argued, was the reason that this time he brought his own Franco-American interpreters to Greenville.[15]

Masass quickly abandoned his proclaimed faith in the document itself, complaining that Delaware and Wyandot villages had received few of the annuities promised to them in the Fort Harmar agreement. Additionally, he pulled a wampum belt from his bag and showed it to the council. The written treaty may have represented the details of the annuities, he argued, but the belt symbolized something more—the promise of friendship forged between Americans and Indians.[16] Masass tried to play the political middleman, speaking to both sides—first bowing to Wayne's demands and then criticizing American policies to gain status among his own people. He also spoke from two different perspectives—one rigidly guided by written treaties and a second based on oral storytelling and wampum. In essence, he tried to balance two competing methods for recording the past.

Oral histories were central to indigenous society; communities constituted rich linguistic locations where leaders rose to power based on oratorical ability. Tribal and intertribal dialogue centered on debate and openness, rather than the relatively closed system of discourse encouraged by Americans. When they met in closed tribal councils, Indian leaders accepted advice from elders, councilors, and female chiefs. Elders at Delaware councils sat behind the main body "and when necessary" spoke up to explain "the proceedings of any previous council."[17] Shawnee tribal councils appointed women as war and peace chiefs who would often lend their advice to "prevent the unnecessary efussion [*sic*] of blood."[18] Robert Yagelski has argued that the "variety of narrative devices" employed by Indian diplomats at treaty negotiations "suggest that only the best storytellers in a tribe were sent to negotiate multicultural alliances."[19] Conversely, American negotiators entered treaty councils with strict instructions from their superiors and often merely repeated their demands over the course of occasional monthlong negotiations.

When they engaged Indian leaders in rhetorical contests during councils, American officials entered into an unfamiliar dialogue where they were forced to recognize that talented Indian speakers outmatched them. Americans often responded by mimicking Indian uses of metaphor and storytelling, especially when it came to the language of fictive kinship. Indians and Europeans had long used ideas of fictive kinship networks to describe everything from economic trade to political negotiation in the lower Great Lakes. Indian communities often assigned each other kinship titles that represented their roles within a larger fictive network. For example, the Delawares considered the Shawnees as their grandchildren and demanded respect from them; in return, the Shawnees expected their grandfathers to protect them and advise them during councils. Sometimes these fictive networks manifested themselves in the physical orientation of council proceedings. At Greenville, the Shawnee chief Blue Jacket made a point of switching seats in order to sit next to his Delaware grandfathers and Wyandot uncles. For the most part, kinship monikers were meant to describe mutual obligations rather than an actual spatial orientation.[20]

The chiefs first tried to establish a fictive kinship with Wayne at the Treaty of Greenville, even as the general tried to "speak Indian." Wayne opened nearly every day of talks by telling the chiefs that the United States wished to "take them by the hand." This figurative gesture might have symbolized a military alliance, an extension of aid, a sign of equality, or the hand of a father guiding or protecting his children—the details of indigenous metaphors used during council meetings were often negotiable.[21] And they probably expected that it meant something important. Considering that Native orators were often important members of their communities, there is little reason to believe that Indian leaders viewed Wayne as anything less than a powerful agent of the U.S. government. But powerful American negotiator did not necessarily translate into omnipotent sovereign. Why would Indians recognize him as anything more than equal? Through a horribly ethnocentric and teleological lens, modern onlookers have concluded that Indians were simply enamored by Wayne's military prowess.

Chief Te-ta-boksh-ke was the first to recognize Wayne as his fictive "brother." For the Delaware leader, the title signified an equal relationship. Within the larger fictive kinship network, brothers held relatively equal obligations, but modifiers were often added to intimately describe the responsibilities of each party. Most of the Indian chiefs at the council called Wayne their "elder brother," slightly altering the relationship. Older brothers could demand respect from their younger siblings, but elder family members also held an additional obligation to protect their younger family members in the same way that uncles, fathers, or grandfathers held much stronger obligations toward protecting and guiding their younger nephews, children, or grandchildren. The details of the relationship between Wayne (the elder brother) and the gathered Indians (his younger siblings) were open to interpretation. Thus Wayne and the Indian leaders spent much of the negotiations trying to define the obligations of this relationship. Despite the insistence of modern scholars that no real negotiation went on at the Treaty of Greenville, Indian use of the title of "brother" implied that they were not willing to concede wholly to the Americans. Instead, Native leaders attempted to use the council to renegotiate their position with the Americans. In many ways they succeeded, but Wayne and the American leaders at Greenville understood little about the extralegal and cultural obligations to which they agreed when they accepted their roles as fictive brothers.[22]

Perhaps most important to Native leaders, Wayne acknowledged the legitimacy of indigenous oral history when he exchanged wampum with

Indian delegates. Americans rarely understood the authority that Native
people placed on the skill of reading beaded belts and strings. Although
it had been used as a medium of trade, wampum served a greater importance for Indians in diplomacy. Chiefs carried the belts from the councils
to their indigenous communities and used them as mnemonic devices
for telling and retelling the history of previous councils and important
events. Because Native people lived in an oral culture, wampum served
as important tools in historical recordkeeping, just as the textual copies of treaties did for Americans.[23] As an example of how history and
wampum were linked, the Miamis believed that they remembered little
about their early history because a box containing the belts and pipes of
the tribe accidently had been destroyed during their rout of Harmar's
invading army. When a handful of Miami leaders were interviewed years
later, they argued that their tribal history had been erased with the loss
of the belts.[24]

Although some tribal leaders had abandoned using wampum with
Americans because they felt Americans failed to understand its significance, Indian leaders at Greenville returned to the beaded belts and
strings as a medium of historical storytelling. To open his speech to
Wayne, Wyandot chief Tarhe pulled out a blue belt and used it to tell the
story of how the British had persuaded him to side with them in previous
wars. He told Wayne that he had accepted a hatchet from the British and
plunged it into the general's head during the Revolution, but now he
envisioned himself gingerly removing the hatchet "with so much care"
that the American would not "feel pain or injury." He pointed to a blue
string that he held in his hand and told the American general that the
blood from this incident remained on the ground, but Tarhe promised
to take up the bloody soil and bury it in the cavity of a tree. The Wyandot
leader also promised to replant the tree in hopes that his children would
never know what happened. He then pulled a white belt from his bag
and told Wayne that he used it to clean the blood from all those involved
and wipe the tears from the general's face. He offered to use the belt to
open the general's ears and prepare his heart for the truth about to be
spoken. The Wyandot chief continued throughout his speech to pull
belts and strings from his bag, using each to tell a story that chronicled

the history between the Wyandots and their American neighbors.[25] He then gave them to Wayne.

Wayne might have been expected to reject Tarhe's narrative as whimsical, but he did not. Instead, the general tried to demonstrate his sincerity by participating in the ceremony and employing wampum of his own to tell stories. He presented belts and strings to the chiefs as he used them to tell his own version of the region's history. Moreover, he promised Tarhe that he would examine the "belts, speeches, and boundaries" given to him by the chief and compare them to the bound volumes that he carried with him. Wayne assured Tarhe that they would "agree with the records" in his possession.[26] American officials recognized the authority of Native oral histories by recognizing the ceremonial aspects of the councils as legitimate. Indigenous leaders viewed councils as spiritual engagements where compacts were forged in the name of the Great Spirit. Cultural customs, such as smoking the calumet and dancing, bridged the meaning between spiritual ceremony and diplomatic negotiation. The willingness of officials to participate in these events signaled to Native leaders that the Americans understood the deeper meaning of the signed compact.[27] Wayne accepted the premise of the indigenous customs when he told the chiefs he had "performed every necessary ceremony, to render propitious" the "renovated friendship" between the Americans and the Indians of the Great Lakes.[28] Indians used the ceremonial aspects of the treaty council to bless the verbal agreements and the signed text, and they expected the Americans to respect this sacredness when it came time to perform the obligations agreed to at the council. Although they left the negotiations divided, the Indian leaders nonetheless believed they shared an understanding with the Americans that the articles of the treaty would not be broken.

In the years that followed the signing of the Treaty of Greenville, Indians and Americans came to dispute the meaning of the document as they both attempted to interpret in their own way the history of Indian-white relations unfolding before them. Many Indian leaders understood their relationship with American officials in dualistic terms combining a promise to adhere to written stipulations and a more ambiguous sense of responsibilities based on a language of fictive kinship. Americans appeared to accept their trust relationship with Native peoples by verbally promising to uphold obligations they knew would go unfulfilled. By the nineteenth century, federal officials in the lower Great Lakes came to see these responsibilities as optional.[29] The "system is to live in perpetual peace with the Indians," President Thomas Jefferson wrote to Indiana territorial governor William Henry Harrison, "by everything just and liberal which we can [offer] them within the bounds of reason, and by giving them effectual protection against wrongs from our own people." If that did not work (and he assumed it would not), Jefferson instructed Harrison to seek land cessions from the tribes and encourage them to move out of the region. He believed that western traders and government agents eventually would drive Indian leaders into debt. "When these debts get beyond what individuals can pay," he informed Harrison, "they become willing to lop them off by a cession of lands. They will perceive how useless to them are their extensive forests, and either incorporate with us as citizens of the United States or remove beyond the Mississippi." Jefferson masked his nefarious plan in benevolence. "But in the whole course of time," he warned the governor, "it is essential to cultivate their love."[30]

Harrison agreed with Jefferson's assessment that land acquisition was the quickest way to civilize the Indians and separate them from the rabble of western white society, but problems abounded. He needed to use the flexibility of language and interpretation to justify new policies of dispossession, which ran counter to the text of the Treaty of Greenville. This was especially true, as many of the Indian leaders insisted that future land cessions required universal Indian approval as outlined in the treaty itself.

Indian leaders turned time and again to the written words of the treaty in charging American officials with corruption. Following an 1804 land cession treaty signed at Vincennes, William Patterson (a Delaware spokesperson) traveled to Fort Wayne and told the Indian agent there that Harrison had committed fraud in negotiating the treaty. Patterson argued that Harrison had told them that the paper "was an instrument of writing to keep peace and friendship" and convinced them that it simply acknowledged Miami claims to lands around the White River. Patterson pretended to "know nothing" of land cessions that involved the Delawares and insisted that the additional annuities they accepted (which Harrison claimed signified the "sale") were gifts meant to "brighten the chain of friendship," not payments in exchange for land. Moreover, Patterson told government agents that the Delaware did not even "own" the land; instead, they insisted that they shared custody with all the tribes who had signed the Treaty of Greenville.[31] The Delawares knew they were being used.

By voicing his concern at Fort Wayne, Patterson actually followed the protocol for grievances outlined in the 1795 Treaty of Greenville. Article Nine of the document stipulated that Indian tribes who objected to American actions needed to raise the complaint with either the president or their local agent. The actions of the Delaware representative traveled up the chain of command, first to the local agent, then to the secretary of war, who ordered Harrison to hold a new council with the Delawares, Potawatomis, and Miamis to discuss the treaty (although he expected Harrison to reach the same outcome). The secretary of war instructed Harrison to convince the tribes that the treaty was "open and fair," suggesting that Harrison should punish anyone he found making "false or improper representations" of what happened at the original treaty council.[32] Harrison canceled the council, however, because he felt it threatened his own "dignity and authority." Instead, he sent agents to renegotiate with individual tribal villages.[33] Harrison's circumvention of a general treaty council marked a turning point in early relations with the Indians. By ignoring the process for adjudicating complaints outlined in the Treaty of Greenville and dismissing the orders of his superiors, Harrison demonstrated a new strategy of land acquisition based on coercion and a refutation of Indian claims.

Still, American officials could not easily refute every Indian leader who opposed treaties or American policy. Montgomery Montour, a Delaware who served on the side of the patriots during the Revolution, sent a petition to Secretary of War Henry Dearborn claiming that some of the Delaware chiefs whose names were attached to treaties signed at Vincennes (1805 and 1806) in fact "were not present" at those treaties but were at "a great distance" from them. He said that some chiefs had become upset when they learned their names had been affixed to the documents.[34] Dearborn agreed, but he could not explain why the disputed names were on the treaties. Hoping to resolve the problem, he promised to send "friendly aid" to the offended chiefs and proposed that each family involved in the dispute receive one hundred acres of land.[35]

Harrison ordered government agents to the tribal villages and met individually with the disaffected Indian leaders. Many chiefs, however, refused to allow officials to approach their villages, telling them instead that they would speak at Fort Wayne when the tribes came together to collect their annuities. Suspicious that he was being undermined by traders and agents (who had married Indian women or were the offspring of at least one indigenous parent), Harrison accused Indian agent William Wells at Fort Wayne of instigating the hostility by pouring whiskey down their gullets. He also blamed Indian traders John Conner and Peter Audrian for agitating the Delawares and accused them of playing a "cunning game" with the tribes in order to exploit them. His rejection of Wells, Conner, and Audrian as suitable negotiators might be viewed as a break from older accommodation policies that relied on cultural mediators to reconcile disputes. Instead, Harrison demanded that he alone be able to dictate new American policies and interpret for himself the past actions of the region's people.[36]

Harrison's attempt to rewrite the history of previous treaty councils and the promises made there stood at the heart of both William Patterson and Montgomery Montour's complaints to the secretary of war. In the years that followed the Treaty of Greenville, this issue of who could and who could not interpret the events of the immediate past emerged as a central point of contention between Native leaders and the governor. For his part, Harrison excelled at reinterpreting events so they would correspond with his goal of acquiring additional land for white settlement. While he served as territorial governor, violence exploded in the western parts of Indiana Territory. Indians attacked whites and one another. The Kickapoos, staunch critics of American policies, murdered the brother-in-law of the accommodationist Kaskaskia chief, Ducoigne. The attack symbolized a growing dissatisfaction among Indians who correctly viewed increased American efforts to acquire Indian lands as a direct violation of the spirit and letter of the Treaty of Greenville. A growing number of Indian leaders pointed to annuity chiefs and accommodationist Indians as the allies of Americans in this extermination campaign.

Messengers like the Shawnee Prophet and Tecumseh capitalized on the growing resentment felt by a beleaguered Indian population.[37]

The history of the Treaty of Greenville council and the shared understanding of what that compact stood for, both in writing and in the mutual obligations forged through Native council protocol, emerged as the nexus for disagreements. Most Indians viewed the treaty's intent as the basis for a permanent peaceful relationship between whites and Indians. Indian leaders who discovered fellow tribesmen violating U.S. laws brought the perpetrators to U.S. officials so that entire tribes would not be accused of breaking their treaty obligations. Article Nine outlined a system of reprisal, which outlawed "private revenge or retaliation," but the section also provided justice for "injuries done by individuals, on either side." American officials tried to fulfill their role of paternal fathers or protective older brothers by attempting to curb retaliatory violence; however, they failed to control escalating instances of blind revenge on either side.

New federal guidelines ordered western agents to record white complaints against Indians and use their powers of "persuasion & of force" to prevent bloodshed, but they expended little effort in tracking down whites who had committed hostile acts upon Native Americans.[38] For example, whites punished horse thievery more than any other crime, as horses provided men with the means to travel great distances, haul supplies to their isolated families, and be used in times of war to mobilize armies. In the early years of the western territories, a white person convicted for the first instance of horse thievery was ordered to pay the court an amount in the value of the horse and receive upwards of 200 public lashings. By 1807, as a growing number of horse thieves disrupted the western life, territorial officials legalized corporal punishments for first-time offenders or those who "knowingly" received stolen horses, including execution.[39] Whites who stole horses from other whites were hanged, and Indians who stole horses from whites were hanged, but white settlers who stole horses from Indians received different punishments. Despite the importance of horses to Indian societies in the lower Great Lakes, white judges preferred to humiliate whites who stole Indian horses rather than hang them; one individual received lashes "inflicted in the most public streets of town" while wearing a sign that proclaimed

"I STOLE A HORSE FROM INDIANS." The editor of a local newspaper hoped it would serve as an "example of justice" and prevent a renewed war between settlers and Indians. It was far from equal punishment.[40]

Indian leaders pushed their tribesmen to abide by the law of the Treaty of Greenville, even as Americans failed to uphold their treaty obligations. Indian chiefs (knowing that their actions would lead to the execution of their tribesmen) handed over Indians who stole horses and tried to return stolen property to American officials.[41] Chiefs often argued that the offenders were not part of their tribes but vagrants who traveled around the area causing problems. They assured American agents that they would do everything in their power to return stolen horses and punish the culprits or turn them over to U.S. officials. A few chiefs toured the region encouraging other Indians to prevent hostilities by delivering criminals to white authorities. In 1799, American settlers complained that Indians along the Ohio River robbed supply boats and killed the crews. Shawnee chief Blue Jacket visited Shawnee villages along the river and verbally berated the offenders. Meanwhile, American leaders pushed their own citizens to prevent retaliatory violence.[42] Still, white gangs combed the countryside indiscriminately killing Indians in retribution for attacks against white people and property.

When serious crimes were committed against Americans by Native people, Indians maintained their commitment by testifying against fellow tribesmen in white courts; they felt it was their sacred duty to uphold the previous agreement. For example, in 1801, Delaware Indians turned over two villagers accused of killing a white man along the Ohio River. Lawyers pieced together the basic details of the story. Three Delaware men met a white man on the south bank of the Ohio River, where they agreed to help each other cross. After fording the river, the party decided to camp on its northern shore. Following a short nap, the four men mounted their horses and started to leave camp. Just as the horses and men began their journey, one (or perhaps more) of the Indians shot the white traveler in the back.[43] A Delaware chief persuaded one of the accused Indians to testify against the others, where he told a jury that he had mounted his horse first followed by the others. Before traveling far he heard gunshots behind him, and as he turned, he saw the white man fall from his horse. He testified that his fellow Delaware travelers, Wa-pikinomouk and Matayhikan, jumped off their horses and stood over the corpse, verifying that he was dead. The witness claimed to know nothing of the plot to kill the man and, since he was on the lead horse, admitted that he did not see the actual shooting. Wapikinomouk refuted the testi-mony and argued that the other two Indians were drunk and killed the man for no reason. But his story came into question when jurors asked him to describe the procession of horses and men. Wapikinomouk con-firmed his accuser's version of the events as he placed him at the head of the procession. Consequently, jurors convicted Wapikinomouk and Matayhikan, and the judge sentenced them to death. When they turned in other Indians or persuaded tribesmen to testify in white courts, Na-tive leaders hoped that Americans would reciprocate by ensuring equal justice. That rarely occurred.[44]

In November 1808, Judge Henry Vanderburgh presided over the trials of Marengum (a Delaware man accused of killing a white man) and Eisha Hicks (a white woman who had killed a white man). A jury found Maren-gum guilty of murder and sentenced him to die. The Delaware man ar-gued that "a white man in his situation would have got clear," but the jury considered him "a dog." He may have been right. Hicks avoided a death sentence, even though Judge Vanderburgh pronounced her crime "one of the most shocking and barbarous murders ever perpetrated." Before he read her verdict, Vanderburgh told Hicks, "The crime whereof you stand convicted is one of the most flagrant and outrageous acts of man-slaughter the whole history of jurisprudence can produce." Nonetheless, the judge followed the jury's recommendation and ordered her branded on "the hand with a hot iron with the letter M" and released.[45]

Perhaps Hicks avoided the death penalty because a squeamish jury re-fused to execute a woman, but such inequitable punishments appeared to be the norm, not the exception. In 1802, a jury concluded in their findings to the courts that a white man in Clark County had murdered an Indian in cold blood, yet they acquitted him. Another jury found a white man innocent of killing an Indian, "altho it was evident that it was a cruel and unprovoked murder." William Henry Harrison believed that, since a "great many of the Inhabitants of the Frontiers considered the murdering of Indians in the highest degree," it would be difficult to stop Indian homicides or punish perpetrators. Consequently, little was done to correct the justice system.[46]

Harrison conceded that, even when they were convicted and sentenced, it was impossible to bring whites to justice for killing Indians. William Red was accused of shooting an unarmed Delaware man whose only crime had been knocking on the white man's door. The courts convicted Red of murdering the Indian, but before he could be sentenced, Red escaped from the Knox County jailhouse. Believing that punishing the murderer would generate "beneficial consequences" when it came time to negotiating with local Indians by demonstrating the United States' commitment to upholding the Treaty of Greenville, Harrison tripled the reward (from $100 to $300) for Red's capture. Nonetheless, the accused evaded all punishment.[47]

Harrison must have known the amplified financial reward would do little good. Years earlier, three white men who killed an Indian eluded capture until Harrison, hoping to use the case as a symbol of the United States' commitment to the Treaty of Greenville, offered $300 for each of their captures. Like the later case, the reward failed in both symbolism and practicality.[48] When Harrison sent an agent to apprehend the men in Kentucky, local citizens and the state governor aided the criminals. Despite serious obstacles, the murderers were returned to Indiana Territory, but soon thereafter escaped from the highly permeable Knox County jail. The three fugitives successfully eluded territorial officials, until years later they themselves were murdered while poaching game on Indian lands in the Missouri Territory.[49]

Governor Harrison insisted that he had no control over whites in the region, although he demanded submission by the region's Indians. He admitted that the claims made by Indians to justify retribution—that whites killed their people, settled on their lands, destroyed their game, and got their men drunk to cheat them out of their money—all were probably true. He also recognized that the Treaty of Greenville provided for the "same punishment for offences committed against Indians as against white men." But experience showed him that there must be "a wide difference in the execution" of the law. In 1806, Harrison told the territorial legislature that the "doctrine" of distinguishing between "the murder of a White man and an Indian" should cease; yet he ultimately concluded, "Too long has this fine Country possessing all the advantages of Climate Soil and situation been the home of the uncultivated Savage. It is about to assume the Character to which it was destined by nature. A virtuous and industrious people will soon render it the abode of Wealth Civilization and science."[50] Harrison's real goal, as outlined to him by Jefferson, was to clear Native peoples from the soil and extend America's reach westward. His version of the region's law, administration, and history led to that end.

By 1809, the philanthropic veneer of early-nineteenth-century American Indian policy fell away, revealing Harrison's unabashed quest for land acquisitions. In that year, thousands of Delaware, Potawatomi, Miami, and Eel River Indians descended upon Fort Wayne to collect their annuities and meet with the governor. Harrison called the tribes together to discuss a new treaty, and both sides understood that land cessions would be raised. But they also knew that the topic would cause tension. Harrison pledged "to shut up the liquor casks" until the council concluded (as he had earlier accused Indian agent William Wells of using liquor to unduly influence Indians leading up to the council). The Miami delegation, led by Little Turtle, rose to defend their rights and reminded the gathered Indian leaders that the Treaty of Greenville had established the precedence of shared custody of the lower Great Lakes among all gathered tribes. They "declared their determination not to sell a foot of land" and said it was time "to stop the encroachment of the whites" who pushed Indians into selling lands for less than their true value. Harrison pledged that the president would "never make another proposition" for them to sell their lands and assured them that he, in particular, would "never be the cause of breaking the chain of friendship" that bound the Indian tribes together as one nation.[51]

When it seemed as though no progress could be made, Harrison whetted the wheels of diplomacy by distributing two kegs of whiskey to each of the tribes. Soon thereafter, he persuaded some of the chiefs to notarize his version of events by signing a new land cession treaty. From that moment onward, Harrison simply dismissed those who raised objections and used liquor to gain Indian cooperation. The governor still needed to persuade Indian leaders to reject the anti-cession rhetoric spouted by

Little Turtle and the Prophet if he planned to gain more land cessions through treaties. "Mellowed with wine," the Mississinway Miami chief Pecan argued that the British were to blame, not the Americans, as he asked fellow Indians to oppose the Prophet and side with Harrison.[52] Little Turtle tried to warn the council that the Americans only wanted more land, but he soon discovered that Harrison had "bought" most of the chiefs with whiskey. The demise of Little Turtle's authority was emblematic of the subversion of the Treaty of Greenville; American officials grew accustomed to ignoring both the agreement and Indian leaders who turned to the language of the treaty to lodge complaints.[53] Moreover, the emergence of Harrison as the face of Indian policy in the West, and the Prophet as his indigenous antithesis, marked the beginning of an end to the language of the middle ground, as older leaders found themselves being tuned out.

Earlier in the decade, the Shawnee Prophet had gathered disgruntled Indians near Greenville to protest American failures to uphold the treaty negotiated there in 1795. He blasted chiefs who accommodated American officials and launched attacks against Indians friendly to Americans by charging them with witchcraft and persuading local leaders to execute the accused. Harrison sent Indian agent John Conner with a message reminding the Prophet that the Indians promised to "live in peace and friendship" with their "brothers the Americans" at the Treaty of Greenville. Despite a long record of broken promises and unfulfilled obligations, Harrison instructed Conner to read the entire text of the treaty to the Shawnee leader and ask him, "Which of these articles has your father broken?"[54] He cared not what the Prophet answered.

Harrison refuted the argument that increased land cessions and his own actions at Fort Wayne were driving disgruntled indigenous peoples into the Prophet's movement, but those complaints were precisely what the Prophet and his brother Tecumseh used as the basis of their recruiting. They rejected the treaty made by the Delaware, Miami, Potawatomi, and Eel River chiefs at Fort Wayne and warned Americans that the United States should stop trying to acquire land from the Indians "without the consent of all the tribes."[55] For their part, Americans "read" the growing resistance in bizarre geopolitical terms. They believed that since a large number of Indians seemed willing to uphold their treaty obligations by handing over criminals and ceding lands, the only explanation for Native resentment must be British interference. Harrison became paranoid that British agents constantly plotted to attack him. As Native leaders lodged complaints about Americans who violated the Treaty of Greenville, American officials deflected charges and obsessed about British complicity.[56]

In an address to the General Assembly of Indiana Territory on September 27, 1808, Harrison argued that recent land cessions had been acquired "by fair, equal, & reciprocally advantageous treaties." Other countries, he contended, would have seized the land "by violence." He tried to cloak his own improprieties by changing the context within which a history of Indian-white relations would be compared. All the wars and hostilities between the United States and the Indians, he argued, had been the result of "foreign influence" and not American shortcomings. A few years earlier President Jefferson had told the Miamis that the Treaty of Greenville had marked a change in American policy toward the Indians.[57] He had begged them to reject British influence and instead adopt "temperance, peace, and agriculture." Harrison revised this history and provided a new focus that excused his inability to uphold older treaty obligations or listen to the opposition.[58]

The messianic movement started by the Prophet and Tecumseh most vividly illustrated the dissatisfaction of Native leaders with Harrison's policy of land acquisitions, but historians who have chronicled the events surrounding the Prophet's pan-Indian movement often overlook a war of words that took place between Native leaders and Harrison in local newspapers. In 1811 and 1812, Indian agent John Johnston aided tribal leaders in seeing their responses to Harrison in print. In written and spoken discourses, which appeared in newspapers across the lower Great Lakes, Native leaders not allied with the Prophet attempted to present their interpretation of recent events. In August 1811, Johnston invited members of the Shawnee and Wyandot Nations to a council at Upper Sandusky, Ohio, where he hoped their words would "quiet the fears of our citizens in this quarter." Johnston recorded their speeches and, apparently with their consent, sent them to Cincinnati to have them published in the *Liberty Hall*; other newspapers in the lower Great Lakes, including the Indianapolis *Western Speculator*, later reprinted them. Shawnee chief Black

Hoof told readers that the Great Spirit had commanded them to "live in harmony and peace" with Americans. He promised that he had no intention of joining the "bad Indians" at Prophetstown and further denounced the Prophet as a man who attempted to "poison their minds." Black Hoof attempted to draw parallels between his view of the Prophet and Harrison's inability to control unruly western settlers: "It is hard and difficult for us to manage our bad people—we have no power over the Prophet to do any thing with him—we have done our best with him. . . . You know you cannot manage your bad people. . . . [Likewise] it is therefore utterly out of our power to do anything with him."[59]

In addition, the Shawnee chief reinterpreted the responsibility of the United States and insisted that they care for Indians in the region. "We are standing here, and view ourselves as one man with the whites," he told Johnston and the American diplomats at Upper Sandusky; "the treaties have always considered us as Americans, and that we look upon ourselves to be now." Black Hoof told his audience, both at the council and in the newspapers, that the Shawnees expected whites to recognize them as devoted citizens of the United States. "There is only one Great Father," he said, "and there is no difference in his eyes respecting the colors of skins." Furthermore, he pledged the Shawnee Nation's allegiance to the United States in times of conflict. "If war breaks out between you and Great Britain, we are determined to follow your advice," Black Hoof promised. (The Americans had asked for the Shawnees merely to remain neutral.)[60]

Harrison viewed the Prophet and British influence as major regional threats and demanded a response from the other tribes in the region. The governor sent runners to gather the Miamis and Potawatomis at Fort Wayne. There he had assistant Indian agent John Shaw produce a written copy of his message, which was delivered to the council by William Wells. The responses of the chiefs at the council were recorded on paper, in anticipation that they would be delivered to Harrison. The chiefs may have also assumed, as was becoming more common, that their words would be printed in local newspapers. In fact, when Potawatomi chief Oseemit rose to speak at the council, he must have known others would read his remarks, because the chief asked specifically that his speech not be "written down."[61] Miami leaders now viewed their published speeches as an opportunity to correct Harrison's interpretation of the recent past and craft one of their own.

Wea chief Laprusieur castigated Harrison for accusing all of the lower Great Lakes tribes of joining the Shawnee Prophet at Prophetstown. "You are deceived," he told the governor. "You said we were of his party. I hold you and the Shawanoe both by the hand; I hold him slack." Laprusieur recognized two competing historical interpretations of recent events. "You have both told me one story: that, if I would adhere to you, that my people (the women and children) would be happy." He warned Harrison, "We are now anxiously waiting to see which of you tells the truth." Despite recognizing the fluidity of these stories, the Wea chief proclaimed some of the story indisputable. He directly challenged the governor's assertion that Native leaders had abandoned their obligations of the Treaty of Greenville: "You have called upon us to fulfill the treaty of Greenville. In that treaty it stipulated that we should give you information, if we knew of any hostile design of a foreign power against each other. I now tell you that no information from any quarter has reached our ears to injure any of your people, except from yourself."[62]

Miami Chief Little Turtle likewise referenced the Greenville accord and offered his own interpretation of recent events. "The transactions that took place between the Indians and white people at Greenville are yet fresh in our minds," he told Harrison. "At that place we told each other that we would in the future be friends." Little Turtle claimed that the Miamis had done everything in their power to cultivate and defend that friendship and further declared, "These are yet the sentiments of your children, the Miamis."[63]

Still Harrison viewed the Indians gathered at Prophetstown as detrimental to the interests of the United States. In October 1811, he led a military force of nearly one thousand men up the Wabash River. Before they could reach the Indian settlement, Indian warriors attacked the soldiers. In the early morning hours of November 7, the Shawnee Prophet instructed his followers to attack Harrison and soldiers who were readying breakfast and preparing for their final push toward Prophetstown. The Battle of Tippecanoe, as it has come to be known, ended with the deaths of sixty-two Americans. Despite national newspaper reports, which called the ambush a "complete defeat" and a "most distressing disaster,"

Harrison claimed victory, as a detachment of men sent to Prophetstown the following day found the settlement abandoned.[64]

Americans and Indians disagreed about the meaning of Harrison's campaign. Harrison, of course, announced that his "victory" meant American dominance over the places and people of the Great Lakes, while Native leaders scrambled either to explain their involvement at Prophetstown or denounce the movement altogether. A spokesman for the Kickapoos argued that their "intention was not to strike the white people, but the Prophet told them many lies, and made them do it." He vowed that the tribes would "throw the tomahawk on the ground" and cease fighting "with the white people."[65] As he had done before, Indian agent John Johnston distributed the speeches made by Indian leaders, this time at Fort Wayne, to local newspapers. He hoped that their words would confirm to white settlers "their firm determination to maintain (inviolate) the several treaties" signed between the tribes of the lower Great Lakes and the United States. Moreover, he suspected that the Indians would "assassinate the Prophet and his brother" when the opportunity presented itself.[66]

Shawnee chief Black Hoof again reiterated his pledge to the U.S. government and chronicled the history between his tribe and the Americans since the Treaty of Greenville. "It is the same we have always told you," he told interpreter John Shaw. "We wish to have peace and friendship as long as we can." "What was there said [at the Treaty of Greenville]," he promised, "we have not forgotten, but is still fresh in our minds." Black Hoof demanded that the speech be recorded and distributed to a broader audience. He told Johnston, "We want our speech to be known everywhere."[67]

After two years of bloodshed in the region between Americans, British soldiers, and Indian warriors during the War of 1812, Harrison demanded that tribes who had once declared their allegiance to the United States again meet at Greenville to confirm their alliance in writing. The negotiations, or lack thereof, that took place at Greenville in the summer of 1814 demonstrate the remarkable changes that occurred in how Americans sought to dominate the conversation. Most important, it illustrates their demand to control the interpretation of the region's recent past.

In the summer of 1814, Indian agent John Johnston arrived at Greenville in order to prepare the treaty grounds. Johnston eyed an "elevated spot" along a nearby creek and commanded a group of soldiers to erect a council house on the location. William Henry Harrison arrived two weeks later. As the general inspected the grounds, he had an aide fetch Johnston. Harrison asked the agent to move the council house and flag-staff about 150 yards, so that it stood on the exact spot where the 1795 Treaty of Greenville negotiations had taken place. He explained that the "ground was consecrated to him by many enduring recollections, which could never be effaced from his memory." He also wanted "all the details of the great treaty about to be held, to conform as near as could be to the one which had preceded it."[68]

The move was more than nostalgia; it represented Harrison's attempt to control the historical narrative at the new treaty council. Many of the Indian chiefs from the first treaty had died, giving him the benefit of claiming firsthand knowledge of every major event concerning Americans and lower Great Lakes Indians since the first treaty. Harrison believed that something more than military victories had led to this moment; Americans claimed ownership of the very language of Indian affairs. The middle-ground world of competing empires and powerful Indian confederations was disappearing, and American officials believed their words alone would thereafter be respected as the ultimate voice of authority. The new council at Greenville signaled the culmination of a decade-long war of words, a clash of epistemologies, and an outright difference in the interpretation of the region's past.

Secretary of War John Armstrong had instructed Harrison to forge "a peace, sincere and lasting, between the contracting parties," but he warned the general not to discuss new boundaries or commitments with the Indians.[69] It was clear that Americans, aware that the strict obligations outlined at the first treaty had caused problems, sought to forge a more ambiguous document that would list Indian responsibilities but leave latitude for later American officials. Armstrong outlined three objectives for Harrison: (1) secure a "peace, sincere and lasting, between the contracting parties"; (2) forge "an alliance between the said parties, in prosecuting the present war against Great Britain; and (3) ensure the "extinction of the Indian title to the tracts" ceded in treaties since the first treaty.

The resulting document resembled a skeleton of the first treaty, only briefly outlining general commitments. Exploiting his historical capital, Harrison told the chiefs that he was standing on the very spot where he stood at the first treaty council (as an aide to General Wayne). He then retreated to an older language of philanthropic paternalism, which allowed him to reject specific claims of impropriety by Indian leaders. Since 1795, he explained, Americans had fulfilled their general obligations as paternal protectors. He claimed that Indians influenced by the British had caused all the problems between whites and Indians, not Americans. After blaming the Indians for violating their pledge from the Treaty of Greenville to remain neutral, Harrison challenged the chiefs to provide a single instance when the United States had not executed their obligations. But what responsibilities was he talking about? No matter the complaint, Harrison had an answer.[70]

Eel River chief Captain Charley rose to launch charges against Harrison and the Americans. He explained that officials at Fort Wayne had failed to protect his people when war broke out. Captain Charley reminded Harrison that the Eel River Indians, who were camped outside the fort, retreated when hostile Indians approached to fight the Americans. When the women and elder chiefs returned, they found their villages destroyed and their warriors wounded—not by opposing Indians, but by the Americans. He argued that he tried to keep his tribesmen neutral, as stipulated by the previous treaty, but when they discovered that the Americans had destroyed their villages, they had no choice but to join Britain's Native allies. "I concluded we were in a precarious situation," Charley told Harrison. "It resembled a wild horse, surrounded on every side by people, endeavoring to catch him, and at last, all fall on him and kill him. When we saw you coming, and found you made the stroke on us, we concluded we were no longer at liberty to choose."[71]

Harrison explained that the villages were burnt so that the enemy could not use the corn and supplies. Several days later, Captain Charley tried to continue his harangue by blaming the Americans for the loss of his tribesmen at Fort Wayne, but this time he was stopped.[72] Unlike earlier treaties, where Indians were allowed to raise complaints and complete speeches, Harrison and his allies made sure that oppositional voices were silenced. Johnston interrupted the chief and recounted how

Indians who were attacking Fort Wayne killed his brother. He blamed the Miamis for his brother's death. It became clear in the altercation between Captain Charley and Johnston that if American officials could not outdebate Indian leaders, they would simply shut them up. Harrison joined Johnston and chastised the Eel River chief for being a half-breed Frenchman and called upon the other chiefs to "disavow" him.[73] Wyandot chief Tarhe responded by removing two British silver medals from around his neck, cut them in half with a large knife, and declared his allegiance to the United States. Harrison praised Tarhe for his honesty and promised to reward those who signed the treaty with "a quantity of whiskey." Others would go thirsty.[74]

The second Treaty of Greenville has long been overshadowed by its more celebrated predecessor, as historians have argued that the 1795 treaty effectively ended indigenous negotiating power.[75] But these types of deductions underestimate the resilience of indigenous societies and their contributions to debates about the fate of the region. They also ignore the important changes in how whites and Indians spoke to, and about, one another in the early nineteenth century. An examination of the two treaties and the verbal contests that occurred between them add to our understanding of how language and historical interpretation were used as tools of colonization and dispossession. Still, to place too much emphasis on the ability of Native leaders to shape the minds of American officials overlooks the ability of agents, like Harrison, to simply ignore them by the end of the War of 1812. Ultimately, turning a deaf ear to differences of interpretation proved to be the most powerful option for Americans looking to extend their power over the lower Great Lakes.

This new type of American Indian policy left few options after the war. American officials and western settlers came to believe that Native people either had to become like them or leave altogether. In other words, they had to blend into the landscape or vanish from it. Either way, American officials saw little value in having whites and Indians cohabit the lower Great Lakes. But federal agents were only part of the story. American settlers did not always agree on who deserved the right to inhabit the West. The debate over proper settlement began at the same time that government officials in the early nineteenth century worked to create a unilateral language of American expansion that excluded Native people.

CHAPTER 2

"Between Savage Cruelty and Opulent Speculation"

Petitions and the Shifting Language of Settlement

While American officials and Indian leaders waged a war of words and employed historical memory as a weapon during treaty councils, white settlers quarreled with one another over who should be permitted access to lands once they were ceded. Never doubting that Indians would eventually leave the lower Great Lakes, white speculators and settlers engaged in a fierce debate over the role of the nascent federal government in distributing newly acquired public lands. From the late eighteenth to the early nineteenth century, speculators labeled settlers who chose illegally to occupy private and public lands as squatters, banditti, or white savages. Squatters countered by accusing speculators of engaging in greedy schemes that gambled away the livelihoods of hardworking, honest western settlers. Within such debates emerged another form of shiftiness in language—one that often masked what was happening on the ground. This verbal warfare took place between the covers of travel journals, on the pages of western newspapers, and in the text of settler petitions. Like the romantic image of the vanishing Indian, that of the noble and esteemed pioneer, who entered an abandoned landscape and shaped it by the sweat of his brow, emerged as a fictive representation of real-life historical actors. Surprisingly, even the seemingly steadfast image of the American settler was malleable in these early years and open to interpretation. Outsiders first tried to differentiate between types of western settlers, labeling them as frontiersmen, settlers, actual settlers, squatters, or pioneers. Each description was used to either indemnify or celebrate the particular person or group to which it was attached. The hard-fought verbal contest eventually led to an acceptance of the American settler and pioneer as a symbol of American democracy.

Settlers had not always been seen as the vanguards of American progress. In fact, before the War of 1812, they faced a difficult struggle in presenting themselves as noble citizens. Travel writers who visited the region often painted a gloomy picture of early frontier life. One such author, Gilbert Imlay, refused to believe writers who described early settlers as individuals who extended civilization into the lower Great Lakes. His observations of the region led him to conclude that "every mark that is human" in the West exhibited the "feature of barbarism."[1] Another writer, Thaddeus Harris, believed that the superabundance of loamy soils, wild game, and untapped natural resources had turned hardy agrarian settlers into lazy backwoods hunters. Instead of profiting from the wilderness, he argued, American settlers were becoming more like their indigenous neighbors. Furthermore, he believed that the pursuit of game kept them from cultivating the soil and caused them to "acquire rough and savage manners."[2] Other observers agreed that these early settlers were no better than Indians—especially squatters who illegally occupied public lands. The acting governor of the Northwest Territory, Winthrop Sargent, believed that squatters chose illegal settlements over legal ones because they preferred to live "free as the Natives" rather than abide by civilized laws.[3] Travel writer Fortescue Cuming claimed that the squatters' "habits and manners" mirrored those of Indians; more telling, he believed, the settlers' rustic cabins looked "no better than Indian wigwams."[4]

Government officials agreed and launched campaigns to rid the western territories of the perceived nuisance. In the 1780s, American soldiers combed federally held lands north and west of the Ohio River seeking out illegal settlers. In 1785 General Josiah Harmar sent detachments to "drive off all surveyors or settlers of the lands of the United States."[5] Soldiers marched 70 miles from their outpost at Fort McIntosh, on the eastern edge of the Ohio country, burning the homes and destroying the crops of squatters. Later that year, Harmar ordered artillery captain John Doughty to lead troops 140 miles down the Ohio River to establish a post whereby the army could "answer the valuable object of removing the intruders from the public lands."[6] Illegal settlers, the general argued, needed to be so "frequently removed from the public lands" that 160 soldiers under the command of Captain John Hamtramck were in constant deployment searching for squatters and torching their homes.[7]

Many Americans simply believed that illegal western squatters purposefully abandoned civilized life to engage in rugged and uncouth ones. Evangelical preachers often used the image of western barbarism to promote their own campaigns, regardless of whether or not they had evidence to make such claims. Missionaries argued that western preachers were necessary not only to convert Indians but also to reclaim the savage settler and rambunctious frontiersman for the sake of Christians everywhere. They referred to backwoodsmen as "white savages" and argued that squatters hindered American progress rather than aided it.[8]

Easterners who traveled west argued that evidence of the corrupting powers of life among Indians and the wilderness abounded everywhere. Newcomers to early-nineteenth-century Vincennes, in present-day southeastern Indiana, believed that the town illustrated the awesome ability of the wilderness to corrupt. American officials complained that the filthy conditions of village life made it "no better than an Indian camp." Daily gunfire sprayed through the streets, threatening both the "personal safety of passersby" and those hiding "in their houses" from stray bullets. Dead horses, dogs, and hogs lined the narrow streets and attracted packs of canines that fed on the putrid carcasses. Other visitors complained that hordes of uncontrollable squirrels decimated untended fields.[9] One federal official, assigned to work in Vincennes, complained that the village lacked the basic necessities to perform his job, including paper, pen knives, erasers, and folders. He furthermore believed that idleness and "want of activity" drove men in the town to violence and vice.[10]

So what did those who condemned western settlers propose as an alternative? Companies of men in the East argued that organization and order were necessary elements of successful western settlement—only through vigorous planning and foresight could Americans prevent the type of disorder that abounded in Vincennes. The early organizers of present-day southeast Ohio had ideas for replicating and improving upon eastern towns and villages. According to their plan, industrious investors would purchase large tracts of land and prepare it for orderly settlement; they argued that speculation was key to exploiting western resources without succumbing to its deleterious effects. Manasseh Cutler, one of the organizers for the Ohio Company, outlined these goals in his report, *An Explanation of the Map which Delineates that Part of the Federal Lands, Comprehended between Pennsylvania West Line, the Rivers Ohio and Scioto, and Lake Erie; Confirmed to the United States by Sundry Tribes of Indians, in the Territories of 1784 and 1786, and Now Ready for Settlement.*[11] Published prior to the Ohio Company's settlement at Marietta and meant as an advertisement for the company's lands, the pamphlet detailed the group's vision for orderly settlement. Cutler maintained that a merchant or industrious person could take advantage of the region's "natural fertility" with "less expence, risk and insurance" than in other parts of the country, because the lands north of the river were "the most healthy, the most pleasant, the most commodious and most fertile spot" on earth. He posited that "a man may clear an acre a day, fit for planting with Indian corn," and the lands could "be reduced to proper cultivation with very little labour." The trees "growing very high and large, but not thick together," needed "nothing but girdling."[12] Moreover, Cutler posited, the orderly minded associates of the Ohio Company would oversee it all.

Cutler's report highlighted the difference between perceived notions of proper and improper settlement, as he lauded the Ohio Company's efforts to promote a "regular and judicious manner" of western advancement that would "serve as a wise model for the future settlement of all the federal lands." He also explained that "a continuation of the old settlements" would leave "no vacant lands exposed to be seized by such lawless banditti as usually infest the frontier of countries distant from the seat of government." In other words, he believed that western expansion should be dictated by the aims of moneyed men and land speculators.[13]

Some local territorial officials disagreed and encouraged legislation that would encourage a more expedited version of settlement, which would push Indians off their lands. They proposed "preemption laws"— legislation that would allow "actual settlers" to purchase public lands, which they had improved, at a minimum price. Previously, Congress had established a system of land sales that required surveyors to survey lands and bring them up for public auction before anyone was permitted to settle on them. Preemption would circumvent that process. Congress identified "actual settlers" as individuals who had moved west, settled the lands, improved plots by felling trees and planting crops, and built a home after gaining title to it.[14] In 1800, William Henry Harrison (then a delegate to Congress) made suggestions for new public land policies that aided "actual settlers" by reducing the minimum purchase size and instituting a credit system for land purchases. Only one-fourth of the total price was required at the time of purchase. He argued for the bill on the House floor because it "prevented speculators receiving the advantages resulting from offering the lands in large quantities" and encouraged "actual settlers to purchase" small claims.[15] Prior to this exception, speculators were able to purchase settled lands at government-run public auctions—thereby evicting actual settlers from their improvements. Harrison probably supported the measure for two reasons. First, actual settlers occupied lands near Indian Country and could be used to persuade American Indians to cede their claims, as far-off speculators would not provide that pressure. Second, eastern speculators interfered with Harrison's own speculation in western lands (charges abounded that he had others purchase large tracts on his behalf).[16]

While some local officials promoted squatter-friendly legislation, most federal politicians and popular writers contrived to attack squatters as lawless banditti. Through the first decade of the nineteenth century, Congress generally outlawed intrusions on the public lands and even authorized the president to use military force to prevent illegal settlements.[17] Squatters flooded Congress with petitions trying to change their minds. Thus began one of the great debates among Americans in the lower Great Lakes over who held the right to settle the region. To defend themselves against military removal, the verbal assaults of land speculators, and the written tracts of land company propagandists, squatters turned to the one outlet available to them: petitions. They believed that actual settlement advanced the cause of extending the American empire westward. Petitioners emphasized their devotion to the nation and told Congress that, while "great numbers" of previous western settlers had abandoned the United States in order to join the "despotic Governments" of the far west (Britain in the northern Great Lakes and Spain west of the Mississippi River), they had not.[18] As Spanish officials had tried to court them, they argued, they decided to "throw themselves on the Justice and magnanimity" of Congress rather than betray their country.[19]

The history of squatter petitions illustrates a war of words that accompanied changes in national policy and popular attitudes toward western settlement. Delineating truth from fiction in these petitions begins by tracing major shifts in the language used by petitioners to describe themselves. In the years preceding the War of 1812, the American West still resembled a colonial world; European powers, the American government, and numerous Indian tribes competed for control of the region. Early petitions reflected an older, yet operational, colonial rhetoric. Petitioners proclaimed President Washington "his Excellency" and recognized themselves as "faithful subjects of the United States."[20] Others begged Congress to recognize their claims and "afford such encouragement and protection" that they had come to expect from their "British proprietors." Petitioners wrote in a language that expressed deference to would-be readers, as they tried to convince congressmen that they deserved recognition as inheritors of a Revolutionary ideal that guaranteed men the right to pursue happiness and accumulate property even if it cost a few dollars in federal revenues.[21] In almost every case in these early years, petitioners simply referred to themselves as "inhabitants" of the western territories beseeching officials for help.

Western settlers labeled themselves as such because nineteenth-century concepts of citizenship required a person to possess a number of qualifications: landownership, suffrage, social ranking, tax-paying status, or military service. These were all credentials that squatter-petitioners lacked.[22] The requirement for landownership rested on a set of older colonial assumptions about a special bond between property holders and a nation that protected their property, but those ideals began to wane as fewer and fewer Americans could claim the necessary requirements to be considered full citizens. Demographic changes, primarily an increase in urban artisans and propertyless western settlers, created a disparity between the general populace and officeholders. Consequently, states began to reconsider suffrage qualifications. Prior to the War of 1812, Delaware, Maryland, South Carolina, and New Jersey each eliminated property-holding standards, while other eastern states accepted different kinds of personal property (savings, buildings, and estate values) as alternatives to cumulative acreage.[23]

Eastern and western pressures forced federal officials (who controlled political decisions in the territories) to reconsider voting qualifications in the area north and west of the Ohio River. The 1787 Northwest Ordinance had required a voter to own fifty acres of land or similarly valued property. As eastern states removed property requirements, western settlers begged Congress to do the same for them.[24] Ohio, the first state carved from the territories, eliminated property qualifications in its state constitution. In 1808, Congress modified suffrage requirements in the Indiana Territory to allow individuals with town lots worth $100 to vote for the territorial general assembly.[25] The following year, Congress eliminated all property qualifications for the territory and permitted any free white male over the age of twenty-one the right to vote for territorial assembly member and the delegate to Congress if he had paid a county or territorial tax.[26] They extended the same right to Illinois Territory in 1812, after petitioners there presented Congress with statistics on the paltry number of eligible voters in the territory. In one district with 12,200 inhabitants, no more than 300 legally possessed enough acreage to vote.[27] Western petitioners viewed the possibility of a few controlling the many "with the aversion natural to free men."[28]

As voting requirements allowed more westerners to participate in elections, squatters began to petition Congress, not as inhabitants but as citizens of the United States. This seemingly minor alteration in language represented something much larger. Petitioners no longer pandered to the government for leniency and preemption, nor did they defer to the authority of their representatives in Washington. Instead, they demanded the right of preemption as an extension of their rights as citizens, and they criticized the government for even depriving them of their "original right of Inheritance." Petitioners believed that they had been "cruelly oppressed" by a federal regime that kept them from enjoying the "realities of Independence" by rejecting their demands for preemption. They contended that the government would benefit from a general accessibility to cheap or free land, because it would "produce loyalty in each citizen, prevent Rebellion, remove animosities, Cement a union, and promote happiness throughout each department of the family of the United States." One group suggested that Congress give every eighteen-year-old man or female head of household a section of the public domain, limiting the amount that anyone else could hold to two hundred acres "by Improvement."[29]

In demanding action, squatters highlighted their position as both "actual settlers" and citizens; they no longer apologized for their illegal occupation of public lands. Instead, they blamed government inefficiency for their lawlessness. Petitioners argued that the federal government failed to put lands up at auction in a timely fashion. Some painted an unsettling picture of patient settlers waiting for a local land office to open, only to be attacked by Indians. Nevertheless, Congress repeatedly rejected the squatters' claims and reiterated the long-held position that preemption promoted disorder and encouraged "future violations."[30] They preferred the model of the Ohio Company. Jeremiah Morrow, member of the Committee on Public Lands, argued that "promiscuous and unauthorized settlements on the public lands" injured "the public interest" and destroyed "the effect intended to be produced by the law" (i.e., revenue for Congress).[31]

The violence surrounding the War of 1812 provided squatters with additional opportunities to claim citizenship. If loosened voting requirements could not persuade congressmen and the general public to support their cause, perhaps tales of defending their families on the violent frontier might. Moreover, the focus of the nation on the western frontier allowed them to distance themselves from labels used to describe Indians. Petitioners highlighted their service in defending the frontier against Indian violence to shed the "white savage" stereotype.[32] In Illinois, where suffrage had yet to be extended to those who owned no land, the War of 1812 provided squatters with an opportunity to reaffirm their image as virtuous citizens rather than barbarous intruders. The federal government found it difficult to recruit and maintain troops during the war, so it promised suffrage rights to volunteers. Military service long had been used as a qualification for voting, and land was used as a reward for service, especially when the government could not afford to pay troops for their enlistments. As war raged in the lower Great Lakes, squatters used their service as "defenders of the frontier" to sue for preemption.[33] Perhaps understanding Congress's preoccupation with revenue, petitioners argued that their presence in the territories meant that the federal government required fewer troops to defend the country against the "inroads of the Savages," thereby saving Uncle Sam money.[34] In 1813, Congress rewarded this argument by passing a preemption law that allowed squatters to register their claims with the local land office, but congressmen ultimately refused to condone all forms of illegal settlements and warned future violators that they would be punished.[35]

Conflict during the War of 1812 took a particularly hard toll on westerners; even those who had purchased lands fell behind on payments as enemies, including unruly American militiamen, stripped their fields. Additionally, the collapse of local agricultural markets prevented those who could harvest their crops from profiting much from them. Petitioners returned to the image of the West as a frontier meeting place between savagery and civilization to highlight the differences between them and their indigenous neighbors. They argued that "frequent interruptions, depredations, and massacres" kept them from tending their fields and harvesting their crops, and they told Congress they often were forced into blockhouses to escape "all the dangers and privations of Savage War."[36] Squatters painted a grim picture of a West where Indians roamed the frontiers looking to "slaughter, rape, and plunder" innocent families whose husbands had either left to serve in the military or fallen to the "Savage Waraxe and Scalping Knife."[37]

Such petitioners flooded Congress with letters complaining that the 1813 Preemption Act failed to address the concerns of "actual settlers" in the West. Entire communities, they argued, were forced to live together to protect against Indian attacks. This prevented them from filing claims or improving their lands.[38] Others argued that the war forced them to "Cultivate Lands in common," and since the act only allowed whole sections to be entered, they could not file for preemption.[39] Violence, precipitated by Indians, they argued, had forced them to abandon their ultimate goal of aiding the United States in extending its empire westward. One group, calling themselves the Society of True Americans, argued that "not one in twenty" persons could afford the minimum price because the war had emptied their pocketbooks.[40] Others complained that they had volunteered for local militias and been unable to file petitions because the deadlines fell while they were away from home serving their country.[41] Together, these petitioners presented a clear message: Indians and foreign enemies stood in the way of American progress.

Postwar petitions focused on the squatters' role in ridding the western landscape of Indians. Petitioners argued that as frontier citizen-soldiers they were indeed participants in proper American expansion rather than obstructions to it. Unfortunately for squatters, the close of the War of 1812 fueled a new influx of settlers into the lower Great Lakes, and the overwhelming number of new arrivals—many settling illegally on government lands—forced the federal government to renew its anti-squatting stance. In 1815, James Madison issued a presidential proclamation authorizing the use of military force in removing illegal intruders from the public domain.[42] Still, petitions kept arriving in Washington. One group of petitioners suggested that twenty to thirty thousand squatters had laid aside the plow and picked up a rifle to defend their country during the War of 1812.[43]

Americans for many years had used North America's indigenous population as a creative reflection against which they could highlight their perceived superiority, but squatters used their position as national citizens to add other elements. They argued that a good government should protect them from both Native Americans who threatened their families and ambitious speculators who threatened to steal their property. Squatters considered themselves "free amerrican Citizans" and begged the government to guard their "Liberties & rights" by protecting their property, including their labor.[44] Squatters believed they had already lost a considerable amount of property to the "Wily intrigues of a ruthless foe" because the government had failed to defend them from Indians.[45] They refused to stand by idly while their improvements were "likely to become an object to the unprincipled ambitious speculators."[46] Petitioners contended that the inaction of the federal government suspended them "between savage cruelty & opulent speculation," and they beseeched Congress to intervene in order to "prevent for the future so black a crime from entering the Volumes of Modern record."[47] Still, Congress rejected their requests.[48]

Perhaps congressional resistance to preemptive legislation resulted from the dishonesty and deception that often resided just below the surface of the language of squatter petitions. Signers were often far from innocent victims. A casual glance at early petitions reveal the signatures of prominent individuals who did not need preemptive legislation to defend their land claims. As Indiana (1816) and Illinois (1818) formed constitutional conventions in the second decade of the nineteenth century, individuals who had previously claimed to be poor squatters often represented their communities at the conventions. As delegates to state constitutional conventions, these individuals since have been lifted from obscurity. Subsequent histories reveal them not as penniless squatters but as prominent individuals (even at the time that they signed petitions claiming to be unfortunate souls struggling to make it on the rough frontier). For example, Washington County, Indiana, voters selected John DePauw as a delegate. Only a year earlier, DePauw had affixed his name to a petition from a group of squatters who warned Congress about the ruthlessness of "unprincipled ambitious speculators."[49] DePauw never had been a squatter. Instead, he had worked as a land agent selling lots in the town of Salem at the time of the petition.[50] So why would he sign a petition lambasting his own occupation? He may have seen his squatter neighbors as future clients or voters (voters in Washington, Orange, and Jackson counties elected him as their representative shortly after statehood). Later, he made a strong but unsuccessful bid for the governor's office, gaining large support from the area where he lived.[51]

Voters in Harrison County, in Indiana Territory, elected Davis Floyd and Dennis Pennington, two former petitioners, as delegates to the convention. Again, neither man seemed to have illegally settled on public lands. In fact, they both appear to have been substantial landholders and territorial politicians. Davis Floyd moved to Indiana in 1801 and served as county recorder and sheriff as well as representative to the territorial legislature. A bit later, Floyd joined a group of investors who wanted to construct a canal at the falls of the Ohio River. One of those investors, Aaron Burr, persuaded Floyd to join him in a project to invade Spanish possessions and forge a new colony in the West. Burr's ambitious scheme drew sharp criticism, and a circuit court in Mississippi Territory issued arrest warrants for both Burr and Floyd. With friends on the bench, Floyd served a three-day sentence and was released. His credibility plunged in the years following the conspiracy, and he may have signed squatter petitions to retool his image and gain support from his neighbors. It appears to have worked. Floyd's neighbors elected him to the General Assembly and nominated him for judge following the convention.[52]

Harrison County voters also sent Dennis Pennington to the convention. Pennington had moved to Indiana earlier in the decade accompanied by his new wife, Elizabeth English, who had been released from Indian captivity only months prior to their wedding. Within a few years, they moved to the area around Corydon in Indiana Territory, where Pennington served three commissions as justice of the peace, sat in the territorial house in 1812, and vigorously campaigned against the movement to allow slavery into the territory. Despite signing a petition on behalf of squatters, he had never been one. Pennington, like Floyd, may have affixed his signature to the petition as a symbol of solidarity with his neighbors, whom he hoped would vote him into office. After the convention, voters propelled him to the state senate.[53]

Other squatter petitioners came from a variety of backgrounds, many of which appeared to have few connections to preemption rights. Some, such as Miles Hotchkiss and George Fisher, owned inns and taverns, while others, like Pierre Menard, were retailers.[54] While none of these men personally needed their lands preempted from sale, the population boom promised by cheap or free land would have directly benefited their businesses. It was never clear which petitioner was and which petitioner was not a squatter. Men like William Biggs certainly appeared to be the real thing. He served under George Rogers Clark during the Revolution and, after short stay in western Virginia, decided to travel west and settle near Kaskaskia. Although he appeared to represent the honest frontier squatter, Biggs did not need the government to preempt his lands from sale—he already owned them.[55] Westerners from all backgrounds signed squatter petitions. Politicians, innkeepers, ferry operators, millers, and landholders who honestly wanted to aid their neighbors affixed their names to these documents, as did politically savvy community leaders who viewed squatters as potential constituents.

Congress assigned two commissioners, Michael Jones and Elijah Backus, to travel to the lower Great Lakes and investigate the authenticity of claims made by petitioners.[56] A closer examination of their investigation highlights the deception and outright nefarious intentions behind some petitioners' claims. It also suggests reasons why congressmen were reluctant in extending blanket protection to individuals who claimed to be actual settlers. In 1804, a group of settlers in what would become Illinois Territory argued that "various turns of fortune" had brought them onto the frontier, including an unfortunate case where Indians had taken many of their wives and children into captivity.[57] They pleaded for Congress to grant them preemption rights to the lands where they settled and excuse their innocent intentions, but the congressional investigation concluded that the petitioners were far from innocent settlers.

The most troubling documents centered on ancient land grants—issued to foreign-born persons who had settled in the region prior to the American Revolution (before it was the American West). Many of those claimants either had died or moved to Spanish-held territories west of the Mississippi, as they did not trust that the United States would honor their property rights following the Revolution.[58] Ambitious American entrepreneurs stepped into the vacuum to capitalize on this chaos. French settlers tried to sell their ancient claims to anyone who would offer them hard specie; after all, they figured the papers were worthless.[59] Local territorial officials swooped in to purchase tracts for themselves at preposterously low prices. In some areas, Frenchmen sold 400-acre head-rights for between $30 and $200 and 100-acre militia head-rights for $6 to $14—the minimum price at public auction was set at $2 per acre.[60]

In the years preceding the investigation, local leaders John Edgar and Robert Morrison, who signed the previously mentioned 1804 petition, attempted to use their remoteness and lack of government oversight to control the local land market and seize political autonomy. They believed they could accomplish their goal by linking their scheme to the increasingly popular squatters' movement. Although they allied with territorial governor William Henry Harrison on the admission of slavery, the group launched a campaign to rid themselves of his management by dividing the Indiana Territory in two (at the time Indiana Territory included all of present-day Illinois). After the Louisiana Purchase, the group started a separatist campaign to break free from the Indiana Territory and join the newly created Louisiana Territory. They believed territorial division would allow them to pursue their quest for more land and power beyond the watchful eye of federal officials like Harrison. The two vocal and charismatic men forged a coalition of westerners under a banner that promoted "opposition to the territorial administration, and Illinois for Illinoisians."[61]

The group successfully wrestled control away from Harrison's supporters and created a virtual fiefdom in what would become the Illinois Territory. By 1807, a handful of the leading landholders, all claiming political allegiance to Edgar and Morrison, held nearly every important local office in Kaskaskia. This allowed them to promote land policies that advanced their own self-interests.[62] When the investigations began, the Edgar-Morrison faction framed it as unnecessary interference by colonial rulers. In fact, they argued a previous board already had investigated the claims. But their complaints could not hide the fact that they all had participated in widespread corruption and fraud. The commission discovered that the previous board, made up of Edgar-Morrison allies, had liberally recognized applications and extended landownership essentially to anyone who resided in the area or served in the militia, despite the fact that the laws under which they were appointed restricted their authority to recognize only settlers with evidence of settlement before the Revolution. Over the span of six years, the new commission considered more than 2,500 claims and found that the most egregious crimes were committed by a small group of inhabitants connected to Edgar and Morrison.[63]

John Edgar led the group both in political prowess and shameless ambition. The commission discovered that Edgar had filed twenty-one double entries—in one case submitting two identical claims to the territorial governor, getting his signature on both, changing the section and quarter designations on one, and then filing both with the local land agent. In other cases, Edgar forged the signatures of officials or paid men to file false affidavits that stated the signatory had sold Edgar their ancient land grants. Thanks to Edgar, the commission reported that "a class of professional witnesses with elastic memories sprang up and did a thriving business" in and around Kaskaskia. The commission concluded that Edgar had filed forged documents for 7,249 acres, perjured statements for 49,246 acres, and inadequate claims for over 73,000 additional acres. The commission's final report eventually drove him out of politics and ostracized him within the community.[64]

Many of Edgar's friends, including Robert Morrison, Robert Reynolds, John Reynolds, George Fisher, William Kelly, James Gilbreath, and
multiple members of the Whiteside family, had also signed the 1804
squatter petition. The land commission examined over 300,000 acres
claimed by the group.[65] Judge Robert Reynolds drew the harshest condemnation from the commission: they labeled him in the final report
as a "forger and perjurer." Reynolds had filed over 26,000 acres worth
of claims, of which the commission recognized only 477 as legitimate.
They found that he issued perjured statements for over 10,000 acres,
and at one point had forged the names of two judges with whom he
shared the bench. In one case Reynolds forged a grant to himself from a
fictional woman.[66] The actions of Edgar's other cohorts were equally dis-
honorable. Out of 17,000 acres, the commission could not find a single
entry submitted by William Kelly that had not been forged, perjured, or
unsubstantiated. Kelly joined Edgar associates John Reynolds, William
Whiteside, and James Gilbreath, each of whom had their claims summarily rejected. Overall, the commission denied nearly 77 percent of the
claims made by members of the Edgar-Morrison group.[67]

The system of public land dispersal up to that time required the federal government to auction off lands at a public venue, with the hope that
interested parties would drive up the price and the federal government
would profit. Squatters had long argued that the lands in question had
not come up for auction fast enough, therefore forcing them to settle and
improve them prior to sale. Speculators like Edgar and Morrison proved
equally disruptive to western sales. In 1817, the Senate Committee on
Public Lands concluded that uneven settlement was "an intercourse by
which the civilized man cannot be improved" and the Indian was "de-
praved—not being sufficiently enlightened to receive a favourable impression from the virtues of civilization." Furthermore, senators on the
committee argued that the inability of Congress to control western settlement exposed Indians to the "contagion of its [America's] vices."[68]

Congress could not dismiss the possibility that preemption and the
encouragement of "actual settlement," legal or illegal, offered an alternative to the cumbersome bureaucracy of the public land system, within
which a reliance on the shallow pockets of public land purchasers threatened to bankrupt the federal government.[69] By 1817, both squatters

and speculators proved obstacles to federal attempts to profit off western lands. Congress had been reluctant to allow squatters to purchase the lands privately, fearing that they would ultimately lose revenue. But a report by the General Land Office in 1816 showed that the government had made a mere ten and a half cents more per acre by selling public lands at auction than by selling them for the established minimum price.[70] The commissioner of the Land Office, Return Jonathon Meigs, calculated that the difference between auctions and sales totaled $685,473.48 for the sale of all public lands northwest of the Ohio River and within the Mississippi Territory.[71] Congress responded by drafting a preemption bill that same day that allowed squatters to purchase their claims for the government-approved minimum price.[72]

These reports revealed only the surface of the problem, as later studies exposed that the General Land Office's accounts were "greatly in arrear" and that many individual balances had remained "unsettled from seven to ten years" earlier. Many of the accounts, the comptroller of the Treasury informed Congress, were "intricate and generally very large" and required "from ten to fifteen days . . . for the best accounting clerks to examine one of them."[73] In 1817, the U.S. government sold 1,412,631.16 acres northwest of the Ohio River for $3,097,253.39, but government receivers deposited only about a third of that amount. By the beginning of 1818, individuals owed $6,184,973 for purchases made over the previous decade and a half, and although the federal government sold an additional 1,245,106.59 acres in the first three quarters of 1818, the outstanding debt of individuals rose to $7,290,489.55. The cost of the public land system began to outweigh the benefits. Still, Congress passed only a single temporary, retroactive preemption measure.[74]

In the years following the War of 1812, settlers flooded into the lower Great Lakes, and increasing numbers of illegal settlers came to articulate their struggles in the form of petitions. They borrowed from the language of earlier petitions, but this new wave of squatters began to draw public sympathy, especially as newly formed western state legislatures drafted public memorials in support of their squatter constituents.[75] State legislatures in Indiana and Illinois drafted memorials instructing their representatives in the nation's capital to "use every exertion" to protect squatter improvements and lower the price of western lands.[76]

Perhaps wary that corrupt individuals were still cloaking themselves as squatters in the petitions, federal officials passed a series of retroactive *but temporary* preemption laws throughout the 1820s and 1830s.[77]

Western congressmen came to the rescue of the "hardy sons of the West" and extolled the virtues of the actual settler.[78] The popular vision of pioneering helped western politicians pass preemptive measures, but stories about the frontier squatter also began to gain the folksy characteristics of the vernacular hero. One anecdote recounted the events of a public auction where a speculator began outbidding a squatter. A roomful of squatters seized the dapper gentleman, passed him over their heads to the back of the auction house, and threw him into the street.[79] Other stories elucidated the meaning of so-called squatter justice. They explained that if a squatter was convicted of intimidating another buyer or threatening him, the local jury—packed with men sympathetic to the squatter—would either find him not guilty or fine him very little. Western writers assured potential settlers that there was "not the least danger of losing title or life" in the West because "every thing relating to the whole business" of squatter settlements was "understood in the whole community, and mutual laws which they have framed for their own management" restrained violence and were meant to "protect each settler in his rights."[80]

More than two decades of squatter petitions to Congress helped provide a language for describing the merits of the western settler and the squatter. Petitioners had challenged the stereotype of the western settler as a solitary bachelor hacking his way westward through the dangerous wilderness.[81] Instead, they had highlighted their families, farms, and communal relationships. Travel writers and easterners often had painted portraits of human declension in the West and warned of the threat of "going Indian." But while squatters admitted that some frontiersmen embodied such unseemly traits, they insisted that their motivations were driven by the "desire natural to the human mind" of acquiring acreage enough to "rear their tender offsprings in a comfortable manner."[82] Petitioners contended that actual settlers, legal or illegal, helped create a western society based on the building blocks of American society—the family—and a place where Americans could "enjoy the comfort and advantages resulting from Civilized Society and Religious worship."[83]

Evidence here sustains the squatter's claims that pioneering was a family affair. By 1800, 1,533 people lived around the area of Vincennes. Of this population, nearly 47 percent were under the age of sixteen and almost one-third under ten. Farther west, in Kaskaskia, 42 percent of the population was under sixteen. These statistics suggest, at least in the long-settled frontier outposts where the majority of westerners lived, that settlers were mostly family men and women. In fact, women outnumbered men around Vincennes.[84] These statistics also reflected the demographics of squatter petition signers. While some petitions cloaked the speculator identities of their signers, petitions signed exclusively by men also hid large families behind the names of each individual. Thirteen squatters who signed a petition for relief from government removal appeared on an 1810 census of Harrison County, Indiana Territory. These thirteen households shared sixty-nine children under the age of sixteen, and only one household lacked at least one child under ten. In at least one case, census data appears to support the claims of petitioners who argued that they had journeyed "thro' a Wilderness without inhabitants," while transporting "Provisions as well as families."[85]

Westerners believed that once their territories entered into statehood, frontiersmen and squatters would be recognized as full citizens. The Northwest Ordinance established progressive stages for the western lands on their way to statehood, but these stages of government were also "read" as stages of civilization: territorial status carried with it the initial vestiges of civilization—legislatures, courts, and ordered settlement— while statehood marked the final metamorphosis from frontier chaos to full-fledged civilization. After all, new states, according to the Northwest Ordinance, were supposed to enter the union "on equal footing" with the oldest eastern ones.[86] Squatters thought the inhabitants and citizens of those states would likewise enter as equal citizens.

At the same time, Jacksonian infatuation with the "common man" posed a dilemma: popular visions of western heroes often returned to the image of the bombastic frontier hunter, not the meek farmer.[87] Part of the new manifestation of the rough-and-tumble frontiersman, in fact, was a result of what many Americans viewed as the overrefinement of westerners into puritan agrarians.[88] Stories about men like Davy Crockett, Major Jack Downing, Simon Suggs, and "Big" Bill Otter portrayed the

Jacksonian "common man" as a rugged, racist, and individualistic coun-
terpoint to the Jeffersonian yeoman.[89] Cincinnati's *Western Monthly Review*
disapproved of the "Jack Downing and Davy Crockett taste" of popular
stereotypes and argued that the half-horse, half-alligator vernacular heroes did not seem to describe the settlers they knew.[90] In a strange turn
of fortune, western settlers in the lower Great Lakes, who had fought for
nearly two decades to shed the type of violent characteristics attached to
Jacksonian men, now found a nation embracing precisely those traits.[91]

The image of the "actual settler," crafted by petitioners and politicians
in the 1820s and 1830s, provided a mellow alternative to this crude Jacksonian folk hero. Western writer Timothy Flint argued that actual settlers
had been classified for too long as "gougers, ruffians, demi-savages, a
repulsive mixture in the slang phrase, of the 'horse and the alligator.'"
He believed it was the "rough, sturdy, and simple habits of the backwoodsmen" pioneers that laid the foundation for "independent thought
and feeling deep in the breasts" of Americans.[92] Flint claimed he "heard
a thousand stories of gougings, and robberies, and shooting down with
a rifle" before he went west, but he witnessed the backwoodsman as "an
amiable and virtuous man."[93] Travelers like Flint helped guide the American gaze away from the frontier ruffian toward the noble farmer. Other
observers helped. After hearing tales about frontier barbarism and a
world populated by miscreants, later travelers discovered a region typified by relative refinement and civility. Unlike their early counterparts,
travel writers in the 1820s and 1830s began to report the heightened
importance of community camaraderie and the family to western settlers and highlighted the community events, like cornhuskings, apple
cuttings, and quilting bees.[94] These images of western life helped craft a
new popular image for western settlers.

Western newspapers hailed the western farmer as the ploughman
and praised him for his devotion to family and community. This image
bridged the Jeffersonian virtuous farmer and the Jacksonian "half horse,
half alligator" man.[95] Writers venerated the farmer as "independent and
yet so free from vanity and pride. So rich and yet so industrious; so patient
and preserving in his calling, and yet so kind, social, and obliging." Eventually, the farmer became a leading symbol of Jacksonian democracy.

By the 1830s, the struggle for preemption became synonymous with the plight of the western settler. Squatters and squatting no longer held the pejorative implications that they had in previous decades. Illegal settlers proudly claimed the moniker and organized communities around the appellation. In self-organized villages across Indiana and Illinois, illegal settlers formed "squatter organizations" or "squatter unions" and drafted "squatter constitutions." Squatter rights and preemption also became the fixation of western politicians. In 1837, representatives from western states launched an extended campaign to reintroduce squatter rights on the floors of Congress. The debates in the Senate and House of Representatives over preemption reveal just how pervasive the image of the squatter as actual settler and pioneer had become. Both sides of the debate hashed out the meaning of western settlement and made the final connections between pioneering and general thoughts about American progress, forever linking the two together.

Still, some congressmen held on to older notions of proper settlement. Ohio senator Thomas Ewing, chairman of the Committee on Public Lands, echoed the decades-old argument that the policy of preemption was "monstrous in itself" because it justified ignorance of the law. Ewing also believed that speculation had "good as well as evil consequences," but "accumulated capital" had produced some of the most remarkable changes in the West. It "opened harbors, drained swamps, built wharves, and erected warehouses, transferring business and bustle and comfort and intelligence of an old and cultivated community into the very heart of our remote western forests." Still, Ewing would not vote for a measure "against the small capitalist, the farmer, the mechanic, the laborer, *for the special benefit of any class of speculators; however great their power, or democratic their professions.*"[96]

Ewing argued that the culture of squatting was too violent for the government to condone. He suspected that settlers, unbound by proper laws, would brutally attack one another for choice lots. Ewing explained that a friend (in the House of Representatives) informed him of a dispute over land in the lead-rich districts of Illinois where members from two parties killed one another over access to specific tracts. The lands and mines switched hands several times before the widow of one victim killed the last male claimant. Ewing used the story to connect squatters back to the lawless frontier.

The senator claimed that the squatter organizations that dotted the lower Great Lakes misrepresented the realities of western life. To illustrate his point, he pointed to the Lake County (Indiana) Squatters' Union, an organization comprising nearly five hundred squatters who drafted a constitution that called upon each member to defend the property rights of the others. He argued that organizations like the Lake County Squatters' Union placed "a false face" on the subject of squatting and gentlemen who represented the squatter "generally as poor men, seeking a freehold and a home, willing to pay for the land on which they settle, but unable to do so, because the lands are not in market, and cannot be purchased" had been fooled.[97]

In subsequent debates, Ewing argued that the improvements made by squatters were "merely *colorable*, for the purpose of enabling the individual to get the land" and trick the U.S. government. Most squatters simply built "a little pen of rails" and sowed "oats or turnips or radishes upon ten or twelve square feet of ground" and called them improvements. Furthermore, preemption laws produced the largest "crop of fraud or perjury" the government had ever seen. Ewing echoed claims made earlier by Henry Clay, who had argued that preemption laws produced "the most stupendous frauds."[98]

Ewing blasted the Lake County squatters and read their constitution before the Senate. He argued that their commitment to gain claims at any cost was evidence of the violent and barbarous manner of squatters in general. Ewing warned the Senate that squatters were capable of atrocious behavior and that the actions of the Lake County Squatters were treasonous because their Union was a "Government established in a Government—*imperium in imperio*," not "subordinate to the laws of the union, but in opposition to them."[99]

Indiana senator John Tipton countered Ewing's remarks by defending the Lake County squatters. In fact, he claimed to have known them personally and attested to them as "an orderly, peaceable, and respectable body of men" who "have gone into that country with a view to better their condition; and who will blame them for it? They engage to employ at the public sales all the same means in their power to obtain their rights, by which I understand them of course to mean all lawful means." Tipton explained that he was "a personal acquaintance with Solon Robinson," the organizer of the Lake County Squatters' Union, and believed "him to be an upright, honest, and honorable man." "Can you expect that these people shall stand still," he asked his fellow senators, "and let the speculators come and turn their wives and children out of doors?"[100]

Ewing believed that squatters and speculators colluded to keep money from the government coffers. He found it curious that his fellow senators "who denounce speculators" the loudest likely were "deeply engaged in the vocation" that they condemned, including Tipton. Ewing's tirades may have been personal assaults on those in Congress who had helped make him a lame duck senator—a Jacksonian Democrat who defended squatters and championed preemption had recently beaten the Ohio senator at the polls. Still, in his remaining days in office, Ewing sought to expose his fellow senators who engaged in speculation while defending squatters; he believed they told boldface lies in order to save their jobs.[101]

During the following congressional term, Democratic senator Robert Walker replaced Ewing as chair of the Committee on Public Land. He bucked the traditional argument against preemption and proclaimed that squatters indeed were valiant American citizens who deserved protection. "The settler who left the comforts of civilization to seek a new home, reclaiming the lands from their rude state, subduing the forest and building his cabin in the before untrodden wilds of the wilderness," he contended, "was surely entitled to such a preference." Walker dismissed cases of fraud as minor prices to pay in the effort to promote the general settlement of the West and reward actual settlers over the interests of speculators. Walker exalted squatters and prayed that God would allow him to "go on adding" to the "glorious Republic State after State."[102]

Illinois senator Richard Young not only supported preemption for squatters but also fought to expand the meaning of the actual settler to include blacksmiths, poor farmers, and even those who had yet to improve the public lands. He argued that any "meritorious persons" who wanted cheap land for their personal use should receive it from the government. Young viewed settlement as an action not limited to agricultural interests. His wide interpretation came to describe a variety of westerners, including farmers, doctors, merchants, and even some speculators.[103] When the proposed legislation reached the House floor in 1838, Indiana representative Ratliff Boon, former Indiana governor and chair of the Committee on Public Lands, shocked fellow representatives when he revealed that he himself had been a squatter. The congressman rose to defend the "rights and interests of [his] fellow-citizens" and explained to colleagues that he could "judge more correctly the many privations which is [sic] experienced by those who, at different periods of time, have settled upon the public lands in the Western wilds," because he had been in their shoes. He explained how his penniless family decided to move from Kentucky to southern Indiana in the hopes of finding cheap, if not free, land. He believed (perhaps erroneously) that "the greater portion of the entire population of those States and Territories settled upon the public lands before they became purchasers." Boon posited that his life story demonstrated how illegal settlement produced men who were attached to their country and considerate of their communities, not "*lawless intruders and land pirates.*"[104]

Congressional debates moved the image of the squatter-as-pioneer to the center of the meaning of American democracy and progress. The case of the Lake County Squatters' Union, whom Tipton raised as an example of the advantage of squatter settlement, provides a particularly interesting case of how the shiftiness in language used to describe and defend western settlers came to obscure the realities of western settlement. On March 19, 1839, nearly five hundred members of the Lake County Squatters' Union attended the public land auction at LaPorte, Indiana, many of them brandishing firearms. They huddled around three well-dressed men sitting behind shrewdly constructed tables under the shade of a large elm tree. Curiously, not a single one of the armed men cast a bid. Instead, Solon Robinson, William Kinnison, and A. McDonald, the dapper gentlemen at the tables, waited until a tract was announced, then quickly gleaned enormous land registers sitting before them until they spotted the tract.[105] Once found, they cast a single bid at the government-approved minimum price: the guns and glares of five hundred armed men behind them prevented competitive bidding.

Many of the Lake County squatters had arrived in northwestern Indiana over the previous two decades, illegally settling on public and Indian lands. Prior to the auction, they had made improvements and organized their own community, all out of sight of federal officials. In addition to conspiring to squash competition at the public land auction, the settlers already had established a town center (complete with a village store, grist mill, and town hall—admittedly several of them in the same building), assembled a Union, and drawn up their own constitution. The Reverend Timothy Horton Ball, a young boy at the time, recalled that "armed men were among them—to use force if necessary to secure the right which each squatter claimed of buying his own quarter section at one dollar and a quarter an acre."[106] Their leader, and the original organizer of the Lake County Squatters' Union, Solon Robinson had in fact never been a squatter and did not need the organization to claim his lands in Indiana. But he does represent how the increasingly popular language of western settlement and the popular image of the squatter permitted men like him to embrace and embody the squatter cause.

Solon Robinson was born in Tolland, Connecticut, in 1803, long after the first American settlers crossed the Ohio River. His father died when Solon was only six years old, and the young boy changed guardians until, at the age of fifteen, he requested that his uncle Vine Robinson (a merchant and county judge) look after him. In his hometown of Brooklyn, Connecticut, Vine introduced Solon to elite members of the community. As he worked in his uncle's storehouse, he chatted with many of the town's wealthier residents, learning through conversations the fundamentals of business and how to act as a gentleman. He carried his ambitions westward and in 1827 moved to Cincinnati, where he married Mariah Evans, a well-educated governess from Philadelphia. Little is known of Solon Robinson's life until 1830, when he reappeared in Indiana with his wife.[107]

In 1830 the Robinsons purchased eighty acres at the Jeffersonville Land Office.[108] Over the following three years, the couple accumulated land through private sales, including the purchase of foreclosed lands from settlers who fell delinquent on tax payments.[109] In 1831, as newly appointed road commissioner, Robinson hired men to clear a thoroughfare that passed by a large portion of his property.[110] The ambitious Robinson used the opportunity to start dividing his land and laying out a platted town. Initially, he advertised the sale of sixty-four lots, offering ten of them to men of "the most useful mechanical trades." Additionally, he announced that he would donate two lots and 10 percent of the revenue from the land sales to build a school for the community.[111] A year later, Robinson advertised the opening of a "log cabin tavern," which doubled as a storefront. Between 1831 and 1834, he built a "House of General Agency," opened a circulating library, and offered his personal services as an auctioneer to help residents settle disputed estates.[112]

Yet, by late 1834, Robinson's experiment had failed, as he could not sell enough plots to recover his initial investment. To avoid being associated with the failed town, he sold what he could and moved his family several hundred miles away to public lands in the northwestern corner of the state.[113] He came to believe that his mistake in southern Indiana centered on his personal investment in the lands themselves. Robinson hoped he could profit in northwest Indiana by being the first to establish the necessary businesses for frontier survival—mills, stores, and taverns—without having to outlay the expenditures of financing all settlement in the region.[114]

Despite owning little land in northwestern Indiana, outside of his personal residence and farm, Solon Robinson named the new settlement Robinson's Prairie and began using Indiana newspapers to advertise the surrounding public lands, which he did not own. Robinson was a relentless promoter; he extolled the land as the "*first* fine country" that he had seen in the West and argued that, instead of being an unattractive wilderness, the land wore "the appearance of an old settled country." He told readers that land was "rising in value most wonderfully," but warned potential settlers not to wait, because "the influx of 'new comers'" was "beyond calculation." In another letter published in Hoosier newspapers, Robinson apologized for not writing sooner because his cabin had been "so constantly crowded with 'land hunters.'"[115] He used the letters to heighten public interest in the public lands around his own.

As more and more illegal settlers flooded onto the public lands around him, Robinson found what he sought. He became the community's father, progenitor, and leader and opened a general store near his home. When state legislators divided the region into counties and townships, the community elected him justice of the peace: a few years later he became clerk of the court.[116] But Robinson's most important contribution to the community, and the one that garnered him the most power, involved his organization of the Lake County Squatters' Union. Before the auction, the Lake County squatters, like many of those who came before them, petitioned Congress for preemption rights. They argued that "all the land that had been offered for sale by the General Government had been taken up by speculators and land jobbers."[117] On July 4, 1836, members of the community met under a shade tree in Robinson's front yard to organize an association and draft a constitution; three years later they would organize to purchase their lands at public auction.[118]

Solon Robinson represented the growing number of people who employed the identity of the western settler for political reasons and personal gain. By the 1830s, squatting had become a popular label used to embrace preemption rights. It had lost its stigma and connections to frontier violence and, instead, became attached to the images of "actual settlers" of the West. Between 1830 and 1836, as temporary preemption acts became law, squatters appeared in droves at local land offices and claimed nearly 2.25 million acres of the public domain.[119] Between 1831 and 1841, when Congress passed a perpetual preemption law, nearly nine hundred individuals showed up at the Quincy, Illinois, land office alone proclaiming themselves squatters.[120]

By the 1840s, the image of the western settler and the squatter had been transformed into an even greater American icon: the pioneer. From the 1840s through the end of the century, the image of the noble pioneer would come to replace the squatter and actual settler. Politicians such as William Henry Harrison used these images to remold themselves into romanticized characters of the western experience. Numerous political biographers produced the story of Harrison's life leading up to the 1840 presidential election. Nearly all of them recounted the story of a young man, connected to the Revolution through his father, who "abandoned his professional pursuits" and dedicated "his life to the defence of his country."[121] They commended the "ambition of those daring spirits" that broke the silence of the wilderness with "the shout of the Christian warrior" and praised those who fought for their nation, yet returned to the fields after conflict, reminding them that "as long as the leaders of the Roman armies were taken from the plough, to the plough they were willing to return."[122] As one writer put it, Harrison "may truly be said, to have begun with the great west, and to have grown with it."[123] Harrison's image as a "log-cabin" resident was birthed from mythical frontier experiences, while his brick home in Vincennes (the first brick building in the Indiana Territory) demonstrated his ambitious attempt to re-create the plantation estate of his father rather than his desire to live like the common western settler.[124]

Harrison used the morphing images of western life to draw a large number of Democratic, squatter-friendly westerners (including Solon Robinson) into the ranks of the once-despised Whig Party. The "Log Cabin and Hard Cider" campaign stretched across the states of the former Northwest Territory. Robinson called for "every 'log cabin' in the state to send at least one delegate to the 'log cabin candidate's' convention" and told readers of the *Indianapolis Semi-Weekly Journal*, "I am no 'Bank Aristocrat,' I am a humble occupant of a log cabin, and I have been all this day grubbing bushes."[125] Between twenty and thirty thousand Hoosiers attended the convention held on the battleground of Tippecanoe.[126] Later that year, Harrison spoke for over an hour at the site of colonial Fort Meigs before more than twenty thousand midwesterners who shouted slogans and sang songs celebrating the "farmer of North Bend" and the "hero of Tippecanoe."[127] Robinson presided over a Whig senatorial convention in Valparaiso that adopted the resolution, "We have our political log cabin already raised, that next August we will roof it in, that next November we will chink locofocos into the cracks, and that next March we will move into it."[128]

Robinson likewise used the shifting rhetoric of western settlement to transform his own image. Despite explaining to a friend in 1832 that he was "pretty well known as a landlord," Robinson proudly boasted in 1841 that his community recognized him as the "King of Squatters."[129] Throughout the rest of his life, Robinson worked to sustain this image by publishing pieces on farming. He was so prolific that one historian has labeled him the "most important agricultural writer" of the mid-nineteenth century.[130] Harrison never got the chance to extend his image (he died shortly after taking the oath of office), but eulogizers left mourners with a unified image of the deceased president. One clergy member proclaimed, "He was no aristocrat in democratic disguise; but, a people's man, he went among the people in the people's dress and with the people's manners."[131] They remembered him as a boy who "grew up

to manhood amidst the soul-stirring scenes of the Revolution" and traveled west for "love of country and fidelity to her welfare," retiring to "his
quiet farm house on the Ohio."[132] Romantic images of a man who ambi-
tiously sought control over the territories of the Old Northwest and set
out to conquer its indigenous population.

In 1844, Jordan Pugh, speaking at the fifty-seventh anniversary of the
settlement of Ohio, asked his audience to remember "when the tangled
thickets, the rank and unwholesome vegetation of a rich and virgin soil,
overshadowed" the ground where they stood; when "first the leaves of
the forest were rustled by the tread of civilized man; when the first stroke
of the woodman's axe, or the crack of the hunter's rifle, broke the silence of the wild—a silence which had never been invaded save by the
noise of the wild beast as he sprung from his lair, or by the whoop of savages as he glided on to the predatory war." "Where the Indian danced his
war dance, knowledge now gathers its votaries," he contended, and "Art
and Religion" replaced the Indian's "barbarous rites." Pugh reasoned
that "Religion and Knowledge and Civilization . . . disciplined the rude
forms of the red man, and erected . . . the social systems of another, an
educated, an elevated race." He exalted western settlers as "aged divines
who lighted fires upon God's alter in the wilderness" and invited the
crowd to join him in a chorus of "Honor to the pioneers!"[133]

The language of settlement, which emerged from treaty councils at
the end of the War of 1812, helped Americans imagine a western world
where settlers entered an empty landscape. It also established a revision-
ist history of American Indian affairs that stressed the United States'
benevolent past toward Native peoples and justified their dispossession
and displacement. By painting a portrait of western settlement as the
natural extension of American progress westward, this narrative of anti-
conquest laid the foundation for subsequent stories. Simultaneously, the
verbal contest produced a language of settlement and anti-conquest that
stressed the pioneer as the iconic western settler, entering a vast empty
landscape left behind by Indians. It allowed Americans who competed
with one another over lands in the West to find common ground and link
themselves together as pioneers. Powerful images of the vanished Indian
and the noble Pioneer came to symbolize America's nineteenth-century
errand into the wilderness and the expansion of American democracy.

Yet symbolism rarely mirrored the truth. Individuals who traveled into the lower Great Lakes in the early to mid-nineteenth century discovered an entirely different world, still marked by the hands of both Native and non-Native peoples. Despite their creative vision, American settlers through the 1840s were faced with a troubling reality: Native Americans still populated what was supposed to be an empty landscape.

PART TWO

Clearing the Middle Ground

And I, and I stand alone the last of my race
I fear I've no longer a home or a place
Since my friends have all fallen neath the conquerors sway
Yes the steal of the white man hath swept them away

And I, and I soon must follow, the Great Spirit calls
To some far distant home where the brave never fall
To some far distant place, to some far peaceful shade
Where the steal of the white man can never invade

—"Indian's Lament" (author unknown, ca. 1840s), Buzzard
Family Papers

Remarkably, the Miami Indians continue today not only as a rec-
ognizable community of Indians in Indiana, but also as a group
aggressively seeking restoration of full status as a federal Indian
tribe. Craft activities flourish, and the Twigh Twee Drum, a group
of male singers, perform at various ceremonies and events in the
Midwest. Hundreds of people attend spring and fall general meeting of the tribe, as well as Miami reunion every August since 1903.

—Stewart Rafert, *The Miami Indians of Indiana: A Persistent People,
1654–1994*

CHAPTER 3

"The Long Looked for Storm"
Writing, Religion, and Removal

One Indian community in Ohio did not fit the early-nineteenth-century image of the vanished Indian: the Wyandots. Schoolchildren in the Buckeye State know them as the last tribe to leave Ohio, but the focus on their removal in 1843 obscures a complex history whereby Native leaders used the malleability of western language to their own advantage. By the end of the War of 1812, the Wyandots attempted to create a place-story of their own—one that pointed to their incorporation into a larger American community. Historians in the past few decades have done much to remind us that Native peoples were active agents in the history of the lower Great Lakes, but this typically has not been true for the period between the end of the War of 1812 and the "removal era" of the 1830s and 1840s.[1] Even Richard White's seminal work *The Middle Ground* ends with a foreboding message for Native peoples in the Great Lakes in the postwar period: "The middle ground itself withered and died," he concluded. "The Americans arrived and dictated."[2] Great Lakes historians often follow this direction and skip ahead to removal, glossing over the years between the War of 1812 and the 1830s, but such selective hindsight overlooks the role of Native peoples in shaping their relationships with Americans during those years, and it especially masks the difficulties faced by whites in physically clearing the landscape of indigenous peoples. It also underplays the connections between pre- and postwar years by ignoring centuries of contact between Native peoples and Euro-Americans, which influenced Wyandot strategies during the removal era.

For nearly two centuries, the story told by Americans about the present-day states of Ohio, Indiana, and Illinois has been one of state-hood development. This linear narrative represents the history of the region as a progression from a colonial middle ground advancing to statehood, when settler societies dotted the landscape and Indians merely existed in memory. But the story of the Wyandots complicates the narrative of anti-conquest in its very chronology—they remained within the borders of the Buckeye State for four decades after its founding.

In October 1831, James Gardiner, the U.S. Indian agent assigned to negotiate a removal treaty with the Wyandots, accompanied an expedition of Wyandot leaders to Cincinnati and watched them depart on a steamboat heading west. The Indian agent had met tribal leaders and negotiated the skeletal works of a treaty over the previous months at the "Grand Reserve"—a 150,000-acre reservation in the central part of the state that Gardiner desperately wanted to place in the hands of white settlers. Although he was confident that a final agreement could be reached, the Wyandots demanded a concession: they wished that a delegation of Indians be permitted to visit their new home in the West before signing the document. Gardiner acquiesced and informed Secretary of War Lewis Cass that the tribe had selected William Walker, Jr.—whom he described as a "white man" and merchant—to lead the party. Before they left, the Indian agent entrusted Walker with a note for $1,000 to pay for expenses incurred during the travels.[3]

Early the next year, rumors reached Gardiner that Walker and the exploring party were "*highly pleased with the country assigned them.*" On January 4, 1832, Gardiner boasted to Secretary Cass, "I flatter myself that I shall be able in four or five weeks, to present you with a definitive treaty with this sagacious, intelligent and *crafty* tribe of Indians." He explained that Walker (whom he trusted as delegation leader) and the expedition were expected to return shortly. Although he admitted that Walker may have been "*one of the nation,*" Gardiner declared "a more suitable person" could not be found. Despite the fact that Walker was one-quarter Wyandot, Gardiner clearly identified him as white rather than Indian, going as far as describing the exploring party as consisting of "four of their men [Wyandot], and their white friend [Walker]." That same day, he informed Elbert Herring in the Office of Indian Affairs that "when notified of their arrival" he would immediately travel to the reservation and conclude the treaty for "final cessions of all the Wyandot lands in Ohio."[4]

Gardiner's excitement soon turned to despair. Within twenty-four hours of reporting that a treaty was imminent, he discovered that the Wyandot exploring party already had returned to their reservation and were deliberating without him. Additionally, new sources in southern Ohio, who had spoken with the expedition on their trip back to the Reserve, told him that the Wyandots were ready to abandon the idea of removal altogether. Despite telling people in St. Louis that they were pleased with the lands in the West, William Walker informed officials in Dayton, Ohio, that the Wyandots "were determined *not to cede*" their reservation.[5]

In an interesting twist, Gardiner quickly blamed the expedition's leader for his own failure in finalizing the treaty. The agent complained of a double-cross and accused Walker of refusing to take the delegation to the designated lands. In fact, he claimed that they "*never saw the country* . . . and spent but one night in the woods*." Gardiner posited that Walker stood at the center of a ruse "matured at Upper Sandusky" the previous summer and designed to filch "from the Government the money for such a tour, and then making *just such a Report*." A day after endorsing Walker as suitable (and white enough) for the job, Gardiner had changed his story. He told Lewis Cass of "much discontent" among the Wyandots with the "persons chosen as Delegates." He accused Walker of distributing letters to important Ohio politicians that "spoke in contemptuous and sarcastic terms of the '*Indian Paradise.*'" Gardiner insisted that "all the emigrating tribes had been '*most shamefully imposed upon.*'" He also claimed that Walker, despite previous promises, failed to alert him first of the delegation's findings. "Whites [Methodist missionaries] and partly whites [now speaking of Walker]," Gardiner believed, had concocted the entire charade because they were "the only gainers by [the Wyandots'] continued residence in Ohio."[6] The entire situation must have been embarrassing for a man who previously declared his trust in the suitable "white man," only to discover that the mixed-raced delegate turned the exploring party and the Wyandots against him.

William Walker's thwarting of removal efforts was more than the story of a mixed-race Wyandot taking advantage of a gullible American agent.

Although divisions among Wyandot leaders carried over from the years before the War of 1812, three years of violence and bloodshed in the lower Great Lakes during the war had upset the organization of tribal governance and created opportunities for cultural go-betweens, like Walker, to broker agreements between whites and Wyandots and capture positions of power within the Wyandot Nation. Walker's understanding of both Wyandot and American diplomacy derived from his experience as a member of the Wyandot Nation and lessons learned from his white and Wyandot parents, who emerged before the War of 1812 as influential voices among the Wyandot community. In important ways, Walker represented both the continuation of Wyandot strategies that predated the war and new approaches, which resulted from postwar reconfigurations of the Wyandot Nation. Moreover, he symbolized an individual who understood how to voice these changes in a way that did not directly contradict the efforts of whites in conquering the Great Lakes landscape. The Wyandots were able to remain in Ohio long after other tribes migrated west by voicing their tribal mission in terms that complemented white progress rather than impeded it. But this process did not leave the Wyandots untouched or unchanged.

The Grand Reserve, which Gardiner wanted and Walker fought to protect, was not the ancestral homeland of the Wyandots. For nearly three centuries, the Wyandots had been a people on the move; their migration, from the eastern Great Lakes across Canada and then to Ohio, had fractured the tribe both politically and geographically. Before the War of 1812, Wyandot communities dotted the landscape from Detroit to modern-day central Ohio. In those years, Wyandot leaders viewed Americans as the least likely of allies. As late as the 1790s, they almost unanimously resisted an American presence in the lower Great Lakes, and by 1794, Principal Chief Tarhe had helped lead Wyandot warriors in a failed attempt to defend the region from American intruders at the Battle of Fallen Timbers. After an American victory, however, Tarhe's attitude toward Americans changed, especially as shifting imperial hands in the lower Great Lakes made opposition to an alliance more difficult. The following summer, at negotiations for the Treaty of Greenville, Chief Tarhe, speaking on behalf of the Wyandots, Delawares, and Shawnees, told General Anthony Wayne that the tribes would agree to ally themselves with the United States. He believed that Americans would thereafter act as fathers to the gathered tribes, granting them protection from harm and respecting tribal boundaries. On one hand, he instructed other Indian leaders to "be obedient" to their new father; on the other hand, he warned that Wayne should "take care" of *all* his "little ones" and be careful not to "shew favor to one, to the injury of any."[7]

Poor conditions among the Wyandot villages may have convinced Tarhe and other Wyandot leaders that they needed help beyond what government agents were able to provide. Shortly after signing the treaty, Tarhe openly welcomed Quaker missionaries into his Wyandot community, and when that failed, he asked Presbyterians to open a mission. In 1798, Quaker missionaries witnessed the deleterious affect of alcohol on the Wyandot Nation. Drunken and mostly naked Indians greeted them with outstretched arms, bearing open bottles of whiskey and rum. Indians who had gathered "about the chief's house . . . were fighting, and nearly all were engaged in some excess or violence." The missionaries were especially startled by instances when "two, and sometimes three, were mounted on a single horse, riding at full speed, and apparently without any object, in every direction—the one behind carrying a bottle of rum, and the one before, endeavouring to guide the horse." The missionaries found that among the more than two hundred Wyandot families living in central Ohio, none could provide them with "a single morsel of meat."[8]

The Wyandot Nation had once consisted of at least twelve clans, but Quaker missionaries recognized only seven when they visited the Wyandot "national council." There they discovered a fractured system of governance, where matters "merely regard[ing] a town or family" were "settled by the chief and principal men of the town," while larger matters that concerned the entire Wyandot Nation were "deliberated on and determined in a national council, composed of the different tribes, attended by the head warriors and chiefs of the towns."[9] Subsequent missionaries recognized additional clan affiliations (perhaps ten or eleven), but by the end of the War of 1812, only seven clans were represented at tribal councils.[10] Differing clan and village affiliations produced a variety of opinions about how the Wyandot Nation should handle outsiders, including missionaries.[11] Centuries of interaction with Europeans and decades of warfare between Englishmen and Americans had significantly changed the composition of the Wyandot Nation, leading to scattered and diverse Wyandot villages that dotted the lower Great Lakes' landscape by the nineteenth century. Sexual relationships between French traders and Wyandot women had produced a growing number of mixed-race children, and warfare with Americans, coupled with the inclusion of white captives into the nation, meant that a sizable number of outsiders had been integrated within the tribe. Moreover, marriages between the individuals described above led to a generation of younger Wyandot members with tenuous biological but deep kin and clan-affiliated ties to the community itself. By the War of 1812, an impressive number of Wyandots on the Grand Reserve could trace their ancestry to an entangled web of French, Wyandot, Delaware, English, German, and American parentage.[12]

Some Wyandot leaders openly refused aid from American missionaries and agents, creating divisions among Wyandot leaders that eventually led to conflict and violence. In 1806, younger tribal members, seeking to separate themselves from leaders who openly welcomed American missionaries and agents, invited the Shawnee Prophet, Tenskawatawa, to conduct a witch hunt. As principal chief, Tarhe was forced to defend four Wyandot women accused of witchcraft, ultimately saving them from execution, but the event created deeper divisions between pro-American and anti-American Wyandot factions. In 1810, a cohort of Wyandot leaders led by the war chief Roundhead defied Tarhe and delivered the calumet to Tenskawatawa at Prophetstown, announcing their allegiance to the Shawnee Prophet and his British allies. Tarhe responded by replacing Roundhead as war chief, but the move only led to more tension among Wyandot communities. This time, Wyandots living near Lower Sandusky executed two women accused of witchcraft, while Roundhead's followers near Columbus, Ohio executed Wyandot chief Leatherlips for refusing to join the Prophet's cause.[13]

Other Wyandot chiefs, such as Tarhe and Between-the-Logs, encouraged indigenous visionaries from the East. In 1806 (and again in 1808), several Wyandot communities welcomed the Seneca prophet Handsome Lake to their villages. He preached both a revivalist message of returning to indigenous spiritual and cultural customs and the acceptance of white agriculture, education, and living conditions as a means of securing Wyandot autonomy. In the years that followed, Tarhe, Between-the-Logs, and others joined Native leaders, such as Blackhoof and his Shawnee faction, in welcoming white missionaries and government agents into their villages in central and north-central Ohio. In exchange for goods and guidance, these leaders pledged neutrality in conflicts between the British and Americans in the West.[14] A few Wyandot villages near Detroit who tried to remain neutral during the war found it impossible to dodge feuding British and American armies. British officials forced William Walker, Sr., and his family to move from Brownstown (south of Detroit) to Canada. As they left, the British burnt their home and confiscated their possessions. While some of the Wyandots living near Detroit joined the Prophet, Walker and others declared themselves captives of the enemy. William Walker, Jr., may have accompanied his father to Canada; he was eleven or twelve years old at the time and only recently had returned to Brownstown with his brothers after attending a Christian mission school near Lower Sandusky.[15]

The aftermath of the War of 1812 reshaped the Wyandot community, as Wyandot leaders faced the daunting task of trying to maintain tribal autonomy amid increasing pressures from Americans to assimilate or perish. At the second treaty council held at Greenville (when Harrison instructed Johnston to reposition the Council House), Brownstown chief Ronioness, who had previously fought alongside the British, agreed to join the Americans. Tarhe followed by presenting William Henry Harrison with two British medals that previously marked the Wyandot alliance with the British.[16] The political realities of the postwar era forced a sizable number of Wyandots to rethink an alliance with the Americans even though individual Wyandot leaders disagreed about what that relationship should look like.

Against that backdrop, John Stewart (a mulatto and self-trained Methodist preacher) arrived at the doorstep of William Walker, Sr., newly appointed U.S. Indian subagent and interpreter for the Wyandot villages around Upper Sandusky. Stewart hoped to covert the Wyandots to Christianity. Walker suspected that Stewart was a runaway slave, so he initially refused to interpret his message to the Wyandots, directing him instead to the door of Jonathon Pointer, a former slave and captive of the Wyandots who had joined the nation. Pointer tried to dissuade Stewart from preaching, arguing that "many great and learned white men had been there before him, and used all their power, but could accomplish nothing." Nonetheless, he agreed to interpret. White traders, who "wanted to continue profiting from the liquor trade to the Wyandot," tried to convince tribal members that "as he was a colored man, the whites would not have him preach for *them*, although they considered him good enough to teach *Indians*; and that it was a degradation to the nation to have a colored man for their preacher." For their part, members of the Wyandot Nation who were open to conversion appeared to worry little about Stewart's race.[17]

Wyandot leaders who had followed the Shawnee Prophet before the war were especially unwilling to open the Wyandot Nation to the influence of missionaries, but they were not alone. Catholic converts also were reluctant to grant access to Methodist missionaries. Jesuit priests had been working to convert the Wyandots for over a century, most recently when communities of Wyandots had resided near Detroit. Although French priests largely had abandoned them in the previous decades, Stewart discovered that the Catholic Wyandots were some of the hardest to convert.[18] They refused to stop praying to the Virgin Mother, abandon their rosaries, and forgo participation in syncretic Catholic and indigenous ceremonies that he thought of as hard-to-break pagan practices.[19] Stewart's arrival exposed tensions between leaders who had long debated the level of access that outsiders should be granted among Wyandot villages.

In 1816, the year that Stewart arrived at the home of William Walker, the Wyandots experienced the deaths of Chief Roundhead and Principal Chief Tarhe. The deaths signaled a shift in tribal governance, as it opened opportunities for the voices of younger leaders to emerge. Still, these younger voices continued to reflect older, often conflicting ideas about the relationship between the Wyandot Nation and Americans. Over the next few years, the reaction of Wyandot leaders to American agents and missionaries often resonated with the influence of older leaders (a few of whom still participated in tribal governance) and indigenous prophets from before the War of 1812.

Stewart, along with Jonathon Pointer as his interpreter, spent most of

1816 and early 1817 preaching to a growing congregation of Wyandot followers. In early 1817, he temporarily left the Wyandots to visit family in Tennessee, and when he returned he found renewed opposition to conversion. Two prominent chiefs, Two-Logs and Mononcue, had argued in his absence that the Great Spirit would abandon the Wyandots if they "forsook him" by following Stewart.[20] Wyandot Nation member John Hicks contended, "We are willing to receive good advice from you, but we are not willing to have the customs and institutions which have been kept sacred by our Fathers thus assailed and abused."[21] Mononcue confided in Hicks, "I have some notion of giving up some of my Indian customs; but I can not agree to quit painting my face. This would be wrong, as it would jeopardy [sic] my health." Throughout the summer of 1817, Wyandot leaders appeared to reject Stewart's message, as they hosted dances, partook of feasts, raced horses, and participated in games of chance.[22]

In Stewart's absence, white traders also had regained influence among the Wyandots and renewed the sale of alcohol, resulting in one prominent Wyandot young man being "killed in a drunken frolic."[23] Decades of trade with Americans before the war, and a military alliance with them during it, had allowed Indian traders to gain incredible influence among the Wyandot community. They tried to convince Wyandot leaders that Stewart could not help them, as he was a black man and marginalized by the white American community.[24] Despite the influence of (and perhaps as a reaction to) white traders, some Wyandot followers welcomed Stewart back. William Walker, Sr., Mononcue, Between-the-Logs, and John Hicks eventually changed their minds and embraced Stewart's message. They may have viewed missionaries (and the promise of more missionaries to come) as a better alternative to alcohol peddling traders. Walker and his wife, Catherine Rankin, played a pivotal role in encouraging Wyandot leaders to welcome Stewart back. William Walker, Sr., who initially was hesitant to introduce Stewart to the Wyandot Nation, now told them "that he believed Steward [sic] was a good man, and if licensed and encouraged would be a blessing to the nation."[25]

In order to combat intrusions onto Wyandot lands and consolidate tribal power in Ohio, the Wyandots adopted additional strategies. In the autumn of 1817, Wyandot leaders (along with other tribes) met with

American officials at the rapids of the Maumee River (near modern-day Toledo, Ohio). Together they agreed to cede title to more than three million acres in Northwest Ohio, in exchange for an annuity of $4,000, a twelve-square-mile reserve (the Grand Reserve), and a nearby one-square-mile tract that included a cranberry bog. Wyandot leaders sought to consolidate power and landholdings at the Grand Reserve, centered at the pro-American villages during the late war, in an attempt to maintain tribal autonomy and prevent further cessions. Although they could not grant land to men like William Walker, Sr. (they refused to recognize him as a member of the Wyandot Nation), American officials granted an individual plot to Catharine Walker on the edge of the Reserve for the Walkers to live.[26] The consolidation of lands acted as a means of protecting the Wyandot Nation, as it established boundaries that could be regulated by the tribal council. Additionally, American officials agreed to appoint a government agent to the Wyandot reserve to oversee the construction of a sawmill and gristmill and to employ a blacksmith for the tribe.[27]

Government promises were not fulfilled quickly and may have further convinced Wyandot leaders to gamble on missionary assurances for aid, supplies, and an alternative to the destructive practices of Indian traders. Following the treaty in 1817, and another in 1818, American officials failed to appoint a government agent to supervise the improvements guaranteed in the treaties. Nearby, Indian agent John Johnston in Piqua attempted to coordinate the building of a mill and blacksmith shop, but failing health and distance between his location and the Grand Reserve retarded progress.[28] Indian agent John Shaw, appointed to the Grand Reserve, did not arrive until the end of 1820. When he did, he listened to Wyandot tribal leaders complain of whites who trespassed on Indian lands and stole their animals. Shaw also found that whiskey flowed onto the reservation. On one hand, the early converts may have questioned their decision to welcome outsiders onto the reservation; on the other hand, they needed Indian agents and white missionaries if they were to be successful in reaching their greater goal of economic and political autonomy.[29]

The group of early converts, including Walker, Between-the-Eyes, Mononcue, and John Hicks, viewed their conversion and the role of mis-

sionaries on the Grand Reserve as part of a larger strategy of acculturation that they hoped would temper pressures by Americans to relinquish
more of their lands and curb the negative influence of traders.[30] Scholars
have often highlighted the eagerness of Methodists in expanding their
influence in the region, but few have sought to understand why Wyandot
leaders welcomed Stewart back after rejecting him.[31] In doing so, the
Wyandot leaders who were open to the idea of a mission on the Grand
Reserve may have reflected a strategy from an earlier time. When he
visited them in 1806, the Seneca prophet Handsome Lake had warned
the Wyandots of impending doom. "Judgments [were] coming on the
nations," he told them, "unless they reform."[32] He outlined what this reform should look like; it centered on a "social gospel" that included temperance, social unity, "good feelings toward whites," preservation of a
tribal land base, an acculturation policy that emphasized education, and
domestic morality. Between-the-Logs, who advocated for the Methodist
mission, had embraced Handsome Lake's message before the war and
even traveled from Sandusky to New York to invite the Seneca prophet
back to Ohio.[33] Handsome Lake's earlier message of openness toward
Anglo education and temperance resonated in the newer call for a mission among the Wyandots.

By 1818, Mononcue, Between-the-Logs, and John Hicks were defending Stewart vigorously against the attacks of other Wyandot chiefs.[34]
Mononcue and Between-the-Logs had been drawn particularly to the
Methodist call for temperance. After witnessing the devastating consequence of alcohol introduced by Indian traders who had denounced
Stewart, Mononcue concluded that he could "compare whiskey to nothing but the devil; for it brings with it all kinds of evil."[35] Years earlier,
Between-the-Logs had murdered his wife while intoxicated; now he used
his personal travails to entice other Wyandots to convert to Methodism
and join the Mission.[36] By 1818, Between-the-Logs had decided that Stewart offered an inroad toward salvation and, more importantly, redemption from his personal demons.

John Hicks's conversion offers further insight into reasons why Wy-
andot leaders might have followed Stewart. The son of German parents,
Hicks had been taken captive at a young age and was adopted by the
Wyandot. With no biological connections to the Wyandot Nation and

two teenage children who had already adopted Anglo names, Hicks may have seen the presence of the Methodist missionary as an opportunity for his sons, Francis and John, Jr., to gain an Anglo education. Less than a year after denouncing Stewart, but only a few months after affixing his name to the second of two cession treaties, John Hicks joined Between-the-Logs, Mononcue, Stewart, and William Walker, Sr., in attending the Methodist Quarterly Meeting in nearby Urbana, Ohio. They asked that Stewart be licensed to open a mission on the Grand Reserve; Methodist officials responded by agreeing to expand the size and scope of its missionary efforts.[37]

In February 1819, help arrived on the Grand Reserve by way of additional missionaries. Methodist leaders sent Reverend Moses Henkle to aid Stewart. The Wyandot congregation grew slowly over the first year, but Henkle and Stewart already were outlining their plans for expanding the mission. They told their new converts that they needed to construct a meeting house "to worship in, and let no foolish feasting & dancing be done in it." The Methodist leaders saw an extirpation of Wyandot rituals as central to their purpose, but Wyandot converts asked for something else: they wanted a school and teachers. The Methodists delayed sending a teacher, claiming that they had "no good Master ready" and did not want "a bad man to teach" the children of the Wyandots. Still, the role of education clearly remained on the minds of those who were willing to welcome Stewart and Henkle on the condition that they provide suitable educational opportunities for their children.[38] Help came soon enough.

Reverend James Finley arrived at the Reserve in 1821, and his arrival marked a significant turning point for the Methodist Mission and the relationship of the Wyandot Nation with the U.S. government. Finley had watched the mission's progress since 1819, when he took over as head of the Methodist district that oversaw the area where the Grand Reserve was located. After witnessing the failures of both government agents and previous missionaries to erect buildings and open a school, he decided to move to the Reserve to play a more direct role in shaping the mission. From Finley's arrival until 1843, when the Wyandots left Ohio for Kansas, he and William Walker, Jr., joined in a linguistic fight to preserve the Wyandot Reserve and isolate it from the negative influences of its white neighbors. But part of that resistance required the Wyandot Nation to open its borders to elements of what was deemed "positive" white influence.

Within six years of John Stewart's arrival and a year after Finley appeared at the Reserve, the Methodist Mission had expanded to include a mission house, mills, a blacksmith shop, and a small schoolhouse. One of Finley's first decisions involved assigning the young William Walker, Jr., to teach at the school. The new minister recognized Walker as a person "who belonged to the nation, and could speak the language."[39] Walker followed the examples of his parents by promoting Methodism and the aims of the mission. Moreover, his ties to the Methodist Church initiated a long friendship with Reverend Finley, especially after 1823, when the senior Walker died. William and his brother Isaac became trusted confidants of Finley, as they emerged as important cultural mediators between the mission and federal agents.[40] The friendship between Finley and Walker can be seen in the letters that passed between them. While each man held slightly different aims for the mission, they both worked feverishly in their letters to defend each other's work.

Wyandot aims for economic and political autonomy were reflected in the stated goals for the Methodist Mission. Missionary Charles Elliott (who replaced Finley for one year in 1822) believed that Wyandot children should be taught to "become industrious farmers, good citizens, intelligent men, tender parents, affectionate husbands, and obedient children." The same year, Finley echoed Elliot's sentiments in an article he penned for *Methodist Magazine.* "I want to grasp all the children," he wrote, "and learn the girls to knit, spin, weave and the art of housewifery; and the boys agriculture; and all of them to read the Holy Scripture."[41] Throughout the 1820s, white settlers pushed in from all sides of the Grand Reserve, but unlike most white settlers, Methodist missionaries who carried Bibles also brought much needed cash, supplies, and educational opportunities for the Wyandots. Money led to improvements, improvements led to greater sustainability, and with sustainability came the promise of autonomy. For some Wyandot leaders, the missionaries offered an avenue toward persistence and survival in the region, even if it came at the cost of allowing the missionaries to exert their control over the Reserve.

Initially, American officials agreed and hoped that missionaries would succeed in converting Native peoples into Christians and Americans. But by the late 1820s, impatient government agents believed that mission schools fell short of turning the Wyandots into acceptable Americans citizens—something the Wyandots probably never wanted or expected.[42] Years before Andrew Jackson signed the Indian Removal Act, politicians and land-hungry white settlers pushed for the dispossession of Ohio's Native populations. Like the petitioners discussed in the previous chapter, white settlers in Ohio petitioned their state legislature, and the state legislators attempted to wield their influence to encourage removal. Despite pressure from government agents, Methodist missionaries at the Wyandot reservation tried to ward off removal, in constant fear that they might forgo the progress already made in "civilizing" and converting the Indians. During his early years at the mission, Finley served both as superintendent to the missionary and subagent for Indian affairs. But eventually religious and government interests clashed, and as early as 1825, Finley complained that the greatest threat to his work was removal. "This moving plan about Indians," he wrote a friend, "has retarded our work much."[43] Michigan's territorial governor and superintendent of Indian affairs in charge of the Wyandots, Lewis Cass, tried to calm Finley: "The law providing for holding treaties with the Indians, with a view to their removal west . . . has not passed," Cass told him. "And should it pass, there is nothing compulsory on the Indians. . . . A very few years longer of improvement would place the Wyandots in a situation, for which no one would wish them removed."[44] Secretary of War Thomas McKenney likewise assured Finley that "no steps will be taken to *compel* the Indians to emigrate." But he warned that the "future happiness and prosperity" of the Wyandots depended on them "having a country of their own" in the West, and he instructed Finley to "suspend any extensive improvements" at the mission.[45]

The message of government officials—proceed as normal but anticipate removal—weighed on the young minister. As mission superintendent, Finley resisted removal as detrimental to his campaign of "civilizing" the Indians. As government agent, he was instructed to consider the interests of both Christian and non-Christian Wyandots with the non-Christian members of the Nation increasingly pushing for removal.

Eventually, the contradictions of holding both offices led to his dismissal from the government post. In 1825, Walker's brother Isaac (government-appointed interpreter) complained that the positions stretched Finley too far. Cass responded by appointing his own brother, Charles Cass, to act as subagent.[46]

Finley plodded ahead, voicing his concerns to leaders of the Methodist Church and to Walker. Shortly after the mission undertook the policy of placing Indian children in white homes, Finley wrote a friend: "Enemies have raised up against us supposing that the Methodist and Mission Establishment will prevent the Wyandots from selling their land." Finley's concerns revealed the ways that outsiders linked the missions with the resistance to Indian removal. In the eyes of pro-removal advocates, Finley, the mission, and men such as Walker were part of a larger problem whereby religious authorities chose Indian converts over the interests of white pioneers.[47] In the years immediately preceding removal, as white authorities and a growing portion of the American public became increasingly skeptical that missionary work could "save" Indians, a group of Wyandot leaders became increasingly convinced that the missionaries were their only hope of continued autonomy in Ohio.

Walker viewed the mission's work as synonymous with the physical and economic improvement of the Grand Reserve and hoped that economic progress might prevent further American pressures to remove. Yet he grew increasingly skeptical that this was possible by merely displaying outward signs of improvement; it required a special political tact. His skepticism had been shaped by his knowledge of earlier divisions within the Wyandot community, his parents' role in welcoming and promoting the missionaries at the Grand Reserve, and his personal friendship with the Reverend James Finley. They each provided him additional insights into the future direction of American Indian policy and how the Wyandots might want to negotiate the highly corrosive world of Indian removal politics.

Finley cited Walker as evidence of the success of the Methodist missionaries. The Wyandots' "approximation to the Whites is Much more than that of any other People of the Forrests they are very Much Mixed with the americans. . . . Many of the Principal families that compose this tribe are the forewith [sic] one half or one quarter white and have numerous white relatives living in the state." Finley believed that Walker represented a portion of the Wyandot Nation who, regardless of race, should be considered American citizens. He concluded that "the approximation of the Wyandot to their white neighbors was 'perhaps the Reason' they were so rapidly mixing," and he had "no doubt" that they would "continue to mix until . . . swallowed up" by the white population.[48]

Walker's decisions in the removal era reflected the increased influence of mixed-race members of the Wyandot Nation and the political restructurings within the nation that had allowed this to happen. Changes within Wyandot tribal governance aided leaders, such as Walker, who endorsed the aims of the mission and rejected calls for removal. The Wyandots living at the Grand Reserve represented a mere fraction of the nation that initially had migrated to the lower Great Lakes, and by the late 1820s at least two of the clans were so much reduced that they failed to send a chief to the tribal council. As early as the 1790s, tribal leaders had to cope with the devastating consequences of war with the Americans, as the loss of a significant number of warriors from the Deer clan (from which principal chiefs were selected) warranted a tribal council decision to choose future leaders from the Porcupine clan. Numerous marriages between female members of the Wyandot community and Euro-Americans, coupled with the loss of warriors and older chiefs, had elevated a growing number of mixed-race children, like Walker, to positions of power.[49]

After Chief Deunquot died in 1826, clan leaders hostile to the Mission appointed the unconverted leader, Warpole, to act as interim principal chief. To their surprise, he then proclaimed his conversion to Methodism and an alliance with the Mission. Clans friendly to the Methodist missionaries delayed the permanent election until they could garner enough support to change the method by which the principal chief and his counselors were chosen. They removed hereditary requirements and agreed instead to hold a yearly popular election.[50]

In the early years of the mission, tribal leaders who opposed religious conversion found it difficult to reject outright physical improvements. In 1821, pagan Chief Deunquot signed a petition authorizing the construction of a mission school at Upper Sandusky. In 1825 Chief Warpole (who initially opposed conversion) signed a petition to have Finley acquire

70,000 bricks to be used in the construction of buildings for the mission. In 1826 Chief Ronioness, who had fought alongside the British in
the War of 1812, signed a certificate complimenting Finley on his work
and assigning the Methodist missionary a Wyandot name. Nevertheless,
despite bringing much needed supplies and improved economic conditions to the Grand Reserve, the presence of the missionaries eventually
tore the Wyandot Nation in two. Many Wyandots, including some tribal
leaders, aggressively opposed Christian conversion and increasingly
viewed the missionary's goals as synonymous with those of the U.S. government. Moreover, Wyandot leaders witnessed bickering between American agents and missionaries throughout the 1820s, as Indian agents and
subagents battled over the political and economic gains of overseeing
the Grand Reserve. In the minds of some Wyandot leaders, missionaries (including Finley) became (perhaps unfairly) associated with a growing web of American lies and deceit. The division of the Wyandots also
presented a problem for Walker, who encouraged both Christian and
non-Christian Indians to resist dispossession. By supporting the Mission,
Walker hoped to ensure economic support from Methodist donors and
government coffers; his actions also drew the ire of those who opposed
the religious aims of the missionaries.[51] Both men also believed that the
efforts of the Wyandots needed to be advertised to the outside world in
order for them to gain the support of a popular audience.

    Under mounting pressures to remove, the missionaries stressed the im-
portance of Wyandots both converting and welcoming physical changes
to the Grand Reserve. Finley and Walker believed that the extirpation of
indigenous spiritual practices was necessary to solidify conversion and
make permanent the progress of improvements. In 1824, when Finley
fell ill and had to leave the Mission, a group of Wyandots held "a great
dance—and a great *Wabanow.*" Walker, who remained at the Reserve and
reported this all to Finley, could only assume that the leaders used the
dance as a move to gain popularity and political stature among the unconverted, thereby supplanting individuals like himself from positions
of power. When he returned, Finley and Charles Elliott, the missionary
who temporarily took his place, moved (with Walker's aid) to end indigenous ceremonialism. They also worked to limit news of the incident to
the Reserve. Walker preached to the unconverted and emphasized the

need for them to join the Mission, but he also worked to conceal his role in reporting the incident to the missionaries, instructing Finley to "let no person" see the original letter.[52] Walker played a delicate role in mediating between the two sides. He understood that political and religious divisions were often linked in the minds of Wyandot chiefs, as two distinct groups of political leaders emerged on the Grand Reserve—the "Pagan Party" and the Christian converts. Ultimately, Walker believed he could promote the physical progress of the Mission while concealing his heavy-handed role in the extirpation campaign.

A reexamination of Walker's actions during the 1831 fiasco with James Gardiner reveals how Walker used his knowledge of both American and Wyandot diplomacy to delay removal by posing as a pro-removal advocate. Gardiner may have been right: Walker never planned to allow the Wyandots to trade their reserve for lands in the West. Far from embracing the idea of removal, Walker keenly identified American pleas for Wyandot removal as the thinly veiled desires of land-hungry whites and manipulative government agents. The most damning evidence that the exploring party and Walker never intended on moving west can be found in the correspondence between Walker and Finley that preceded the expedition. In these letters the gulf between words and actions becomes clear. On May 21, 1831, months before Gardiner identified Walker as a helpful ally in convincing the Wyandots to remove, an irritated William Walker scrawled an angry letter to his friend: "Bribes are in tow—corruption will be introduced to the utmost extent." He told Finley that he believed Gardiner was "characterized by true Jackson tyranny and corruption with all its blasting effects" whose actions revealed "all the skill, chicanery, and adroitness of a well trained diplomat." He lamented, "The long looked for storm, which has been gathering and thickening over our devoted heads, is now commencing its ravages on our nation."[53]

Yet when the time came, Walker convinced Gardiner that he supported the government's position on removal, so much so that Gardiner reported to his superiors that a removal treaty was all but assured. As the treaty negotiations came to an end in October 1831, Walker was the one who prodded Wyandot leaders to demand that an exploring party be allowed to examine their lands. The strategy of deploying an expedition to appease American agents, while secretly working to thwart removal attempts, may have manifested in Walker's mind years earlier. In 1826, Indian agent John Johnston had penned a letter to Wyandot leaders at the Grand Reserve informing them that the secretary of war would authorize him to fit exploring parties to examine lands in the West in the hopes that Ohio's Indians would remove voluntarily.[54] Walker wrote to Finley at that time, mocking Johnston's letter: "Oh ye fugitive sons of the forest," he imagined Johnston saying, "where can ye find an abiding place to rest your wearied limbs and sing the songs of your father in peace? Unhappy people! Never will the white man yield till the Pacific Ocean drinks of your blood."[55] Despite Johnson's reputation of being an ally to the Wyandots, Walker mocked him as a land-hungry white man. The Wyandots passed at the opportunity, as Finley, perhaps prodded by Walker, defended the Mission to his superiors and received assurances from men like Cass that progress at the mission would ensure their continued residence in the state. A few months earlier, Cass had written to Finley and promised, "If your Indians continue to improve as they have done, and manifest a wish to adopt the opinions and institutions of the whites, no power will compel them to remove."[56]

When Gardiner arrived to negotiate the 1831 removal treaty, Walker secretly vowed to Finley that he would defend the Grand Reserve and mission. Outwardly, he must have presented himself as open to removal, but in private correspondence with Finley, Walker never wavered in his devotion to preserving the mission. He was more concerned that he would fall victim to an angry American government once his hand in thwarting the removal treaty was revealed. If Walker and Finley stood in the way of the federal government's removal efforts, the president likely would take measures to "remove the obstacle"—that is, Walker and the mission. Moreover, Walker feared he would "be sacrificed" because he refused to "be made to subservor [*sic*] to the unhallowed purposes of the '*reign of terror*.'"[57] Certainly, Gardiner was upset with Walker's seemingly changed heart, but many Wyandot leaders—especially converts associated with the Mission—later voiced their approval of Walker's efforts through actions of their own.

The changes in political leadership aided the Wyandots in challenging American hegemony and removal efforts throughout the 1830s. As early as 1830, Finley's longtime ally (and Walker's former boss) Lewis

Cass came out in support of removal; he believed that the Wyandots could not hold onto their reservation as whites moved in from all sides of the Grand Reserve, a situation that he claimed would bring "destruction upon the Indians." In 1832, Wyandots at the nearby reservation at Big Springs sold their land and joined their brethren at Upper Sandusky. Two years later pressure mounted as the Ohio state legislature passed a resolution calling for the removal of the Wyandots, and Indian agents returned to the Wyandot reservation to initiate the drafting of another removal treaty.[58] Ohio governor Robert Lucas traveled to the Reserve and authorized another exploring party to travel west and scout lands for their potential relocation. Although William Walker did not accompany this expedition westward, he served as interpreter between Lucas and the chiefs, at times inserting his own opinion to the Wyandot leaders. Lucas discovered that the Wyandots had passed a law forbidding "any discussion among individuals of the tribe relative to the sale of their lands, under a severe penalty."[59] The law represented the consolidation of power within the hands of chiefs friendly to the aims of the mission and opposed to removal; it also highlights the strategy employed by Walker and his allies of consolidating power on the Grand Reserve and promoting economic improvement in order to ensure national Wyandot autonomy rather than the previous system of village autonomy. Again, the negotiations resulted in the Wyandots disapproving of the lands in the West, with Walker standing at the center of the anti-removal movement.

In 1836, Christian converts used the new system of popular tribal elections to endorse the political aims of Walker by electing him principal chief. As chief, Walker seemingly switched strategies as he approached government agents with a plan to sell part of the Wyandot landholdings in spite of the tribal law he had endorsed. Willing to accept any indication that the Wyandots might leave, Robert Lucas agreed to purchase sixty sections on the outskirts of the Grand Reserve. Some Indians and whites may have viewed the maneuver as hypocritical, but the sale should not be read as a prelude to removal. In 1834 and 1835, the Wyandot mission had witnessed a series of serious setbacks. Flooding in previous years had decimated crops in the fields and "destroyed some of the Reserve." The corn crop had been "nearly exhausted" after feeding the hogs, and the supply of oats was virtually used up to feed horses and other "stock hogs." Profits from the sale of the five-mile-wide strip of land on the eastern edge of the reserve helped finance the rebuilding of mills, roads, schools, and "other public objects for the improvement" of the reservation.[60] Walker hoped that the proceeds could be used to strengthen the mission and ensure its continued existence, but further setbacks and reprehensible government actions thwarted Walker's efforts.

The federal government had discovered that the fracture between the Christian and non-Christian parties of the Wyandots provided an opportunity to remove half the Wyandots from the Grand Reserve, as rumors circulated that the so-called Pagan Party wished to leave. In essence, they planned to circumvent Walker and the mission-friendly Wyandots in favor of the Pagan Party. Less than a year after ceding the cranberry bog to the federal government, Walker dejectedly wrote his friend James Finley, who had left the mission years earlier for health reasons. "I could wish, if wishing do any good, . . . give you a flattering account of the condition of the Mission." Throughout the 1830s, the federal government cut finances to the mission, and white supporters, equating the possibility of removal to the futility of the mission, sent fewer and fewer supplies. Moreover, new missionaries held less power than their predecessor, James Finley. Walker glumly noted that the Mission along with its new missionaries now looked "like a den of robbers and land pirates, haunted by owls, cormorants, and satyrs." He bemoaned its "most deplorable condition." Walker reported that since government funding for the Mission dwindled, the Wyandots lived in horrid conditions, with "no bedding, no clothes, and as dirty as Swine."[61] The federal government immediately sought to take advantage of the situation.

In 1837, Indian commissioners visited the Grand Reserve, persuading whoever would sign a removal treaty to do so. They held no councils. Instead, they organized meetings with smaller groups of individuals or families, plying some of them with alcohol in return for their signature. According to Walker, commissioners left the treaty at the local tavern and allowed "straggling Wyandott" to sign it as they passed through— "signing the treaty was then made the price of a glass of grog!" Federal officials seemed "bloody bent in breaking up the nation," Walker wrote, "but we shall continue inch by inch, and rather than yield, 'perish in the last ditch.'"[62]

In 1838 Congressmen William Hunter and N. H. Swayne were appointed government agents in charge of pushing the Wyandots to remove. Hunter hoped that the approval of Christian Wyandots would
expedite the removal process even while non-Christian Wyandot leaders traveled to Washington in hopes of negotiating their own removal
treaty.[63] Treaty talks occurred sporadically over the next year. Hunter,
who lost his seat in Congress, nonetheless assumed the position of special
Indian commissioner and returned to the reservation to pursue removal.
In 1839, the Wyandots, again led by the advice of Walker, asked permission to send an exploring party westward before signing a treaty. The
commissioner of Indian affairs again acquiesced. William Walker did not
join this exploration, but his brother Matthew did. After several weeks
spent scouting areas in present-day Kansas, the Wyandot party asked that
more Wyandot leaders be allowed to visit the site they deemed appropriate. This time Walker's other brother, Joel, accompanied six others
westward. The exploring party agreed to a removal treaty, but the Senate rejected it in 1840. The following year, Indian agent John Johnston
returned from retirement to negotiate a new removal treaty with the Wyandots. At that time, the Wyandots agreed to move to an area across the
Missouri River from Westport, Missouri. In 1843, James Finley returned
to the Reserve for a final sermon and reminisced about better days at the
Mission. On July 11, 1843, nearly seven hundred Wyandots (including
William Walker) left the Grand Reserve.[64]

Reverend James Finley later remembered Walker as a friend who
aided him at the Mission. In 1857, the missionary published a reminis-
cence of his time at the Grand Reserve, entitled *Life among the Indians*,
where he identified Walker as "the teacher" who "sought and found the
Lord." His memories of Walker were colored by their work together re-
sisting removal and encouraging conversion. Long after he left the mission and more than a decade after the Wyandots left Ohio, James Finley
recalled, "I plainly saw that there was a storm ahead. I made use of every
exertion to prevent it, by keeping up our prayers and class meetings;
and was fully and ably sustained by the mission family." He singled out
Walker and Robert Armstrong as his allies and remembered them "as
armor-bearers" of the mission.[65] Whether the minister recognized it or
not, Walker had benefited from a half century of change among the

Wyandots, whereby tribal leaders reorganized the Nation in hopes of sustaining their autonomy amid the corrosive world of Indian removal politics; he also represented a history of prophecy by indigenous leaders attempting to predict the "storms" that threatened Wyandot autonomy. For the Wyandots, the end of the War of 1812 had not marked a direct line to removal. Many members of the tribe believed that new strategies, based on old ideas, could lead to an autonomous Wyandot Nation within the state of Ohio. Instead, after 1843, they fought to establish that nation elsewhere, beyond the Mississippi River.

The rhetorical strategies employed in Ohio failed to work in the West. The shiftiness in language that had allowed the Wyandots to remain in Ohio, even as settlement moved on into Indiana, did not follow them to Kansas. Once settled in Kansas, Wyandot leaders petitioned Congress to allow them to elect a delegate. Congress rejected their proposal. The following year, they asked that the area be organized into a new territory that would welcome white settlement and encourage economic develop-ment. The Wyandots elected William Walker, Jr., as governor of the provi-sional territory. Again they were denied. The Wyandot Nation splintered into factions. In the decades that followed, Wyandot members scattered again. Some families accepted allotments in Kansas, others moved into Indian Territory to live on the Seneca reserve, while still others moved to Canada to live with family and friends there. By the 1860s, the Wyandot Nation, which began the century as a confederation of scattered villages, again found itself spread across North America.

William Walker and James Finley's campaign to employ the lan-guage of settlement as a means of convincing outsiders that the Mission could incorporate the Wyandots within the larger Ohio community ul-timately failed because whites were unwilling to accept a continuation of middle ground accommodation. Instead, Ohioans wanted to be able to demonstrate a clean break between colonial occupation and state-hood development. Through words and deeds, they stressed the futility of Native attempts to thwart removal and tried to reassert a narrative of conquest that offered few other possibilities. Still, whites in other lower Great Lakes' states faced difficulties in completing the physical removal of the regions' indigenous population. While the Wyandots eventually concluded that their best option for maintaining autonomy lay in the

West, other Native communities in the lower Great Lakes successfully thwarted attempts at removal and remain there today. Continued Native occupation of the region required a creative rendering of the place-story of the region. In north-central Indiana, American communities became especially adept at crafting narratives, which overlooked the realities of the cross-culture world around them.

CHAPTER 4

"Led by a Touch of Romantic Feeling"

Art, Science, and Depictions of the Vanishing Indian

For nearly three decades, dating back to William Henry Harrison's treaty councils, American officials had been trying to persuade tribal leaders to cede lands in northern Indiana. Emboldened by the passage of the Indian Removal Act in 1830, they increasingly pressured tribes to relinquish lands in exchange for reservations in the West. In 1837 George Winter, an Englishman and an artist, arrived in the bustling north-central Indiana town of Logansport to catch a glimpse of what he thought were vanishing Indians. Truth be told, Winter did not need to hurry. Removal was never quite completed in Indiana. Examples of unfinished conquest like those in Indiana did not conform to popular notions of western settlement, which concluded that the frontier needed to be cleared of indigenous people before proper white settlement could commence. Winter's experience in the Wabash Valley of nineteenth-century Indiana illustrates how the production of local knowledge helped white settlers remake the history of the region and reestablish a place-story that stressed the passive erasure of Native people while emphasizing white efforts toward progress.

Despite contentions that the end of the War of 1812 opened the region to unbridled white settlement, nearly half the state of Indiana had not been ceded to whites by the 1830s. Instead, Miami, Potawatomi, and European American influences helped color the landscape and shape the region's history. The influence of these groups could also be seen in daily life along the Wabash River. This complex story of cross-cultural communities could have been adopted as the place-story of the region, but it was not. In its place, white settlers crafted a reductionist history

that pitted white Hoosiers against American Indians and called for the
removal of the region's indigenous population, which the settlers depicted as primitive and unqualified to remain. George Winter, an occasional writer and a prolific painter, contributed both words and images
to illustrate this story of erasure.

Although historians have long identified him as simply an Englishman, Winter had lived in the United States seven years by the time he
started writing about Indiana's Indians. In 1830, he stepped off a passen-
ger ship and onto a New York City wharf. His father and most of his siblings had migrated to the United States a decade earlier, but George had
not. Instead, he remained in England, determined to become a professional artist. Noted painters offered to instruct him, but neither Winter
nor his family could afford the cost of professional training, so he spent
much of his teenage years visiting London's famed art galleries and imi-
tating the works of Europe's great painters. After several years of struggling to establish a career, Winter cast aside his aspirations and joined
his brother John in setting sail for New York, a place where he would find
art schools more accepting and less expensive.[1] Little is known about his
years in New York, but we know that Winter attended the newly established National Academy of Design and gained some formal training in
the art of painting. His stay in New York City was short. By late 1835 or
early 1836, Winter had joined the rest of his family in Cincinnati, where
he opened a portrait studio.[2]

Winter stayed only briefly in Cincinnati, first moving to Middletown,
Ohio, and then to Logansport, Indiana, where he later recalled that he
had "been led by a touch of romantic feeling to see and sketch the Indians of the Wabash [River]."[3] Logansport was an early Indiana canal town,
whose population boomed as individuals arrived hoping to benefit from
increased commerce that often accompanied the opening of a canal.
Consequently, the hamlet attracted entrepreneurs looking to open businesses ahead of the rush. While the canal meant prosperity for some, it
promised disaster for others. The influx of settlers threatened to disrupt
the tenuous decades-old relationship forged between white traders and
Indians. Long before Americans arrived in the area—even before the
United States existed—Euro-Americans and Indians had coexisted in
mixed-race communities along the Wabash and were mutually depen-

dent on one another for trading furs. New arrivals probably found the older arrangements and cross-cultural feel of Logansport at odds with their expectations. These beliefs must have, in some way, also affected Winter's views of the area.

Winter's reasons for moving to Logansport reflected larger ideas about western settlement. White settlers anticipated that the arable land around the town would serve as the backbone of a booming agricultural community, while businessmen hoped that the area's new inhabitants would visit their grain mills, mercantile shops, and houses of entertainment. These visions shared one commonality: neither of them included a spot for the area's Native population. Thus Logansport's creation story began when incoming settlers imagined a place-story that excluded Native actors. It was at that moment George Winter decided to migrate to the frontier. His decision was driven by his desire to record the region's "vanishing" Indians on canvas. In this way, his work might be viewed as ethnographic evidence that reveals the multiethnic history of the region. On the other hand, Winter also traveled to Logansport to profit from the opportunities that accompanied the economic boom of a canal town. In other words, he wanted to sell his paintings. Consequently, we must read his works beyond their stated intentions. While Winter may have "been led by a romantic feeling," he was also led by a desire to reap the rewards of the larger colonial project that sought to remove Indians.[4]

Still, scholars primarily have used Winter's Indian paintings and sketches as ethnographic evidence of indigenous adaptation and persistence. R. David Edmunds cites Winter's work as verification that the Potawatomis and Miamis had made "significant changes" during the seventeenth and eighteenth centuries, proving "remarkably adaptive" and combining "traditional tribal values with many new ideas offered to them by Europeans." Susan Sleeper-Smith believes that Winter's painting of a Miami woman, D-Mouche-kee-kee-awh, is an example that "confirms both the affluent appearance of nineteenth-century Indians as well as the ways in which persistence, like the fur trade, was facilitated by kin networks that linked traders and Indians."[5] Many of the interpretations drawn by scholars of American Indians decontextualize Winter's paintings and overemphasize his role as an Indian artist and ethnographer, ignoring his proclivity to self-promote. By teasing apart the ethnographer from the entrepreneur, we might see the role of individuals such as Winter in reshaping the place-story of Logansport and the Wabash River valley. His career and his images of Indiana's Indians offer deep insights into the interconnectedness of race, science, and colonialism in antebellum America.

The Logansport community had already begun to suggest the inevitability of Indian removal in the years before Winter's arrival. Consequently, Winter not only shaped the community's perceptions through his artwork but also echoed popularly held notions about the soon-to-be "vanished" Indians. Prior to 1837, politicians and writers had filled local newspapers with words to describe this picture.[6] It was within this environment that his work became instrumental in crafting a new narrative of western expansion.

Westerners tried to transform the image of the countryside from one characterized as a dangerous wilderness filled with Indians to one depicted as a serene pastoral landscape where hardy farmers filled an empty frontier. In Indiana and elsewhere, settlers increasingly faced a different reality, as they lived, traded, and farmed among the thousands of Indians who lived around them. As more whites moved into areas like Logansport, they concluded that they either had to mask a prevalent indigenous presence or force Indians to remove.[7] Local newspapers, a major source for information and entertainment, echoed these statements. A poem published in an 1831 issue of Logansport's *Cass County Times* provided few alternatives to removal.

> And where is the home
> Of the Red man to be?
> The pale face will come,
> The Chieftain will flee.
> His empire is fled,
> His scepter departed,
> His prowess is dead,
> His tribe broken-hearted.
> The white man is near,
> His shadow is death:
> And the red nations fear
> Who sleeps underneath.
> His feet move to crush:

He looks, and they fly;
He speaks, and they hush;
He arms, and they die.[8]

Poems like this suggested that Americans did not need to forcibly remove Indians. Instead, they indicated that Native "empires" would simply
flee before the shadow and footfall of Americans. In that way, poems like
the one above helped define a narrative of anti-conquest that distanced
the action of forced removal from those individuals who called for it.
Still, the last stanza of the above example served as a warning for those
tribes or leaders who refused to follow their preordained fate, as it suggested that if forced to act, whites would "arm" and Indians would "die."
Although this particular poem, written outside of Indiana but republished in Logansport's newspaper, did not directly reference the lower
Great Lakes, it embodied the sentiments of local whites and reflected
local attitudes about removal in the period directly after the passage of
the Indian Removal Act. Other local authors echoed these sentiments.

Settlers in and around Logansport often ignored signs of Indian
persistence as they advocated for removal. Even before the first group
of Miamis agreed to move west, one writer in the *Logansport Telegraph*
anxiously awaited the opportunity to acquire a few acres of the "first
rate quality" Miami lands. Moreover, he argued that "experience, the
surest guide in all things," convincingly had "shewn that the red men"
could "neither be happy, prosperous, nor contented, when surrounded
by, and liable to the daily encroachment of the white population." Despite a local economy that had long been dependent on trading furs with
the Miamis and required both whites and Miamis to learn each others'
customs, languages, and cultures, the author explained that the Miamis
were "ignorant of our language, averse to enduring the labor attending
an agricultural life, deprived by our laws, of the rights of citizens," which
all caused them to "sink into idleness, brutality, and intemperance."
Whites, he argued, should reclaim the lush farmland from wasteful and
ignorant Indians.[9] Such arguments became common in newspaper columns around Logansport.

One writer to the *Cass County Times* in 1833 crafted his own revision-
ist history of the region. After halfheartedly mourning the bygone days

when Indians and whites supposedly lived in peace, he proceeded to attack the character of all Indians in Indiana and call for their immediate
removal:

> There is no subject, in which the people of this country are so
> deeply interested, as the removal of the Indians. Everyday con-
> vinces us more and more of the necessity of their removal beyond
> the sentiments of the whites. These people are not what they used
> to be. The time was when they were sober, honest and industrious;
> but since their intercourse with the whites, they have become dis-
> sipated, dishonest and idle. With few exceptions they have given
> up hunting, and instead of giving chase to deer, they are found
> lounging about our villages, scillig [sic] or pawning their knives,
> guns and blankets for whiskey! . . . Justice to the citizens, and to the
> Indians themselves, requires that something should be done.[10]

By crafting a narrative that highlighted the degeneration of Indian
and white relations as the result of Native idleness, the author cleverly
created a story that justified white actions by blaming local Indian communities for forcing whites to remove them. Moreover, the author presented local whites as helpless bystanders in the devolution of Indian
communities—tenets of a narrative that cast white pioneers as passive
actors in a larger and seemingly natural colonial process.

Impatient Hoosiers called for the expedient removal of Indians in the
decades leading up to Winter's arrival. The northern part of the state
was home to thirty-six Potawatomi and twenty-three Miami communities,
and as white settlers pushed into the region, they beseeched government
officials to remove the more than 3,500 Indians who lived there (roughly
the same number of whites who lived in the area in the early 1830s).[11]
When government officials could not persuade Native leaders to concede lands as quickly as the public would have liked, whites bemoaned
the efforts of "shrewd traders" and inept agents and claimed that the
Miamis and Potawatomis had become bad neighbors.[12] Moreover, they
tried to use events farther west to characterize their experience with
the tribes. Local writers claimed that while it once had been possible to
distinguish between "good" and "bad" Indians, recent outbreaks of violence (or at least reports of violence) on the western border of Illinois

blurred those distinctions. Fear spread across the lower Great Lakes in 1832, when chief Black Hawk led his Sac and Fox followers into Illinois and present-day Wisconsin to protest removal.[13] Reports of Indian violence filled newspaper columns farther east. Indianans, Ohioans, and Kentuckians read reports daily about atrocities committed by western Indians. One writer in Logansport believed that the "conduct of the Indians in Illinois" would "open the eyes of ignorant and credulous people, East of the mountains."[14] While some Hoosiers believed that the Indians of Indiana could be easily compared to tribes farther west, some Indian sympathizers argued that the reports were a "farce" and blamed Indian agents at Chicago for "unnecessarily alarming the people throughout the whole frontier borders."[15]

Regardless, anxious westerners used the Black Hawk ordeal to demand removal and warned of the impending doom that a continued Indian presence in the lower Great Lakes spelled. Hyacinth Lasselle, editor of the *Cass County Times*, sounded jingoistic calls for action in a poem he penned for his paper.

> March, march, hear ye the Savage yell,
> Far to the North where war whoops are sounding,
> March, march—let's onward to battle,
> Where Black Hawk and warriors, the helpless are slaying.
> There mothers are weeping, and daughters are screaming,
> The wilds re-echo, with their shriek of despair.
> Your fathers, your mothers—your aid they're imploring,
> To save them from tom'hawk, the knife, and the spear.
> Bright is the laurel, entwin'd for the brave,
> Pure by the tears, for the hero who falls;
> Honor'd forever, the youth who will save
> His country from foes, when to battle she calls.[16]

By drawing a distinction between "good" and "bad" Indians, American settlers recalled an older colonial era when whites and Indians shared control of the region and launched campaigns against foreign enemies and their indigenous allies. But the story that whites told themselves about nineteenth-century western settlement did not leave the possibility for such actions. Instead, a new narrative was supposed to trace an

advancement from colonial status to statehood. By the 1830s settlers in
Ohio, Indiana, and Illinois explained that there was "more danger" in
not being able to "discriminate between the friendly and unfriendly Indians" within their borders than there was in forcibly removing Indians
from their states. In Indiana, settlers had already begun to imagine a
state without the Miamis and Potawatomis, but the presence of Indians,
either bad or good, forced them to recognize the incompleteness of
statehood and demand removal. Furthermore, they argued that whites
who were still stuck in an older frontier mind-set were to blame for the
continued presence of Native people. They claimed that selfish white
traders had interfered with removal, especially those "few persons" who
cared "not for the welfare of the country" but only wanted to "make a
living off them by trading and bartering."[17]

By 1834, American agents had persuaded the Miamis to open more
than 200,000 acres of their reserved land to white settlement. The treaty
did not, however, call for the Miamis to leave Indiana.[18] Instead, American agents demanded additional cessions. Indian agents engaged in removal negotiations with tribes throughout the lower Great Lakes. By the
mid-1830s, American officials had come to view Indian removal as an
inevitable component of western expansion. In fact, a census report in
1836 provides insight into the thoughts of government agents on the
subject. Census takers left no possibility for Indians to remain in Indiana, as they classified lower Great Lakes' Indians as either "Indians Emi-
grated" or "Indians to Remove." But the long process of treaty negotiations and councils revealed serious flaws in American thinking. Treaty
negotiations were slow and often seemed quixotic because tribal leaders simply refused to accept their supposedly imminent demise. In the
minds of many lower Great Lakes Indians, removal was not inevitable.
Consequently, many westerners came to imagine a landscape without
Indians, even as Indians fought to be part of that landscape.[19]

Towns and villages located near Indian communities exalted their
efforts to expunge elements of savage frontier life. Newspapers publi-
cized reports that chronicled the physical changes of their settlements
since whites had come in great numbers. One editor in the canal town
of Delphi, Indiana, proudly boasted that "the citizens of this place have
effected, in one year, a work in the wilderness, which have taken others,

judging from what they have done, in some of the older counties, at least fifteen years." He argued that the village had been only one year earlier "situated as it then was, in the heart of the Indian country." But since, townspeople had erected forty to fifty buildings, including "a large brick building 25 by 50 feet, two stories high, designed for a Masonic Hall."[20] Across the lower Great Lakes, writers exalted the physical transformation of Native spaces into bustling towns and villages. They also believed that the backwoods were "receding" and rejoiced that American "*States, Cities, Towns, Villages, etc.*" had "sprung into existence" far west of Pittsburgh, which had only a few decades earlier been on the margins of American expansion. One western writer posited that "should the same spirit of internal improvement continue," their "*red brethren*" who "roam[ed] through the wood . . . unconcerned about their future destiny" would be pushed "far beyond the *Rocky Mountains*."[21]

One of the most remarkable aspects about the transformation of northern Indiana was the ability of white Americans to ignore the realities of life along the Wabash River. In 1835, John Brown Dillon, editor of the *Telegraph* and friend to George Winter, spoke before an Independence Day crowd in Logansport about the importance of remembering the past. Dillon beseeched the people of Logansport to look around them and thank those who helped advance the success of the republic through physical improvements. "Our immense forests are falling before the power of a hardy, free, and independent population," he told them. "The wilderness is beginning to blossom as the rose; the towns and hamlets are springing up, in civilization and refinement, even while the footprints of the uncultivated Aborigines remain fresh upon the soil." Dillon's use of the phrase "fresh footprints" ignored the fact that the Miamis had merely ceded lands in northern Indiana, not departed. In fact, Miami villages surrounded Logansport, and individuals from the Miami community frequently visited the small canal town to complete routine errands, especially conducting business with powerful trading companies that were headquartered there. It is even plausible that a number of Miamis were in Logansport on the day that Dillon lamented their absence.[22]

A few months before Winter arrived in Logansport, the *Telegraph* published a poem, "The Aborigines," which asked,

> Where are they—the forest rangers,
> Children of this Western land?
> Who to greet the pale-faced stranger,
> Stretched an unsuspecting hand?

Citizens of Logansport could have answered this query easily by pointing to Native individuals in their midst; but they instead chose to ignore the Indians and portray northwestern Indiana as an area where white progress already had supplanted Indian culture. Long before it was true, the white community essentially adopted the poet's tragic response:

> None are left to deplore them,
> None are left their names to tell.
> Only nature bending o'er them
> Seems to sigh FAREWELL—FAREWELL.[23]

Throughout his stay in Indiana, Winter recorded his impressions on canvas, in his personal journal, and on the pages of local newspapers. His work provides counterevidence to earlier claims that Indians had simply vanished. The accounts of his initial shock at discovering vibrant and persistent Indian communities in place of primitive and vanishing Indians revealed a world far from the abandoned landscape described in poems and editorials. In one of the first entries to his journal, Winter remarked that the Indians he encountered were not ones he "had seen through the imagination or fancy." Instead, they were "clothed in varied colored *draperies*, each one in accordance with his own particular *conceit*; instead of the *shaven* head, and scalp lock towering from the centre of the cranium—his head was wrapped around with a shawl of many Colors. Turban fashioned—à la turk, presenting a picturesque appearance." On paper and canvas, he voiced his intention to document the unexpected.[24]

Winter's first encounter with Indiana's indigenous population, and his entrance into the local community, can be traced to his experience documenting a court case in Logansport. In fact, he spent most of his first year in the village covering the case, which involved misappropriated annuity payments to the Potawatomis. The judge, after hearing that Winter was a painter, asked the Englishman to render a portrait of the Potawatomi speaker Iowa. Shortly thereafter, Winter opened a studio next to Ewing and Walker's "Indian trading establishment," where he hoped that the busy street traffic that included wealthy traders and Indian chiefs would produce clients. He located the studio near the courtyard where traders had erected accommodations for Indians who traveled to Logansport to collect (and spend) their annuity payments.[25]

His initial clients were not Indians. Colonel Abel Pepper, removal agent for the United States, and his staff first commissioned Winter to paint their portraits. This fortuitous meeting shaped the rest of Winter's career. First, Pepper praised his talents as a portraiture artist and shared his delight with other prominent members of the community. This undoubtedly helped bring additional sitters to Winter's studio. Second, the colonel invited him to attend removal negotiations being held at nearby Lake Keewaunay. After the council, he penned several pieces for the local newspaper. In one of his first articles, Winter claimed, "Until my arrival at this place I had never seen an Indian; and it was with no little delight a long awakened curiosity was gratified."[26]

Winter began much like others who made their careers as Indian painters. George Catlin traveled westward in at least five trips between 1830 and 1836 to study Native people and capture their images on canvas. In his travels, and through his paintings, Catlin also contrasted his accounts against the expectations of his audiences. In 1837, the same year that Winter arrived in Indiana, Catlin exhibited nearly 600 Indian portraits as part of his Indian Gallery. Newspaper reports lauded Catlin as an expert on Indian culture and history. Like Winter, Catlin first promoted his artistic endeavor by penning articles about his experiences for newspapers. He also used his firsthand experience traveling throughout the West to lend credence to his paintings. Scholars have since argued that Catlin used these claims to accuracy and authorial authenticity rather than aesthetic appeal in order to promote his artwork. "The relationship between observation and knowledge," historian Steven Conn has argued, "was a central component in nineteenth-century science." He believes that Catlin's claims to observation helped boost his stature as a "scientific painter."[27] As Catlin traveled with his collection around the country, his Indian Gallery morphed from a static representation of Indian images to a performative experience where he presented public lectures on Indian life and culture and displayed objects that he had

collected throughout his travels. Catlin even dressed in "authentic" Indian garb, telling stories of Indian cosmology. The painter's significance
derived from his personal experience interacting with Indian societies
rather than from his artistic merits.[28] Winter, perhaps taking a cue from
Catlin, also began collecting; necklaces and ear bobs worn by Native sitters can be found in his archived collection.

Winter also modeled himself after men like Catlin by sharing his experiences in the pages of newspapers. In that way, he employed his personal
experience to promote his artistic visions. Throughout his first years in
Logansport, Winter wrote extensively about his astonishment and the
gulf between what he expected to see and what he saw in Indiana. Many
Indians wore "frock coats, cut after the most approved fashion," he proclaimed, and they had "banished the 'scalp lock.'" He zealously awaited
any future interactions with his indigenous neighbors, professing that
"reality had exceeded anticipation." Winter confronted a problem that
Catlin did not. According to the stories produced by white settlers and
pioneers, Indians were not supposed to exist in Indiana, let alone mirror
the dress and living conditions of the region's white inhabitants. How
could Winter reconcile his observations of Indian persistence with an art
market that demanded Indians to be portrayed as primitive people who
had all but disappeared? To sell paintings, he had to conform to popular
notions of a vanished Indian. Yet he also relied on his reaction of shock
and astonishment to establish his accounts of "authentic Indians." In
other words, Winter had to convince his potential customers that his
paintings depicted a vanishing race and convince a reading audience
that his accounts of unexpected Indians were reliable.[29]

Winter's state of amazement, as it concerned seeing unexpected Indians, was shared by earlier arrivals to Logansport. In 1834, one individual
wrote of his astonishment in a local newspaper that "considerable numbers" of Indians roamed about town. "The red men, you know, are objects of curiosity, 'away down in old Virginia. Not so here," he explained.
Less than a year before John Brown Dillon lamented the disappearance
of the region's Miami and Potawatomi populations, the same author
wrote that Indians "visit town daily: sometimes in great numbers, dressed
fantastically in the finest broad cloth, and having their ears, noses, arms,
&c, ornamented."[30] Winter produced numerous sketches and water-

colors of the region's indigenous inhabitants during his first two years in Logansport, as he tried to shop his portfolio around to local government agents who were known to collect such images. Winter campaigned for government contracts by declaring his paintings as documents of ethnographic and historical value. After learning that Henry Schoolcraft proposed the creation of a "Cabinet of Indian relics, costumes, etc." for the Department of the Interior, Winter wrote to his friend Colonel Pepper, asking him to audit some sketches and inquire whether the government might purchase them. He also offered to transform the sketches into full oil paintings if the government so desired. For the next decade Winter pestered federal officials about purchasing his paintings, but they refused.[31]

In hindsight, Winter's hope that the federal government might purchase his paintings may seem a fool's errand, but the federal government had long been the largest collector of works involving Native subjects. The government's acquisition of such works also represented the intersection of art and science. Between 1843 and 1863, the government included over 700 western scenes (many of which included Native people) in published reports. They also commissioned artists and natural scientists to travel throughout the West to record Native customs and document Native life in the form of images. Many of the paintings used by modern ethnographers who study Native cultures come from artists employed by the federal government, including Samuel Seymour, Titian Ramsey Peale, Henry Rowe Schoolcraft, and Thomas McKenney. But not all Indian painters were on the federal payroll. In fact, George Catlin had also tried desperately to sell his Indian Gallery to the federal government but failed despite several congressional resolutions proposing their purchase. Ultimately Catlin's financial hardships forced him to take his exhibit to London and Paris where he tried to make a profit and escape American debt collectors.[32] Winter, however, adapted to the local markets, and his paintings, especially those conducted after his first few years in Logansport, reflect popular perceptions of Native people rather than serve as accurate ethnographic records of Native life.

Like Catlin, Winter published pieces for local newspapers marketing his work as both authentic representation and ethnographic evidence. These comparisons eventually drew the editor of the *Indiana Magazine of*

History, George Cottman, to declare Winter the "Catlin of Indiana." But Winter's tireless self-promotion in the 1830s and his reinvention over the subsequent decades also point to a different life: one of a thrifty entrepreneur who adapted to public opinion and altered his work to meet expectations. As such, his sketches and paintings represent larger discussions about the intersection of art and science that helped Hoosiers imagine a narrative of clean indigenous dispossession and innocuous settlement.[33]

In the summer of 1838, Logansport bustled with activity, as federal officials, traders, and curious spectators flooded into the small hamlet in preparation for the forced removal of Potawatomis from the Wabash River valley. Authors filled newspaper columns with pieces advocating for and justifying forced removal. Yet removal was more complicated than merely moving people west. It took incredible organization, coercion, and often duplicitous actions by American agents. By August Colonel Pepper demanded that Chief Menominee and the Wabash River Potawatomis leave for Kansas.[34] As removal, at least of the Potawatomis, shifted from possibility to reality, Americans in Logansport attempted to detach the Potawatomi community from the land.

On August 11, white settlers gathered in Logansport to discuss an "expedition to the Devil's Lake," after rumors surfaced that a strange creature might inhabit its depths. According to the local newspaper, a "well-known" gentleman in the community had witnessed "some animal raise its head, three to four feet above the surface of the water," and survey its surroundings. The anonymous source further described the creature as "having the characteristics of [a] serpent; color dingy, and with bright yellow spots," and explained that it had paused briefly and stared directly at him from several hundred yards away. Community leaders called the meeting to discuss a strategy of catching the animal.[35] The crowd, which included both John Brown Dillon and George Winter, concocted an elaborate plan to capture the "Lake Monster." After listening to community leaders and drafting several proposals, members of the group decided that they would anchor eight lines, equipped with hooks attached to floating buoys, into the depths of the lake. They elected a group of individuals to serve as an expedition party, who would deploy the lines and bait them with "meat or large fish." Before they left, however, Winter sketched "a drawing of a plan for the capture of the Leviathan" that could be used as a blueprint for crafting the trap.[36]

When they gathered in Logansport to discuss the "Lake Monster," Winter and others were doing more than fantasizing about a large snake; they were also attempting to belittle the connections that Native communities held to the land. The Potawatomis and Miamis of northern Indiana believed that something mysterious indeed inhabited the same lake, which they called Lake Manitou. Within those communities the lake held special meaning. "Such is the terror in which [the lake] is held that but few Indians would even dare to venture in a canoe upon its surface," reported Winter in the *Telegraph*. "The Indians will neither fish, nor bathe in the lake; such is the powerful conviction that 'Man-i-tou,' or the Evil Spirit, dwells in its Chystal [*sic*] waters."[37] Winter did not directly state that the Man-i-tou of the Devil's Lake was a serpent, but the community certainly implied that connection, as they plumbed its depths in search of the Lake Monster.

Serpents were integral symbols within both Miami and Potawatomi cosmologies. Miami elders told stories of a warrior from their tribe, Young Thunder, who traveled to the falls at Niagara and engaged in an epic battle with a "wonderful serpent, of immense size, of black colour and having on his head two horns as large as those of the Elk." A similar story existed within the Wea communities about two Miami boys who jumped on the back of a giant serpent in order to stop it from ravaging the countryside. According to the story, the boys set fire to the beast's horns, which burnt inward, frying his brain. Giant serpents and mammoths appeared within local indigenous cosmologies, especially the Miamis. They believed that both creatures had once required the actions of warriors to subdue. While mammoths were more prevalent in stories told by tribes like the Shawnees, serpents appeared often in Miami and Potawatomi legends.[38]

The Miamis both feared and revered serpents. According to one story, a Miami boy who was traveling with his family wandered off—distracted by a small bird that flew into the forest. He chased it, wanting to capture the bird and make it his lunch, but it flew beyond his reach. Distraught, the boy turned to rejoin his family, but soon realized that he was lost. Frightened and alone, he started to worry. Then a voice called to him,

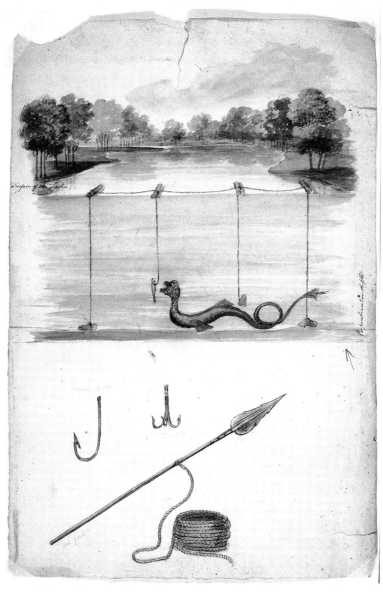

George Winter, *Trapping Lake Monster.* Courtesy of Tippecanoe County Historical Association, Lafayette, Ind. (Catalogue # M-82)

comforting him and telling him that his safety was assured. The voice then informed the boy that he and his tribesmen from that moment forward could kill all the deer, bears, or raccoons of the forest to satisfy their needs. The boy, too afraid to turn toward the voice up to this point, finally did so. To his surprise, he discovered that the voice belonged to a snake that was hanging from a tree. When the boy returned to his village and told them about his experience, the Miamis thereafter banned the killing of snakes. Furthermore, they believed that the mysterious serpent had been responsible for a renewed abundance of game in the forests near where they lived.[39]

The Miamis and Potawatomis also viewed other spaces within Indiana as sacred. Joseph Allen, a government surveyor sent to Indiana to begin parceling land for white settlement, observed that both of them refused to settle at a spot near the forks of the Wabash River because they believed that a spotted rattlesnake, representing a celestial deity, lived along one of its banks. He was amazed that the Miamis refused to "even pass by it within a small distance." Instead, they used the area around the forks to bury their dead.[40] White settlers and surveyors believed these actions were irrational, because the area around the forks of the Wabash seemed advantageous for locating a fort or trading post. Historian Claudio Saunt found a similar process occurred in the American Southeast, where Europeans and Americans employed enlightenment philosophies and scientific reasoning to conclude, "Myth, like the people who produced it, was childlike, irrational, and primitive."[41]

Whites found such stories quixotic and sought to use science to disprove Miami and Potawatomi myths. At first, they tried to explain the existence of the Lake Monster in scientific terms rather than as the product of indigenous spiritual beliefs. When an eighteen-inch Mastodon tooth was discovered near Logansport, Winter suggested that perhaps a real yet unnaturally large snake lived in the Devil's Lake. "The existence of a monster in this lake," he wrote, "is not an object of more surprise to us than the remains of the Mastadon."[42] Could the natural sciences explain the Lake Monster? Certainly Winter believed so. He argued that the occasion presented an opportunity "worthy the consideration of every scientific mind" and believed that the discovery of a new species would be an "object of interest to science, the naturalist, and [the] philosopher."[43]

The citizens of Logansport had not been the first American community to claim sighting abnormally large serpents.

In the decades prior to Potawatomi removal, sea serpents had become the object of great speculation among natural scientists, both in the United States and England. In 1817, reports surfaced that a sea serpent had been spotted in Gloucester Bay (Massachusetts). Over the course of the following year, scientists debated its existence and whether or not it had been a hoax. The controversy drew national attention. Scientific associations, like the Linnaean Society, sought to gain valuable information from capturing and studying the creature. The late summer of 1818 opened "serpent season," as fishermen off the New England coast dropped lines and nets hoping to capture the beast. Their efforts produced numerous stories of close encounters and mistaken identities, as several fishermen produced large fish they claimed might have been the sea serpent. The scientific searches also led to fantastic stories produced by witty and disbelieving playwrights who mocked the entire endeavor.[44] By 1838, fish stories about large serpents were seen as just that: fish stories. Additionally, by the time that the Logansport community debated the existence of their serpent, the general scientific community had moved beyond tall tales of sea serpents. So why did this frontier community, decades removed from the national obsession with sea serpents and more than a thousand miles removed from the sea, develop its own infatuation with the Lake Monster?

In the years prior to Potawatomi removal, science and scientific taxonomy, whereby life on the planet could be organized into hierarchal classifications, had begun to be used to categorize human life. Not only could Americans around Logansport use scientific endeavors, like the search for the Lake Monster, to contrast their superior scientific knowledge against that of the supposedly primitive minds of indigenous peoples; they could also use science to position themselves at a higher biological position. In 1837, eastern phrenologists visited Logansport to deliver seminars on the science of human taxonomy.[45] American phrenology derived from eastern natural scientists who had adapted European scientific theories of polygenesis—the belief that the races of the earth descended from unrelated ancestors. Craniologists and phrenologists believed that the science of reading human skulls provided adequate data to classify human races. Samuel Gordon Morton, a Philadelphia physician, later produced his results in *Crania Americana*—an endorsement of phrenology. These studies purported that American Indians did not possess the biological capacities to rise above their suspended state of primitivism.[46]

In Logansport, the search for the Lake Monster served two purposes. First, it provided an opportunity for the community to dislodge Native connections to lands they sought to conquer. And, second, it allowed them to highlight their scientific superiority in an effort to justify removal. Articles about the Devil's Lake and its reptilian inhabitant spread across the country. While some editors simply republished articles from the *Logansport Telegraph*, including Winter's pieces, a handful of newspaper editors challenged the claims of the frontier village. Newspapers in Boston, New York, and even Cincinnati debated the presence of the Lake Monster.[47] The editor of the *Maysville* (N.Y.) *Sentinel* doubted "not only the existence of the monster of Lake Manitoo, but the existence of the Lake itself."[48] The *Telegraph* reprinted this last condemnation and challenged the editor to travel to Indiana to visit the lake himself. Even the newly established *Logansport Herald* questioned claims about the Lake Monster that appeared in its competitor.[49] In response, the *Telegraph* issued an article penned by George Winter attempting to end the debate; the article also included a drawing by the artist.[50] His cartoonish caricature of a grinning eel-like creature revealed underlying issues connected to the search for the Lake Monster. Winter's drawings and writings demonstrate how the community used the entire episode to belittle the Potawatomis, who were in the process of being forcefully removed, and the Miamis, who they hoped would depart shortly.

A poem published in the *Telegraph* illustrates the connections between the community's version of the Lake Monster and that of the local Native communities. Titled "To the Northern Monster," the poem could easily have been addressed to either the Potawatomis or the Miamis.

> Dear Mr. Monster, Devil, Fish, or Snake,
> Or whate'er other cognomen you wear,
> Your neck's in danger in the 'Devil's Lake,'
> Unless you keep your head below the air.
> An expedition soon will scour your range,

To take and kill you in your own dominion;
Oh! Homicide! or Snakicide! most strange!
Supported, too, by popular opinion.
Look out, old Scratch! a head & tail's at stake.
Keep dark and low. How deep's your famous lake?

How many hundred years, you old Infernal,
Have pass'd since in Manitto you began to revel?—
Keeping the harmless fish in fear eternal,
And scaring young papoosies like the devil!
When, with her lover, the poor Indian girl
Roam'd near your lake, the fairest of Earth's daughters,
Say, did you not your long tail often twirl,
And pop your ugly head above the waters?
And was it not for thee right glorious fun,
To see the nude and tawny lovers run!
How many legends could your skinny Grace
Unfold to mortals, if you had a tongue!
The loves, and wars, of that strange Indian race,
Who never knew from what far land they sprung. . . .

Look to thyself, old Monarch of the North!
Thy lake will soon be filled with hooks and ropes,
And many a tempting bait to lure thee forth,
That men may crush at once your head and hopes.
I do not wish to see thee come to harm,
Old Imp—and ergo you had better DIVE:
Your presence makes the weather rather warm;
The best thermometer stands now at 95;
But if you will not take a timely warning,
Why, I'm your most obedient. Good morning.[51]

The hype over the Lake Monster masked the violence of removal. As
the Logansport community scoured the Devil's Lake in August and September, armed military escorts marched the Potawatomis westward. The
forced removal held deadly consequences for the Potawatomis and has
since been dubbed the "Trail of Death." Once the Indians were removed,
the local community's interest in both the Potawatomis and the Lake
Monster waned. In September 1838, the *Logansport Telegraph* announced
an end to the search for the serpent.[52] According to the article (penned

by Winter), a local resident had netted an abnormally large fish, thereby solving the mystery. An article chronicling the removal of the Potawatomis from Indiana appeared next to the report.

Art, science, and history mutually reinforced a concept of American progress and westward expansion that forecasted the erasure of America's indigenous peoples. This sentiment drove Americans and Europeans westward in the hopes that they might capture an accurate portrait of a people destined to disappear. Artists like George Catlin and George Winter embodied this spirit as they traveled west, seeking to capture the fleeting images of Native people. They hoped that their art might aid science and inform future histories. Yet, despite claims to objectivism and empiricism, American historians provided romantic accounts of human progress in ways that were not so different from their European colleagues. Artists who painted Indians provided these historical narratives with visual representations that supported claims to the inevitable demise of western Indians. And an explosion in print media in the 1830s created an inchoate marketplace where authors debated the validity and authorship of accounts on western life, especially as it pertained to Native Americans. Eastern authors claimed that those who traveled west became infatuated with their subjects and allowed their romantic visions to cloud their works. Westerners claimed that eastern writers simply could not capture a true representation of western people without actually traveling west. Claims to "truth" became central to these debates.[53]

George Winter's authorial works in the *Logansport Telegraph* established him as a western writer at the same time that he was attempting to launch his career as a western painter. He claimed to have found a different kind of "authentic" Indian. By doing so, he was trying to capitalize on the larger discussion going on between historians, travel writers, and other artists, who each claimed that authenticity and firsthand experience were key to the value of one's work. But Winter faced a paradox. If all travelers to the West claimed "accuracy" or "truth" from their firsthand observations of Indians, how could Winter's observations be different? As we have seen with the incident of the Lake Monster, Winter's role in promoting western settlement and helping to justify removal also shaped his thoughts on the subjects he attempted to paint: American Indians. Winter may have claimed authenticity, but the Englishman also shared American beliefs in the advancement of Euro-American progress. In fact, as an Englishman, Winter may have been more likely to impart romantic ideals into supposedly historical accounts and pander to fickle American audiences who demanded vivid portraits of western life. Winter certainly interjected popular beliefs about Indians, and thus himself, into his work.

What complicates our understanding of Winter further is the discord between his public writings and his private thoughts, as recorded in journals not meant for publication. At the same time that Winter professed to producing truthful renditions of Indiana's Indians, he romanticized their removal in private. In 1838, again during Potawatomi removal, Winter penned "To a Decaying Trunk; or, Reflection upon an Old Tree." The somber sonnet bemoaned the death of an ailing oak and, at the same time, seemingly reflected upon the demise of the local indigenous peoples in the process of removing.

> Venerable, leafless and decaying old trunk! Thou hast withstood the lightning's flash and the wanton storm. Thou standest proud monarch of the forest still, erect, and in various hues relieved by the young green, and tender progeny around thee. Time has been with thee, and thy days are numbered. Old tree! Thy vernal honors have disappeared.

Winter continued, connecting more directly the history of the tree to removal.

> Yes! Once decaying trunk! Thy sinuous and heavenward extending branches bore a noble and massive leafy crescent that waved in the gentle breeze and flung around an ample shade wherein the Red man oft have set in grave consultation and mutually avowed their hate as they viewed the white man's wigwams in infant "Logan" [Logansport] springing up mysteriously quick in the aboriginal domain and which too truly foretold the melancholy truth that ere many summers the moccasins tread would be obliterated from the verdant carpet of the forest.
>
> Noble tree of the forest! Like man thou hast had thy infancy, childhood, youth, and age; but more than man thou hast experienced the seasons, each in due succession. Thou didst not commence thy youth too early for thy venerable and aged aspect proclaims no premature decay.[54]

As he worked to dislocate Native connections to the land in his public writings about the Lake Monster and Devil's Lake, Winter also began embedding them in his artistic landscapes. His effort to connect Indians with nature, making the demise of both an inevitable consequence of American progress, actually revealed itself in his newspaper articles. In describing a Potawatomi burial in the autumn of 1837, Winter framed his observations within a portrait of the natural environment that surrounded the burial site. Reporting on the burial, Winter took time to reflect, "The Indian country near these lakes is strangely beautiful." Still measuring what he saw against what he expected to see, Winter singled out "one old warrior, who might have been the grand-father of the girl," who, it seems, had forgotten "that cold, stern indifference which marks so strongly the Indian character." Perhaps confused by the seemingly unconventional expression of the Indian's emotion, Winter redirected his attention to the beauty of the setting, inadvertently inserting the real people that he saw into the pastoral landscape of his mind's eye. His dual fascination with Native people and nature carried into his final reflection on the funeral: "Beautiful is the resting place of a nameless daughter of the forest, who was buried in silence on the banks of Lake Ke-wah-na." Despite his claims that he traveled to Logansport to learn as much as possible about the Potawatomis and Miamis who lived there, he knew surprisingly little about them. Instead, the Potawatomis who attended the burial were no more subjects of his study than their surroundings; the Potawatomis, like the deceased girl, simply became part of the scenery that he hoped to capture on canvas.[55]

Winter did not make his career as a newspaper reporter or a fisherman of lake monsters. He painted. Yet his paintings, which have long been used as accurate representations of Indian life, were also imbued with Winter's romanticism. Far from renditions of western life, his paintings, at least those that he sold, were carefully constructed and manipulated pieces. But he believed that his life as an observer and his life as a painter needed to be linked if he hoped to sell his paintings. Winter's *Indian Burial Kee-waw-nay Village 1837* demonstrates how he took liberty in changing scenes he saw into the scenes that he painted. Like most landscape artists in the early to mid-nineteenth century, Winter traveled into the field with the basic tools of the trade: pencils and sketch pad

George Winter, *Indian Burial Kee-waw-nay Village*. Sketch. Courtesy of Tippecanoe County Historical Association, Lafayette, Ind. (Catalogue # G-347)

George Winter, *Indian Burial Kee-waw-nay Village 1837.* Courtesy of Tippecanoe County Historical Association, Lafayette, Ind. (Catalogue # M-81)

with perhaps a few watercolors. Only later would travel artists commit these images to canvas.[56] In the case of the Potawatomi funeral, Winter conducted a quick sketch of the work with pencil. The fact that a separate watercolor of the burial exists suggests that it was conducted later than the initial sketch. In fact, it has been suggested that the watercolor was not produced until the 1860s, when Winter was compiling his notes and producing illustrations for a journal about his experiences that he hoped to publish. In this particular painting, Winter made one minor alteration that perhaps symbolized a major change in the painting's ethnographic significance. In the original pencil sketch, the Potawatomi gentleman standing in the near right corner wore an open jacket, ruffled shirt, and additional adornments. In the watercolor, executed years later, the entire upper dress of the individual was changed, so that he was only wearing a shawl. Did the difference in dress mean something? Who was this man? It is quite likely that Winter did not know. The images of the Potawatomis were merely illustrations for his larger work, which had more to do with him than it did with the people he painted.

Winter's account of the Potawatomi burial came by chance, as he visited a series of councils held between Indian agent Abel Pepper and the Potawatomis. Like his written account of the burial, Winter's observations of the treaty councils had the effect of embedding the Indians in the landscape, as he spent nearly a quarter of his journal entry describing the "wild and uncultivated country," which included the "foliage of the forest trees," "innumerable and various species of wild flowers," and "rank grass waving under the influence of a gentle breeze." He juxtaposed his description of Indians with his observations on the natural landscape. As he put pencil to paper and produced his sketch of the scene, intending to commit it to canvas later, he treated individual Indians in the same manner that he treated the trees and shrubbery in the background: they were malleable subjects of his paintings.[57] Winter prepared a painting from his sketches for the War Department and boasted to Pepper that his paintings derived from his direct observation at the council, although he admitted at the time of the council "there was not an ample scope to give the likenesses of the actors in the scene," so he rendered only "a *general* character of them." In his examination of the painting, scholar Christian Feest concluded that the details of some of the individuals in the scene were drawn from sketches and portraits Winter had conducted in the year prior to the council.[58]

Winter's council painting drew from a variety of studies, and he took liberty in repositioning actors. An entire grouping of Indians who appeared in the background of the original sketch fail to appear in the painting. Moreover, Winter seemed more focused on the artistic merits of the painting than accurately creating a snapshot of the moment. In a letter to Pepper, he described how he cast the "principal light" upon the Indian speaker Na-waw-kay, who stood "conspicuous in his white counterpane coat and red silken sash," and positioned several notable Indian leaders, whose images were taken from earlier studies, in an "oblique line" immediately behind the vividly dressed speaker.[59] We cannot be sure if Winter's image of the council even depicts the correct attendees,

George Winter, *Council of Keewaunay*. Courtesy of Glenn A. Black Laboratory of Archaeology and the Trustees of Indiana University.

let alone where they stood or what they wore. In this manner, the work re-sembled popular genre paintings more than ethnographic recordings. Winter's use of individual studies made his paintings composite pieces, which mirrored the work of other 1830s genre painters. Although his early work was meant to be a recording of real events and people, his later pieces more closely represented artists of non-Indian subjects. George Caleb Bingham produced romantic pieces of western life that engaged the politics of everyday life and challenged the image of de-generative westerners. His paintings of jolly boatmen and western civic characters likewise were drawn from individual sketches, which were then organized, repositioned, and cast onto a single canvas. In this way, Bingham's work was not meant to be a direct representation of daily life. Instead, it was meant as an artistic interpretation, guided by aesthetic expression. While he claimed that his early work was illustrative of life in Indiana, the canvases Winter produced for the public market were similar to Bingham's composite pieces.[60]

Winter struggled, like many of his contemporaries, to forge a living from painting. By the early 1840s, it became clear that he would not be able to support his family off the sale of paintings with Indian subjects alone. The government had refused to purchase his depictions of the Po-tawatomis and Miamis, and few people offered to employ him as a por-trait painter in the frontier outpost—the real lifeblood of a struggling artist. By 1844, government officials threatened to sell his lots in Logans-port because he had not paid his taxes.[61] While he spent his first few years in Indiana painting the images of Native people, he spent the bet-ter part of his career selling landscape paintings. Eventually he learned how to combine the two in order to appeal to a fickle art market. Still, he spent the 1840s and early 1850s experimenting with different forms of artistic expressions.

In the 1850s he became desperate and asked his brother Charles, who lived in Ohio, to finance an Indian Gallery in Cincinnati. He tried to convince him that his Indian paintings would sell in the larger market of the Queen City. His brother decided otherwise and used his life savings to open a general store instead. Undaunted, Winter asked his brother to donate a few lanterns and lighting equipment from his new store so that he could use them for an "Elydoric Paintings and Dissolving Views" exhibition. These shows included enormous canvases (nearly 15 by 10 feet), which were projected upon a wall using the gas lamps. Winter hoped to use profits from the shows to fund his Indian Gallery.[62] Although the historical record is silent on whether or not Charles sent the lamps, he opened the exhibition for a short time. Still, the Indian Gallery never materialized.

In subsequent years, Winter abandoned any claims to authenticity and virtually admitted that his later paintings were romantic and inaccurate portrayals of a "vanishing people." Many artists, including Winter's famed contemporary, English landscape painter J. M. W. Turner, penned poetry and stories in the margins of their sketchbooks, but by the 1840s and 1850s, Winter often copied these thoughts and accompanying poetry directly onto the descriptions of his paintings, hoping they would lure purchasers. Writing to one prospective buyer, Winter used romantic images of the "vanishing Indian" in an attempt to entice him to purchase a copy of *View upon the Wabash.*

The time for [the Indian's] emigration by "treaty" had expired, the whitemen were gathering thick around them, which was but a sad necessity for their departure. Still they clung to their homes. But the flames of the torch were applied—their villages and wigwams were annihilated. The principal chiefs were secured by the strong arm of authority, and led or rather driven captives out of the land at the point of bayonet! It was truly a melancholy spectacle, that awoke a deep feeling of sympathy for their unhappy fate. They have gone, and how soon forgotten![63]

His description was as much about lamenting the loss of Native people as it was a celebration of white conquest. Winter ended his letter with a poem.

The whiteman came and the Indian passed
Like withering leaves as an autumn blast,
The glorious forest was felled at last,
And house by house
The village rose
And the fields were cleared
And the road was made
But the Elm was spared for a friendly shade.[64]

According to Winter, the sympathetic story so touched the potential buyer that he was persuaded to "literally empty" his pockets to procure the painting.[65] Of course, Winter told the final part of this story to another patron, hoping he would purchase a similar work.

Unlike his earlier watercolors, where Native people were the focus of the painting, Winter's later oil paintings simply used Indians as secondary subjects within larger sweeping landscapes. His friends advised him to abandon painting real Indians altogether. One critic believed that "a nigger dance, . . . a paw-wow of drunken Indians, or a portrait of the girl that ran away with the Fakir of Siva would have more attraction." On a trip to Cincinnati to sell a group of Indian paintings, Winter sold only two, which barely covered his travel expenses. When he showed up at Reverend R. B. Tefft's office (the man who earlier supposedly unloaded his pockets for Winter's work) with paintings in hand, Winter discovered that the Reverend had forgotten their meetings and had already left town.[66] One friend trying to comfort Winter told him, "You must not be deterred . . . your experience has already shown you, that the public taste in the *fine arts*, is very precarious, indeed that it is an *ignoramus*, and you must 'administer to such a taste' in such a manner as will *take their money*." He warned Winter that "the red man at home surrounded by the scenery of his mature forests" would not sell. Like other confidants, his friend advised Winter to "administer to their tastes" if he wanted to sell paintings to the general public. Winter's ethnographic work would "not always be unproductive," the friend assured him; he assumed that someone eventually would surface who would "appreciate such truths."[67]

Winter never stopped painting Indians, but he kept reducing their centrality to works that he presented for sale. In the art market of the nineteenth century, Winter often included his paintings in private distributions. Art distributions were popular venues for artists looking to make a name in the art world, as they would supply paintings to a general distribution and clients would purchase tickets for a raffle where winners would either choose a work from the collection or be assigned a specific work from the offering. Sometimes distributions would offer chances on individual paintings. In any case, they usually provided some money for the artist. More important, they gave them exposure among collectors. If a painting became popular, an artist might find himself/herself commissioned to have their paintings made into lithographs, whereby they might make some substantial money. Winter participated in these distributions but often complained that the revenue from the tickets rarely covered his expenses. In 1854, he attempted to hold his own distribution in Lafayette, Indiana. But the results were disappointed, as the winning tickets for at least three of the twenty paintings had gone unsold.[68]

Beginning in the 1840s, Winter tried to dump the mountain of paintings gathering in his studio by offering them in larger regional art union distributions. These sales offered subscribers the chance to "win" paintings. Art unions sold yearly certificates to members to help fund struggling artists, and a few lucky members received pieces of art purchased by the union. The Western Art Union in Cincinnati bought some of his paintings, but the more lucrative and widely popular American Art Union in New York City refused to purchase any. When they were purchased, his mainstream landscape paintings were received favorably. Winter's landscapes (30 by 20 inches) received estimates between $30 and $50, which was comparable to work from artists like George Caleb Bingham ($30 and $70). But Winter lacked quality pieces that brought top dollar. His larger, more expensive paintings were valued around $100, while Bingham's most celebrated works brought triple that amount—*The Jolly Flatboatmen* originally sold for $290. Moreover, by not being included in the national distributions, Winter lost the opportunity for having pieces selected to be lithographed; Bingham sold an original copy of a painting to the American Art Union for $1,200 so that it could be turned into a lithograph.[69]

Whether through lotteries or distributions, Winter began offering more landscapes than Indian paintings. And when they did appear in paintings, Indians served more and more as objects embedded in the landscape. Winter described a large canvas (50 by 38 inches) depicting Lake Mucksin as "a scene in Indiana, being a representation of Autumn. . . . It is rendered interesting by the introduction of several Indian groups." While Indians appeared in the painting, Winter clearly did not view them as the most important aspect; he spent as much time describing the "picturesque" frame as he did describing the Indians. As he began promoting his new studio in Lafayette, Winter referred to himself less and less as an Indian artist. Instead, he promised visitors that "lovers of

George Winter, pencil sketch of women washing clothes. Courtesy of Tippecanoe County Historical Association, Lafayette, Ind. (Catalogue # G-417)

fine art" could expect to find "a large collection of oil paintings, among
them many picturesque views of Indiana."[70]

Furthermore, the large landscapes, which included Native subjects,
were not representations of real scenes. Instead, they were almost entirely composed of composites from sketches made years, sometimes
decades, earlier. In one landscape, which depicted Indian women washing clothing along the banks of the Wabash River, the individuals within
the painting are not identified. Winter took great liberty in *Scene Along
Wabash River*, repositioning the subjects, even in relation to his sketches.
For example, he altered the positions of the woman washing a shirt in
the right foreground and the woman nursing her child on the rock. In
the painting they are separated by two women on their knees washing
clothing, while they appear side-by-side and alone in a pencil sketch conducted decades earlier. Other individuals within the painting may have
come from other sketches taken from Winter's trip to Crooked Creek in
August 1837.

Eventually, Winter stopped promoting his paintings of Indians as ethnographic evidence and instead produced paintings that conformed to popular tastes and exhibited fully the idea of the "vanished Indian." Consequently, he began producing images of the archetypal and completely fictionalized American Indian. Unsurprisingly, perhaps, he found success with this approach. In the 1850s and 1860s he painted multiple copies of a piece entitled *Spotted Fawn*. The painting depicted a scantily clad Indian woman crossing a stream. As she jumped from stone to stone across the water, her long black hair flowed behind her, and she clung to a piece of vibrant red cloth that was draped irreverently across her partially exposed breasts. Winter based the figure on John Gadsby Chapman's popular painting *The Chief's Daughter*, and a copy of Chapman's work still resides in Winter's personal papers. Winter included his

George Winter, *Scene Along Wabash River*. Oil on Canvas. 38 × 54 inches. Copyright 2010. Courtesy of Gerald Peters Gallery, Santa Fe, N.M.

George Winter, *Spotted Fawn*. Courtesy of Conner Prairie Interactive History Park, Fishers, Ind.

version of *Spotted Fawn* in at least seven art distributions and in at least four sizes.

Dealers, friends, and family informed Winter that *Spotted Fawn* was worthy of replicating and selling. One purchaser of the painting, Winter discovered, held it "among the greatest of her earthly possessions."[71] The owner of several art studios wrote Winter in 1848 to inform him that not a single piece of Winter's work had sold in his New York City gallery, but he assured Winter that copies of *Spotted Fawn* occupied "the very best kind of position" in his Louisville studio.[72] Later that year, Winter's sister-in-law informed him that people in Fort Wayne, Indiana, where she lived, had been talking about his paintings, especially *Spotted Fawn*. She requested a copy of the painting along with some other "pretty pieces" of Indians to show.[73]

It probably helped that the painting came with a romanticized story about its subject. In his notes accompanying the painting, Winter recalled the story of Spotted Fawn. She was an Indian princess, he concluded, who had fallen in love with a French trader of whom her father disapproved. The painting depicted the young woman sneaking away from her Indian community to meet her European lover. Although not depicted in the painting, Winter explained a tragic end to the story. Upset that his daughter had run off to be with the Frenchman, the chief decided to murder him before they rendezvoused. Firing his musket in the direction of a figure believed to be the Frenchman, the chief discovered that his daughter had cloaked herself in the Frenchman's clothing while attempting to avoid capture.[74]

The image and story of Spotted Fawn supported popular tropes that justified white conquest. The Indian princess chose to "escape" Indian society, leaving her community and embracing white culture in the form of a European lover, as the Frenchman acted as a foil for the peaceful interaction between Americans and Indians. Scholar Susan Scheckel argues that the eroticized Native woman, as portrayed in popular renderings, demonstrated the centrality of femininity and the superiority of white masculinity represented by "the idealized female Indian" choosing white over Native associations. "This very recognition," Scheckel posits, provided "proof of her feminine virtue" and served as "the basis of her idealization," providing "an implicit justification of conquest."[75]

Despite the habit of modern historians to read his journal, paintings, and other writings as objective documentary evidence, most of Winter's known work on Indiana's Indians was compiled or produced decades after he made his initial observations. Beginning in the 1860s, the artist began collecting historical information about the Indians he had painted

from popular sources like those written by Henry Rowe Schoolcraft.[76] In
these later journals, Winter claimed that the Indians he observed in the
1830s did not conform to his expectations when he arrived in Indiana. He
insisted, "Many painters have painted Indians from the imagination. . . .
I know, until I saw the red man . . . how sorely I was misled." In 1871, he
compiled his notes and watercolors on the Indians of north-central Indiana into a journal, hoping to market it to publishers. When that failed,
he sent a copy to his close friend Horace Biddle. Winter's note that accompanied the unpublished journal reflected the connections between
his personal beliefs and popular opinions.[77]

> I dedicate these effects of pen and pencil, however unpretentious
> they may be—having had so long a time—the assurances of your
> sympathy and appreciation of my labors in artistic distinctions from
> alliteration and the desire to presume the likeness, habits, and cus-
> toms of some at least of the unfortunate race of redmen, whom I
> have seen and know personally, and alas! August falling away from
> earthly existence without the natural sympathy for their sad and
> inevitable extinction.[78]

Winter's lamentations on the extinction of Indiana's Indians was partially misplaced. Unlike the Wyandot of Ohio, Indian removal in Indiana was never completed. Instead of relying on old sketchbooks from
the 1830s, Winter could have continued painting Indians living in Indiana throughout the 1840s, 1850s, 1860s, and even the 1870s. Yet his
later work presented a romanticized and historicized Indian—one that
predated the 1840s. Consequently, his writings and paintings served the
purpose of narrating a story of western settlement that justified and nat-
uralized conquest. His work also represents powerful intersections between science, historicism, and the aesthetic in the place-storytelling of
the lower Great Lakes. As early as the 1820s, westerners across the region
began to imagine a West without Indians. Winter, other western artists,
race scientists, and early historians provided evidence that the clearing
of the middle ground, via Indian removal, was inevitable and necessary.
As congressmen and petitioners debated the importance of pioneering,
men like George Winter provided Americans with an image of a cleared
western landscape open for the pioneers to settle and farm. Winter's
work could have exposed the persistence of Native communities in the

lower Great Lakes, but his habit of promoting himself, the Logansport community's assumptions about the inferiority of Native people, and the pressures of a hostile art market kept the realities of a multicultural world hidden. The story of Miami woman Frances Slocum, one of his sitters, best exposes how this process of historical amnesia worked to clear the middle ground.

CHAPTER 5

"They Found and Left Her an Indian"

Captivity Narratives and the Whitening
of the Middle Ground

Another story from Indiana generated national interest at approximately
the same time that Americans debated the existence of the Lake Monster. Like that previous story, this one appeared as local citizens pushed
government agents to remove Native Americans. But, unlike accounts of
the creature living in Devil's Lake, the story of Frances Slocum, a white
captive living among the Miamis of Indiana, neither quickly dissipated
from the public consciousness nor could easily be used to signal an end
to Native presence in the lower Great Lakes. Instead, the malleability of
Frances Slocum's story over time allowed white communities to establish
another type of place-story—one that downplayed their personal role in
the dispossession of Native peoples and instead focused a seemingly natural and inevitable flow to western settlement centered on racial superiority. Over the course of the late nineteenth and early twentieth century,
authors manipulated Slocum's story to highlight her whiteness and present the place-story of the Hoosier landscape as one drawn in contrasting
colors of red and white. Doing so allowed them to present a narrative of
anti-conquest, which ignored persistent and visible Native communities
that lived (and in some cases continue to live) among them.

On an autumn evening in 1835, the elderly, diminutive Miami woman
Maconaquah (Young Bear) welcomed a weary white Indian trader into
her home at Deaf Man's Village.[1] The village consisted of stables, a corn-
crib, fenced pastures, and a double-log cabin occupied by the family.
According to the visitor, George Ewing, the indigenous woman joined
him near the cabin's hearth after her family went to bed. He surmised
that, sick, tired, and perhaps wanting to confess before she died, Young

Bear revealed a secret to him that she had kept for nearly half a century: Indians had taken her from her white family as a child.[2] His "discovery" launched a national search for Young Bear's eastern relatives that eventually raised the woman from obscurity to national recognition. Ewing, informed by Young Bear that she had once lived among white people in Pennsylvania, wrote to eastern newspaper editors who subsequently published Ewing's letters. "There is now living near this place," he wrote the postmaster at Lancaster, Pennsylvania, "an aged woman, who a few days ago told me, whilst I lodged in the camp with her one night, that she was taken away from her father's house."[3] Two years later, Ewing received a letter from Joseph Slocum, who was living at the time in Pennsylvania, inquiring about the woman. Slocum wondered: could she be his sister Frances, the "Lost Sister of the Wyoming"? He packed his bags and set off for Indiana.

White authors have recounted tales about Frances Slocum many times over the past century and a half. And while these stories appear to mirror the many other captivity narratives that dominated eighteenth-century and (to a limited extent) early-nineteenth-century American literature, the narrative of Maconaquah's capture, discovery, and later life differs in important ways. These differences reveal dynamics about gendered constructions of race in the nineteenth and twentieth centuries that others do not. Moreover, Frances Slocum's story has been written and rewritten as a captivity narrative and, as such, has come to obscure our understanding of Native history in Indiana. This rewriting demonstrates how a shiftiness in the language of conquest enabled Americans to redraw the boundaries of whiteness and conceal stories that directly challenged a narrative dependent on the clearing of the middle ground.

Historically, captivity narratives have served as powerful fables that stress the undesirability of race mixing and place the events of colonization, settlement, and conquest into narratives of violent conflict.[4] But modern scholarly treatments of the genre raise the possibility of seeing beyond typical nineteenth-century bifurcated categories of race that stress opposition. Historian June Namias believes that "the captivity drama presents us with an intersection of cultures" as intermarriages rest at the center of many of these stories.[5] In the case of Frances Slocum, however, writers have historically underplayed the violence of her captivity and seldom focused on Slocum's marriages to two indigenous men. In fact, they rarely discuss her half-century living among the Indians at all. Instead, writers spilled much ink upon paper trying to explain how the elderly Frances Slocum had either "gone Indian" or retained her claims to whiteness, in the process revealing nineteenth-century American anxieties about the fixed nature of racial categories.

Late-nineteenth-century biographers who disseminated the story of Frances Slocum focused on instances that illustrated a bifurcated world where racialized differences between white and red were drawn firmly. Earlier authors had not always done so. Instead, early visitors, family, and community members were certain that Frances Slocum had "gone Indian." As scholar Robyn Wiegman reminds us, the relationship between race and gender "is not a 'natural' reading of bodies in their obvious and unchanging visual differences."[6] After the shock of Slocum's initial "discovery" had dissipated, authors trained their observations to highlight signs of domesticity, thereby linking examples of domestic behavior to whiteness.

Historians have spent the past several decades uncovering the cross-cultural world of the Great Lakes region, finding documentary evidence left by white Euro-Americans proving the existence of vibrant and persistent indigenous communities.[7] In fact, historian Susan Sleeper-Smith has examined Deaf Man's Village and argued that the indigenous and mixed-ancestry community "attested to permanence and persistence." She contends that Indian villages in central Indiana "began consciously to construct themselves as white in an attempt to remain on their lands." Moreover, Sleeper-Smith believes, "This was the strategy that a politically savvy Deaf Man's Village pursued when Mo-con-no-qua, the widow of Deaf Man, publicly revealed that she was a white captive."[8] This chapter does not attempt to engage the argument of whether or not Frances Slocum purposefully used her identity as a white captive to skirt removal. Instead, it attempts to explain how white writers in the years following her "discovery" manipulated the story of her life to aid in the cultural conquest of the lower Great Lakes by finding evidence of her whiteness in perceived signs of white domesticity.[9]

Since Young Bear and the inhabitants of Deaf Man's Village seldom speak in the historical record, our best glimpse into this complex world comes from outside visitors, like George Winter. The journal of his visit to the village (mostly unpublished during the nineteenth century) documented a culturally diverse world in northern Indiana. This was remarkably different than the report of Slocum's "discovery," which appeared in the same newspapers that printed stories about the Lake Monster.

In the world documented by Winter, interracial relationships were not just a reality; they were necessary for the survival of the multicultural community that surrounded Logansport. Although Winter initially believed that Frances Slocum had been converted irreparably into a Native woman, he simultaneously recorded evidence (conceivably unaware of its significance) that pointed to a web of interracial relationships that characterized the cross-cultural world of northern Indiana. Winter experienced a world of cultural and economic exchange, where a multitude of indigenous, European, and American hands colored the landscape. Places like Deaf Man's Village looked more like a cultural mosaic than a sharply drawn frontier boundary where uncivilized and civilized people clashed. Historian R. David Edmunds believes that Winter's observations have since provided evidence for "significant changes" made by the Potawatomi and Miami nations during the seventeenth and eighteenth centuries and demonstrate just how "remarkably adaptive" indigenous societies were at combining "traditional tribal values with many new ideas offered to them by Europeans."[10]

Winter encountered people of mixed ancestry throughout his trip. His canal boat pilot, Captain Bygosh, came from the "French voyageur class" and, outside of guiding canal boats, participated in "Indian trade, Indian councils, and Indian payments." Although Bygosh served as a Potawatomi and Miami interpreter, Winter tells us, his English was "very limited," and he could only speak, not write or read, his native French language. Winter hopped off the canal boat and proceeded on foot past Osage Village, where log cabins stood beside wigwams.[11] As he approached Deaf Man's Village, Winter met a familiar face: Captain Jean Baptiste Brouillette.

Brouillette symbolized the cross-cultural world of the lower Great Lakes—produced by centuries of cultural exchange and interracial sexual unions. Born of a French father and indigenous mother, Brouillette acted as a cultural mediator for the Miamis and Potawatomis of Indiana.

He was also Young Bear's son-in-law and lived with the extended family at Deaf Man's Village; he was the only adult male figure living in the two-room cabin. Winter had first met him in Logansport two years earlier at an annuity payment distribution. At that time Captain Brouillette allowed Winter to paint his portrait. But, at this moment, Brouillette was on his way to visit the local magistrate to report the theft of a hog—he held the hog's head in his lap as evidence against the white man he suspected had butchered the animal.[12]

Deaf Man's Village bore the characteristics of the cross-cultural world of the lower Great Lakes, as it displayed the riches accumulated by Young Bear's husband through resourceful dealings with French, British, and American traders and embodied the influence of a multitude of indigenous and Euro-American actors. Both the demographic composition and physical space of Deaf Man's Village testified to the presence of various racial and ethnic influences. Although Winter believed the place resembled one of the "forest mansions" that pioneer farmers built after their "interests expand[ed]" and families became "enlarged," he still identified it as "The Wigwam."[13]

George Winter, *The Deaf Man's Village.* Courtesy of Tippecanoe County Historical Association, Lafayette, Ind. (Catalogue # OV3-53)

Winter recorded all of this in his personal journal, but didn't make the connections between Slocum's actions and the world she lived in. In fact, nearly every visitor who came to see Young Bear recorded their impressions of the woman but failed to connect the relative opulence of Deaf Man's Village to the cross-cultural world through which they traveled to reach her. Unfortunately, the bulk of Winter's extensive notes on the region's indigenous population—precisely those portions that evidenced the complex, cross-cultural world of north-central Indiana—did not make it into print during his lifetime. Biographers in the nineteenth century, telling Young Bear's tale as the captivity of Frances Slocum, overlooked the multiple intermarriages and the multiethnic composition of the village. Instead, they commonly labeled signs of cross-cultural interactions as solely indigenous.

One September morning in 1837, Joseph Slocum began the final leg of his journey from Peru, Indiana. He and his brother Isaac, an interpreter, and a curious local guest mounted their horses and set off for Deaf Man's Village. When they arrived, Young Bear "received them with great reserve, coolness, and indifference," while Joseph, overwhelmed with emotion, collapsed to the floor and wept. Joseph supposedly recognized Young Bear instantly as his sister: a disfigured finger resulting from a childhood accident confirmed her identity. Still, he found it difficult to ignore the dramatic transformation. Most middle-class white Americans believed that women were unable to control their emotions, but Young Bear seemed to exhibit no outward signs of passion.[14] Her initial lack of reaction predictably caused confusion among her white visitors: here was Joseph and Isaac's sister, apparently devoid of the very Anglo traits that defined white womanhood.

Local community members and outside visitors who first commented on the saga of Frances Slocum began reporting her story as that of a white woman "gone Indian." Early visitors spoke and wrote openly about the transformation from an innocent white girl to an elderly indigenous woman, who showed "all the coolness and reticence of her adopted race."[15] Transplanted English artist George Winter first captured her image on canvas. Shortly after arriving in Logansport, Isaac and Joseph Slocum commissioned him to paint her portrait. When he first visited Slocum, Winter remarked, "Though bearing some resemblance to her [white] family, her cheek bones seemed to have the Indian characteristics—face broad, nose bulby, mouth indicating some degree of severity, her eyes pleasant and kind." Moreover, he attributed her clothing choices to indigenous designs—red calico shirt, black petticoat, long red leggings "winged" with long green lace, and earlobes adorned with large silver "bobs"—despite evidence that these fashions were products of a widespread trading network that blended Euro-American and indigenous styles.[16]

Even Young Bear's white family initially agreed that their sister no longer looked or acted like a white woman. Young Bear outright rejected notions that she knew about her white past. Hoping to confirm that the elderly Miami woman was his sister, Joseph asked if she remembered her name. She said no. Young Bear only agreed that people may have once called her Frances after Joseph prodded a little deeper. The men, disappointed and perhaps dejected, left her in the cabin and surveyed Deaf Man's Village later that afternoon on their own. When they returned, Joseph found his sister seated on the floor "at work at a deerskin." He was aghast. Frances appeared uninterested in her visitors, instead focusing on the work at hand. In fact, she only acknowledged their presence when prompted by the interpreter.[17]

Joseph invited Young Bear to Peru so that she could meet her sister, but she initially refused to go. She obliged, but only after consulting with Francis Godfroy, elder chief of the Miamis. Young Bear's visit to Peru provided the family and the community further evidence of her indigenous conversion. Local newspaper writers (apparently expecting Slocum to have weathered five decades of "living among the Indians" without exhibiting any mark of cultural change) shockingly reported that she arrived in Peru "on horseback dressed in full Indian costume riding Indian file with her [Indian] relations thro' town."[18] Young Bear stopped at the inn, where Joseph and Mary stayed, and presented them with the hindquarters of a newly slain deer. The gift, a traditional ceremony of reciprocity, was met with open jaws followed by uncomfortable silence. Young Bear refused to speak to her family members until Mary accepted the gift by embracing it in her arms.[19]

Joseph asked Young Bear if she had "ever tired of living with the Indians." "No," she responded quickly, "I have always had enough to live on, and have lived well. The Indians always used me kindly." Perhaps not happy with her answer, Joseph prodded his sister about her desire to be saved from her captors. "I never thought anything about my white relatives," she told him, "unless it was a little while after I was taken."[20] He pleaded for her to return to Pennsylvania, but Young Bear rejected his repeated requests. "I cannot," she forcefully told him. "The Great Spirit has permitted me to live so long because I always lived with the Indians. . . . My husband and my boys are buried here, and I cannot leave them. On his dying day my husband charged me not to leave the Indians!"[21]

Frances Slocum's brothers came to Deaf Man's Village not only to identify their aged sister but to "rescue" her from captivity. Joseph wrote to a friend in Pennsylvania, "[We] have tried every means in our power to induce her to return with us, to see at least the spot from which she was taken, but such are her manners, her habits and customs, that I fear everything will prove ineffectual. She is perfectly conscious of her condition and feels the peculiarity of her history."[22] Perhaps the brothers expected a reaction from their sister based on the voluminous captivity literature of the previous century. These narratives, scholar Susan Scheckel argues, provided "an instance of 'virtue in distress' that is significant to readers in its capacity to reveal the innate virtue of the sufferer and to stir sympathy."[23] The stories may have guided the Slocum brothers to the inevitable conclusion that they had to rescue their sister from the clutches of her captors. Yet these narratives could not have prepared them for what they found in Indiana. It appeared to her white family that Deaf Man's influence kept Young Bear tied to her indigenous community, as she refused to be saved. But she certainly did not view her lifetime experiences in terms of a captivity narrative; she told her siblings about her adoption into her Native communities and insisted that she belonged with them. In fact, Young Bear suggested to one visitor that her ancestors included the Potawatomis.[24]

Young Bear's insistence on a Native identity undermined the assumption of concrete racial categories; she demonstrated few cultural signs of whiteness despite her white ancestry.[25] Her story threatened to expose racial categories too fluid and unstable to justify conquest and, perhaps more important to the region, Indian removal. The physical and literary effort to remove Indians "into a romanticized, mythic 'elsewhere'; far to the west in the place of the setting sun," begun in the decades preceding Indian removal rested on a schizophrenic belief in the efficacy of civilization campaigns and a growing confidence in the biological inferiority of indigenous peoples.[26] The seemingly complete physical transformation of the young Frances Slocum to the elderly Young Bear threatened to expose the flaw in this logic and endanger the entire colonial project. Rebecca Blevins Faery argues that "the prospect of white women's intimacy with Indians, the underlying danger in the scene of captivity, continued to pose a threat to white identity and the success of the white project to control America."[27] Frances Slocum refused to be rescued and, more disturbingly, professed her devotion to her dead Indian husband. Consequently, the reactions of early visitors, family members, and the local white community had been marked by both anxiety and confusion.

After their initial encounter and the failed attempt to coax her back to Pennsylvania, the Slocums tried to save their sister from moving farther west via removal. They did so by stressing Young Bear's whiteness, but even these attempts resulted in mixed messages about the certainty of racial categories. Miami leaders and American agents had signed many agreements over the previous decade outlining land cessions and providing reservation lands for individual families. For example, an 1838 treaty exempted elderly Chief Jean Baptiste Richardville and his family from removal, and an 1840 treaty permitted the family of recently deceased Miami trader Francis Godfroy to remain in Indiana on a 640-acre reserve. Congressional members from Pennsylvania and Indiana (at the urging of the Slocum family) embraced the story of a young, innocent Pennsylvanian girl violently stripped from her peaceful home and miraculously discovered in faraway Indiana. "Frances Slocum was taken from her white friends when a child," Pennsylvania congressman Benjamin Bidlack told his fellow house members. "She is now desirous of dying among her red friends, where she has lived for half a century, without being compelled to remove west of the Mississippi. Let her first and last request be granted."[28] The resulting measure represented the early confusion held by Americans about Slocum's identity. In 1845, lawmakers passed a resolution allowing Slocum and her extended family reprieve from the removal treaties, but they treated the inhabitants of Deaf Man's

Village as an indigenous community rather than as a white settlement: granting them reserved lands and annuity payments.[29]

Slocum biographer John Meginness, writing in the late nineteenth century, made a strong case that the congressional mandate was unnecessary. He argued that Frances Slocum never actually "owned" Deaf Man's Village. Instead, Meginness posited that the 1838 treaty that granted Chief Richardville his reserve also assigned Deaf Man's Village to O-zaw-shing-qua, Young Bear's widowed daughter. This may explain why O-zaw-shing-qua was easily able to bequeath the lands to her descendants in later years.[30] Perhaps government officials feared that attributing the lands and annuities to Frances Slocum would concede her conversion as an indigenous woman, so they placed the reservation in her mixed-ancestry daughter's name.

Early firsthand observations, which were marked with an anxiety about how to deal with visible evidence of the fluidity of racial categories, informed the accounts of Frances Slocum's captivity that made their way out of Indiana. Much like the Logansport community, outsiders remarked on the shocking "discovery" of a white woman who had been transformed into an Indian. In 1842, Reverend John Todd first directed a national audience to the saga of Frances Slocum through his book *The Lost Sister of the Wyoming* (referring to the area in Pennsylvania where she first lived). He startlingly proclaimed, "What a change, from the fair-haired, pale-faced little girl, to the old, jealous, ignorant, suspicious savage!"[31] Todd compiled his account from a combination of interviews with the Slocum family, family letters, family journals, and newspaper accounts (including those written by George Winter). Consequently, Todd's account reflected the same notion held by early witnesses that Slocum had been transformed into an indigenous woman. Like earlier eyewitnesses, Todd suggested that exposure to Native life had "colored" Frances Slocum. "She was rich," he wrote, "and much respected and beloved; but she was a poor, darkened savage!"[32]

Todd's contemporaries agreed. In 1845, Charles Miner, yet another Slocum biographer, believed that "time and education had made her of another race."[33] Five years later, Benson J. Lossing told readers of the national publication *A Pictorial History of the Revolution* that Slocum's face

exhibited "nothing but Indian lineaments."[34] Most notably in this period, a famed nineteenth-century poet and opponent of Indian removal,
Lydia Sigourney, penned her own account of Frances Slocum's story.[35]
By the 1840s, Sigourney had become nationally known for poems that,
according to scholar Paula Bennett, sentimentalized Indians as "noble
warriors, venerable patriarchs, grieving mothers, and chaste maidens."[36]
Her poems chastised government removal policies as overly ambitious
and inhumane. Scholar Nina Baym has argued that Sigourney drew
from the torrid history of European-Indian relations in New England,
which included the Pequot Wars, to conclude that "the Anglo-American
national character was defined by how whites acquired the land they
needed and [by] what happened to the Indians afterward."[37] Baym believed that Sigourney intended her poetry, which sympathized with the
plight of Native people, to motivate Americans to treat Indians better
in the West. Published in 1849, her poem "The Lost Lily" followed this
theme by chronicling Slocum's life from her capture in the Wyoming
Valley of northern Pennsylvania to her family's visit to Indiana.

Although Sigourney never named Slocum as the poem's subject, she
began the piece with an account of a young woman's capture from the
same Wyoming Valley where Slocum was taken. "Fain would I tell a tale
of Wyoming in days long past." The poem traces Slocum's journey into
the wilderness and recounts the death of her mother at the hands of her
captors:

> The frail mother, tax'd
> With the loved burden of her youngest born,
> Moved slowest, and they cleft her fiercely down.[38]

Sigourney continues with a story more fiction than reality. In this account, Slocum's father receives news on his deathbed that his daughter
may have survived in the West. As he passes, he asks his other children
to visit her.

> Mourning the lost. At length, a rumour came
> Of a white woman found in Indian tents,
> Far, far away. A father's dying words
> Came o'er the husbandman, and up he rose,
> And took his sad-eyed sister by the hand,

> Blessing his household, as he bade farewell,
> For their uncertain pilgrimage.[39]

The remaining ninety-six lines of the poem chronicle her brother's visit to Deaf Man's Village, although Sigourney never uses the names of the Slocum family nor the location names in Indiana. Like most accounts of the 1840s, Sigourney's fictionalized record of the first encounter between the Slocum siblings highlights the shock of finding a woman "gone Indian." But unlike previous accounts, Sigourney suggests that hints of Slocum's whiteness transcended her near-five decades of living among Indians.

> At length they reach'd a lodge
> Deep in the wilderness, beside whose door
> A wrinkled woman with the Saxon brow
> Sate [*sic*] coarsely mantled in her blanket-robe,
> The Indian pipe between her shrivell'd lips.
> Yet in her blue eye dwelt a gleam of thought,
> A hidden memory, whose electric force
> Thrill'd to the fount of being and reveal'd
> The kindred drops that had so long wrought out
> A separate channel.[40]

Despite the Sigourney's initial account that the Slocums from Pennsylvania recognized an inherited whiteness in their long-lost sister, the author also suggested that Frances Slocum, now known as Maconaquah, challenged those assumptions.

> A trembling nerve
> Thrill'd all unwonted at her bosom's core,
> And her lip blanch'd. But two daughters gazed
> Reproachfully upon her, to their cheek
> Rushing the proud Miami chieftain's blood,
> In haughty silence. So, she wept no tears;
> The moveless spirit of the race she loved
> Had come upon her, and her features show'd
> Slight touch of sympathy.[41]

In the poem, Sigourney allows Frances Slocum to speak.

> Slowly she spake:
> I do remember, dimly, as a dream,

> A brook, a garden, and two children fair,
> A loving mother with a bird-like voice,
> Teaching us goodness; then a trace of blood,
> A groan of death, a lonely captive's pain;
> But all are past away.
> Here is my home.[42]

Frances Slocum rejected her brother's pleas to return to Pennsylvania. By doing so, Maconaquah rebuffed her whiteness. To emphasize these points, all of which were meant to challenge popularly held notions about Indian removal, Sigourney has Maconaquah directly criticize the actions of whites in the 1830s and 1840s.

> Upon my head
> Rest sixty winters. Scarcely seven were past
> Among the pale-faced people. Hate they not
> The red man in their heart? Smooth Christian words
> They speak, but from their touch we fade away
> As from the poisonous snake.
> Have I not said
> Here is my home? and yonder is the bed
> Of the Miami chief? Two sons who bore
> His brow, rest on his pillow.
> Shall I turn
> My back upon the dead, and bear the curse
> Of the great Spirit?[43]

Sigourney's poem mirrored ideas about Frances Slocum's dramatic psychological and physical transformation that were first captured in her biography written by John Todd. "How striking the difference between the heart that has been educated and trained up under heathenism," Todd wrote, "and the same heart trained under the light of the Gospel. It is not the tawny skin of the lost sister to which I refer, it is not to her living in the log cabin and sleeping on the ground, it is not to her catching her pony and riding him *á la Turk* when she wishes to go abroad, but it is to the whole character. The soul seems to be sunk and almost destroyed. The sweet sympathies of the heart are not there, and no chords in the bosom respond to the touch of affection and love. The intellect sleeps, and is powerless."[44]

Subsequent stories about Frances Slocum marked an increasing focus

on her whiteness, while downplaying or outright ignoring her immediate indigenous family. Few, if any, of these stories included new information, because Todd stole most of the primary evidence required to
compile such stories. Shortly after their visit to Deaf Man's Village, Todd
had approached the Slocum family for source material and interviews,
which they graciously granted him. Sadly, he never returned the written
records to the family, and all subsequent accounts, which cite such material, derive from *The Lost Sister of the Wyoming*.[45] Instead, subsequent biographers simply retold the story of her captivity, focusing more and more
on portraying Frances Slocum as a white woman or fictionalizing their
stories to challenge the very process of removal that threatened to force
her west. Most biographies acknowledged her daughters and son-in-law,
but none recorded the true measure of the extended family that lived
at Deaf Man's Village, consisting of at least twenty-five individuals (both
indigenous and mixed-race) ranging in age from six to seventy-eight.[46]
As they expanded the definition of whiteness to include Frances Slocum
and shield her mixed-ancestry family from removal, white Americans
also tightened the boundaries of whiteness to exclude the remaining
Miamis who were pushed westward. The whitening of Frances Slocum
made it easier for other nineteenth-century westerners to emphasize the
biological superiority of whites and justify Indian removal.[47]

Frances Slocum's biographers since the mid-nineteenth century have
suppressed the realities of Deaf Man's Village by categorizing her life as
a captivity story. Yet, on the surface, the story does not follow the typical
captivity narrative. The initial story written about her captivity by Rev.
John Todd in 1842 appeared long after the popularity of the genre began to decline.[48] Moreover, early-nineteenth-century captivity literature
had moved from stories of Indian atrocities to a sentimentalism of its
subjects by either valorizing masculine white heroes or sympathizing
with white heroines who were "usually passive, waiting to be rescued by
male heroes."[49] Frances Slocum neither wanted to be rescued nor waited
passively for her male heroes to arrive. Furthermore, scholars have long
surmised that most captivity narratives share three narrated moments:
the capture of the subject, the captive's life among Indian captors, and
the successful or failed attempt to rescue and reincorporate the captive
into white society.[50] But Frances Slocum's story differs dramatically, for

we are told how she was captured, how she was found, and how she rejected attempts at rescue, but we rarely get a glimpse into her life spent
living among the Miamis. Even Sigourney's poem, which includes a statement made by the main character about her husband and sons, skips
from her capture to her "discovery." None of the poem chronicles any of
her fifty-plus years living with the Miamis.

A *Narrative of the Life of Mrs. Mary Jemison* (1824), like the story of Slocum, refuted the parable of the redeemed captive by recounting Jemison's marriage to Indian captors (more than once) and her refusal to
leave her Native community to return to her white family. But a sizable
portion of this book was devoted to narrating Jemison's life among an
indigenous community.[51] June Namias argues that Jemison's story poses
an opportunity to examine "a new cross-cultural American family on the
frontier" and suggests that the story provides "possibilities for cooperation rather than conquest."[52] But nineteenth-century white Americans
certainly did not see it that way at the time. Susan Scheckel believes
that the Jemison narrative "actually undermine[d] the nationalistic
project by revealing . . . the boundaries of identity to be permeable and
the ascendancy of Euro-American culture to be questionable."[53] Thus
nineteenth-century Americans worked to convert the story into something that could be used for nation-building by offering a parable about
the dangers of frontier life. James Seaver, editor of the Jemison narrative,
made certain to highlight moments where Jemison struggled to maintain
her whiteness, giving examples of her either trying to keep her English
tongue or secretly practicing Christianity. Scholar Ezra Tawil concluded
that the Jemison narrative performed in a way that other captivity narratives could not, as "it defined the captive's race as something that could
not be lost or taken away."[54]

Frances Slocum's story mirrored the Jemison narrative, as it involved
a woman who lived most of her life among Indians, married Indians,
birthed and reared children in an Indian community, and refused to
return to her white family. But it also differed in important ways that
threatened to expose contradictions in the justifications for Indian removal. Unlike the popular stories published about Mary Rowlandson,
Mary Barber, or Mary Jemison, Slocum narratives usually revealed little
about her life among Indians. Perhaps this was because she told very little

of her story directly to whites. John Todd included a pithy 14 pages (out of 160) chronicling what he called "Her Own Story" in *The Lost Sister of Wyoming*. The bulk of his volume discussed the Slocum family, the settlement of the Wyoming Valley by whites, her discovery, the Slocum family's trek to visit their sister, their initial meeting, and life after her discovery.[55] In fact, most nineteenth-century narratives about Slocum centered on her initial capture, "discovery," and post-"discovery" life.

Todd's *Lost Sister* supposedly contained a transcript of Young Bear's only recorded interview with her white family. In fact, an examination of later biographies reveals the use of Todd's account, as the language of subsequent biographies matches his original. Moreover, few other authors republished it in its entirety, instead excerpting passages from Todd's transcript. Still, Todd warned his readers that Young Bear became "especially cautious" when she witnessed her family "produce writing materials in order to note it down." In fact, he stated that the account published in his book was "the substance of her account of herself." It is not clear whether his emphasis on calling it the "substance" of the account meant it was a verbatim transcript, a paraphrased account, or a later recollection of the interview.[56]

Nonetheless, if we accept the short interview with Young Bear as reliable, then it becomes clear that Young Bear tried to recast her life in terms of cultural exchange rather than contestation or survival, much as Sigourney suggested in her fictionalized poem, whose language does not indicate that it was based on Todd's published interview. Despite white reports that she didn't know she had been an Indian captive, Young Bear told her white family that she "well remember[ed]" the day she was taken from her family but only briefly mentioned the details of her capture—a moment exhaustingly narrated by her biographers. Remarkably, Young Bear did not recount that her first days of captivity were marked by trauma. Instead, she told visitors, "The Indians were very kind to me; when they had anything to eat, I always had the best, and when I was tired, they carried me in their arms."[57] These sympathetic views toward Indians were not uncommon in captivities of the nineteenth century, but the way that authors buried Young Bear's few words within the text made them almost invisible.

Ultimately, the very elements normally chronicled by most captivity narratives—life among the Indians—in this case threatened to expose contradictions in the language of conquest by pointing out the instability of racial categories in the case of Frances Slocum. This explained why Sigourney's account differed from others by placing words in Maconaquah's mouth and having her directly criticize American policies. Perhaps, had Slocum returned to her white family, authors could have spoken more openly about her marriages to Indian men and her rearing of mixed-ancestry children. But Young Bear's refusal to be saved was linked inextricably to each of these, because she vowed to stay near her deceased husband. Instead, subsequent stories about Frances Slocum refocused the story to highlight elements of her whiteness. Thus these stories could both refute suggestions that whites were not biologically superior to Indians (why did Slocum not want to return to her white family?) and explain why Slocum and her large extended family were exempted from removing west (were her children considered white or Indian?).

Few accounts of her life appeared between 1860 and 1880, but narratives that focused most directly on Frances Slocum's whiteness emerged in the late nineteenth and early twentieth centuries, as Americans turned to their pioneer pasts and reimagined the relationship between race and gender on the frontier.[60] In the 1880s, John Meginness interviewed members of Frances Slocum's white and Indian families. The author proclaimed that his research uncovered "the many contradictory details" of her life. Yet he concluded that his struggle to reveal the real history of the "white woman" underscored that "nothing in the annals of history [had been] more pathetic and impressive than the story of the captivity, life, wanderings, and death of Frances Slocum." Rather than being a true narrative of her life, Meginness's book contained mostly a collection of interviews and documents with occasional narrative interjection.[61] Nonetheless, he presented some of the first evidence used by late-nineteenth- and early-twentieth-century Americans to point at Slocum's inherent whiteness.

In September 1839, Joseph Slocum brought his two daughters to Deaf Man's Village to meet their aunt. The women, Hannah (37) and Harriet (17), recorded their visit in private journals. Some of Slocum's biographers read Hannah's account, including Charles Miner and John

Meginness, who included a copy of Hannah's diary in his 1890 *Biography of Frances Slocum: The Lost Sister of the Wyoming*. But the nieces' reflections on their aunt did not become central to any story about Frances Slocum until the twentieth century. In 1916, Frances Slocum's white grandniece Martha Bennett Phelps decided to publish her own biography of Frances Slocum that included her mother's (Hannah's) diary, so that her "children and grandchildren may hear the story." The women's impression of Young Bear differed from that of her male visitors, who came to "save" her. White men, such as George Winter and John Todd, had obsessed over the physical transformation of Frances Slocum into Young Bear, highlighting an age-old fetishism with indigenous women that centered on commentary about the female physique, skin color, and bodily ornamentation. But Hannah and Harriet eagerly recognized signs of whiteness rather than indigeneity in Deaf Man's Village.[58] These connections centered on signs of domesticity and mid-nineteenth-century white, middle-class notions of femininity. They also provided evidence that Frances Slocum had not been transformed into an elderly indigenous woman.[59]

Phelps compiled and penned *Frances Slocum: The Lost Sister of the Wyoming* with the help of her own daughters. The narrative, highly influenced by Hannah and Harriet's journals, reveals important insights into how later Americans reinvented Deaf Man's Village and Slocum. Scholars of global colonialism have reminded us that patriarchal males did not generate gender inequalities on their own; women likewise participated in forging gendered attitudes and expectations. Margaret Strobel, studying constructions of gender throughout the nineteenth- and twentieth-century British Empire, has concluded, "At the same time, women continuously experienced, sometimes challenged, and sometimes reproduced the economic, political, and ideological subordination of women." Her work on mission women revealed that female missionaries often taught and introduced the same concepts of "Victorian notions of domesticity and female dependence" to colonial subjects that disempowered women within British society. It is not surprising, then, that the two middle-class women, rather than the white men, emphasized signs of Anglo domesticity and femininity among the women of Deaf Man's Village in the years following the "discovery" of Frances Slocum.[62]

As she made a mental checklist of the cabin's contents and later re-corded them in her journal, Hannah Bennett drew deep connections between gender and race: she noted that blankets stored beside the beds in the sleeping area were "folded together," and one space in the sec-ond room "contained cooking utensils," and another area had "the table and dishes." Despite standing inside a two-room cabin, Hannah saw a bedroom, kitchen, and dining room. In essence, she projected a middle-class Anglo-American floor plan over the open spaces of the cabin, thereby converting the "invisible" and unfamiliar spaces into recogniz-able places.[63] The two Slocum women, almost certainly reared in homes that stressed the "pastoralization of housework," read signs of indige-nousness as signs of whiteness.[64] For them the focus on the cleanliness produced by household chores helped reinforce a binary opposition that pitted white female domesticity against Indian drudgery. Frances Slocum's cabin did not feel foreign (or, in other words, indigenous) to her white nieces, because they reimagined it as a familiar white middle-class home.[65]

Hannah also scrutinized the actions of female members in the cabin for signs of familiar gendered behavior. Dinnertime, a common point of reference among all visitors to Deaf Man's Village, offered a key moment for observation. "They spread a cloth on their table," Hannah wrote, "and gave us a very comfortable meal." She assigned special significance to these habits commenting on how they mirrored familiar practices back home, but her sister, Harriet, more directly connected these actions to white female domesticity. She elaborated on their dinner experience: "They spread the table with a cotton cloth, and wiped the dishes, as they took them from the cupboard, with a clean cloth. . . . After dinner they washed the dishes [and] replaced them on the shelves, and then swept the floor." Harriet remarked that they "were surprised at these evidences of civilization."[66]

As she watched her aunt and cousins dip homemade wicks in and out of a wax bath, Harriet believed she witnessed signs of Young Bear's white-ness. Moreover, when the Slocum women began to knit in front of the fireplace, they observed their aunt's peculiar reaction. "Aunt Frances be-came very much interested," Harriet remarked, and "went through the motions of showing her daughters how to spin and reel yarn." It did not appear that either Young Bear or her daughters had ever spooled yarn or knitted—fundamental components of an Anglo-American domestic economy. But the nieces believed that somehow Frances remembered the domestic skills taught to her by her white mother. They celebrated the incident as evidence that their aunt had maintained the basic elements that made her white.[67] Yet Hannah and Harriet failed to realize that by the late 1830s candle making and knitting had become the practices of everyday life on the Indiana frontier for Indians and whites. Indians, British soldiers and settlers, French traders, and Americans had traded goods and cultural practices for many decades. Young Bear could have learned these skills from any number of places and people. Still, for white American audiences, all signs pointed to Slocum's whiteness.

For the Slocum women, Young Bear's efforts to teach her daughters acceptable domestic tasks—cleaning dishes, folding laundry, dipping candles, and spooling yarn—proved that the traits of a white mother and woman existed in the body of Young Bear. One scholar has argued that, for white middle-class Americans, the "glorification of wife- and motherhood was at the heart of one of the most compelling and widely shared belief systems of the early nineteenth century."[68] For the nieces, the interconnectedness of domesticity and race helped them recast Young Bear as white. Ironically, the very focal point of this whiteness, motherhood, should also have reminded them that Frances Slocum had birthed several mixed-ancestry children, leading to the conclusion that their aunt must have been involved in an intimate relationship with at least one indigenous man. This line of inquiry might have led to the conclusion that the vibrant cross-cultural world around them had been the result of years of cultural accommodation, adaptation, and persistence among the region's indigenous peoples. But it did not. Instead, Young Bear's husband, Deaf Man, was never mentioned in the nieces' narratives.

On May 16, 1900, Frances Slocum's descendants (both white and Indian) raised a monument at her gravesite (one that still stands). The giant bronze marker, meant to look like stone, included four panels that separated Frances Slocum's life as a captive from Young Bear's life as an Indian woman. The east panel reads, "Frances Slocum, a child of English descent, was born in Warwick, R.I., March 4th, 1773, was carried into captivity from her father's house at Wilkes-Barre, Pa. Nov. 2nd,

1778, by Delaware Indians, soon after the Wyoming Massacre. Her brothers gave persistent search, but did not find her until September 21st,
1837." The other panels recount the Slocum family's visit to their aunt,
yet acknowledge, through a biblical reference, that "Frances Slocum became a stranger to her mother tongue. She became a stranger to her
brethren, and an alien to her mother's children, through her captivity."[69]
The southern panel recognizes Young Bear as Maconaquah and indicates the existence of her extended Indian family, including her second
husband—suspiciously absent is any reference to her first husband or
two sons who are buried nearby.

    The 1900 ceremony itself and how writers later recounted the events
symbolized the rhetorical separation of the two women. The attendees
included descendants from both Frances Slocum and Young Bear's families. Slocum family members made the long journey from Pennsylvania,
while the children and grandchildren of Young Bear's oldest daughter,
Ozahshinquah, made the short jaunt from Peru, Indiana. Again, this
scene of Miami descendants inhabiting the area around the original site
of Deaf Man's Village could have been used as evidence of the persistence
of Native people in Indiana, but it did not. It could also have been used
to illustrate the complexities of the region's history: one that did not

Postcard, Frances Slocum's Memorial. Author's personal collection.

fit the model of colonialism to statehood, which erased Native peoples from the narrative. In fact, many of Young Bear's great-grandchildren who attended the ceremony bore Anglicized names, a consequence of the family's long history of intermarriages.[70]

In real life, Young Bear connected her identity to her indigenous family, as she made sure to tell her white family that little would change simply because easterners, who claimed to be her long-lost "real" family, arrived at her door. In fact, when interviewed by her brother, she stressed most deeply, both in words and actions, her affectionate ties to her Indian family. She told them, "I have always lived with the Indians. They have always used me very kindly. I am used to them. The Great Spirit has always allowed me to live with them, and I wish to live and die with them." Her final insistence that she would remain in Indiana because, as she told her brother, "my husband and my boys are buried here," highlights the importance she placed on her kinship ties to her Miami community.[71]

As time passed, white authors began to retool the story of Frances Slocum to refocus the narrative on signs of inherited whiteness. Unfortunately, the momentary glimpses into Young Bear's life as an indigenous wife and mother underlying Todd's account were suppressed further by later white authors who focused more and more on her white family and elements of domesticity that supposedly demonstrated Frances Slocum's whiteness. Using elements of the captivity genre and the evidence of Slocum's inherent whiteness, subsequent authors were able to whiten Young Bear in their texts and control her life's story, allowing little of what she wanted to say to enter the narrative.

Perhaps the most lasting consequence of recasting Young Bear's life as a captivity narrative has been the imaginative erasure of her late husband. For many Americans, especially middle-class Eastern audiences who experienced very little contact with indigenous peoples, popular captivity narratives provided them with their first exposure to the issue of interracial marriage.[72] Stories like those about Frances Slocum and Mary Jemison inspired renewed debate about the legality of race mixing: the reaction was rarely positive. Americans discussed more often than they had before the legality of interracial marriages, although the discourse mostly centered on the union between white women and black men.[73]

Recent historical studies convincingly demonstrate that governments have regulated the legal compact of marriage as a means to mediate appropriate sexual behavior and thus prevent interracial relationships. Historian Nancy Cott argues, "Radiating outward, the structure of marriage organizes community life and facilitates the government's grasp on the populace."[74]

Throughout the early nineteenth century, state governments passed antimiscegenation laws outlawing the marriage of whites and blacks, but laws banning the union between whites and Indians never fully developed.[75] Whites shared a long history of sexual relations with Indians— some of the most popular stories about American history centered on these types of relationships (John Smith's fictionalized romance with, and John Rolfe's actual marriage to, Pocahontas).[76] But cultural custom rather than statute largely dictated the appropriateness of interracial affairs between Indians and whites in the West. Indian women across the Great Lakes married white trappers, traders, and settlers to strengthen economic and political ties, while white men used these relationships to fulfill their sexual appetites or ease their need for companionship. But white men rarely thought of sex with indigenous women as only sex. Historian Theda Perdue reminds us that marriages between indigenous women and white men performed an additional practical role for the male; traders "needed wives in Indian country because a man without a wife did not eat except at great expense and with constant uncertainty. Native people divided labor according to gender, with women farming and men hunting, and awarded each the product of his or her labor."[77]

Interracial relationships between Indian women and white men proved fundamental both for white exploitation of the region and for the indigenous struggle for survival.[78] Yet the marriage between the white woman, Frances Slocum, and her Miami husband, Deaf Man, threatened to upset ideas about social order by placing power in the hands of Indian men. Scholars remind us that "white women were economic, social, and sexual possessions of white men; therefore, a nonwhite man who 'possessed' a white woman undermined the gendered and racialized dominance of white men."[79] By acknowledging the marriage between Frances Slocum and Deaf Man, white audiences would have been assigning an incredible amount of power to the late Miami chief. This is perhaps why the story of Deaf Man mostly has been lost in the written historical re-cord, as white authors from the 1830s through today have minimized his role in the story of Frances Slocum, the white captive. Historian Susan Sleeper-Smith contends, "In the intersection of race and nation we see the extent to which intermarriage was subsequently masked by 'pioneer' memories of a 'white' frontier, obscuring both the frequency and im-portance of intermarriage." She has demonstrated successfully how over time Euro-American colonizers defined mixed-ancestry children as In-dian and used ties to nationality to reimagine Indian women married to white men as white citizens.[80]

In the case of Frances Slocum, white authors simply tried to write her husbands out of her history altogether. Young Bear's first husband is virtually invisible in the historical record. In an interview with her family, Young Bear explained, "While I lived with them, I was married to a Dela-ware. He afterwards left me and went west of the Mississippi." Over the years biographers have included this passage, each time altering the de-tails and changing the language.[81] In the early twentieth century, Frances Slocum's white relatives published their own version: "While I lived with them I was married to a Delaware by the name of 'Little Turtle.' He went to the wars and did not come back."[82] Although they assigned the first husband a name, later authors clearly manipulated the text to focus on his absence rather than presence by suggesting a violent and tragic end to the marriage. These brief sentences provide the only written histori-cal evidence for Young Bear's first marriage. This silence speaks volumes about the ways that whites sought to suppress the story of intermarriage in the narrative of Frances Slocum.

Biographers did not include much more information about Young Bear's second husband, Deaf Man (Che-por-on-wah). Mostly, they fo-cused on his death, rather than his life—perhaps making it easier for them to imagine Slocum as a delicate white woman rather than an el-derly Indian widow.[83] In a few short passages, again attributed to Young Bear herself, biographers recognized her second husband. According to Young Bear, "I was afterwards married to a Miami, a chief, and a deaf man. His name was Che-por-on-wah. After being married to him, I had four boys and two girls. My boys both died while young."[84] These words resonate (nearly verbatim) throughout the written historical record. Not much else is written about her marriage to Deaf Man or his life. The two boys disappear almost entirely from the record; we do not know how they died or how old they were when they died. Outside of these few sentences authors mention Che-por-on-wah only after talking about the site of Deaf Man's Village—thereby embedding Young Bear's late husband into the landscape and imaginatively erasing nearly thirty years of marriage.[85]

Had they prodded more deeply into Young Bear's life, rather than her captivity or the death of her husband, white visitors might have heard stories that have since been preserved by her Indian descendants.[86] Chief Clarence Godfroy, her great-great-grandson, shared his family's oral traditions about Young Bear with an interested family friend, Martha Una McClurg, in the 1960s. Young Bear, he told her, "was regarded among the Miami Indians as a good sportswoman. She enjoyed fun and frolic and attended all such gatherings if she was able. . . . A race track was located back of her home. . . . Frances could ride and guide any of the Indian ponies without a bridle or a saddle by placing a blanket on the back of the pony. She was especially fond of riding a bucking pony." In fact, Godfroy told McClurg that Young Bear helped break "outlaw ponies . . . right along with the men of the Indian tribe." The historical record makes clear that two versions of Frances Slocum's life have been preserved. The first, recorded by whites, depicts a solemn and grim old woman, while the second, told by her Native descendants, portrays a vibrant, cheerful individual revered by the Miami community. Godfroy recounted that, when Deaf Man died, the Miami community members went to Young Bear for counsel because she was someone "who they admired and respected just as they had her husband."[87] Why did whites not record these lively stories about Frances Slocum and Deaf Man in the nineteenth century? Perhaps stories of the gender-bending, bucking-bronco-riding Young Bear and her wealthy Miami husband were told but suppressed, as they threatened to disappoint gendered and racialized expectations of white visitors. We will never know. The focus of nineteenth-century authors on Frances Slocum, the captive, certainly has distorted our view of Deaf Man and Deaf Man's Village, and accounts stretching into the early twentieth century have continually recast Young Bear as the white woman Frances Slocum.[88]

George Winter, *Frances with Daughters.* Watercolor. Courtesy of Tippecanoe
County Historical Association, Lafayette, Ind. (Catalogue # OV3-51)

The process of whitening Young Bear continued from the nineteenth
into the twentieth century, even influencing physical depictions of the
"lost sister." Publishers included their own versions of George Winter's
paintings in the frontispieces of their books. As time passed, Frances
Slocum's complexion literally whitened in the images; her rough facial
features, once described by Winter "to have the Indian characteristics,"
were altered—crow's feet softened and wrinkles smoothed.[89] The picture
of Frances Slocum that accompanied Phelps's biography clearly resembled George Winter's painting (the setting, clothing, and posture are
nearly identical), but the woman's face in the later work barely resembles
the elderly indigenous woman captured by Winter in the 1830s.

Frontispiece to Martha Bennett Phelps, *Frances Slocum: The Lost Sister of Wyoming* (Wilkes-Barre, Pa.: Privately printed, 1916).

The woman we know as Frances Slocum, a woman who existed mostly in the minds of white readers, continues to be a source of popular intrigue. Non-Indians continue to appropriate her image and the story of her captivity. The name Frances Slocum now graces a state park and lake in Pennsylvania, another in Indiana, schools in Indiana, and formerly a chain of banks across the Hoosier state: locations of her "capture" and "discovery."[90] Her story continues to be popularly viewed as a captivity narrative and employed in ways that focus on whiteness and ignore the Indian woman Moconaquah.

By teasing apart the story of Young Bear and Frances Slocum we reveal the interconnectedness of race, gender, and conquest in the history of America's western or frontier past. Early visitors and onlookers appeared confused about the instability of racial categories in her case. After all, she appeared to have physically transformed into an indigenous woman. But writers over the nineteenth century rectified this by moving the discussion from her differences to her connections to domesticity. Here, they connected domestic activities with whiteness, thereby linking race and gender. Once Frances Slocum's whiteness could be confirmed, she stood as an example of the biological determinism of race. Ironically, as her white family members and visitors (like George Winter) searched for evidence of whiteness, they also unintentionally recorded the brilliant multicultural world that surrounded them.

The refusal by Americans to acknowledge Slocum's two marriages to Indian men as sites of intimate, sexual unions helped conceal the multilingual, multicultural communities of the lower Great Lakes and supported the justifications for Indian removal that were based on the biological determinism of race. Ironically, the sources that chronicled racist assumptions held by nineteenth-century whites—from George Winter's paintings and journals to the captivity narratives themselves— simultaneously captured the very evidence that can be used to refocus the story. In recent years, historians Susan Sleeper-Smith, R. David Edmunds, and Stewart Rafert have contributed to our understanding of the persistence of Indiana's Miami people by reading between the lines and lifting the ethnographic gems embedded in the historical literature.[91] They have also stressed the need to question popular perceptions of Great Lakes Indians (both historical and modern). Biographer George

Peck, writing a decade after Maconaquah's death, reflected that the Slocum family had "found and left her an Indian."[92] Unknowingly, Peck recognized that the whitening of Young Bear happened more successfully in the minds of white audiences than in reality.

The case of Frances Slocum illustrates how nineteenth-century whites created their own historical accounts and place-stories to promote a vision of western expansion that ignored the complexities of the multicultural world that Americans first entered in the eighteenth century and which continue today. As Americans from Ohio to Illinois started preparing to commemorate the first hundred years of their respective states, they also started to consolidate the disparate local stories of their pasts into cohesive narratives that reinforced a linear narrative of progress from the colonial era through statehood. By the twentieth century, residents of the lower Great Lakes were crafting a larger regional place-story that underplayed conquest and presented white settlement and Indian dispossession as natural processes.

PART THREE

Remembering and Forgetting

The woodman's ax has done its work,
The forest has been removed;
Where savage Indians, so unbeloved,
Held their dances where we men walk.
Made ready for the husbandmen,
The fertile soil to cultivate
The choice products of the land,
To increase his good estate.
The bears and panthers, wolves and deer,
Unmolested used to roam
The wildwood which in days of yore,
They no more dare to come.
Wild turkey, deer, and raccoons, too,
Were plenty in those days;
They fed where they chose to go,
And frolicked in their plays.
But now the place so free to them,
No longer gives them room;
And all who 'scape the eyes of man,
Have found another home.

—*Early Life and Times of Boone County, Indiana* (1887)

CHAPTER 6

"With Strong Hands and Brave Hearts"

Remembering the Pioneer

The narrative of statehood development that has come to dominate the place-story of present-day Ohio, Indiana, and Illinois developed fully by the end of the nineteenth century. As with the case of the Frances Slocum story, Americans in the lower Great Lakes constructed new narratives to underplay the violence of conquest and assert the inevitability of American hegemony. This process took time, especially as the nation, including the lower Great Lakes, became entangled in the physical battles of the Civil War and political attempts at reconstruction. The Reconstruction Era witnessed its own imaginative rendering of the national narrative, centered on national reconciliation. As historian David Blight has shown, the postwar decade culminated with a new narrative of national reunion rather than one of a reconstructed South. Although this process did little to shape the history-telling of the lower Great Lakes, its emphasis on the role of veterans in saving the republic certainly played a part in how the pioneer period would be remembered.[1] As Civil War veterans made claims about saving the republic, individuals who had originally settled in the lower Great Lakes but had not fought in the war demanded that their own efforts in creating the nation not be forgotten. In 1876, as Reconstruction waned and the nation prepared to celebrate its centennial, a generation of old settlers and those who claimed to be pioneers emerged to claim their role in the founding of the American West.

The nation's centennial offered a unique opportunity for America's "island communities" to incorporate themselves within a larger national narrative.[2] Moreover, as a centennial movement, it required them to reflect upon the significance of their past by connecting the local to the national. On May 25, 1876, President Ulysses S. Grant, with the help of Congress, issued a joint proclamation, asking people in each state to "assemble in their several counties or towns on the approaching centennial anniversary," where they were to "have delivered on such day a historical sketch of such county or town from its formation." Moreover, Grant called for an additional copy of these local histories to "be filed in the office of the librarian of Congress to the intent that a complete record may thus be obtained of the progress of our institutions during the first century of their existence."[3] In the lower Great Lakes, the proclamation inspired local historians to chronicle a century of progress that centered on the American pioneer.

In Indianapolis, John Brown Dillon, later dubbed the "Father of Indiana History," addressed a Fourth of July crowd by reading Grant's proclamation and positing, "If the future historian shall be assisted in his work by a careful examination of these historical sketches, they ought to contain . . . some authentic and definite statements of facts." He noted that the "hardy adventurers who passed westwardly over the Allegheny Mountains . . . to lay the foundations of civilized settlements in a vast wilderness were strong-hearted and strong-handed men and women." Dillon labeled them "pioneer settlers of the 'West'" who "carried with them, severally, some contribution to the general store of pioneer knowledge."[4] Dillon, and others like him, focused on the character of the pioneer rather than the frontiersman as the symbol of American progress. More than simply document the history of the past, Americans in the lower Great Lakes memorialized, venerated, and celebrated it.

In preparation for the international Centennial Exposition in Philadelphia, the Buckeye State went to work planning its contribution. The Ohio Board of Centennial Managers argued that Ohio had been but "a forest when Independence was achieved," but it had since become the "Mother of the States of the Northwest."[5] Presumably, the hard work of pioneers had made that possible. The following year, the board proclaimed success. "The Centennial Exposition at Philadelphia," they reported, "was intended to accomplish a double purpose. It celebrated, in an appropriate and impressive manner, the hundredth anniversary of

American independence, and afforded a good opportunity for marking the progress made by the American people during their first century of national existence."[6]

Measuring progress required the states to acknowledge their indigenous past. Since Indians were used as a baseline against which progress could be gauged, Indians could easily be forgotten. In a speech given on behalf of Ohio at the exposition, Edward Mansfield proclaimed, "One hundred years ago, the whole territory from the Allegheny to the Rocky Mountains was a wilderness, inhabited only by wild beasts and Indians. The Jesuit and Moravian Missionaries were the only white men who had penetrated the wilderness or beheld its mighty lakes and rivers." Mansfield, like George Winter and others before him, cast Native people as part of the landscape from which Indians had simply disappeared.[7]

Following the nation's centennial, communities in the lower Great Lakes moved to continue the commemoration of the so-called pioneer generation. They gathered in local courthouses, libraries, and homes to organize associations for preserving the memories of settlement. In northwest Ohio, the Old Settlers' Association of Williams, Defiance, and Paulding counties invited Indiana judge Alfred P. Edgerton to speak at their annual meeting. On September 11, 1878, Edgerton welcomed a crowd of old men sporting "gray heads" (like Edgerton) and others too young to grow facial hair. They gathered to honor the area's pioneer generation—some of whom sat amongst them. Edgerton opened the meeting by toasting the spirit of settlers who had "chopped and logged, and cleared, and sown, and reaped their way in honest toil to better the land." "Out of these movers' wagons, and from these cabin homes," he proclaimed, "have come the good and true men and women who have made this wilderness to blossom like the rose." "And this was indeed a wilderness—grand, beautiful, and majestic in its beauty," he reminded them. "In the calm, echoing its bird songs and every footfall of the wanderer though it; waving gently and singing in the summer wind; moaning in the autumn storm, and howling in the winter blasts. Into the wilderness the movers came, and the land wears the smile of culture, civilization, and peace."[8]

Edgerton highlighted the efforts of early settlers who earned the title of pioneer by working together to physically transform the landscape. He claimed, "It is only the earth—the land—that man can change by his labor." Edgerton hoped that the younger generation would recognize "he who had the courage to encounter a wilderness, and the hopes to evolve from it [and] by his own labor build a home of comfort." But he also yearned that they would remember that the pioneer would not "stain his manhood by turning a weary traveler from his door, or by withholding sympathy and aid in sickness," and he challenged them to build upon the work of the pioneers to "make their country grow better and richer."[9]

In an interesting twist, Edgerton expanded the common understanding of what physical progress meant. As Solon Robinson had done with his own image in becoming the "squatter king," Edgerton hoped that those gathered to celebrate pioneers would also recognize the role of entrepreneurs like himself in extending American civilization westward. He argued that Henry Hicks, the namesake of Hicksville, Ohio, should be venerated as a great American pioneer. For many at the meeting, they would not have recognized Hicks as a pioneer. It is not even clear whether or not Hicks had ever stepped foot in the Buckeye State. Instead, he had built a shipping and mercantile empire in western New York by profiting from the influx of goods traveling up and down the Erie Canal. From his home in Buffalo, Hicks imagined the lower Great Lakes as many men had before—a fertile countryside ready for exploitation. In the early decades of the nineteenth century, he formed the Hicks Land Company and sent Edgerton west as his proxy and land agent.[10] Still, Edgerton posited that Hicks's influence in promoting settlement should qualify him as a member of the pioneering generation.

Edgerton also believed Isaac Smith should be considered a pioneer. Smith had been Hicks's business partner and the proprietor of Smith and Macy—Steamboat Owners and Commission Merchants of Buffalo. Like Hicks, he ran his western empire from the far-off shore of Lake Erie, probably never visiting his investments in the West. Of others listed by Edgerton as speculator/pioneers, at least John Bryan had been to Ohio. Bryan served initially as a western agent for the Hicks Land Company (alongside Edgerton) but left to accept a position as Ohio state auditor before switching jobs once again to work as an agent for the American Land Company. His new employer rewarded Bryan by naming one of their boomtowns after him—Bryan, Ohio.[11] Hicks, Smith, Bryan, and Edgerton hardly resembled the cash-poor squatters or actual settlers venerated by earlier Americans as pioneers, but the language of settlement had always been malleable.

Edgerton echoed the long-standing connection that Americans had drawn between pioneering and progress. After all, hadn't the entrepreneurs and speculators laid the groundwork for the corporations and businesses of the Gilded Age? Edgerton simply reframed the concept of progress to include a generation of speculative financiers. How could the older generations impede the new symbol of American progress and civilization? Would they become impediments like the Indians? Edgerton challenged the younger members of the audience to "see that nothing stagnates around them." He warned old settlers, "If they do not improve upon our work and make their country grow better and richer when we are gone, they are unworthy of our paternal care and labor, and should not be inheritors of what they will not improve, and cannot, therefore, save."[12]

"Old Settler Societies," "Old Settler Unions," or "Pioneer Associations" emerged across the lower Great Lakes after the Civil War. Between the war and the nation's centennial, these organizations defined pioneering in more stringent terms than later orators and organization leaders. For example, the Allen County Old Settler Association required members to prove that they had actually settled within one hundred miles of Fort Wayne, Indiana, prior to 1840. As a symbol of his or her rootedness in the soil, each member was issued a cane made from lumber preserved from the original stockade at Fort Wayne.[13] Other groups marked those who settled in the area prior to 1812, others 1826, and at least one association identified old settlers as late as 1846.[14] Edgerton, Hicks, and Bryan most certainly would not have been considered Old Settlers or Pioneers by these standards.

Additionally, the earliest Old Settler Associations did not strictly separate the pioneering period from a time when Native Americans inhabited the region. They were less likely to ignore American and Indian conflict than later accounts, as some of them embraced bloody conquest. In a poem read before the 1869 celebration of the Licking County Pioneers of Ohio, an unidentified poet declared:

The Indian from his wigwam home, with sly and stealthy tread,
Made many a settler's hairs to stand erect upon his head;
The wild beasts of the forest—the wolf, the panther, and the bear,
Fell by the deadly rifle's aim, when held by the LICKING PIONEER!
His hunting shirt of buck-skin, his leggings made of leather,
His cap of coon or fox skin, the tail worn like a feather;
A pair of fancy moccasins he kept so nice for Sunday wear—
A lord in the wild, stately forest then, was the LICKING PIONEER![15]

In 1870, Reverend A. H. Bassett addressed the Mad River Valley Pioneer and Historical Association in central Ohio and argued that the
founders of the nation had "proceeded to found, and build and people
State after State in their Westward progress, not stopping for mountain
barriers or for savage opposition."[16] These early associations seemed to
hint at a messier history for the region, whereby cohabitation occurred.
Yet they also claimed that the success of pioneering existed as a result
of the disappearance of the region's indigenous inhabitants. In the immediate aftermath of the Civil War, perhaps a few old settlers sought
to assert their own military prowess through occasional tales of bloody
conquest. Regardless, stories that admitted to the violence of western
expansion were the exception, not the norm.

As time passed and the nation celebrated its centennial, more romanticized and less violent renderings of historical events entered the public
consciousness. In New Castle, Indiana, the Old Settler Society of Henry
County met at the county fairgrounds to celebrate their past. The gathering included a few who had settled in the region prior to 1825. In a
speech, one old settler proclaimed, "In the early settlement of all new
counties the people are dependent upon each other for favors, and are
more sociable and more inclined to help one another than they are in
older communities." Gone were discussions of violence and conquest.
Instead, the speaker concluded, "To clear the land and prepare it for
cultivation was the first duty of the pioneer, and this required the help
of all."[17] This sense of antimodernism and communal development pervaded the post-centennial years, as Americans questioned the industrial
growth of America rather than the consequences of its colonial past.[18]
How much of the romanticized renderings of the pioneer past are to
be taken seriously is debatable. At meetings such as the 1876 gathering

of the Old Settlers' Union of Clinton County, Indiana, nearly fifty men, including some who had settled the region prior to 1826, "were called upon and gave a short history or anecdote of early times."[19] These impromptu yarns became part of the documented history of the region.

Pioneer and Old Settler Associations encouraged pioneer veneration and stressed the transformation of the physical landscape at the hands of industrious men. Judge R. C. Parsons told a gathering of Pioneer Association members in North Solon, Ohio, that pioneers had included all those who acted as an "agent of change" in the development of the West. He also said that "the very word 'pioneer' awakens a sensation in our bosoms like gazing upon the ruins of a by-gone age." This rhetoric echoed a language of conquest, which posited that pioneers had extended civilization into the recesses of the American West. Parsons proclaimed: "What a great debt do we owe those noble men and women who, through good report and evil report, through perils often by day and by night, amid hunger and loneliness, with painstaking self-sacrifice and noble ambitions, laid low the primeval forests, scattered wild beasts and the still wilder savage; plowed and sowed, and turned the wilderness into a garden; laid broad and deep the foundations on which our free institutions are built, education and religion, leaving to their descendents the land we now enjoy."[20]

A year later, W. W. Andrews addressed the same organization and reminded them that pioneers "were actuated by higher motives" than greed or personal ambition. Instead, they toiled for the nation. Pioneers, he recalled, "reared in Eastern civilization left homes of comfort, and often luxury, and pursued their weary journey until, in the untrodden forest, they settled down and began their great work." They worked to establish the nation, Andrews argued, and to "develop it all and push civilization into its remote places, to create future States and make the Nation prosperous and strong."[21]

Leaders in Indiana tried to forge a statewide association. In 1878, organizers (including John Brown Dillon) succeeded in hosting the state's first convention of the Pioneer Association during the Indiana State Fair. They issued a circular to "Old Settlers" from across the state to join them in Indianapolis. They hoped the gathering would "be the inception of regular annual meetings of the surviving pioneers of Indiana, where they

'who tramped down the nettles' and laid the foundation for this great
and growing state, will meet." They further hoped the assembly of old
settlers and young fairgoers would "renew in spirit and feeling the scenes
of early days, and inspire others who are following in their footsteps with
gratitude to those who 'blazed the way' and 'cleared the opening' for the
blessings we now enjoy." They called upon all "pioneers seventy years of
age, who have been residents of the state forty years" to join them at the
fairgrounds; they even agreed to provide free transportation and waive
the admittance fee.[22] More than seven hundred individuals, averaging
74 years in age, applied for membership, including a 102-year-old man
from Auburn.[23]

Mostly the Pioneer Association of Indiana became a venue for Hoosiers to record the memories of a passing generation that Dillon hoped
historians might use to draft the place-story of the region. During their
first meeting, hundreds of "venerable men and women" gathered at the
state fairgrounds to commemorate early settlement. On the morning of
October 2, 1878, Judge Charles H. Test welcomed them and invoked
the past to sketch a picture of the future. "Religious, moral, and educational institutions of the state" must keep pace "with its material develop-
ments," he warned, and he called upon Hoosiers to pen the "unwritten
history" of the pioneers so that future generations could read about their
"hardships and adventures" and learn from their trials. Test regretted
that the *History of Indiana*, written by John Brown Dillon (in attendance),
presented only the history of the region up to about 1816—a moment
marking the end of the War of 1812 and the transition to statehood. He
hoped that someone would expand that history to include the pioneers
who came later and helped transform the landscape.[24]

Test continued by presenting his own history of the pioneer period
and describing the hardships faced by pioneers—rustic cabins, primitive
conditions, no schools, no roads or bridges, no churches. Still, he argued, they "worked hard and lived hard" and erected the institutions of
civilization in the wilderness. Prior to the War of 1812, Test posited, "The
settler had lived in daily dread, not knowing at what moment his cabin
might be infested by savages and himself and family fall victims to their
cruel and relentless warfare." In his description of the postwar period,
Indians did not exist; they had merely disappeared. Instead, he fully in-

corporated the pioneer saga into his account by chronicling the history of land laws, which were trumpeted by squatter-settlers who challenged the government to grant them access to public lands. "With all these trials and discouragements, I have seen Indiana rise from a population scarcely equal to that of a present-day county town to 2,000,000 people." Test defined "trials and discouragements" differently in the years before and after the War of 1812. Before the war, Indians posed the greatest threat. Later, land speculators and land policy impeded progress, despite the fact that Indians remained in Indiana for decades. Test's version of Indiana history reached every member of the audience, as he had 5,000 copies of his speech printed and distributed to the crowd.[25]

In the afternoon, Hoosier historian John Brown Dillon spoke. He predicted that one hundred years into the future (1978), the citizens of Indiana would likewise "study with a great degree of interest" the history of the pioneers. He told them that English dictionaries defined the word "pioneer" as "one who goes before to remove obstructions or prepare the way for another." Dillon argued that the old settlers in the audience were pioneers because they had faced "dangers, toils and trials" in their attempt to extend civilization westward. Like trees or mountains, he viewed Indians as obstacles who needed be cleared before a pioneer era could begin. Yet Dillon spoke only of Indians when he discussed the eighteenth century. In fact, his speech focused on an era that predated the lives of even those old settlers in attendance. While he lamented that the "old log cabins, which were the dear homes of early settlers," had been "falling into ruins," Dillon really used the distant past to speak about the "spirit of modern progress" initiated by the pioneers, which might continue "its long course" into the future.[26]

Both Dillon and Test focused on pioneering as an action rather than identifying individuals whom they considered pioneers because they sought to use their own efforts as a measuring rod for future progress. They had "done their work," Test said of the pioneers in general, and "cleared away the forests, built their homes, planted their orchards, raised their children, performed every duty towards their country, and passed away forever. . . . They sought to subdue a great wilderness, and found an empire in the west." He proclaimed, "The works in which the old settlers of Indiana, as a class, have made themselves famous are not finished, and these works of human progress and improvement must be carried on through future times by the wisdom, strength, and patriotism of the people of the state." Strangely, Test's pioneers eventually vanished like the Indians—one actor departing before another could arrive. The age of modern machinery and technological progress required them to do so. For Test, both the "vanished Indian" and the "stalwart pioneer" were romanticized characters of the past.[27]

The Pioneer Association of Indiana planned to meet again the following year and vowed to preserve the memories of the pioneer generation, but tragedy struck before that could happen. On January 27, 1879, John Brown Dillon died in Indianapolis. For more than four decades, Dillon had been instrumental in preserving Indiana's history. He also helped keep alive the Indiana Historical Society. It had formed during the removal era when, in 1830, more than half the members of the state general assembly met to create the organization for the "necessity of collecting and preserving the materials for a comprehensive and accurate history" of the state.[28] It floundered in its early years, but leaders collected ephemera from the early period of settlement that was later used in writing histories of Indiana. Dillon (who joined in 1835) began writing his *History of Indiana* as early as 1838. He also served as editor to the *Logansport Telegraph* in the 1830s, when George Winter penned articles about the Lake Monster and Indian removal. Undoubtedly, his past must have forged some of the ideas he held about the history of the state. After leaving Logansport, he worked as the state librarian from 1845 until 1851. Although Dillon personally remained active in collecting documentary evidence, the Indiana Historical Society went dormant until the end of the nineteenth century. The Pioneer Association of Indiana, soon to be renamed the Indiana Pioneer Society, was Dillon's attempt to accomplish the goals of the Indiana Historical Society through a new organization.[29]

In October 1879, the Pioneer Association of Indiana officially adopted the name Indiana Pioneer Society.[30] Again, it organized transportation to the state fairgrounds for old settlers, but it required that county organizations verify individual applicants. The society believed it was "absolutely necessary" that those counties without either county pioneer associations or old settlers' societies form one immediately. They hoped that the hierarchical system of state, county, and local historical societies and associations would provide an outlet for collecting, crafting, and disseminating coordinated histories of the state.[31] They also hoped it would ensure an infrastructure for keeping the statewide organization alive. However, the second meeting of the Indiana Pioneer Society proved to be its last. After paying for the transportation and housing costs of their invited guests, organizers became dismayed as pioneers dodged events organized by the society and spent most of their time enjoying the entertainments of the fair. Some "old settlers" flocked to livestock shows, but most huddled around the exhibits displaying the latest industrial agricultural machinery. In a twist of cruel fate, the old pioneers—vanguards for their generation—were more interested in elements of modern progress than in reflecting on stories of yesteryear.[32]

Local communities in other lower Great Lakes states also began preparing to celebrate and document their pasts. In Ohio, where American settlers first moved after the Revolution, organizers sought to capitalize on the impending hundredth anniversary of the initial settlements made after passage of the Old Northwest Ordinance (1787). As early as 1875, Ohio had created a state archaeological association. But despite gaining a "very commendable number of members" at the time of the centennial exposition in Philadelphia, the organization effectively disbanded following the death of its organizer, John T. Short.[33] On March 12, 1885, prominent Ohio citizens met at the state capitol to establish the Ohio State Archaeological and Historical Society. With Albert Adams Graham as its first director, the Ohio Historical Society issued a circular to old settler or pioneer associations asking them to provide both information about organizations in their area and donations relevant to Ohio's history.[34]

Although the first mission of the Ohio Historical Society was to "prepare for and properly celebrate important historical events, beginning with the Centennial of the First Settlement in Ohio," Graham also believed that the public should donate items to the society that kept "alive the memory of those persons and events that have contributed, or that will contribute, to mold the history and destiny" of Ohio. According to Graham, the purpose of the society was twofold: to document the past and to celebrate it. In so doing, he gave prospective members a general chronology within which Ohio history, and its historical objects, could be categorized. As he asked for donations, he divided them into four distinct periods: (1) "Drawings and descriptions of the mounds and earthworks"; (2) "Facts, illustrating the Indian tribes who once made the forests of Ohio their home"; (3) "Manuscript statements, narratives and biographies of pioneers and old settlers"; and (4) Items "relating to the West in general." Although he included objects associated with the "conflicts between their own tribes and also between themselves and the white races" within the second category, Graham viewed this as a distinctly different period than the one involving pioneers.[35] This suggested a clean break between Ohio's colonial and pioneer pasts.

In December 1885, Graham made this division clearer. In a letter sent to schoolchildren to pique their interest in the upcoming centennial observances, he explained that the French and British occupation, along with the history of Native Americans, should be relegated exclusively to the earlier colonial time period. While Indians and early explorers fought for control of the Ohio country, pioneers settled the country "as citizens of Ohio" and "changed its wilderness character to that of civilization." Indians, French traders, and British settlers did not inhabit the region long enough, he argued, to be considered true occupants. Instead, that task "remained for the sturdy American to found a settlement and a nation." Nonetheless, Graham believed that evidence about Indian occupation existed "in works of adventure, in legends, and in the narratives of explorers and pioneers." He suggested that children study the entire history of the Buckeye State and read books covering all periods. To aid them in that endeavor, Graham included a list of suggested titles, carefully dividing them into three self-prescribed periods of history: French, British, and American.[36]

In the 1885 circular, Graham detailed the history of the failed State Archeological Association, the beginnings of the new Ohio Historical Society, and the problems facing it. Graham called upon leaders to preserve Ohio's history before other states could rob her of her artifacts and fill their own "cabinets and valuable collections" with Ohio's riches. He hoped that their donated historical ephemera would be maintained by the society and eventually displayed to the public.[37] Graham received a deluge of disappointing responses. A few individuals pledged to donate their personal collections of "Indian relics and stone implements," but more offered to sell the society their collections. The leaders of local historical societies outlined their efforts to collect local artifacts, compile historical documents, and record settler reminiscences. But while they offered Graham emotional support and granted him access to their collections, they apologized for not being able to contribute more. Some respondents congratulated Graham for his determination and encouraged him to trudge forward, but shamefully admitted that they could not help at all.[38] Despite the pitfalls of organizing a statewide historical society, Graham received some interesting personal offers. The *Magazine of Western History* responded to his circular by offering him the opportunity to publish a history of Ohio he succeeded in collecting enough material to write it. Like John Brown Dillon, Graham ignored the failure of the state historical society and went on to pen his own history of the state where he lived.[39]

The failure of statewide history organizations in the 1870s and 1880s actually may have been the result of an incredibly popular local movement to commemorate the pioneer era, especially in rural communities. In villages and counties throughout the lower Great Lakes, citizens bridged history and historicism as they celebrated their pasts.[40] In 1883, Judge George Loring spoke before a Marietta, Ohio, crowd as they marked the ninety-fifth anniversary of the town's settlement by the Ohio Company. Loring proclaimed the town a shining example of "great social and civil achievements"; a model for all the "admirers of progress" to gaze upon. "They were obliged, it is true," he said, "to endure the hardships of an existence in the wilderness. . . . But they brought with them all those rights and privileges, all those principles which had made their old homes so dear to them." Loring used the story of the Ohio Company to celebrate a history of the region that exalted progress as much as it documented the actual history of Marietta. Despite settling the town long before the removal era, Loring rarely mentioned the indigenous inhabitants of Ohio. Instead, he focused on Marietta as Ohio's version of the city upon a hill. "Admirers of progress" from around the world, he argued, could view "the great social and civil achievements" that marked a "century of settlement in the state."[41] Loring employed agricultural analogies to explain the early settlement of Marietta. In describing Ohio

Company agent Manassah Cutler's role in encouraging others to move west, Loring said, Cutler had "sent forward the seed, whose imperial harvest now lies before us."[42] This rhetoric of planting served speakers and authors who sought to speak about how pioneers altered the landscape without talking about the violence of conquest itself. Loring was not unique in applying broad, and romanticized, strokes in his attempt to paint the region's portrait.

The souvenir program for the April 7, 1888, public celebration listed forty-eight men who first arrived at the site where Marietta stood. In a skewed depiction of this early event, the authors of the program concluded that "the Indians bade the Pioneers a hearty welcome, but afterwards proved very treacherous and unreliable, characteristics they ever possessed." "These traits did not surprise General [Rufus] Putnam. He had noted treaties made and treaties broken, and also had observed that the Indians were not pleased to see the land cleared and houses built." The authors included the passage as an example of what steadfast pioneers faced in moving west. "The completion of a century, and the outgrowth of that period since the first settlement of the State, together with the marking of these by the hundredth yearly mile-stone, are events well worthy of the notice of every citizen of the State," they believed, but "other reasons" existed "of State and National importance" to warrant a celebration. Indians had not been the only impediment to progress. The authors explained that the Revolution had halted settlement initially, and when the federal government failed to reward veterans for their service in the war, the land around Marietta had become a direct extension of revolutionary ideals. In other words, they believed that Marietta stood as a direct legacy of the American Revolution itself.[43]

Speaker George Hoar posited that the foundational document of the Northwest Territories, the Northwest Ordinance, had helped ensure the success of the western states and should be held with the same regard as the Magna Carta, Declaration of Independence, and the Mayflower Compact. The "spirit" of the document, he claimed, had protected "absolute civil and religious liberty." Unlike other speakers and historians, he completely dismissed the role of Americans in physically conquering peoples who had lived in the region prior to their arrival. "The Indian and Frenchman dwelt here," he admitted, but they "could not hold their place."[44] They simply disappeared.

The seals of the Northwest Territory and the state of Indiana, which reflected the larger place-story by downplaying conquest and stressing the inevitability of American progress, reemerged in the late nineteenth century as citizens across the lower Great Lakes states celebrated their histories. The Seal of the Northwest Territory, first introduced in 1788, features boatmen ascending the Ohio River with the motto *meliorem lapsa locavit*—"He has planted one better than the one fallen"—set in the foreground of an idyllic scene that includes a felled tree.[45] Indiana historian William Hayden English traced the history of the seal and provided readers with a version of it in his 1895 *Conquest of the Country Northwest of the River Ohio*. On the meaning of the seal, he concluded:

> A study of this historic seal will show that it is far from being destitute of appropriate and expressive meaning. The coiled snake in the foreground and the boats in the middle distance; the rising sun; the forest tree felled by the ax and cut into logs, succeeded by, apparently, an apple tree laden with fruit; the latin inscription . . . all combine to forcibly express the idea that a wild and savage condition is to be superseded by a higher and better civilization. The wilderness and its dangerous denizens of reptiles, Indians and wild beasts, are to disappear before the ax and the rifle of the ever-advancing western pioneer, with his harvest, his boats, his commerce, and his restless and aggressive civilization.[46]

The Indiana state seal originated as a modified version of the territorial one. In 1816, the first General Assembly of the State of Indiana adopted Davis Floyd's proposal, which he described as "a forest and a woodman felling a tree, a buffalo leaving the forest and fleeing through the plain to a distant forest, and sun in the west with the word Indiana."[47] Still, the official state seal was not standardized. In the early twentieth century, Indiana historian Jacob Piatt Dunn researched its origins and concluded that the sun should be located as rising in the east to signify the birth of the nation's sixteenth state. Hoosiers have long debated the origins of the seal and its meaning. In Dunn's 1919 book, *Indiana and Indianans*, he argued, "This seal has been the subject of much jest, and of many surmises as to its significance. . . . The woodman represented civilization subduing the wilderness; and the buffalo, . . . going west, . . . represented the primitive life retiring in that direction before the advance of civilization."⁴⁸ Both the territorial seal and the Indiana state versions represented permanent markers meant to commemorate the pioneer period. Lower Great Lakes citizens attempted to erect their own tributes to earlier generations.

Merging history and celebration, Albert Graham's Ohio Archeological and Historical Society resolved to erect "a suitable monumental structure" at Marietta to "commemorate the services of the patriotic men who obtained a valid title to the Northwestern Territory." The society had begged the state legislature over the course of two years to finance a monument that would "inspire a patriotic devotion to institutions and inheritances established for their benefit." Continuing with rhetoric that invoked the agricultural origins of the state, the society argued that the founders "*intended*" to establish civilized institutions in Ohio and "ventured into the wilderness to plant principles as well as cereals." According to the Historical Society, the overcoming of hardships defined the pioneers. "They came in the face of dangers. . . . They built and held their forts against the combined force of twenty-one tribes of savages, supported and encouraged by the emissaries of Great Britain."⁴⁹ In June 1888, the organization met at Marietta's City Hall in conjunction with the city's centennial. The society's president, F. C. Sessions, addressed the organization. "One hundred years ago the advance guard of our present civilization were slowly floating down the river the Indians call 'the beautiful.'" He wondered if the "Pilgrims of the Northwest" could have realized "what one century of time would do" in the territory. He exalted the pioneers who entered a land inhabited by "wild beasts and wilder men." Former president Rutherford B. Hayes, who also spoke at the meeting, believed that the 1876 centennial celebration in Philadelphia had excited the nation and inspired events like the centennial celebration in Marietta. Hayes excitedly hoped more festivities would follow.⁵⁰

In July 1888, Thomas Ewing, former Ohio congressman, addressed the Women's Centennial Association in Marietta. He believed that the first settlers to Ohio brought with them the living memory of the Revolution and the "great charter of freedom." Also adopting romanticized

The frontispiece of William Hayden English's *Conquest of the Country* features both the Northwest Territorial seal and the Indiana State version. The artwork accompanying the state seals echoes the themes of anti-conquest from John Gast's painting, whereby Indians and animals simply flee from the advancement of white progress. English, *Conquest of the Country Northwest of the River Ohio, 1778–1783* (Indianapolis: Bowen-Merrill, 1896), vol. 1.

agricultural analogies, Ewing proclaimed the states of the lower Great Lakes as "the first states planted in the soil of American liberty," which had "ripened in its sun."[51] Often preachy, historical orators in the late nineteenth century melded religious undertones with national or local messages of progress, as many of them had learned their craft from ministers. Historian David Glassberg has argued that the "speakers' religious and patriotic rhetoric reinforced the authority of their historical narrative and offered a common language to address their diverse audiences as a united community of believers." In other words, one had to speak passionately and patriotically in order to be taken seriously.[52] Consequently, individuals who spoke at pioneer associations both recalled the history of the location and worked that history into a greater message exalting the transformative powers of pioneer hands.

When they spoke at meetings and annual gatherings, many old settlers left messages for the younger generation about the future: get moving but be cautious. Some speakers warned that the inroads of material progress might need to be checked by religion and morality. Living in a time marked by political corruption and industrial greed, Judge Samuel Hunt, a speaker at the Marietta centennial, asked his audience to look into the future "with a sublime hope that God will save the nation, save it from men who are dishonest, save it from the designs of men who would destroy it," and ensure that "religion and piety and truth and justice" will be "maintained among us for all generations." He believed the answer lay with the yeoman pioneer of the past.[53]

We might dismiss these highly sentimentalized speeches as products of the celebrations that initiated them, but the ideas and information from orators slipped into the public record and became the basis for many of the self-labeled scholarly or authentic accounts that followed. In fact, modern historians can read the texts to these addresses because they were published for distribution, often by local and state historical societies. When he undertook the task of penning a history of the early settlement of Indiana, William Hayden English, a former congressman and member of the 1850–51 state constitutional convention, discovered that the state library's collection was in horrible condition. According to Lana Ruegamer, who wrote a history of the Indiana Historical Society, "There was no complete set of Indiana state and territorial laws, no card catalogue, and no order to federal publications. A large number of the books [in the State Library], which supposedly numbered 23,000 volumes, were falling apart. . . . The large pamphlet collection was unusable . . . [and] no state archives existed except the files of the secretary of state, which were inaccessible and incomplete."[54] Starting in 1886, novice historians Daniel Wait Howe, Jacob Piatt Dunn, and English helped reconstitute the Indiana Historical Society, focusing on the dissemination of historical material to the masses. All three men were heavily involved in state politics and sought, as many progressives had done, to use history to inform their political decision-making.

More important, at least for the argument of this book, the three men also helped start the Indiana Historical Society Publications. These included tributes to notable Hoosier men, accounts made by old settlers, and speeches given at historical commemorations. In the second volume, they printed General John Coburn's address to the society on the "Life and Services of John B. Dillon."[55] Other material included Robert B. Duncan's "Old Settlers," a reprinting of an 1879 newspaper article about Duncan's disdain for land speculators. Echoing language used in early-nineteenth-century squatter petitions, Duncan wrote, "In most instances the occupant [squatter] got the land occupied; but occasionally an ungodly sinner, with more money than the settler, who did not expect to become a citizen and occupant of the land, but purchased purely for speculation, would out-bid the occupant." He concluded that the threat of ambitious speculators had forged a harmonious community of actual settlers on the frontier void of "tramps, 'vags,' or persons of ill repute." Furthermore, mutual dependence had caused "differences of education and station to disappear, and almost absolute social equality prevailed."[56] In 1905, the society began publishing the *Indiana Quarterly Magazine of History* under the auspices of editor George Cottman.

The success of the Indiana Historical Society marked a renewed interest in history in the late nineteenth century. The possibility of profiting from the appeal of local history did not escape the attention of book publishers. Agents from publishing houses went door-to-door, interviewing residents in order to publish individual county histories. As they gleaned information, agents also spun yarns about the wonderful volumes that would be produced as a result of these interviews. Despite presenting themselves as novice historians working to produce scholarly works, the agents were really salesmen trained to coax unsuspecting individuals into ordering and (when possible) prepaying for a copy of the final product. Known as subscription-based book sales, this method of selling county histories dominated the market in the lower Great Lakes.[57]

From the 1880s until the turn of the century, publishing houses in the lower Great Lakes produced an incredible number of county histories. Bibliographer P. William Filby estimates that close to two thousand county histories have been published since the Philadelphia centennial celebration, many of them in the 1880s and 1890s. This does not include many of the county biographies and atlases, which were similar to the broader county histories and which also saturated the late-nineteenth-century book market. An earlier scholar estimated that more than three thousand volumes, including biographies and atlases, have been published since 1876. For their part, publishers in Ohio, Indiana, and Illinois produced nearly three hundred county histories before 1900.[58] A boom in volume required a new process for authoring and printing the unfathomable number of books expected to be published. The same elements of standardization and administrative streamlining that typified the corporate world of the period influenced the way that the county histories were penned. The books, regardless of publishing house, followed popular formats. Most started with a standardized history of the state or region where the county was located, followed by a chronological telling of the county's organization, and concluded with a series of biographical sketches (an early Facebook) of prominent community leaders. Almost all of the publishing houses relied heavily on the same sources used by local historians. In this way, they echoed the same passionate pleas of contemporary orators. Yet publishing houses sought to present themselves as valid interpreters of the past.

County historians stressed the similarity between their methodologies and those of academic historians. In the late nineteenth century, history departments emerged on campuses across the country. Professors tried to separate themselves from amateur editors, compilers, and writers by stressing authenticity and the unsentimental nature of their work. Historians trained in the German academic tradition revamped the craft of historical writing, stressing methodology and objectivity. They strived to extract history, as a profession, from the clutches of amateurs whom they viewed as old school romantics.[59] Academics stressed a break from romantic accounts of the past, as they considered county histories the work of armchair historians who sought to evoke passion and local patriotism. County historians were able to present themselves as producing a combination of romanticism and proper historical methodologies, which might explain their popularity.

The authors of county histories overtly highlighted their methodologies in the introductions or prefaces to their books. They admitted that "the discrepancies and the fallible and incomplete nature of public documents" made their work difficult, but they insisted that their work represented an "accurate and complete record" of the lower Great Lakes. Authors and editors increasingly pointed to their sources, which they believed made their work reliable. Moreover, they called upon citizens from across the region to contribute "recollections, carefully preserved letters, scraps of manuscript, printed fragments, memoranda," and other documents to base further volumes. Editors promised to dispel any "question of authenticity" by consulting "the best authorities" and brushing "away false traditions" in order to "reveal facts."[60] Authors proudly boasted that "public records and semi-official documents have been searched, the newspaper files of the counties have been overhauled, and former citizens, now living out of the counties, have been corresponded with" in order to produce accurate works. In other words, they claimed to have done the job of a historian. Individual authors attached themselves to the new scientific methodology by insisting they had spent years securing and preserving valuable data, combing "official treaties, records, and documents . . . often at vast expense of money and toil." Some works touted that they had gathered sources from "more than 2,000 Pioneers or their descendants." One author admitted that "a large part of the material" for his history "had to be gathered from the early pioneers or their descendants," but since they "were dependent upon their memories for dates and events," the writer had to "adopt that statement which seemed to him most probable and trustworthy." "No trouble nor expense" had been spared, one publishing house promised, to make its books "complete and reliable." Others promised to produce a "plain, unvarnished tale" of American history.[61] County historians not only convinced their contemporary audiences; academic historians have often used county histories as authoritative accounts and cited them as reputable sources.

Still, county histories were more often than not romanticized accounts. The author of Defiance County, Ohio's history (home of Bryan, Edgerton, and Hicksville) graciously thanked the county's early speculators, including Alfred Edgerton, for providing information about the settlement of the county. Instead of distancing themselves from highly suspect sources, county histories embraced them. Consequently, many authors appeared to reassert the conclusions of earlier romantic or "literary" historians who tailored narratives to highlight American progress. One author proudly boasted that men with "strong hands and brave hearts" who "came to battle with the hardships incident to a frontier life" and "helped clear away the logs and brush" had also penned sections in their county's history. A few publishers even allowed older settlers to craft entire sections of their county's history.[62]

By the mid-1880s, a handful of publishers based in major midwestern cities dominated the subscription-based county history market and helped standardize their product. A few individuals who specialized in subscription sales shuffled between publishing houses or started their own companies. Early in his career, Benjamin Franklin Lewis gathered recollections and acquired subscriptions from small communities for the Appleton Company out of Chicago, while his brother Samuel worked across town for Charles C. Chapman and Company, one of the more prolific county history publishers in the Midwest. In 1880, the Lewis brothers quit their jobs and founded Inter-State Publishing, which focused almost exclusively on county histories; they published the histories of at least fourteen Indiana counties. Elsewhere, the namesakes of Williams Brothers Publishing entered the county history market after working for J. P. Lippincott in Philadelphia. They moved to Cleveland in 1880 and began targeting Ohio counties. By the end of the decade, Williams Brothers had produced the written accounts of more than a dozen Ohio counties.[63]

As competition drove publishers to produce cheaper and cheaper products, county histories became standardized. Borrowing from local historians, editors compiled county histories that often included township sections or biographical accounts that came directly from popular yet untrained state historians. Publishers, no doubt seeking to cut costs, used generalized state histories that could be inserted into each of the state's county histories. They could also be used to thread together the disjointed township and local stories into a greater narrative. County history publishers have left little, if any, evidence about where these standard histories came from, but they do not appear to have been penned in-house. One "History of Indiana" appeared in books published by at least three publishing houses.[64] For example, nearly every county history published by the Lewis Brothers' Inter-State Publishing included this standardized history, although later editions, published under the newly formed Lewis Publishing Company, included an abridged version.

Publishers of county histories in Ohio also included standardized state narratives, including one written by Albert Adams Graham. Graham's "History of Ohio" appeared in no less than seven county histories, including three self-published volumes. His first chapter wove together geology, topography, and Indian history. Graham's account of indigenous history was brief, and Indians mostly appeared as foils to American progress. "No sooner had the Americans obtained control of this country," he explained, "than they began, by treaty and purchase, to acquire the lands of the natives." Graham defended the government's inaction in safeguarding Indian country. "They could not stem the tide of emigration; people, then and now, would go west." Furthermore, he lamented the unfortunate but inevitable demise of the Indian. "Savage men, like savage beasts, are engaged in continual migrations. Now, none are left. The white man occupies the home of the red man. Now, the verdant hills / Are covered o'er with growing grain / And white men till the soil / Where once the red man used to reign."[65] Graham merely recollected that Indians had passed in the wake of progress, not that whites had either forcefully removed them or killed them. As secretary and president of the Ohio State Archaeological and Historical Society, Graham represented the interconnectedness of historical organizations and published county histories.

Early American settlers, like Solon Robinson or the Lake County Squatters, probably would have been surprised to see how entrenched the manufactured story of the pioneer generation had become. Certainly, late-nineteenth-century Americans had altered the story and the icon to fit the modern needs of an industrializing society, but the core of the image remained a useful symbol of the American progressive spirit. "Within one brief generation," extolled authors, "a wild waste of unbroken prairie has been transformed into a cultivated region of thrift and prosperity, by the untiring zeal and energy of enterprising people."[66] Even as late as 1906, one county historian opined, "Gradually the wilderness gave way to the pioneer. His sturdy arm and untiring frame never knew rest until the forest was made to blossom with fruit and grain."[67]

Despite their claims of objectivity, historians routinely supplemented historical methodology with unabashed romanticism. Pioneers, both in poetry and prose, became synonymous with progress; their deeds transcended the actions or abilities of real individuals. As one county historian professed, "Men of stout hearts, strong arms, and determined spirits have already been in the vanguard in the army of progress, the axes of the backwoodsmen have cleared the road; civilization follows them." Historians could not lift themselves above the romantic rhetoric of popular authors. "The seeds they scattered," another county historian quipped, "ripened into the fullness of a plentiful harvest, and schoolhouses, churches, cities, towns, canals, telegraphs, railroad and palatial-like residences occupy the old 'camping grounds.'" But where had the "camping grounds" gone?[68]

Late-nineteenth-century county histories defined pioneering as synonymous with general American progress. Consequently, authors continued to engage in a romanticized "usable past." Moreover, in an age of industrialism and incorporation, publishers provided the technology and markets to mass-produce a story of pioneering that ensured its place in the American consciousness. But the rise of the pioneer as the symbol of progress also meant the demise of its antithesis—American Indians. In the American mind, no space or moment existed where and when these two opposing forces comingled. One county historian grimly concluded, "The inevitable destiny of his race was being crowded westward and to eventual extermination."[69] There could be no middle ground.

CHAPTER 7

"A Melancholy but Necessary Duty"

Forgetting the American Indian

The veneration of America's pioneer generation required a creative re-drawing of early lower Great Lakes geography and memory, a recasting that emphasized the region as an American place of progress rather than a shared Native space. Authors hesitated in providing accounts in which Native Americans and pioneers cohabitated, and they rendered violence out of the place-story of the region. Instead, early histories projected a linear history beginning with the Indians, moving to a colonial period of conquest and confusion, and ending with a pioneer phase when steadfast Americans felled trees and tilled the soil. Somewhere between the second and third stages, Indians simply disappeared. By the end of the nineteenth century, Americans began pointing to the lower Great Lakes as an example of a larger national history of western settlement and American progress. In keeping with a narrative of anti-conquest, they began depicting Native Americans as either primitive peoples of the past or sad victims of the spirit of progress itself.

As local townspeople gathered in Marietta in 1888 to commemorate the early settlement of that place, Cincinnati prepared to welcome visitors from across the nation to attend the Centennial Exposition of the Ohio Valley and Central States, where they celebrated the "establishment of civil government in the Northwest Territory."[1] Citizens from the "Queen City of the West" were particularly adept at organizing large industrial fairs. Although Cincinnati's Alfred T. Goshorn had served as the deputy general for Philadelphia's Centennial Exposition in 1876, much of his experience came from reviving regional fairs in Cincinnati. In 1869, he had approached Cincinnati's Board of Trade and pleaded to restart the annual industrial fairs that had been hosted intermittently by the Ohio Mechanics Institute prior to the Civil War. The Board of Trade, in conjunction with the Cincinnati Chamber of Commerce and the Mechanics Institute, assembled a fifteen-person board of directors to plan the expositions. In total, they spent more than a million dollars on "the erection of permanent buildings in the center of the city" for the annual celebrations.[2]

The annual expositions received praise from around the nation. One reporter, in the *Manufacturer and Builder*, called the Cincinnati industrial fair of 1873 "the best exposition of the industrial arts ever held in this country."[3] Even after the grand spectacle of the Centennial Exposition in Philadelphia, visitors exalted the work of organizers in Cincinnati. Individuals wrote to the editors of the *Manufacturer and Builder* in 1879, reporting that that year's fair began with a "most auspicious" opening ceremony and was held in the most "tastefully arranged" buildings. Witnesses believed that the exposition "proved one of the most interesting and successful fairs that has taken place in that city, the results in every way having exceeded the most sanguine expectations." Furthermore, they believed that Cincinnati had "established for herself an enviable preeminence as a successful exhibition holder."[4] In 1888, they hoped that their experience, along with the erection of permanent buildings, would ensure a successful Centennial Exposition of the Ohio Valley and

Advertisement for the Centennial Exposition of the Ohio Valley and Central States. Author's personal collection.

Central States. "Time, the place, and the occasion should," one writer believed, make the "exposition a most interesting and memorable one—a fitting and dignified memorial to the great historical events" it was "intended to commemorate."[5]

The Cincinnati Board of Directors agreed and decided "that the exposition for the Northwest Territory centennial should exceed any of those previously held" with every attempt made to demonstrate the progress "of art, sciences and industry" in the region "during the first century of their organization by civilized man."[6] They pledged money for the construction of additional buildings that would hopefully act "as a nucleus" for the 1888 celebrations. The cities of Cincinnati, along with Covington and Newport, Kentucky, supported the exposition; and the Ohio legislature authorized the provision of money and the appointment of honorary commissioners. The legislatures of West Virginia, Pennsylvania, Kentucky, Tennessee, Indiana, Illinois, and Michigan additionally passed "resolutions of acceptance, and appointed honorary commissioners." For their part, citizens of Cincinnati raised $1,050,000 for the festivities, as they hoped to return the city to its previous position as the "Queen City" of the West.[7]

The resulting fairgrounds exceeded expectations. The main exposition building was two stories tall and 100 by 300 feet wide with two one-story wings extending from the main hall, each 100 by 200 feet. A two-story Grand Exposition Hall spanning nearly 56,000 square feet was attached to the building. The grounds included a Power Hall (50 by 400 feet) that provided steam power for the machinery in the exposition halls, thirty-two livestock buildings, a 5,000-seat amphitheatre, and a "roomy" two-story main office. For the centennial, Cincinnati's Board of Public Affairs closed the center of the city and granted the committee the use of Washington Park and all the streets between the exposition buildings and the Miami Canal. This setup created nearly 400,000 square feet of floor space with 142,000 feet of wall space.[8] The impressive buildings, the city's history of industrial fairs, and Cincinnati's position as a leader in building agricultural machinery made it the very symbol of progress and prosperity. But the fair also provided Cincinnati and the nation with a unique opportunity to contrast the past with the present.

Unlike industrial fairs, which merely displayed industrial machinery, international expositions included machinery and arts from around the world and presented historical and ethnographic exhibits that directly evaluated modern advancements by comparing them with primitive objects and people. The directors of the Cincinnati centennial celebrations operated in a similar way, as they declared that the object of the exhibition was to "present a panorama of the nation's resources and present state of progressive development, by an exhibition of the products of agriculture, of the various industries and fine arts; also the results of advancement made in the sciences; all the while illustrating the opportunities secured to and the possibilities which wait upon the citizens of the Republic." Indians would stand as the benchmark by which progress could be measured.[9]

The fair, as an international exhibition, drew from the resources of the federal government in its mission. When Cincinnati organized a smaller industrial exposition in 1884 as a buildup to the larger fair, Congress had authorized executive agencies, including the Smithsonian, to provide more than $10,000 toward the acquisition of materials. The Smithsonian had been instrumental in developing the ethnographic exhibits at the 1876 Philadelphia Centennial Exposition, where, as historian Robert Rydell has argued, "The Indians' worth as human beings was determined by their usefulness as counterpoint to the unfolding progress of the ages."[10] Likewise, scholar Bruno Giberti has written that the "managers of the Centennial devised a dual system of classification that was both hierarchical and progressive, and attempted to impose their theoretical order on the built environment of the exposition." Overall, Giberti posited, fairs "permitted the construction of a temporarily organized complex" used to order and organize the human experience.[11] Late-nineteenth-century exposition designers and exhibit curators worked under the assumption that "objects could tell stories" to the casual observer. They believed that "objects, at least as much as texts, were sources of knowledge and meaning."[12] Exhibits at fairs, like the Philadelphia and Cincinnati expositions, chronicled the stages of human progress by arranging displays on the history of mankind from "simple to complex, from savage to civilized, from ancient to modern." In other words, through physical exhibitions, world fairs offered a linear timeline of history where Indians were cast solely in the past.

For the Cincinnati Centennial Exposition, Indians appeared everywhere but only as objects of history rather than as living people. Interior Secretary William F. Vilas suggested that an "interesting exhibit could be formed of articles manufactured at the Indian industrial schools." Consequently, the Indian Bureau forwarded a "collection illustrating the methods employed in the education of Indian children at the government schools, with samples of the work done by the pupils." But the artwork and handicrafts failed to impress the secretary. Fair organizers and Congress agreed. They ordered the Smithsonian Institution to aid in developing additional exhibits for the fair. In the past, the Smithsonian had produced impressive ethnology exhibits for the Philadelphia exposition and had been loaning them to subsequent fairs, including the 1884 World's Industrial and Cotton Exposition in New Orleans. The displays located ethnographic objects from Indians within a broad chronology of global peoples and places. Long before the Smithsonian became known for its museums along the National Mall, the Institute had gained notoriety by building exhibits for international expositions. For the Cincinnati fair, the Smithsonian asked for $50,000 to rework their collections, as they believed it had "somewhat diminished" in popularity since the Cotton Exposition.[13]

The Smithsonian Institution's exhibits at the Cincinnati Exposition were prepared under the direction of Professor G. Brown Goode, assistant secretary in charge of the United States National Museum. The fair directors certainly believed the Smithsonian's exhibit was important in telling the narrative of national progress, as nearly a third of the space— 12,000 square feet—designated for the government at the fair was assigned to the Smithsonian. Their allocation measured 125 by 95 feet with an uninterrupted wall space 13 feet high and 125 feet long. Nonetheless, Goode "outlined an exhibit which would require 20,000 feet of floor space" (the same space assigned the Smithsonian at the Philadelphia Exposition). When he discovered that the area had been reduced, Goode decided to maintain the story of Indian primitivism and "substitute pictures and models for the more bulky specimens."[14]

The Smithsonian's overall exhibit was designed to be "educational in character" and "illustrate the progress made by man in the arts and sciences . . . and the methods employed in modern scientific investigations."

Each display was labeled and arranged "in such a way as to bring out clearly the particular lesson which it was intended to teach." The exhibits were arranged into three categories: "anthropological exhibits, natural history collections, and series illustrating progress in the arts and industries." By the end of June 1888, eight of twelve train cars carrying displays were "either en route for Cincinnati or had already arrived at the exposition." R. Edward Earll, deputy representative for the Smithsonian and the Department of Ethnology, James Morrill, clerk for the Smithsonian, and a team of museum curators, laborers, and mechanics arrived on the train. The final four cars containing photographic exhibits (recently mounted and intended to replace the artifacts left out because of spatial limitations) arrived several weeks later.[15]

Overall, exhibit organizers from the Smithsonian believed that the exposition would present an opportunity for "intelligent visitors" to benefit from the "great educational value" of the displays and argued that "if these departmental exhibits when properly installed in Washington were accessible to all, there would certainly be no excuse for ever sending them to other localities; but as such a vast majority of the people of the country never visit the National capital the practice of sending educational collections to the larger centers of population is perhaps justifiable." Hence the Smithsonian sent its collection to Cincinnati. In doing so, they believed "more good can be accomplished with a limited expenditure of money through the exposition than in any other way." They suggested that the exhibits of the Smithsonian "be so far separated from the other collections as to be accessible to the public without charge."[16] It was clear that both the local organizers and the Smithsonian representatives meant for the exhibits displaying the progress of Americans to be central to the mission of the overall exposition.

Professor O. T. Mason, curator of ethnology, prepared a special exhibit for his department "showing the principal characteristics of the different races of men; and in a more detailed way the tribal relations of the North American Indians and the progress made by them in civilization."[17] The exhibit consisted of a collection illustrating the chemical composition of the human body in the center, broken down into the "various solids, liquids and gases being represented." The rest of the exhibit contained two sections. The first displayed "the classification of mankind into the

races, with their geographical distribution, their cranial and facial pecu-
liarities and the characteristic costumes of the leading nationalities" and
contained "maps indicating by colored areas the distribution of the various races over the face of the earth."[18] Plaster models "of the heads of the
many . . . semi-civilized people of the old world" and full-sized "figures
showing the characteristic costumes of the various nationalities" accompanied the diagrams and maps. The second section contained "hand-
colored photographs showing both profile and front views of prominent
members of the different tribes, with specimens of their war, hunting,
and agricultural implements, cooking utensils, samples of their weaving,
and collections illustrating their art, religion, and pastimes." The majority of artifacts focused on North American Indians included "war-clubs,
bows, arrows, spears, tomahawks, scalping-knives, cooking utensils, samples of weaving, dressed skins, and agricultural implements."[19] These objects could easily be compared to the impressive machines in the industrial building or viewed against the massive building within which they
were housed. The message was clear. Indians were a primitive people: a
people of the past and a people without a future.

Thomas Wilson, curator of archaeology for the Smithsonian, developed another exhibit to "illustrate the methods employed in the study
of prehistoric man." The exhibit included two thousand specimens that
"would best represent man's progress during the early centuries of his existence." The items were arranged "in a continuous series in cases placed
end to end to represent the stream of time during the prehistoric ages."
The display was divided into sections devoted to "a different country or
group of countries. At the top was Great Britain, next below came France
and Belgium, then Italy, Switzerland, the Scandinavian countries, Asia,
Africa, Oceanica, and at the bottom the United States." This arrange-
ment, according to the designers, made it easy to "compare the progress
of man in the different countries." The exhibit displayed the tools of the
various civilizations "showing clearly the steps in human progress from
a lower to a higher civilization." Indians were placed at the beginning of
this timeline.[20]

Edward Tyler, the Englishman known as the founder of modern anthropology, wrote in *Primitive Culture* (1871) that human history moved
"along a measured line from grade to grade of actual savagery, barbarism,

and civilization."[21] This concept of evolutionary and linear progression took root in America. Lewis Henry Morgan, the most prominent nineteenth-century American anthropologist and evolutionary ethnographer, became its spokesperson. His work heavily influenced the efforts of the Bureau of American Ethnology, especially John Wesley Powell, who helped design exhibits for the fairs. These men "embraced some form of 'unilinear' social evolutionarism; each felt that the normal evolution of human societies proceeded through a single progressive sequence of social or cultural stages."[22]

Powell, director of the Bureau of Ethnology, assembled a special exhibit for the Cincinnati fair that included materials from the Zuni and Moki tribes along with an exhibition on the Mound Builders. The first collection included models of the Zuni and Moki dwellings and "samples of their agricultural implements, pottery, basketry, and textiles" alongside artifacts from mounds. Part of the exhibit included a fifteen-square-foot model of a Zuni village. Under glass cases, the curators displayed "textiles, basketry, pottery, agricultural implements, and household utensils." Similarly, they displayed "pottery and other articles" from mounds. All of this pointed to the sophisticated cultures of extinct societies and the degenerative nature of America's aboriginal people.[23]

Even displays on technical progress and industrialism revealed racial assumptions. An exhibit on transportation included a "separate series based upon the different motive powers, including man, the various animals, wind, steam, and electricity."[24] The exhibit featured illustrations "to tell the story of the development, step by step, of the great systems of transportation" and started with an illustration of an Apache woman carrying a basket followed by a photograph of Apache women carrying their children. The images progressed from images of pack mules, horses, birch-bark canoes, wagons, and steamboats to an entire section on the "development of the American locomotive." A section on the "development of the American steamboat and modern steamship" began with a full-size figure of an Indian in a birch-bark canoe followed by a model of a ferryboat—all meant to illicit comparisons.[25]

The linear projection displayed at the fairs not only demonstrated Indian primitivism and placed Native people at the beginning of an evolutionary timeline. The exhibits also marked the final clearing of the middle ground. Displays told the same story over and over again—Indians came before whites; they never lived among them. Evidence abounded for this story. Visitors could view plaster casts of human heads ordered from primitive to civilized; they could observe ornately clothed figures lined up in rows representing the same; they could go to the mechanics building and see primitive tools positioned next to modern implements; they could witness the Zuni and Moki exhibit for evidence that an exotic group of civilized people—the Mound Builders—had once lived in the lower Great Lakes. Nowhere did organizers provide evidence that suggested a cross-cultural world ever existed (or had even been possible), nor was there evidence that Indians could have done anything but vanish before a wave of white progress.

Writers believed that attendance of the Cincinnati Exposition had eclipsed the popular World's Industrial and Cotton Exposition in New Orleans, and visitors commented that nothing like it had been mounted "since the great one at Philadelphia in 1876," although some detractors complained that attendance had paled in comparison to the estimated 55,000 daily visitors to centennial celebration in Philadelphia (nearly 10,000 visitors viewed the exhibits on any given day in Cincinnati).[26] Organizers reasoned that an unusually warm summer and early autumn, the demands of the harvest season on the region's population, and uncooperative railroad executives who refused to reduce their rates had kept more visitors from attending the exposition. Still, the directors applauded the efforts of curators who assembled displays that were "studied with very great care by various classes, notably by students from the institutions of learning in Ohio and adjoining states, and the educational influences upon these cannot be overestimated."[27] On November 8, 1888, eight men arrived from Washington, D.C., to "assist in the work of packing the exhibits." Local mechanics and laborers joined federal agents in readying the materials for shipment. Meanwhile, officials in Washington prepared an exhibit for the local centennial celebration to be held at Marietta, Ohio; a small portion of the Cincinnati exhibits were forwarded to Marietta for the event marking the first American settlement in the Northwest Territory.[28]

The Centennial Exposition of the Ohio Valley and Central States demonstrated the extent to which older ideas about Native Americans and white conquest, including scientific justifications for removal, pervaded late-nineteenth-century culture. Clearly, ideas from earlier periods filtered into the historical interpretations of later accounts. As we have seen in chapter 6, many of the individuals involved in the creation of historical societies, who provided the public with accounts of the past, and historians with the sources to craft their interpretations were closely connected to the celebratory culture of pioneer veneration. Consequently, the line between civic celebration and historical reporting was often blurred. In at least one case, the connection between past and present, celebration and historicism was direct. In 1897, the Indiana Historical Society published a speech given by John Dillon Brown before the organization nearly fifty years earlier. Dillon's address, "The National Decline of the Miami Indians," illustrates how early local historians created a usable past that warranted their own occupation of the lower Great Lakes, while simultaneously lamenting the dispossession of Native people. In other words, it provided the foundation for a place-story and narrative of anti-conquest.

Dillon instructed the crowd of pseudo-historians, "If we look backward, we shall learn . . . something of the slow and sad means by which a vast and beautiful region has been reclaimed from a state of barbarism." To demonstrate his intimate knowledge of the region's past, he read transcripts from seventeenth-century Jesuit missionaries that described the flourishing Indian communities of the lower Great Lakes and then recounted the various means by which whites aided in the destruction of Native communities. The voices of early squatters, speculators, and government officials (all agents of American empire) spilled from Dillon's mouth, as he proclaimed that pioneers were caught in a "conflict between barbarism and civilization" that prevented them from aiding their Miami brethren. The lines had been drawn, he explained, and pioneers found themselves trapped on the side of civilization. "Thus shrouded in darkness, with the lights of civilization and religion beaming around them," Dillon remarked, the Miamis quickly passed "away from the earth forever."[29]

Dillon portrayed Native Americans as hapless victims swept up in the advancement of civilization over the wilderness. Hoosier audience members probably nodded and applauded this familiar narrative of lamentable yet inevitable conquest. But Dillon did not stop there, and in an interesting act of elocutionary ventriloquism, he took up a Native voice. "Men of the white race, you are faithless," he proclaimed. Combining the trope of the vanished Indian with harsh criticism of white western settlement, Dillon scorned the crowd on behalf of the Miamis: "You spoke of peace on earth and good-will to men, but you made war on one another. . . . You did those things for the love of gold. . . . You have violated the treaties which you have made with us. You entered our country by force; you took possession of our lands; you told your warriors to strike us hard; you drove us from our homes; you killed our men and women. . . . Oh! You are a strong, false, false race."[30]

Readers may see Dillon's performance as an early harbinger of modern critics who condemned early-nineteenth-century Americans for committing genocide based on racist assumptions, but Dillon was no soothsayer. He quickly assuaged the crowd's fears. Still in Native character, he asked, "Have civilized nations nothing to say to the departing red man?" Then, on behalf of whites in the audience, he answered with an emphatic yes.[31]

> We found you in a state of ignorance and barbarism. We sent good men among you to enlighten your minds. . . . You disregarded their instruction. . . . We gave you warning after warning of the fate which awaited you if you continued to neglect our advice. We tried to treat you with forbearance, moderation, and humanity even when your tomahawks and scalping knives were red with the blood of our murdered men, women, and children. The land you once claimed was not made to remain forever wilderness, to be used only as a vast hunting ground for the race of red man.[32]

While he outlined a sharp critique of white western settlement, Dillon did so only as a literary device, which allowed him to justify the seamier consequences of American progress. Dillon's speech demonstrates that nineteenth-century Americans were aware of the consequences of conquest, but it also illustrates how they rationalized it. Although he gave his speech in the 1840s, "The National Decline of the Miami Indians" did not become widely distributed until it was printed by the Indiana Historical Society. The fact that Dillon, and his work, straddled these two worlds—that of the pioneer period and the late-nineteenth-century world of remembrance—demonstrates the role of multiple generations in crafting the image of the pioneer and the vanished Indian.[33]

In 1848 John Brown Dillon probably knew more about the Hoosier state than any other human. As a young man he had lived in a pioneer community, witnessing the tide of immigration, the intermingling of whites and Indians on the middle ground, and the eventual removal of the Indians. He had also watched George Winter paint the Miamis and Potawatomis of central Indiana; he published the stories of Frances Slocum in his newspaper; and he watched as schoolhouses and cabins, shops and banks, jails and courthouses rose along the streets of Logansport, Indiana. Dillon both recorded and participated in the transformation of the physical and literary landscape.[34] When he published his book, Dillon claimed to have chronicled Indiana's history by way of "a close examination and an impartial comparison with the statements and views of those who were contemporary writers." He promised to base his history on records and documents, not romanticized ideals. In many ways, Dillon anticipated the movement toward scientific objectivism promoted by county history editors and the history profession forty years later, but his views were also bound in an ethnocentric view of western progress that justified dispossession of Indians and glorified pioneers. By ending his history in 1816, Dillon symbolically terminated the presence of Indiana's Indians in that year, providing a chronological timeline for the clearing of the middle ground.[35]

Although they found Dillon's writing loquacious, late-nineteenth-century historians used *A History of Indiana* as their principal source for their own books. Writers often cited Dillon's *History* because his reputation as the "Father of Indiana History" brought instant credibility to their works.[36] Dillon's influence could even be seen in children's books. William H. Glascock, Julia S. Conklin, and Maurice Thompson provided young Hoosiers with books that praised the work of the pioneer while lamenting the demise of Indians as the natural consequence of national progress. Even the titles echoed this romantic ideal. Glascock titled his work *Young Folks' Indiana: A Story of Triumphant Progress*. In the preface to his *Stories of Indiana*, Thompson proclaimed, "From the first footfall of the white man in her forests down to this hour, our State, as wilderness, territory, and commonwealth, has been a theater for tragedy, melo-

drama, comedy, song, and farce. Upon its stage human life has passed
from scene to scene, always developing, spreading, increasing in power
and value." Julia Conklin echoed these themes in *The Young People's History of Indiana*, explaining in her preface "how an almost limitless wilderness was turned into a great and prosperous State—not in a moment's
time, by the waving of a wand—but by the patient toil of thousands of
brave and sturdy men and women, in a period of less than one hundred
years."

Dillon and his disciples focused almost exclusively on the role of
pioneers in transforming the physical landscape. In the process, they
erased an entire period when Indians and whites lived side-by-side in
the region—a period Dillon knew all too well. A century of physical
and rhetorical battles for control of the lower Great Lakes had led to
a common goal for whites: the dispossession and disempowerment of
the region's indigenous population. The result was a collective amnesia
about the clearing of the middle ground: it had simply happened, sometime between the scenes of history as stage curtains opened and closed.
Conklin summarized the passivity of the moment in the opening of her
book: "They [pioneers] were the genii who swept away the forests, made
their farms, built the cities, and established civilization." By the late nineteenth century, white Americans had come to believe that the Indians
had vanished, along with the middle ground.

Scholars of America's Gilded Age often focus on the seamier issues
of political corruption, an increasingly xenophobic immigration policy,
an expanding chasm between rich and poor, jingoistic calls for military
intervention in the western hemisphere, or the military conflict between
whites and Indians. Most prominently, they have followed the era's own
foremost critics, Samuel Clemens and Charles Dudley Warner, in highlighting the stark contrast between opulence and poverty. Other historians have begun to examine how Americans tried to craft a national
identity out of the cacophony of immigrant voices. Recently, Alan Trachtenberg has placed the image of Native Americans at the center of
late-nineteenth-century American identity formation, arguing that the
"fundamental shift in representations of Indians, from 'savage' foe to
'first American' and ancestor to the nation, was conditioned by the perceived crisis in national identity triggered by the 'new' immigrants."

Essentially, Trachtenberg believes that as they struggled to incorporate the growing immigrant population within American society, Americans turned to the image of the Indian as "first American" in order to fuse together a shared American culture.[37] But this conclusion overplays the creativity of late-nineteenth-century Americans and underplays the influence of earlier whites in helping craft the image of the pioneer, the idea of the vanished Indian, or the erasure of the middle ground. In many ways, this book has sought to demonstrate the power of the "unbroken past" and the continued role of colonialism in shaping popular perceptions of whites and Indians in the American mind.

As we have seen in the previous chapter, popular county histories helped perpetuate and standardize the image of the stalwart pioneers, and they did the same with the vanished Indian. American writers increasingly placed Indians, a symbol of primitiveness, in the period before white settlement. The history of Indiana in the Gilded Age, proclaimed the author of the *History of Franklin and Pickaway Counties, Ohio,* "extends from the scene of plenty and of peace, of well ordered society, of education and good morals, back to the time when all these things were not; . . . to the savagery and wilderness of the periods which preceded the white man's occupancy."[38] This notion—that Indians came *before* whites—had existed in the American conscience for nearly a century, but new forms of storytelling via county histories, new self-proclaimed objective methods of historical documentation via professional histories, and new ways of displaying the past via expositions perpetuated the story in ways that early Americans could not have imagined.

If any individual Indian could have emerged as the symbol of brokering power on the middle ground, Tecumseh was that man. But as any white late-nineteenth-century midwesterner could attest, he had failed, not in trying to accommodate whites but by attempting to resist them. Most important, Tecumseh had died trying. Authors of the region's county histories believed he exhibited "all those elements of greatness which place him a long way above his fellows in savage life"; he was "high-minded, honorable and chivalrous." In fact, they argued, the Shawnee leader predicted his own fate. Indians "would perish," he supposedly declared, and "all their possessions taken from them by fraud or force, unless they stopped the progress of the white man westward; that it must be a war of races in which one or the other must perish; that their tribes had been driven toward the setting sun."[39] This type of language not only foreshadowed the removal of Native people from the region but also established Tecumseh as the symbol of indigenous dispossession. Historian Alfred Cave has concluded, "Tecumseh is easily idealized, for he was indeed handsome, heroic, generous, and, after 1813, dead—the white man's ideal Indian."[40] County historians routinely placed a chapter on the Shawnee leader between their chapters on Indian history and those on the history of whites in the county.

Tecumseh's death marked a turning point for many county history writers; Tecumseh died, one author proclaimed, and "his death disheartened the savages to such an extent that they were willing to make terms of peace."[41] But Indians did not always disappear from the narrative, especially when place-specific histories could not simply ignore local events. For example, Black Hawk's War and Potawatomi removal often received brief, disjointed chapters in their state histories. After all, authors had to explain these events, viewed as anomalies, to their readers. According to the "History of Indiana," Black Hawk's War and Potawatomi removal stood as an ultimate reminder that Indians had left the region.

> In 1830 there still lingered within the bounds of the State two tribes of Indians, whose growing indolence, intemperate habits, dependence upon their neighbors for the bread of life, diminished prospects of living by the chase, continued perpetuation of murders and other outrages of dangerous precedent, primitive ignorance and unrestrained exhibitions of savage customs before the children of the settlers, combined to make them subjects for a more rigid government. The removal of the Indians west of the Mississippi was a melancholy but necessary duty.[42]

Counties far removed from these events simply removed the chapters. Not that it mattered. The chapter on Black Hawk's War discussed very little of the actual events surrounding Black Hawk's protest of removal policies. Instead, authors focused on how indigenous resistance justified removal. Chapters on Black Hawk and Potawatomi removal punctuated the narrative of white progress but for the most part did not disrupt the linear projection of the story. Following a pithy chapter on Potawatomi removal (two pages), the writers of the "History of Indiana" backtracked

204   REMEMBERING AND FORGETTING

to the 1820s in order to discuss land sales; it apparently did not matter
that the Potawatomi remained in Indiana until the late 1830s.[43] The fact
that even those Miamis who removed from Indiana did not leave until after the Potawatomis, or that many of them never left, went unstated. The
voices of George Winter and other writers from the *Logansport Telegraph*
a half century earlier resonated throughout the section on removal. In
fact, authors of the "History of Indiana" clearly pulled their material
from newspaper articles penned by Winter in the 1830s—sometimes pla-
giarizing entire sections of Winter's work.[44]

     Wyandot County, Ohio, faced a similar dilemma. After all, the county
had been founded on the site of the former Wyandot Reserve. The
authors of Wyandot County's history admitted, "Probably no county
in the State of Ohio is richer in historical data concerning its original
inhabitants."[45] Consequently, they included three full chapters on "the
story of the Wyandot Indians, and of other Ohio tribes, from time im-
memorial," but their account of Wyandot history was far from the actual
history of the tribe presented here in chapter 3.[46] "By reason of being
on the extreme borders of civilization, and mixing with the most de-
grading vices," they argued, many of the Wyandots "became the most
debased and worthless of their race, and drunkenness, lewdness and at-
tendant diseases, had reduced them in twenty years nearly one-half in
numbers."[47] Despite including a history of the Wyandot Nation in their
volume, the authors mainly used it as an opportunity to contrast white
advancements. They concluded that when the former reservation lands
were opened to whites, they found it underdeveloped. In this way, they
made local improvements seem more impressive than those in surrounding counties.

     When evidence abounded that Indians had indeed altered the physi-
cal landscape, late-nineteenth-century authors dismissed their labors.
This was especially true as Americans tried to explain how supposedly
primitive peoples dramatically changed the physical landscape by moving
tons of earth and leaving behind impressive mounds and monuments.
Most county histories began with an account of the "vast and vanished
race" that "once occupied and cultivated portions of the soil." Yet they
argued that the Mound Builders "left no literature, no inscriptions as
yet decipherable, if any, no monuments except the long forest—covered

earth—and stoneworks, no traditions of them, by common consent of all the tribes, were left to the North American Indian." The Mound Builders were a curiosity, much as their earthworks had become.[48] Decades earlier William Henry Harrison had speculated on the demise of the Mound Builders in a speech made before the Ohio Historical Society, perhaps influencing later interpretations. "I assume the fact that they were compelled to fly from a more numerous or more gallant people," he concluded. "No doubt the contest was long and bloody, and that the country, so long their residence, was not abandoned to their rivals until their numbers were too much reduced to continue the contest." Harrison both minimized the Mound Builders' influence by claiming them extinct and highlighted the contrast between whites and American Indians by arguing that nineteenth-century Indians descended from a barbaric and violent ancestor who had slaughtered a more civilized society.[49]

As they struggled to make sense of the mounds and the meaning of an advanced civilization in the region, natural scientists and historians simply invented stories about them. Historian Steven Conn argues that the Mound Builders were both "the greatest discovery of nineteenth-century American archaeology" and its "greatest invention."[50] When a few archeologists came close to identifying the Mound Builders as ancestors to the Indians who lived in the region in the early nineteenth century, ethnologists and government officials dismissed the evidence as ludicrous and published their own findings. In 1894, Cyrus Thomas, head of the Smithsonian Institution Bureau of Ethnology's Mound Builder project, published a report that suggested the Mound Builders had never really existed. They were, as Conn has argued, living in "history's shadow": a people without a history, easily dismissed and forgettable. Most county histories simply jumped to what they believed were the next group of indigenous people to inhabit the lower Great Lakes: savage Indians.[51]

Science seemed to support claims made by county historians, as standardized state histories like the "History of Indiana" used the findings of a rising number of pseudo-scientists, such as midcentury phrenologists, early ethnographers, and natural scientists as evidence. For many writers, science supported conquest. The demise of Indians was not genocide; it was scientifically and biologically inevitable. The authors of the *History of Allen County, Indiana* believed that the "cranial structure" along

with the "flattened occipital" and "low and receding" forehead of indigenous peoples proved their inferiority and marked the inevitability of
conquest.[52]

County histories placed individualized local experiences within the
larger framework of linear national progress. The "History of Indiana"
provided a chronological narrative that seemed to suggest that as new
people entered the lower Great Lakes, Indiana progressed from a stage
of primitivism to civilization. It began with an overview of the "prehistoric
races" of the lower Great Lakes, perhaps an exception to the hierarchical progression of the human races in the area. Authors concluded that
the early Mound Builders were replaced by a people who lived in simple
dwellings, depended on hunting and fishing, and sought vengeance
more often than did whites: "war, rather than peace, was the glory and
delight" of the Indians.[53] In fact, the authors of Hardin County's history
admitted that they included a section on the indigenous history of the
region so that progress could be measured. "We do not wish to recall
the history of the aborigines who occupied the locality," they wrote, "to
extol their supposed greatness or to lament their disappearance, but to
compare them with the white race of people who have followed them."[54]
Moreover, they believed, "It was a part of the inevitable that the red man
should depart and the white man take his place."[55]

County historians argued that the Indians who followed the Mound
Builders were vagabonds, not permanent residents of the region. Prior
to pioneer settlement, one author recounted "only straggling and stroll-
ing bands of Indians invaded the territory or locality."[56] "So far as is
known," the author of Brown County, Ohio's history wrote, "no tribe
of Indians ever lived upon its soil." Instead, many writers believed, the
region had merely been the "camping ground of the red warrior."[57] "The
aborigines," another writer concluded, had traversed Indiana's "forests
uninterrupted in their wild pursuits. In its wilderness they chased their
game, they paddled their rough canoes upon its streams, and here and
there they kindled camp-fires, built the wigwam, engaged in their savage
revelries, or fought their battles."[58]

Since authors believed that American Indians were only temporary
residents of the region, moving farther west seemed inevitable. By focusing on Indians as hunters and warriors, white historians were able

to present them as transients, unable to understand the full potential of nature's abundance. Indiana's "wide and tangled forests and its
blooming prairies were the haunts of wild beasts and the home of rov-
ing tribes of Indians. Only here and there were to be seen any traces of
civilization."[59]

> The lazy Indian still he scorns;
> Their squaws and their papooses—
> The things God made them, but no doubt
> For undiscovered uses.
> Where now a dozen turnpikes stretch
> Stiff lines between the meadows,
> He knew a single Indian trail
> That wound through forest shadows.[60]

Despite the fluctuating years that authors placed on the "end of the
Indian," they all conveniently predated Indian removal and thereby
white settlement. Writers argued that Indians, who were once "bold,
fierce, and stalwart," simply disappeared after ceding their lands after
the War of 1812, or the Treaty of Greenville of 1814, or the St. Mary's
Treaty of 1817.[61] By placing the vanished Indian before removal, writers
made the actions of conquest passive; Indians simply "left the county" or
"took their departure" with the "first encroachments of civilization."[62]
Americans did not push them off the land, county historians argued, as
white pioneers conquered landscapes, not people.[63]

Did the wilderness include Indians? Had they, too, been felled by the
woodman's ax? Authors suggested that Indian removal was inevitable,
but how could they explain the role of white pioneers in clearing the
middle ground? Certainly, clearing was an active, not passive, act. One
writer argued, "Gradually the wilderness gave way to the pioneer. His
sturdy arm and untiring frame never knew rest until the forest was made
to blossom with the fruit and grain."[64] The clearing of the middle ground
(a physical space rather than a concept of cross-cultural interaction) became the natural product of extending civilization. The "destiny of his
race," more than one county history proclaimed, "was being crowded
westward and to eventual extermination": unquestionable and unavoid-
able.[65] Writers seemed unwilling to admit that whites had precipitated
removal or even wanted it to take place. One author preposterously

claimed that white settlers were patiently "waiting and watching over the border [Ohio River]" for lands to open up. "Of course not much, if anything, was known of this wild region," another contended, "perhaps not even of its existence, except by the Indians, until about 1812."[66] But "after the close of the war of 1812, Indians made their annual hunting-camps in various parts of the county" and "within a few years they were removed."[67] The author of Darke County, Ohio's history concluded that all Indians vanished from the region by 1816, as he cited the deaths or removal of Tecumseh, Logan, and Black Hoof, and proclaimed that Native people had simply "vanished before the swelling tide of western-bound humanity."[68]

Many writers argued that the concept of a cross-cultural middle ground, where Indians and whites mingled, traded, and shared cultures, had never existed. The line demarked by the Treaty of Greenville, one author believed, served as a "border between whites and Indians."

> It stood like a Chinese wall until the year 1817, separating civilization from barbarism. On one side were fruitful fields, towns, roads, well-clothed people, enjoying the rewards of peace, industry and thrift which good soil, good climate and a beneficent Providence assures every citizen of Ohio. On the other side was the wilderness and squalid poverty—the Indian in his worst estate. . . . But it was impossible that this condition should continue long. The land could not be separated on such a line. It must be all one or the other. Call it fate, or whatever name we choose, the Indian was doomed to be swept aside by the new and superior race. He either must fall in with the marching procession or be left to his fate, by the way side.[69]

Indeed, some writers argued that Indians who resisted removal were destined to perish, and they romanticized the loss of Native peoples through poetry included in their county histories.

> Fought eye to eye, and hand to hand,
> Alas! 'twas but to die!
> In vain the rifle's deadly flash
> Scorched eagle plume and wampum sash—
> The hatchet hissed on high;
> And down they fell in crimson heaps
> Like the ripe corn the sickle reaps.[70]

Not all county histories presented injurious depictions of Indians; apologists existed. The authors of the *History of Logan County, Ohio,* argued that historians had ignored "the fatal effect that one hundred years contact with civilization has wrought" on Native Americans. Indians possessed a right to the soil, they contended, and "in the cool recesses of the woods they had their homes, and here beyond the reach of the luxuries and vices of a corrupt civilization" before whites, with their "greedy designs," stripped them of their homes.[71] Another author believed that Indians were "capable of high attainments, both mental and moral," but had been "corrupted and enfeebled by the vices of society, without being benefited by its civilization."[72] The lamentations of these county histories differed from other accounts in two important regards. Individual authors rather than teams of in-house editors penned them, and they were almost all published by small, independent publishing houses. In other words, they represented a tiny fraction of the hundreds of county histories available to midwestern audiences.

County historians from all backgrounds seemed to mourn the tragic loss of the vanished Indian. "The red man," wrote one, "that met and welcomed him [the frontiersman] to these fertile valleys, has long since gone to the great hunting-ground, or now roams, old and feeble, towards the setting sun."[73] Certainly, for late-nineteenth-century Americans who read daily reports about western Indian affairs, the image of a vanished or vanishing Indian helped comfort them from devastating news of western Indian-white violence, like the Battle of Little Bighorn. "Soon they will live only in the songs of their exterminators," lamented one writer. "Let us be faithful to their rude virtues as men, and pay due tribute to their unhappy fate as a people."[74] The theme was echoed again and again in the county histories: the day was "not far distant when the Indian race, as a race, will become extinct."[75]

The disappearance of Indians was a welcome event for white county history writers, who viewed Native people as an obstacle to American progress. Regardless of the claims made by publishers, editors, and authors that their works employed historical objectivism, county histories still reflected the romantic ideal of American progress. Historical reflection, they believed, offered clues to the structures of human society. American history and identity extended, one author chronicled, "from the scene of plenty and of peace, of well ordered society, of education and good morals, back to the time when all these things were not; from the scene of mental, moral, and material affluence; from the *cultivated* landscape, dotted with farm houses, villa and town, busy and bustling with an hundred industries, back to the time of the lonely log cabin, and farther, to the savagery and wildness of the periods which preceded the white man's occupancy."[76]

Certainly the impact of the exposition in educating the masses in the lower Great Lakes should not be overlooked, but neither should the voices of men like John Brown Dillon, who argued to his imaginary Indian counterpart half a century earlier, "The land you once claimed was not made to remain forever wilderness, to be used only as a vast hunting ground for the race of red men." These were the very sentiments expressed by Theodore Roosevelt in *The Winning of the West* that "this great continent could not have been kept as nothing but a game preserve for the squalid savages."[77] The clearing of the middle ground had taken more than a century, had occupied multiple generations, and had gone through a variety of cultural productions. Surely the story changed from decade to decade, generation to generation, but Americans had used the image of the pioneer and amnesia about a middle ground to justify the dispossession and disempowerment of Native peoples as an act of natural progress. Late-eighteenth-century and early-nineteenth-century American officials used the language of conquest to push for treaties that stripped Indians of their lands. Early-nineteenth-century Americans used the images to gain preemption rights and instigate removal. Americans in the 1830s and 1840s assuaged their guilt about Indian removal by arguing that they played no active part in it. And late-nineteenth-century Americans used the image of the primitive "Other" to measure their own progress and calm fears about the corruptive influences of industrialism. But the story remained the same. Americans employed a war of words that kept Indians positioned in a constant state as colonial subjects. Indians had little input into these stories, and even when they did, as we saw in the case of George Winter or Frances Slocum, few listened.

By the early twentieth century, the narrative of linear progress and the clearing of the middle ground had become the story of America itself. The followers of Frederick Jackson Turner clung to his story of successive stages, which left little room for intercultural interaction, and state cen-tennial parades completed the linear projection of the story by running Indians off the stage when it came time for white pioneers to enter. In 1883, one county historian wondered,

> Are we placed in the dilemma of believing either that our pioneer fathers were rapacious invaders of the lands of the Indians, or that the red men were innocent regardless of their solemn engage-ments? . . . Fortunately, we are not compelled to adopt either al-ternative. Enough has already been said to show that the [War of 1812] was not one in which all the wrong was on one side and all the right on the other. An honest effort was made by the Govern-ment of the United States to observe good faith toward the Indians, and to prevent their lands from being taken from them without their consent in treaties duly ratified.[78]

For late-nineteenth-century Americans in the lower Great Lakes, the answer seemed simple: Indians had always been destined to relinquish their land. By the twentieth century, white Americans clearly believed they had won the war of words.

Epilogue
Centennial Celebrations

> The truth is that time will make truth irrelevant.
> —Andrei Codrescu, "The Future Is Now . . . and Then"

The states of the lower Great Lakes all observed centennials of their statehood in the early part of the twentieth century—Ohio (1903), Indiana (1916), and Illinois (1918). These celebrations illustrated the culmination of more than a century of pioneer veneration and a collective amnesia about the region's indigenous past, all of which informed self-proclaimed objective and scientific historical interpretations. For the hundreds of thousands of Americans who attended outdoor pageants and parades or purchased commemorative books printed to mark these occasions, these cultural artifacts projected a linear narrative that embodied the place-story of a cleared middle ground. Ohio led the way in November 1902, when citizens gathered in Chillicothe, the Buckeye State's first capital, to commemorate the meeting of the state's first constitutional convention. In an attempt to differentiate Ohio's state-sanctioned centennial observation from earlier popular celebrations, Governor George Nash ordered that the 1903 celebration be a "literary and historical event, with no attempt at an exposition." Instead of exhibits and displays, Ohio's grand commemoration would center on a series of orations given by some of the state's leading citizens. Still, he admitted that, if the local Chillicothe community wanted to organize a parade, they should be permitted to do so.[1]

Congressional leaders in Ohio appointed seven prominent citizens to the state Centennial Commission and charged the Ohio State Archaeological and Historical Society with organizing the celebration.[2] The state-sponsored centennial would look very different than the celebration urged by federal leaders in Washington. Congress passed an act in 1899, calling for Ohio to hold an "Ohio Centennial and Northwest Territory Exposition" in Toledo in order to display "the progress and civilization of the American countries." A private group, the Ohio Centennial Company, had been formed to finance the exposition, and Congress asked the Smithsonian Institution and National Museum to furnish "articles and materials as illustrate the function and administrative faculty of the Government, its resources as a war power, and its relations to other American Republics"—as they had done at Cincinnati two decades earlier.[3] Perhaps due to Governor Nash's declaration, the Ohio state assembly failed to appropriate a grant of $500,000 required by the federal government for its participation, so the exposition never occurred.[4] Instead, crowds gathered in Chillicothe for two days to listen to public orators present "in a sequence a history of the state from the time of the establishment of the Northwest Territory."[5] On May 20, 1903, Archibald Mayo commenced the celebration by chronicling the early Indian wars in the lower Great Lakes. In his speech, Native people mostly acted as foils, used to demonstrate the prowess of American military leaders. "After General Anthony Wayne's victory of 'Fallen Timbers' and the Greenville treaty had brought Indian warfare to an end," Mayo concluded, "the Ohio settlements began to receive an influx of Revolutionary officers and soldiers."[6] Little else of Native life was mentioned.

General J. Warren Keifer, chairman of the Centennial Commission and trustee of the Ohio State Archaeological and Historical Society, outlined a chronology whereby Indians lived in a perpetual state of primitive barbarism before Americans arrived. Afterward, white pioneers sought to sow the seeds of democracy in the West. "Here, a little more than one hundred years ago, on these grounds, have been enacted the barbaric scenes incident to wild savage existence. Here Boone, Kenton, and others, of the earliest pioneers, who as advance agents of a coming civilization, fought, and some in captivity, ran the gauntlet. . . . Here, many of the worthy heroic class met and planted settlement."[7] Despite admitting that Indians lived in the region prior to American arrival, the next speaker, Judson Harmon, declared, "The region we are now considering was then wholly unsettled." [8]

Martin R. Andrews, a professor of history and political science at Marietta College, divided early Ohio history into multiple colonial stages. "First among these colonies," he argued, "were the settlements of the Indians, for many of the tribes in what is now Ohio had entered that region within the eighteenth century."[9] "First to compete with the Indians," Andrews posited, "came the ubiquitous squatter."[10] This differed from Keifer by not recognizing the first American settlers as pioneers. Regardless, he concluded that "all honor is due to the body of pioneers who, under such adverse conditions, held fast to the religion and morality of their fathers, and this laid the foundations of stable and orderly government. . . . These pioneers, these legitimate settlers, followed closely upon the trail of the squatter."[11] Rush Sloane, who provided the next speech on the "Organization and Admission of Ohio into the Union and the Great Seal of the State," focused on statehood development alone and failed to mention indigenous inhabitants of the Buckeye State after 1803.[12]

Thomas M'Arthur Anderson, lifelong member of the Ohio State Archaeological and Historical Society, was charged with the task of chronicling the War of 1812—often used as a moment to divide Ohio's Indian and American pasts. After venerating the pioneers, Anderson concluded, "It only remains not to refer to the final result of the contest, so far as the Indians were concerned. By a treaty made . . . in 1817, the Wyandots, Senecas, Delawares, Pottawatomies, Ottawas, Shawnees, and Chippewas sold and relinquished their right and title to all lands north of the Ohio River and agreed to move beyond the Mississippi."[13] He ignored the fact that the Wyandot, as we have seen, used the opportunity to create a reservation within the state, not "beyond the Mississippi." Furthermore, Anderson admitted he knew as much: "I remember, as a boy," he proclaimed, "seeing the last of these Ohio Indians passing Chillicothe on canal boats on their way to their new reservation."[14] Considering that Anderson was not born until 1836, he must have been recalling the 1843 removal of the Wyandot, rather than removals from before his birth.

In all, the orators of the Ohio Centennial proclaimed a distinct difference between a period when Indians inhabited the region and the period that followed, using the War of 1812 as the turning point. Although he didn't directly mention the war, journalist Murat Halstead marked its general influence on clearing the middle ground. "The land was won from a wilderness, whose swarms of savages were implacable," he argued. "The Ohio country was the battle ground for a generation between civilization and barbarism."[15] Despite admitting to a violent form of conquest, he believed American settlers had done Ohio's inhabitants justice. "The chief Indian town in Ohio was Chillicothe," he concluded, and "the whites paid the Indian the compliment of locating the state capital on an old Indian site."[16] For Benjamin Rush Cowen, a member of the Ohio Centennial Commission, Ohio's Indian history mattered not. "The original Ohio man," he declared, "was a pioneer, and his descendents naturally inherited the spirit of the pioneer."[17]

In Indiana, government officials hoped to surpass Ohio's celebrations by expanding their program to all corners of the state. In 1915, the legislature created the Indiana Historical Commission to oversee its planning; the commission included the governor, the director of the Indiana Historical Survey of Indiana University, the director of the Indiana History and Archives of the State Library, five members appointed by Governor Samuel Ralston, and one member appointed by the Indiana Historical Society. Ralston had asked the state legislature to create the commission because Indiana was "proud of her achievements along every line that causes a people to be recognized as great—great in material progress and greater still in moral and intellectual development." He hoped that centennial celebrations could be used to educate Hoosiers about their past.[18]

Government-sanctioned commemorations helped standardize a narrative of state histories, and government officials reacted with hostility when private organizations tried to present alternate civic celebrations. Orin Walker wrote to Governor Ralston in March 1915, informing him that "bankers, manufacturers, business men, and the various clubs and fraternal organizations" had concluded that the state allotment of $25,000 was inadequate to finance a proper centennial.[19] Instead, "a large number of citizens, moved by patriotic motives," organized the Indiana Centennial Celebration Association in the hopes of raising an additional $100,000 "to promote a movement for a fitting celebration of the state's birthday." They hoped to use the money to create "a historical opera

Portrait of the Indiana Historical Commission in 1916. Standing (*right to left*), Charles Moores, Harlow Lindley, John Cavanaugh, and Lew O'Bannon. Seated, James Woodburn, Frank Wynn, Governor Samuel Ralston, Charity Dye, and Samuel Foster. Courtesy of the Indiana Historical Bureau, Indianapolis.

and a historical drama, showing the life of the pioneers and bringing the development of the state down through the last 100 years."[20] Ralston publicly rebuked the association and condemned their actions. When an organization calling itself the National Patriotic League showed interest in assisting with the centennial, Ralston sent letters to mayors instructing them to ignore it. He wrote to the mayor of Muncie, who had been contacted by them, telling him that it looked "very much like" there was a "studied attempt going on over the state to cripple materially the work of the statutory commission."[21] In public he declared all such organizations "repudiated by the duly authorized and organized Indiana Historical Commission."[22] The commission itself condemned competition. When the Pioneer Association of Indiana tried to revive the organization in order to host events, which would include addresses given by professors from Purdue University, the commission declared, "It is a cheap blundering effort to play upon the credulity of the people of Indiana, and make a travesty of their loyalty and patriotism in this Centennial year."[23]

To disseminate news about the centennial movement and promote civic education, W. G. Woodward, director of the Indiana Historical Commission, attended the meeting of Indiana mayors, released numerous news articles, sent letters to all old settler societies, sent more than 1,000 letters to prominent individuals, 400 copies of the centennial bulletin to county chairmen, 500 more to unnamed individuals, 500 letters to members of the Grand Army of the Republic, 100 letters to commercial clubs, 400 letters to school superintendents, and had nearly 5,000 copies of the commission's third bulletin ready to mail.[24] In order to ensure that the civic celebration would not end once the final parade and pageant had ended, the Indiana Historical Commission promoted a continued pageant movement, the creation of a centennial medal, the making of a motion picture about the state's history, the advisement of local historical societies to erect monuments and memorials, the beginnings of a state park system, and the spending of an additional $5,000 to publish historical volumes related to the work of the commission.[25]

Woodward also developed a "course of study in Indiana History for elementary schools." His work, according to the commission, addressed the perceived need to give "pupils a knowledge of some of the fundamental facts in the history of their State." The curriculum drew from the same sources as orators and pageant masters: pioneer and county histories. Ultimately, they deemed that the curriculum was "one of the most permanent and beneficial phases of [the commission's] work."[26] Ralston aided in promoting the educational aims of the commission by calling upon schools in Indiana to use Woodward's curriculum on the day when the public celebrated Admission's Day at the state fairgrounds in Indianapolis.[27] Additionally, the commission supported "centennial exhibits," which traveled around the state so that the past could be "visualized for them in the collection of pioneer relics and mementoes." Schools also held their own pageants, in which they "dramatized events in Indiana history."[28] The education programs made clear that the centennial celebrations, from pageants to published works, were meant to be both didactic and entertaining.

Several years prior to the creation of the Indiana Historical Commission, the state legislature had organized the Indiana Centennial Commission and instructed them to "recommend a site and suggest plans for a permanent memorial."[29] This commission proposed the construction of a state library and museum to commemorate a century of progress and serve as a resource for future generations to learn about their past. After completing their mission, the commission felt obligated to form their own association in order to promote celebrations across the state. On May 3, 1912, they formed the Indiana Centennial Celebration Committee and soon thereafter published *Suggestive Plans for a Historical and Educational Celebration in Indiana in 1816*—a manual that encouraged "a historical pageant which would bring before the eye of the people the development and growth of Indiana."[30] As part of the manual, James Albert Woodburn, professor of history and politics at Indiana University, provided an outline of Indiana history. He suggested that the chronology of the Hoosier past could best be displayed by "a grand spectacular procession through the streets of the capital city."[31] He concluded that the following periods would be represented: (1) "Pioneer Life," which included a depiction of Indian wigwams, early trappers, Jesuit preachers, George Rogers Clark's capture of Vincennes, and the Battle of Tippecanoe; and (2) "The Period of Settlement," which focused exclusively on the foundations of the state government in Indiana. These two periods, firmly separated from one another, again demonstrated an imaginary clearing of the middle ground with the War of 1812 as a decisive moment of change.[32]

Undoubtedly, the educational aims of the Indiana Historical Commission informed the narratives acted out in the state's extremely popular pageant movement. Pageants were true place-stories. William Chauncy Langdon, first president of the American Pageant Association, argued, "In the pageant the place is the hero and the development of the community is the plot."[33] Langdon was largely responsible for the popularity of pageants in Indiana, as, in 1915, Indiana University welcomed him to campus where he taught a course on "the general subject of pageantry."[34] As they prepared to celebrate the state's centennial, the commission employed Langdon as Indiana's "Pageant Master," hiring him to pen *The Pageant of Indiana*. They also distributed a bulletin entitled "Pageant Suggestions for the Indiana Statehood Centennial Celebration" to guide local pageant masters.[35] Communities from across the state held their own outdoor dramas, as local historians drafted versions of the pageant suitable for their location. Langdon wrote two of his own pageants for Corydon, Indiana's first capital, and Bloomington, site of Indiana University.[36]

In 1915, George McReynolds, a history teacher at Evansville High School, offered advice for potential pageant masters in an article, "The Centennial Pageant for Indiana: Suggestions for Its Performance," which appeared in the *Indiana Magazine of History*. Citing Langdon's definition of pageants as place-stories, McReynolds concluded that "a person who has never gone to school can appreciate this form of drama because it portrays only those things that can be easily understood and that have a permanent value. It is a better teacher than the text book; to the pupils an incentive to work; to the people in general a kind of laboratory of history."[37] He also believed that the community dramas should follow the appropriate narrative of Indiana history. Consequently, he included his example of early life in Evansville as a way of demonstrating his version of sequential "episodes" for potential pageant authors to follow. In episode 1, white settlers purchase land from the Piankashaw Indians and William Henry Harrison signs treaties with neighboring tribes to cede lands around present-day Evansville. Episode 2 opens with pioneers entering the county; the Indians never returned.[38]

Other pageants followed similar linear trajectories by presenting short episodes of Native habitation followed by a distinct period of pioneer settlement. Pageant historian David Glassberg argues, "The sequence of historical pageant episodes emphasizes historical continuities over dislocations and conflicts."[39] For most of the Indiana centennial pageants, the moment of dislocation was one of temporal overlap, when white pioneers and Native Americans occupied the same space. For Carl Anderson, author of the Owen County centennial pageant, his narrative opens with an episode that includes an Indian camp pitched in the center of the pageant grounds. Chiefs of the Miami and Potawatomi tribes "lounge about in idleness" as "a group of men congregate to watch two Indian lads wrestle." The scene is interrupted when a covered wagon wheels onto the edge of the stage and two white men hunting a turkey frighten the Indians into hiding. Shortly thereafter, the white men discover the abandoned Indian camp. For a moment cohabitation appears possible, especially when the Miami chief reveals himself and welcomes the men to the camp. But that possibility is lost as the scene ends. In the next scene, set in 1820, only whites enter the stage.[40]

William Langdon solved the problem of valorizing passive conquest by introducing symbolic superhuman characters. In the *The Pageant of Bloomington and Indiana University*, a group of pioneers, the first of which are dressed in buckskin followed by others in the homespun garb of later settlers, are flanked by Indians who begin "attacking them with ferocity, yelling the war whoop, shooting arrows, and brandishing their tomahawks." Just as hope seems lost, women representing "the spirits of Determination rush forward to the rescue." They surround the pioneers and protect them from attacks. The Indians, repelled by the spirits of Determination, exit the stage and "the Pioneers proceed on their way, acclaiming with outstretched arms the future."[41] In one brief scene, Langdon affectively obfuscated the messiness of violent conquest by having the pioneers look to the future rather than the past.

The authors of the *Decatur County Pageant* ended their second episode with the "Guardian of the Wild Things" touching a young Indian with her wand, causing him to fall "to the earth penitent." As he lies on the ground, she says,

> Soon the white man, brave, determined,
> Axe in hand and gun on shoulder,
> Will uprear his little cabin.
> Then ere many moons have vanished
> You must leave this land of hunting;
> Wander ever, ever westward,
> Roaming never to return.[42]

A third episode continues the indigenous history of the county and state through the War of 1812, when, in a moment of chronological revisionism, the authors have Miami chief Little Turtle (who had died at the beginning of the war) proclaim at its end:

> 'Tis the Spirits of the Sunset
> Come to beckon us to Westward
> Come, my children, let us follow.[43]

As usual, the next episode opens with pioneers, this time sitting in a cabin, commanding the stage, with Indians never to return. The cover of the pageant program illustrates the larger argument about primitivism versus progress. In the foreground, a male Indian, wearing a large headdress, sits alone and dejected in a canoe, looking back at white pioneers busting through the wilderness in a covered wagon. In the far distance, a clock tower stretches high above clouds and the forest.

Similar to county histories, pageants that took place in counties where local history complicated this linear projection found other ways to both address history and ignore it. In Cass County, where Logansport was located, the pageant focused heavily on Potawatomi removal rather than highlight the cross-cultural communities that George Winter had described in his journals. According to the pageant's program, "The excitement caused by Black Hawk's war sealed the doom of the Indian in Indiana."[44] In Miami County, where many Miami Indians still reside today, Claude Andrews, the county's centennial chairman, admitted to state organizers, "Our county is yet the home of the descendents of Indians, who were the primitive people here."[45] But Andrews, who also helped write the county's pageant, focused the story of Native people in the county on the story of Frances Slocum. Episodes chronicled Indian removal up to the 1830s, but they were punctuated by the drama of Slocum's story. Moreover, in the prologue to the pageant, Andrews's coauthor lamented:

> Here on the scenes of bloody conflict
> You come this night, to re-enact
> The story of our domain.
> Sweet content replaces olden bitterness,
> And kindly peace the enmities of yore.
> You are inheritors of the earth.
> We are gone—down into the vastness of the Past
> Crushed by civilization's onward march;
> With folded wigwams, toward the setting sun
> We have gone.[46]

By the time they gathered at Indianapolis's Riverside Park to watch *The Pageant of Indiana*, Hoosier citizens had come to accept a standardized linear narrative chronicling their past: one in which pioneers entered an

Cover of program for the Decatur County, Indiana Centennial Pageant.
Courtesy of the Indiana State Library, Indianapolis.

empty landscape and Indians simply disappeared. This place-story of Indiana fit any locale, regardless of the nuances of local history. Moreover, through county histories and state centennial celebrations, it had come to serve as the story of the entire lower Great Lakes.

Officials in Illinois watched their eastern neighbors closely and hoped to host their own centennial celebration in 1918, surpassing both Ohio's and Indiana's in size and historical accuracy. Otto Schmidt, president of the Illinois State Historical Society and chairman of the Illinois Centennial Commission, argued that there were no good state histories except those based on "personal remembrances of somebody." As he reflected on the centennial celebration of Ohio, he lamented, "Ohio fell very flat in its whole celebration but its Historical Society published a little book." Schmidt declared that Illinois's commemoration would differ, because they intended not to depend "upon anybody's work but to go back to the original material."[47] Of course, what Schmidt meant was that the organizers would turn to pioneer recollections and printed sources penned by the region's early settlers; all such documents, as we have seen in previous chapters, employed shifty language.

Illinois had started much earlier than either Ohio or Indiana in planning centennial celebrations. The state legislature created the Illinois Centennial Commission in 1913. Even at that early juncture, the commissioners planned for statewide celebrations and the publication of a five-volume history of Illinois, covering 1673 to 1918.[48] Moreover, the commission proposed additional centennial publications, a memorial building campaign, the erection of historical statues and markers, and a publicity campaign that would ensure that "every man, woman, and child in the State will not only know the general facts of the celebration, but will be familiar with its details."[49] After attending Indiana's Admission Day and *The Pageant of Indiana*, the commissioners issued a report to the Illinois legislature, outlining a plan for their own centennial.[50] The commission proposed three major state-sponsored programs: (1) A Dedicatory Program to Commemorate the Occasion; (2) A Historical Pageant; and (3) a Centennial Exposition. They also warned that proper preparation was necessary to avoid the shortcomings of their eastern neighbors. "Ohio, the first of the States of the Old Northwest," they argued, "failed to observe its first century of statehood adequately to the great lasting regret of its citizens." Indiana fared better, they concluded, but still, "on account of lateness of official action for its Centennial could not enter upon any plans of permanent memorial marking or of great official celebration."[51]

The Illinois Centennial Commission began planning for both a state fair and a centennial pageant. By June 1917, they had hired Thomas Wood Stevens to write a pageant, but tensions developed between Stevens and the commissioners, and they replaced him in November with Wallace Rice, who had penned the centennial pageant for Fort Wayne, Indiana.[52] They named Rice the official state pageant writer and lecturer. By early 1918, Rice had written a pageant for the state and six plays for schoolchildren. The plays, which were distributed to schools across Illinois, were also offered free to any school or organization that wished to host a version of its own. The play, or masque, included six parts, the last of which was written so that communities could incorporate local historical peoples and events. The first five parts, however, outlined a linear history much as Indiana's pageants had done.[53]

On October 4, 1918, thousands of Illinois citizens gathered at the state fairgrounds in Springfield to enjoy Rice's *Masque of Illinois*. Masques, like pageants, were large outdoor dramas meant to present historical narratives, but unlike pageants, masques presented larger abstract ideas about the nation's past. For example, the *Masque of Illinois* opens with a woman representing the state surrounded by other women draped in white who represent "the PRAIRIES, the FORESTS, the RIVERS, and the FLOWERS." In some cases, like when the masque was presented in high schools, the characters were portrayed by single individuals, but in the case of the masque at Springfield, characters were represented by enormous groups of similarly dressed people. One thousand participants crossed the stage at the state fairgrounds, "culminating in a thrilling, patriotic appeal."[54]

The women are soon interrupted by characters meant to represent FEAR, followed by "the INDIAN CHIEF and his BRAVES." FEAR instructs the INDIAN CHIEF, "Lead forth thy braves to show of skill: Shrill murder, horrid torture, needless death." "We are thy children," the INDIAN CHIEF responds, "and our will is thine." Over the following two scenes, French and British traders, trappers, and soldiers unsuccessfully try to drive FEAR, the INDIAN CHIEF, and the BRAVES off the stage. The French eventually concede to the British and allow them to occupy Illinois, but American rebels threaten to overthrow their English rulers.[55] Illinois and the rebels declare:

> Not my king, while, the rising morn beneath,
> My prairies spread their sweet, my rivers run
> Smiling down to the Gulf, my forests toss
> Untrammeled arms above mc, and my flowers
> Perfume this western freedom.[56]

The British military officer responds by calling on FEAR (including his indigenous subordinates) and a new character, HATE, to terrorize Illinois and her inhabitants. VIRGINIANS quickly enter the stage from all directions, defending ILLINOIS and driving the other characters from the stage. Soon thereafter, PIONEER MAIDENS, COLUMBIA, and CONTINENTAL SOLDIERS enter the stage to usher in an era of physical transformation and progress. COLUMBIA then approaches ILLINOIS and places a crown on her head that represents the new characters of LIBERTY, JUSTICE, and LOVE.[57] Like the pageants of Indiana, the masques of Illinois presented a clear and definitive moment of transition between when pioneers came and Indians disappeared.

By the early twentieth century, the story of the clearing of the middle ground had become the story of American progress. "It is thought that the time is not fitting for this celebration, because of the world-war in which we find ourselves," Illinois governor Frank Lowden told his constituents. "I do not share this view. I realize the greatness of the burdens this war imposes on us. We, of Illinois, will bear those burdens more lightly if we shall recall the first hundred years of Illinois' achievements. Our fathers before us, too, bore heavy burdens. They, too, knew what it meant to offer all for a great cause. They, too, faced danger and difficulty. But they triumphed over all, and this great commonwealth—the home of twice the number of free men the United States contained at the close of the Revolutionary War—is the result."[58]

Regardless, Illinois's plans for an elaborate and statewide celebration of its centennial were dashed by both war and disease. By October 1918, the Illinois Centennial Commission had spent only $90,000 of its $160,000 budget (mostly on the salaries of the director and executive officers), and an outbreak of influenza prevented many schools and clubs from hosting their own versions of the *Masque of Illinois*.[59] At the end of the year, the commission reported that at least thirty-five pageants, scheduled in October and November, had been canceled. Moreover, the influenza outbreak had forced the cancellation of numerous other celebrations, ceremonies, and community meetings associated with the centennial.[60] In the end, Illinois's celebration did not surpass either the size or scope of Indiana's movement, nor did it differ in significant ways from the veneration and skewed historicism of other celebrations.

Pageant masters, orators, and state leaders across the lower Great Lakes routinely highlighted the centrality of the pioneer in chronicling regional history. At the same time, the exultation of the pioneer represented a centuries-old struggle to dispossess Native peoples from the region. Stalwart pioneers and noble-yet-savage Indians were linked intrinsically in the linear narrative of American progress. Yet, by the end of the nineteenth century, Native Americans had become a people "without history." Most of what was told about Indians was told *about* Indians, not by them. And when the voices of Native peoples (such as Little Turtle or Captain Charley) tried to speak out in the historical record, they were either ignored or dismissed as incorrect. Modern scholars, especially those looking at empires elsewhere, have demonstrated that people who have been viewed as living without a history have been "subjugated, colonized, and exploited," but they have not vanished.[61]

The history of the lower Great Lakes still relies on a narrative of anti-conquest, whereby pioneers entered a vast and empty landscape while Indians simply disappeared following the War of 1812. This narrative of statehood development may be convenient, but it is far from correct—the histories of the Wyandots, Miami traders, or Frances Slocum remind us as much. Narratives of anti-conquest also hold real consequences for people who have been dispossessed and disempowered, as they often seem unchangeable. Yet this does not have to be the case. In recent years Native American communities, scholars, and leaders have begun to reclaim their place in the historical narrative by telling their own stories. These new indigenous voices have resonated uncomfortably in the ears of many white listeners, as the narratives seem foreign and threatening. For many whites, today's Indians defy expectations: they do not appear primitive, they do not acquiesce to white hegemony, and they do not perform as the obedient colonial subjects as portrayed in the pageantry of American progress. Historical narratives, as this book has shown, long have been used as weapons of colonialism. They might also serve as tools of the colonized to reassert their place in telling the story. Perhaps this is what frightens many Americans who reject alternate narratives proposed by indigenous storytellers, as Indians have emerged as a people with a history.

Nearly two centuries ago, William Henry Harrison moved a flagpole and council house in a seemingly innocuous attempt to gain an advantage at the second Treaty of Greenville, but that symbolic move proved to be more significant. By 1814, whites had begun to control how the story of the lower Great Lakes would be told. Over the course of the next century, they chronicled a self-proclaimed "authentic" and "objective" version of the place-story of the region. Americans have long overlooked the fact that mastery of this narrative historically has involved a war of words, one that is far from over. Attempts by Native American communities to reclaim a shared history and assert that they have not simply been swept from the landscape remind us that the place-story of the lower Great Lakes is malleable yet today.

Abbreviations Used in the Notes

ASPIA
: Walter Lowrie and Matthew St. Clair, eds. *American State Papers, Documents, Legislative and Executive of the Congress of the United States (1789–1838), Class 2, Indian Affairs.* 2 vols. Washington, D.C.: Gales and Seaton, 1832–34.

ASPPL
: *American State Papers, Documents, Legislative and Executive of the Congress of the United States (1789–1838). Class 8, Public Lands.* 8 vols. Washington, D.C.: Gales and Seaton, 1834–61.

CCT
: *Cass County Times*

CHS
: Chicago Historical Society

GWMSS
: George Winter Manuscript Collection, Tippecanoe County Historical Society, Lafayette, Indiana

Hayes
: Rutherford B. Hayes Presidential Library, Fremont, Ohio

IHS
: Indiana Historical Society, Indianapolis

ISL
: Indiana State Library, Indianapolis

LDC
: *Lafayette Daily Courier*

LT
: *Logansport Telegraph*

NARA
: National Archives and Records Administration

OHS
: Ohio Historical Society, Columbus

OWU
: Ohio Wesleyan University

Rice Papers
: Wallace Rice Papers, Newberry Library, box 8, folder 162

Schmidt Papers   Otto Schmidt Papers, Chicago Historical Society, box 9, folders 3 and 4

SIA, RU 70   Smithsonian Institution Archives, Record Unit 70, Exposition Records of the Smithsonian Institution and the United States National Museum, 1875–1919

SMR Papers   Samuel Moffitt Ralston Papers, Lilly Library, Indiana University, Bloomington, box 6, folder June 1–15, 1916

Sun   *Western Sun* (Vincennes)

TP   Carter, *Territorial Papers of the United States*

Notes

INTRODUCTION

1. "Indiana Centennial Jubilee," booklet, October 2–15, 1916, William Barker Mss., Indiana State Library, Indianapolis, box 3, folder 1. Also see daily schedule in Lindley, *The Indiana Centennial, 1916*, 280–82.

2. "Parade Gala Affair," *Indianapolis Star*, October 3, 1916.

3. Meredith Nicholson, "Author Finds Inspiration for Young and Old in Historical Spectacle at Riverside Park," *Indianapolis Star*, October 5, 1916.

4. "Many New Features in Last Pioneer Parade," *Bloomington Daily Student* (Indiana), May 17, 1916.

5. Lindley, *The Indiana Centennial, 1916*, includes summaries of the pageants and parades conducted by each of Indiana's ninety-plus counties.

6. Because this book takes language as a serious tool in the process of colonialism, it borrows heavily from the lineage of cultural historians who trace their work back to Michel Foucault. For the intersection of language, knowledge, and power, see Foucault, *The Archaeology of Knowledge* and Foucault, *Power/Knowledge*, 125. For the connection between the written word and nationalism, see Anderson, *Imagined Communities*. Foucault defined Discourse or Episteme as "the total set of relations that unite, at a given period, the discursive practices that give rise to epistemological figures, sciences, and possibly formalized systems." See Foucault, *The Archeology of Knowledge*, 38, 191, and *The Order of Things*, xx. I view discourse in terms described by Sonja K. Foss, Karen A. Foss, and Robert Trapp as "a cultural code, characteristic system, structure, network, or ground of thought that governs the language, perception, values, and practices of an age." See Foss, Foss, and Trapp, *Contemporary Perspectives on Rhetoric*, 216. For other studies of language and colonialism, see Bhabha, *The Location of Culture*; and Bhabha, *Nation and Narration*.

7. Thomas, *Colonialism's Culture*, 2.

8. Limerick, "Making the Most of Words," 182.

9. Ibid., 168–69. Recent scholars have uncovered these alternative narratives and Native voices as a means of criticizing the larger colonial project. See Konkle, *Writing Indian Nations*; and Smith, *Conquest: Sexual Violence and American Indian Genocide.*

10. Sleeper-Smith, *Indian Women and French Men*; Murphy, *A Gathering of Rivers*; Tanner, *Atlas of Great Lakes Indian History*; Rafert, *The Miami Indians of Indiana*; Cayton and Teute, *Contact Points*; Barr, *The Boundaries between Us*; and Richter, *Facing East from Indian Country.*

11. Historian Sean Wilentz has argued in his Pulitzer Prize–winning book that a "momentous rupture occurred between Thomas Jefferson's time and Abraham Lincoln's that created the lineaments of modern democratic politics." Before Arthur Schlesinger Jr. questioned the origins of Jacksonian democracy half a century ago, Wilentz contends, historians viewed "American democracy as the product of an almost mythical frontier or agrarian egalitarianism." See Wilentz, *The Rise of American Democracy*, xvii, xix. Despite disagreeing on who was responsible for changes in this period, Democrats or Whigs, or even being able to agree on what changes were most important, a long list of scholars point to this period as one of dramatic and unparalleled change. For competing versions of this period, see Sellers, *The Market Revolution*; and Howe, *What Hath God Wrought.* Howe contends that we ought to stop calling the period the "Market Revolution" altogether.

12. Howe, *What Hath God Wrought.*

13. Hooper, *Adventures of Captain Simon Suggs*, 12.

14. My use of "the middle ground" might better resemble what scholar Leo Marx describes as "somewhere 'between,' yet in a transcendent relation to, the opposing forces of civilization and nature." See Marx, *The Machine in the Garden*, 23.

15. White, "Mutual Misunderstandings and New Understandings," 306.

16. Thrush's *Native Seattle* has been inspired by the movement in New Western History that emphasizes regional and local studies, rather than trying to explain settlement as a national process or the frontier as a physical place. By fixing oneself in a region and examining how people shaped that place's history, these historians promise to highlight both change and continuity by uncovering a locale's "unbroken past." They have also opened the door for the possibility of rich interdisciplinary work. For the seminal works in New Western History, see Limerick, *Legacy of Conquest*; White, *Land Use, Environment, and Social Change*; Worster, *Rivers of Empire.* Some historians have tried to recast the frontier as a sight of intercultural exchange. See Cronon, Miles, and Gitlin, "Becoming West: Toward a New Meaning for Western History"; Aron, "Lessons in Conquest; Faragher, *Rereading Frederick Jackson Turner*, 237–41; Klein, "Reclaiming the 'F' Word, or Being and Becoming Postwestern." For a recent version of this approach, see Adelman and Aron, "From Borderlands to Borders." For different directions in frontier

studies, see Drinnon, *Facing West;* Jennings, *The Invasion of America;* Faragher, *Women and Men on the Overland Trail;* and Jeffrey, *Frontier Women.*

17. Aron, *American Confluence,* xix.

18. Basso, *Wisdom Sits in Places,* 7.

19. Cayton and Gray, *The Identity of the American Midwest,* 11. More recently, scholars from across the humanities have directly tackled the issue of place in regional studies. See Mahoney and Katz, *Regionalism and the Humanities.*

20. O'Brien, *Dispossession by Degrees,* 4.

21. O'Brien, *Firsting and Lasting,* xii–xiii.

22. Roosevelt, *The Winning of the West,* 1: 104.

23. Pratt, *Imperial Eyes,* 9.

24. Taylor, *The Turner Thesis.*

25. For those disappointed with Turner's frontier significance, see Taylor, *The Turner Thesis;* Billington, *America's Frontier Heritage;* Caughey, "The Insignificance of the Frontier."; and Elkins and McKitrick, "A Meaning for Turner's Frontier."

CHAPTER 1. "A PEACE, SINCERE AND LASTING"

1. Limerick, "Making the Most of Words," 168.

2. Knox outlined his thinking about Indian affairs as a foreign policy issue in three reports to the president on May 23, June 15, and July 6–7, 1789. All in *ASPIA,* 1: 7–8, 12–14, 15–54. For Knox's ideas about federal policy, see Nichols, *Red Gentleman and White Savages,* 81–83. The unwillingness of American officials to recognize Native title to the land extended from a "doctrine of discovery," which predicated that Europeans and Americans ultimately held claim to the region and the right to purchase lands from its Indian inhabitants. See Wilkins and Lomawaima, *Uneven Ground,* esp. 36–41.

3. Pickering to Wayne, April 8, 1795, in Knopf, *Anthony Wayne,* 398–403. Italics are Pickering's. For similar instructions and the discussion they produced, see Wayne to Pickering, March 8, 1795, in ibid., 386–90; Pickering to Wayne, April 15, 1795, in ibid., 405–406; Pickering to Wayne, May 7, 1795, in ibid., 413; Pickering to Wayne, May 30, 1795, in ibid., 422–23. For Pickering's influence on early Indian affairs, see Nichols, *Red Gentleman and White Savages,* 129–36.

4. These scholars often adopt teleological arguments that present American policymakers as forward-thinking individuals who planned for the acquisition of Indian lands and Indian removal from their very first interaction with indigenous peoples. See Hurt, *The Indian Frontier,* esp. 106, 115–16. Horsman, in *Expansion and American Indian Policy,* states, "There seems little reason to suppose that they intended this boundary [Treaty of Greenville] to be permanent" (102). Horsman also argues that we should not condemn these officials for their intentions as a belief in white progress clouded their vision. See Horsman, *The Origins of Indian Removal.*

5. Andrew Cayton believes, "All of the participants in the Greenville nego-tiations thought that the events of the summer of 1795 were about much more than establishing boundaries." See "'Noble Actors' upon 'the Theatre of Hon-our,'" 238. Robert Owens argues, "Greenville held great significance for the Americans, both symbolically and legally. It had not been enough to simply gain Indians' marks on the treaty. They wanted Indians' open acknowledgement of American sovereignty and a retroactive endorsement of the righteousness of the American cause." Owens, *Mr. Jefferson's Hammer*, 32.

6. Horsman, "American Indian Policy in the Old Northwest, 1783–1812," 35–53. For the general change in Indian treaty-making, see Jones, *License for Empire*, esp. 120–86. For the connection between prerevolutionary diplomatic Indian practices and Knox's Indian policies, see Onuf and Sadosky, *Jeffersonian America*, 160.

7. Henry Hamilton, "Journal of the British Expedition to Vincennes, 1778–1779, TS Mimeograph Transcript," entries for October 26–27 in Hamilton Col-lection, Houghton Library, Harvard University, Cambridge; and *ASPIA*, 4: 564.

8. Pickering earlier recognized that the Indian signers of the Treaty of Fort Harmar held only "the shadow of a title to it," which was why he maintained that Wayne assemble a "full representation of all nations claiming property in the lands." See Pickering to Wayne, April 8, 1795, in Knopf, *Anthony Wayne*, 394–403.

9. *ASPIA*, 4: 568–69.

10. *ASPIA*, 4: 568.

11. *ASPIA*, 4: 568–69.

12. *ASPIA*, 4: 574–77. On the intersection of Indian and Euro-American ways of communication, see Lepore, "Dead Men Tell No Tales," and Murray, *Forked Tongues*, esp. chapter 2.

13. *ASPIA*, 4: 568–70.

14. *ASPIA*, 4: 574–77.

15. *ASPIA*, 4: 568–70.

16. For an overview of Indian reactions to the treaties, see Howard, *Shawnee!* and Weslager, *The Delaware Indians*, 319–20.

17. Heckewelder, *History, Manners*, 163–67.

18. Howard, *Shawnee!* 47 and 109; Hulbert and Schwarze, *David Zeisberger's History*, 94–102.

19. Yagelski, "A Rhetoric of Contact."

20. *ASPIA*, 1:571. For Blue Jacket's role in Indian resistance leading up to the Treaty of Greenville and his participation in the treaty negotiations, see Sugden, *Blue Jacket*, 172–87, 200–207. For the role of fictive kinships in Indian diplomacy, see Fenton, "Northern Iroquoian Culture Patterns," in Trigger, *Handbook of North American Indians*, 15: 312–13; Galloway, *Old Chillicothe*, 177–79; Howard, *Shaw-nee!* 113–14; Jones, *License for Empire*, esp. chapter 1; Parmenter, "Pontiac's War,"

618–19, 635–38; Trowbridge, "Meēārmeear Traditions," 38–39, 46–48; White, *Middle Ground*, 322–51; White, "The Fictions of Patriarchy," 66–67; Williams, *Linking Arms Together*, 68–69, 72–73.

21. *ASPIA*, 4: 564.

22. *ASPIA*, 4:564, 572–75.

23. For the use of wampum in indigenous cultures, from trade medium to mnemonic devices, see Beauchamp, "Wampum Used in Council and as Currency"; Ceci, "The Value of Wampum among the New York Iroquois"; Foster, "Another Look at the Function of Wampum in Iroquois-White Councils"; Jacobs, "Wampum, the Protocol of Indian Diplomacy"; Merrell, *Into the American Woods*, 187–93; Merritt, *At the Crossroads*, 205, 210–12; Miller and Hamell, "A New Perspective on Indian-White Contact," 311–28. Richter, *The Ordeal of the Longhouse*, 32–49, 84–85, 276–77; Salisbury, *Manitou and Providence*, 147–52; Snyderman, "The Function of Wampum"; Speck, "The Functions of Wampum among the Eastern Algonkian"; White, *Middle Ground*, 96–98; and Williams, *Linking Arms Together*, 51–53. Many tribes used wampum in extraordinary numbers. The eighteenth and early nineteenth-century missionary David Zeisberger commented, "An allegiance or league is hardly arranged between two peoples with less than twenty belts of wampum. Often thirty or more are required." Hulbert and Schwarze, *David Zeisberger's History*, 32. The Shawnee were one of the few Indian nations that did not use belts in this mnemonic fashion. Their collective memory relied on an oral tradition outside of wampum use. C. C. Trowbridge writes, "They have no belts commemorative of any events in their history nor do they pretend to preserve these as is customary among other nations, although they are used in many occasions." See Trowbridge, "Shawnee Traditions," 9. Instead, the Shawnee used ceremonial customs such as dances to mark time. For example, the "bread dance" symbolized the beginning of planting season. See Galloway, *Old Chillicothe*, 189–94.

24. For the loss of Miami belts, see Trowbridge, "Meēārmeear," 10.

25. *ASPIA*, 4: 571.

26. Ibid.

27. For the idea that Indians viewed treaties as "sacred texts," see Williams, *Linking Arms Together*, 40–61.

28. *ASPIA*, 4: 573. Masass said that the great calumet came from Lake Superior and represented the spreading of the works done in previous councils. He showed Wayne a belt and strings that marked the nine villages that he traveled to after the Treaty of Fort Harmar and told about the council. *ASPIA*, 4: 572.

29. For an overview of the fluctuating trust relationship and trust responsibilities of the United States, see Wilkins and Lomawaima, *Uneven Ground*.

30. Jefferson to Harrison, February 27, 1803 in Esarey, *Governors Messages and Letters*, 1: 70–71. The policy of land acquisition is further elaborated in The Secretary of War to Governor Harrison, June 21, 1804, in *TP*, 7: 203–204. Jefferson

told Indians that the new relationship between the American government and Indians began when whites took them by the hand at Greenville. Jefferson to Miamies, December 1808 in *TP*, 328–30; and Jefferson to Delawares, December 1808, in *TP*, 330–335. Also see Onuf, "'We shall all be Americans'"; Carter, "A Frontier Tragedy," 3–18; and Dowd, "Little Turtle and the Origins of a Great Native Debate," 5–21.

31. Delaware Indians to William Wells, March 30, 1805, in Esarey, *Governors Messages and Letters*, 1: 117–18; William Patterson, a Delaware, to Wells, April 5, 1805, in ibid., 1: 121–23. It was not the first time that the Delaware were involved in a dispute with Harrison. A year earlier, Delaware chief Buckongahelas interrupted Harrison at a council in Fort Wayne, declaring land cessions by the Piankashaws unjust. The Shawnee delegation became so infuriated that they left the council altogether. See Owens, *Mr. Jefferson's Hammer*, 78–80.

32. William Patterson, a Delaware, to Wells, April 5, 1805, in Esarey, *Governors Messages and Letters*, 1: 121–23; Secretary of War to Harrison, May 24, 1805, in ibid., 1: 130; Harrison to Secretary of War, May 27, 1805, in ibid., 1: 132–34.

33. For overview of the treaty, see Dawson, *Historical Narrative*, 47–54.

34. Memorial and Petition of Montgomery Montour, December 26, 1806, in *ASPIA*, 1: 744.

35. Opinion of Henry Dearborn to Memorial of Montgomery Montour in ibid., 1: 744. Although they argued that the Delaware held no claim to the land, American officials acknowledged a de facto right of occupation within the text of the treaties. The Treaty of Grousland signed on August 21, 1805, stated that the "Miami tribe, from whom the Delawares derived their claim, contend, that, in their cession of said tract to the Delawares, it was never their intention to convey them the right of the soil, but to suffer them to occupy it as long as they thought proper; the said Delawares have, for the sake of peace and good neighborhood, determined to relinquish their claim to the said tract." Ibid., 1: 696–97.

36. Harrison to Secretary of War, March 3, 1803, in Esarey, *Governors Messages and Letters*, 1: 76–85; Harrison to Secretary of War, April 26, 1805, in ibid., 1: 125–26; Indian Council, June 21, 1805, in ibid., 1: 137–39; Gibson and Vigo to Harrison, July 6, 1805, in ibid., 1: 141–46; Harrison to Secretary of War, July 10, 1805, in ibid., 1: 147–51; and Secretary of War to Harrison, October 11, 1805, in ibid., 1: 169–70. Most of these cultural mediators depended on a continued Indian presence as their economic means. Many served as traders, Indian agents, or interpreters.

37. For violence in 1807, see Jones to Harrison, May 4, 1807, in ibid., 1: 211–12; Harrison to Menard, May 18, 1807, in ibid., 1: 213–14; and Harrison to Kickapoos and Kaskaskias, May 19, 1807, in ibid., 1: 215. For the report concerning Ducoigne's brother-in-law Gabriel, see Harrison to Secretary of War, May 23, 1807, in ibid., 1: 216–17. The Kickapoo had complained to Harrison two years earlier when Chief Pawatamo reported on Americans who stole the bells off his horses and threatened to kill his son. As we have seen, Harrison could do little to

punish whites who terrified Indians. Perry and Bond to Harrison, December 10, 1805, in ibid., 1: 176–77.

38. General Wilkinson to St. Clair, March 28, 1797, William Hayden English Papers, IHS, box 30, folder 2.

39. *Centinel of the Northwest Territory* (Cincinnati), September 19, 1795, March 25, 1796.

40. For the punishments for horse theft, see An Act Respecting Certain Crimes and Punishments, August 24, 1805, in Philbrick, *The Laws of Indiana Territory, 1801–1809*, 118; An Act Respecting Crimes and Punishments, September 7, 1807, in ibid., 235–55; and An Act to Amend an Act Entitled "An Act Respecting Crimes and Punishments," October 26, 1808, in ibid., 267.

41. Examination of Thomas McCulloch, March 1, 1797, William Hayden English Papers, IHS, box 30, folder 2.

42. For accounts of Indians returning horses, see *Sun*, July 8, 1809; Secretary of War to Governor Harrison, July 2, 1804 in *TP*, 7: 204–205; entry for October 10, 1810, in Thornbrough, *Letter Book of the Indian Agency*; and letter from General Anthony Wayne to Northwest Territorial Governor Arthur St. Clair, August 19, 1795, Ayer Collection, Newberry Library, MS 966, folder 3.

43. Minutes and Proceedings of a Court of Oyer and Terminer held at Kaskaskias for the County of Randolph, November 10, 1801, William Hayden English Papers, IHS, box 30, folder 4.

44. Indictment of Wapikinomouk and Matayhikan, September 1801; Examination of Johnny, October 29, 1801; Examination of Wapikinomouk, October 29, 1801; Minutes and Proceedings of a Court of Oyer and Germiner held at Kaskaskias for the County of Randolph, November 10, 1801, all in IHS, box30, folder 4. For a slightly different account of the incidents found in the local papers, see *Kentucky Gazette* (Lexington), November 6, 1801. The editor there reported, "One of the Indians discovered a nest of Yellow Jacketts [*sic*], and attempted to put the White Man on the nest," but Harrison proved too strong and instead pushed one of the Indians on the nest. The "two Indians shot him through the body" once they reached the other side, and the third confessed the entire incident to the tribe. The Yellow Jacket story does not appear in the transcripts of the trial.

45. *Sun*, November 26, 1808.

46. Thornbrough and Riker, *Journals of the General Assembly*, 113n; and Esarey, *Governors Messages and Letters*, 1: 25–26.

47. For the 1806 William Red case, see Woollen, Howe, and Dunn, *Executive Journal of Indiana Territory*, 44; Proclamation Offering a Reward for the Arrest of the Two Men Who Had Broken Jail at Vincennes, June 21, 1806, in Esarey, *Governors Messages and Letters*, 1: 190; and Harrison to Prince, July, 1806, in ibid., 1: 191–92. For Harrison's reaction to the escape, see Harrison to Dearborn, July 11, 1807, in ibid, 1: 222–25. William Red's name may have been James; both names

appear in reports of the case. Message of the Governor to Legislature, November 4, 1806, in Thornbrough and Riker, *Journals of the General Assembly*, 110–13.

48. Harrison to Henry Dearborn, July 15, 1801, in Esarey, *Governors Messages and Letters*, 1: 25–31.

49. The circumstances of the Delaware murders can be found in Dawson, *Historical Narrative*, 7–12, 31–33; Woollen, Howe, and Dunn, *Executive Journal of Indiana Territory*, 17–18; and Esarey, *Governors Messages and Letters*, 1: 25–26, 48–49. For additional complaints made by Indians about injustices of the legal system, see ibid., 1: 27; Dawson, *Historical Narrative*, 7–8; and Woollen, Howe, and Dunn, *Executive Journal of Indiana Territory*, 13. Robert Owens chronicles the Davis Floyd expedition and additional complaints in *Mr. Jefferson's Hammer*, 60–62.

50. Message of the Governor to Legislature, November 4, 1806, in Woollen, Howe, and Dunn, *Executive Journal of Indiana Territory*, 110, 113.

51. Journal of the Proceedings at the Indian Treaty at Fort Wayne and Vincennes, September 1 and October 27, 1809, in Esarey, *Governors Messages and Letters*, 1: 362–378; Harrison to Secretary of War, October 1, 1809 in ibid., 1: 358–359; Sugden, *Tecumseh*, 179–90. Robert Owens argues, "The Fort Wayne treaties of 1809 represent the zenith of Harrison's negotiating style. They utilized all of his most effective tactics." See *Mr. Jefferson's Hammer*, 204. A year before the treaty, Harrison helped demote Wells from Indian agent at Fort Wayne to interpreter. See Carter, "A Frontier Tragedy."

52. Esarey, *Governors Messages and Letters*, 1: 25–26.

53. The editor of the *Sun* argued that Little Turtle's "opposition is of no consequence,—his influence is gone forever." See *Sun*, November 18, 1809.

54. For Conner's speech, see Drake, *Life of Tecumseh*, 100–102. Harrison's speech was published in the *Sun* on July, 2, 1808. The Prophet to Harrison, June 24, 1808, in Esarey, *Governors Messages and Letters*, 1: 291–92. For the Shawnee settlement at Greenville, see Sugden, *Tecumseh*, 128–33.

55. As quoted in Hill, *John Johnston*, 27. See also Edmunds, *The Shawnee Prophet*, 31; Edmunds, *Tecumseh*, 43–45; and Sugden, *Tecumseh*, 107–109. Tecumseh's speech to Harrison was printed in the *Sun*, August 4, 1810. See Tecumseh's Speech to Governor Harrison, August 20, 1810, in Esarey, *Governors Messages and Letters*, 1: 463–68. This is the famous, or infamous, speech where Tecumseh and Harrison almost came to blows. Harrison to Eustis, August 22, 1810, in ibid., 1: 459–63.

56. Gregory Dowd has aptly demonstrated how American officials ignored the movement as a product of British influence rather than a Native struggle for unity. See Dowd, *A Spirited Resistance*.

57. Jefferson to the Miamies, December 1808, in Esarey, *Governors Messages and Letters*, 1: 328–330.

58. Speech to 2nd General Assembly, September 27, 1808 in Thornbrough and Riker, *Journals of the General Assembly*, 166–67.

59. *Western Speculator* (Indianapolis), September 7, 1811.

60. Ibid.

61. Ibid.

62. *Western Speculator,* September 28, 1811.

63. Ibid.

64. Quotes are from the *U.S. Gazette,* as quoted in the *Sun,* December 28, 1811. For accounts of Battle of Tippecanoe, see Edmunds, *Tecumseh,* 159–60; Owens, *Mr. Jefferson's Hammer,* 217–24; and Sugden, *Tecumseh,* 226–36.

65. *Sun,* December 21, 1811.

66. *Western Speculator,* December 28, 1811.

67. Ibid.

68. *ASPIA,* 1: 828–36. Also see Conover, *Concerning the Forefathers,* 32, 52–53, and Wilson, *Around the Council Fire,* 22.

69. John Armstrong to Harrison, in *ASPIA,* 1: 827; Journal of Proceedings of the Treaty at Greenville, 1814, in *ASPIA,* 1: 828–29.

70. *ASPIA,* 1: 828–36; Conover, *Concerning the Forefathers,* 32.

71. Speech of Captain Charley, July 10, 1814, in *ASPIA,* 1: 830.

72. Speech of Captain Charley, July 15, 1814, in *ASPIA,* 1: 832.

73. For Johnston's account of his brother's death, see Johnston to Armstrong, August 24, 1814, in U.S. Office of Indian Affairs, Piqua Agency, Account and Memorandum Book, 1812–1876, Yale University, Beinecke Rare Book and Manuscript Library.

74. *ASPIA,* 1: 834.

75. Robert Owens is one of few historians to pay significant attention to the 1814 treaty; see Owens, *Mr. Jefferson's Hammer,* 235–39.

CHAPTER 2. "BETWEEN SAVAGE CRUELTY AND OPULENT SPECULATION"

1. Imlay, *A Topographical Description,* preface.

2. Harris, *The Journal of a Tour,* 59.

3. Sargent to Secretary of State, January 20, 1797, *TP,* 2: 587

4. Cuming, *Sketches of a Tour to the Western Country,* 118.

5. Harmar to Secretary at War, June 1, 1785, in Smith, *St. Clair Papers,* 2: 6.

6. Harmar to Secretary at War, October 22, 1785, in ibid., 2: 12.

7. Harmar to Secretary at War, July 12, 1786, in ibid., 2: 14. For more reports of Harmar's exploits against illegal settlers, see Harmar to the President of Congress, May 1, 1785, in ibid., 2: 3–5; Report of the Secretary at War Relative to Intruders on Public Lands, April 19, 1787, in *TP,* 2: 26–27; Rohrbough, *Land Office Business,* 14–16; Rohrbough, *Trans-Appalachian Frontier,* 48; and Cayton, *Frontier Republic,* 4–11.

8. Bushman, *The Refinement of America,* esp. 383–90; Samuel Holden Parsons, quoted in Cayton, "The Northwest Ordinance from the Perspective of the

Frontier," in Taylor, *The Northwest Ordinance*, 7. See also Nichols, *Red Gentlemen and White Savages*, esp. intro.

9. *Sun*, August 20, 1808; *Sun*, September 3, 1808; *Indiana Gazette*, August 28, 1804; and Maga and Ahmad-Maga, "Forgotten Scourge," 67–78. It is interesting to note that frontier settlers focused an incredible amount of time and money to tackling the "squirrel problem." Squirrels were so numerous and destructive to the settlers' crops that local governments allowed men to pay taxes in dead squirrels rather than money. In Ohio, taxpayers chose between a $3 tax or 101 dead squirrels. Settlers hunted in groups; one hunter would shoot the den of squirrels from a tree, and then the others would swoop in, killing the dazed animals with clubs. A group of hunters could kill more than 7,000 squirrels in one day.

10. Badollet to Gallatin, January 1, 1806, in Thornbrough and Riker, *The Correspondence of John Badollet*, 54–65.

11. Cutler to Winthrop Sargent, March 24, 1786, in Cutler and Cutler, *Journals and Correspondence of Rev. Manasseh Cutler*, 1: 187–88; Samuel Parsons to Cutler, July 16, 1788, in ibid., 1: 388–91. Cayton writes, "Ignoring the presence of Indians—and despite the risk to their lives and prospects—they saw their new state as a blank canvass on which they could paint a magnificent future of prosperity and harmony." Cayton, *Ohio*, 2.

12. Cutler, *An Explanation of the Map*, 5–10. Many of the later accounts are based on his recollections of the company. See Hildreth, *Pioneer History*, esp. vol. 1. For general overview of the Ohio Company and other speculative adventures established by eastern entrepreneurs, see Livermore, *Early American Land Companies*; and *Centennial Souvenir of Marietta, Ohio*. Some emphasized the egalitarian motivations of the eastern companies. See Bond, *Civilization of the Old Northwest*, 9–12; Hulbert, *Records of the Proceedings of the Ohio Company*; Rohrbough, *Trans-Appalachian Frontier*, 66–70. For the economic motivations of the Ohio Company Associates, see Shannon, "The Ohio Company and the Meaning of Opportunity." Also see Cayton, "'A Quiet Independence.'"

13. Cutler, *An Explanation of the Map*, 13–14.

14. *Annals of Congress*, 6th Cong., 1st sess., 1800, 651.

15. For Harrison's participation in committees concerned with land policy, see *Annals of Congress*, 6th Cong., 1st sess., 1799–1800, 209, 477, 510, 513, 527, 529, 532, 539, 540, 587, 656, 660; 2 STAT 73–78. Historians have often portrayed Harrison's actions in romantic terms, but his actions should not be read as entirely altruistic. See Bond, *Civilization of the Old Northwest*, 282–86, 293–94; and Buley, *The Old Northwest Pioneer Period*, 1: 102–104.

16. It is possible that he supported the legislation in an attempt to drive out large land companies, like the Ohio Company, who sought to accumulate vast holdings and impose local government hierarchies. Harrison's political career in Indiana Territory centered on his zealous control of local politics; he would have viewed organized land companies as a personal threat. Additionally, he par-

ticipated in land speculation and may not have wanted to compete with outside land companies that could outbid his own collection of friends. For Harrison's explanation of his speculative ventures, see *Sun*, September 19, 1807. By 1812, some of Harrison's landholdings were auctioned because he had failed to make payments on them. *Sun*, October 6, 1812.

17. For Jefferson's views, see Onuf, *Statehood and Union*, 29–33; *An Act to Prevent Settlements Being Made on Lands Ceded to the United States, until Authorized by Law*, 9th Cong., 2d sess. (March 3, 1807). Ironically, this act also allowed those settled on the lands to record their claims with the local register: an early form of preemption relief (becoming "tenants at will").

18. Petition to Congress by Residents on the East Side of the Scioto River, August 22, 1799, *TP*, 3: 62, 63.

19. Petition to Congress of the Territory, February 20, 1801, *TP*, 3: 123.

20. Memorial to Congress by Inhabitants of Randolph and St. Clair Counties, *TP*, 7: 592.

21. The American Inhabitants of the Illinois to Governor St. Clair, May 23, 1790, *TP*, 2: 252.

22. Kettner, *The Development of American Citizenship*, 28. There were court cases in Ohio, Indiana, and Illinois to determine the difference between citizens and inhabitants. See *Johnston v. England* (1817); Pollack, *Ohio Unreported Judicial Decisions*, 149–59; and Rosberg, "Aliens and Equal Protection."

23. Collier, "The American People as Christian White Men of Property"; Keyssar, *The Right to Vote*, ix, 5, 11–12, 22–23, 46–50; Kruman, *State Constitution Making*, 87–98; Lutz, *Popular Consent and Popular Control*, 99; and Williamson, "American Suffrage and Sir William Blackstone," 552–57. For the relaxation of property qualifications, see Keyssar, *The Right to Vote*, 11–12, 45, 47–48, esp. tables on 328–36 and 351–55; Steinfeld, "Property and Suffrage in the Early American Republic"; and Wilentz, "Property and Power."

24. Taylor, *The Northwest Ordinance*, 47–49, 118.

25. 2 STAT 469; *Annals of Congress*, 10th Cong., 1st sess., 1808, 2834; and *TP*, 7: 526.

26. *Annals of Congress*, 11th Cong., 3rd sess., 1809, 1347–48.

27. Kettleborough, *Constitution Making in Indiana*, 58–59; and Illinois Territory, see 2 STAT 741

28. Petition to Congress by Inhabitants of the Territory, March 24, 1812, *TP*, 16: 203–204.

29. Memorial to the President and Congress by Citizens of the Territory, December 6, 1812, *TP*, 16: 272–75.

30. Petition to Congress by Citizens of the Territory, December 16, 1812, *TP*, 16: 276–78; Petition to Congress by Citizens of the Territory, 1812, *TP*, 16: 205–208; and Petition to Congress by Citizens of the Territory, February 1, 1814, *TP*, 8: 287.

31. Preemption Rights in the Illinois Territory, December 28, 1812, *ASPPL*, 2: 731.

32. By midcentury, "inhabitant" was the equivalent to an illegal alien. For the connection between the terms "Indian" and "Inhabitant," see Wolfley, "Jim Crow, Indian Style," 167–202. In fact, some Indians (unlike the squatters) owned enough land to qualify otherwise under older voting requirements. Lee, "Indian Citizenship and the Fourteenth Amendment," 199–206; and Cohen, *Handbook on Federal Indian Law*, 157–58.

33. Petition to Congress by Inhabitants of the Territory, March 24, 1812, *TP*, 16: 203–204.

34. Petition to Congress by Citizens of the Territory, February 1, 1814, *TP*, 8: 282.

35. *An Act Giving the Right of Pre-emption in the Purchase of Lands to Certain Settlers in the Illinois Territory*, 12th Cong., 2d sess. (February 5, 1813).

36. Application of the Indiana Territory for the Relief to the Purchasers of Public Lands, September 21, 1814, *ASPPL*, 1: 888.

37. Memorial to Congress by Citizens of the Territory, November 26, 1814, *TP*, 8: 318.

38. Petition to Congress by Citizens of Illinois and Indiana Territories, September 30, 1814, *TP*, 17: 29–30.

39. The petitioners' request to purchase shared parts of the same claim was rejected by Congress. See *House Journal*, 9: 463, 525; and 14th Cong., 1st sess., 56, 187. Western politicians and land office agents wrote eastern officials complaining about the restriction to whole sections. See Edward Tiffin to John Caldwell, March 6, 1813, *TP*, 16: 302–303; Sadrach Bond to Tiffin, December 18, 1813, *TP*, 16: 379; Tiffin to Bond, December 20, 1813, *TP*, 16: 388; and Caldwell to Tiffin, June 21, 1814, *TP*, 16: 434–36.

40. Resolution by the Society of True Americans, June 6, 1813, *TP*, 16: 341–43.

41. Petition to Congress by Citizens of the Territory, December 15, 1815, *TP*, 17: 261–63. At least one group of petitioners may truthfully have been prevented from filing claims due to militia service. Several signers of an 1816 petition answered an advertisement in March 1813 that called for volunteers. This was only a month after the preemption act passed through Congress. The implementation of land policies in the West was notoriously slow, so it was possible that these men were unable to file with the local register before they left to join the local Rangers. Petition to Congress by Citizens of the Territory, January 2, 1816, *TP*, 8: 367–68. For the local call for volunteers, see *Indiana Gazette*, March 6, 1813.

42. Madison, "A Proclamation," December 12, 1815, in Richardson, *Compilation of the Messages and Papers of the Presidents*, 2: 557–58.

43. Memorial to Congress by Citizens of the Territory, February 17, 1816, *TP*, 8: 389–90.

44. Petition to Congress by Citizens of the Territory, December 15, 1815, *TP*, 17: 261–63.

45. Memorial to Congress by Citizens of the Territory, January 16, 1816, *TP*, 3: 368–69.

46. Memorial to Congress by Citizens of the Territory, February 1, 1815, *TP*, 8: 331–35.

47. Memorial to Congress by Citizens of the Territory, November 11, 1814, *TP*, 8: 317–19.

48. The House Committee on Pubic Lands summarily rejected these claims and argued that offices had just been opened in the territories to handle the influx of settlers. See Report of the House Committee on Public Lands on Sundry Petitions, January 18, 1816, *TP*, 17: 289.

49. DePauw signed the Petition to Congress by Citizens of the Territory, February 1, 1814, *TP*, 8: 281–82; and Memorial to Congress by Citizens of the Territory, February 17, 1816, *TP*, 8: 389–90. For DePauw's background, see Cockrum, *Pioneer History*, 392; and Carmony, *Indiana*, 30–31.

50. He advertised for town lots in the local newspaper. See *Western Eagle* (Madison), February 11, 1814, and October 24, 1815. For members of the convention, see Kettleborough, *Constitution Making in Indiana*, 1: 83–125; Carmony, *Indiana*, 151–60. At least eight of the forty-one members of the convention signed squatter petitions in the years leading up to statehood.

51. Carmony, *Indiana*, 30–31.

52. Thornbrough and Riker, *Journals of the General Assembly*, 973–77; Cayton, *Frontier Indiana*, 239–40, 246; Cockrum, *Pioneer History*, 392–93; Carmony, *Indiana*, 456–57; Owens, *Mr. Jefferson's Hammer*, 132–35.

53. Thornbrough and Riker, *Journals of the General Assembly*, 1002–1004; Ray, "A Recollection of Dennis Pennington"; and Carmony, *Indiana*, 29, 86, 282, 335. Several counties in Illinois also sent petitioners to their constitutional convention in 1818. See *Illinois Constitutional Convention of 1818*, 327, 341–42.

54. Local officials fined Miles Hotchkiss for repeatedly violating liquor laws at his inns and taverns. In 1805, courts found him delinquent in paying for three tavern licenses; the violations may have eventually led to his removal as coroner for Randolph County. See Philbrick, *The Laws of Indiana Territory*, cxx, cxxxiii, cclxxiv. For Fisher, see ibid., cxx, ccxxx. For Menard, see ibid., cxx, lxxxv–vi.

55. Biggs was appointed sheriff of St. Clair County in 1790, sat on the bench from 1800 until 1806, and served in the territorial legislature from 1805 until 1809. After statehood, Biggs represented St. Clair County in the Illinois legislature. For his background, see Alvord, *Kaskaskia Records*, 445; Cockrum, *Pioneer History*, 341–42; and Philbrick, *The Laws of Indiana Territory*, lxxix n. 3, cclxi.

56. The act establishing the committee can be found *ASPPL*, 1:285–86. Also see 2 STAT 278.

57. Memorial to Congress by Inhabitants of Randolph and St. Clair Counties, December 12, 1804, *TP*, 7: 243–47. The family of at least one of the more than two hundred signers had been murdered by Indians nine years earlier. Indians killed petitioner Robert McMahon's wife and children in 1795 and took him prisoner. He escaped and became a notable community figure, serving for six years as a judge. Reynolds, *The Pioneer History of Illinois*, 193–97; and *Combined History of Randolph, Monroe, and Perry Counties, Illinois*, 67.

58. Confirmed Claims in Kaskaskia District. See *ASPPL*, 2:174–202. For ancient grants, see *ASPPL*, 157–58, 211–14.

59. Treat, *National Land System*, 102, 120; and Alvord, *The Illinois Country*, 419–20.

60. *Combined History of Randolph, Monroe, and Perry Counties, Illinois*, 101; and Alvord, *The Illinois Country*, 420. Alvord says one person told him that a Frenchman sold his claim for a jug of whiskey.

61. Alvord, *The Illinois Country*, 423; and Philbrick, *The Laws of Indiana Territory*, xxiii–xxv.

62. For delinquent taxes, see Philbrick, *The Laws of Indiana Territory*, cxx.

63. Alvord, *The Illinois Country*, 420.

64. *ASPPL*, 2: 138–39, 148–54, 206, 215–17, and 230–38. For an overview of claims and factions, see Philbrick, *The Laws of Indiana Territory*, lxxx–xcv. Indictment quoted in ibid., xciv. For the commissioners' final report, see *ASPPL*, 2: 123–26. Also see Alvord, *The Centennial History of Illinois*, 1: 421; and Treat, *National Land System*, chapter 9. The commission reviewed 197,720 acres worth of John Edgar's claims and rejected over 130,000 acres.

65. On December 2 and 3, 1805, the Edgar-Morrison faction filed two petitions as squatters, asking for land grants and lower prices. They were presented to Congress on January 13, 1806. See *Annals*, 9th Cong., 1st sess., 339; and Philbrick, *The Laws of Indiana Territory*, xxxii n. 1, lxxvi n. 4.

66. Philbrick, *The Laws of Indiana Territory*, lxxxviii; and *ASPPL*, 2: 128, 129, 136.

67. *ASPPL*, 2: 149, 151.

68. Senate, Committee on the Public Lands, "An Exchange of Territory with Any of the Indian Tribes," *Senate Journal*, 14th Cong., 2nd sess., 1817, 3.

69. *House Journal*, 14 Cong., 1st sess., 367.

70. Meigs to Registers of Land Offices [and U.S. Congress], April, 1816, *TP*, 8: 415–16.

71. U.S. Congress, General Land Office, *Letter from the Commissioner of the General Land Office*.

72. *An Act Relating to Settlers on the Lands of the United States*, March 25, 1816, 3 STAT 260–61; and *An Act Concerning Pre-emption Rights Given in the Purchase of Lands to Certain Settlers in the State of Louisiana, and in the Territory of Missouri and Illinois*, April 29, 1816, 3 STAT 330–31.

73. U.S. Congress, House, *Letter from the Chairman of "the Committee on Unsettled Balances."*

74. U.S. Department of the Treasury, *Letter from the Secretary of the Treasury, Transmitting Statements of the Sales of Public Lands during the Year 1817.*

75. Two of the more vocal western politicians on the committee were Christopher Rankin (Mississippi) and Jonathon Jennings (Indiana). Rankin proposed a measure in 1824 for the relief of squatters. See Further Relief to Purchasers of Public Lands, January 12, 1824, *ASPPL*, 3: 641. Jonathon Jennings fought for legislation that specifically targeted groups of illegal settlers in Indiana. See Pre-emption Rights Granted to Certain Settlers in Michigan and Indiana, February 29, 1828, *ASPPL*, 5: 104.

76. Application of Indiana in Relation to Pre-emption Rights, and the Lands Acquired from the Pottawattamie Indians, February 2 and 4, 1833, *ASPPL*, 5: 696; Application of Illinois for the Rights of Pre-emption to Actual Settlers within Her Limits, January 11, 1833, *ASPPL*, 5: 671; Application of Indiana for an Extension of the Act Granting Pre-emption to Actual Settlers, January 14, 1836, *ASPPL*, 8: 383.

77. For congressmen opposing preemption, see Pre-emption Rights, April 23, 1824, *ASPPL*, 3: 720; and Settlers on Public Lands and the Right of Pre-emption, January 18, 1826, *ASPPL*, 4: 332–33. For temporary preemptive legislation in this period, see *An Act to Grant Pre-emption Rights to Settlers on the Public Lands*, 4 STAT 420–21; *An Act Supplementary to an Act to Grant Pre-emption to Settlers on the Public Lands*, 4 STAT 496–97; *An Act Supplementary to the Act "Granting Pre-emption to Settlers on the Public Lands," Approved the Twenty-ninth Day of May, Eighteen Hundred and Thirty*, 4 STAT 603–04; *An Act to Revive the Act Entitled "An Act Supplementary to the Several Laws for the Sale of [the] Public Lands,"* 4 STAT 663–64; and *An Act to Revive the Act Entitled "An Act to Grant Pre-emption Rights to Settlers on the Public Lands," Approved May Twenty-nine, One Thousand Eight Hundred and Thirty*, 4 STAT 678.

78. Jones, *Illinois and the West*, 227.

79. Tatter, *The Preferential Treatment of the Actual Settler*, 276–77.

80. Jones, *Illinois and the West*, 227.

81. Western settlers struggled to defend their masculinity. Early American manhood often was connected to the ownership of personal property, paternal protection of the home, military service, or social deference, but public images of the western settler often portrayed him as intemperate, greedy, profligate, and prone to violence. Political scientist Mark Kann argues that the founding fathers "deployed a grammar of manhood that provided informal rules for stigmatizing disorderly men, justifying citizenship for deserving men, and elevating exceptional men to positions of leadership and political authority." The importance of family lay at the center of constructions of manhood, but the label of banditti or white savage carried connotations that robbed illegal settlers' possibilities for family life. Kann, *A Republic of Men*.

82. Petition to Congress from the Inhabitants of the Scioto, February 1, 1798, *TP*, 2: 638.

83. Petition to Congress by Residents on the East Side of the Scioto River, August 22, 1799, *TP*, 3: 62. For additional examples of these arguments, see Petition to Congress of the Territory, February 20, 1801, *TP*, 3: 122–28; Memorial to Congress by Inhabitants of Randolph and St. Clair Counties, December 12, 1804, *TP*, 7: 243–47; and Petition to Congress by Inhabitants of St. Clair and Randolph Counties, September 15, 1808, *TP*, 8: 591–96.

84. Census information can be found in Woollen, Howe, and Dunn, *Executive Journal of Indiana Territory*, 83. The demographic breakdown for Vincennes mirrored other western communities in the census. In Kaskaskia, 42 percent of the population was under sixteen (this counts forty-seven slaves whose ages were not recorded and may have been under the age of sixteen: if slaves are excluded from the demographic, children under sixteen made up 47 percent of the population—same as Vincennes). The biggest difference in the population of the two land office villages was the ratio of women to men. In Kaskaskia, men outnumbered women nearly two to one. Even the ratio of women over sixteen to men or sixteen was disproportionate, as women only made up 37 percent of the adult population. In Kahokia, 47 percent of the population were children sixteen or younger; men outnumbered women as they did in Kaskaskia (but less than two to one).

85. The Harrison County statistics can be found in Walter S. Beanblossom, "Early Records of Harrison County, Indiana" (census data compiled February 1975), Newberry Library, Chicago. Census data was compared to a database of nearly two thousand signatures compiled by the author. The petitioners in the Harrison County census included William Barnett, Thomas Berry, John Boone, Philip Conrad, Benjamin Crabill, William Davis, George Gresham, John Henson, Richard Heth, Abraham Huff, William Kendall, Dennis Pennington, George J. Pfrimmer, John Pittman, James J. Smith, Jacob Stephens, John Tipton, and Jacob Zenor. Petition to Congress from the Inhabitants of the Scioto, February 1, 1798, *TP*, 2: 638.

86. Onuf, "From Constitution to Higher Law."

87. Saxton, *The Rise and Fall of the White Republic*, 77–83.

88. For the popular image of the rugged and often rancorous "common man," see Hooper, *Adventures of Captain Simon Suggs*; Smith, *My Thirty Years Out of the Senate*; Stott, *History of My Own Times*.

89. Hutton, *A Narrative of the Life of David Crockett, by Himself*, v–lvii; and Heale, "The Role of the Frontier in Jacksonian Politics," 405–23. Crockett eventually abandoned the Democratic Party partly because Democrats in Congress—some from his home state—rejected his squatter legislation. His autobiography was the product of Whig efforts to garner him votes for reelection and a possible bid for the White House. For an older yet still useful account of Crockett, see Shackford

and Folmsby, *A Narrative of the Life of David Crockett of the State of Tennessee.* For the "stage version" of Crockett that propelled him to celebrity, see Tidwell, *The Lion of the West.*

90. *Western Monthly Review* 2 (November 1828): 366. See also "Writers of the Western Country," *Western Monthly Review* 2 (June 1828): 11–13.

91. A good overview of these images can be found in Johns, *American Genre Painting,* 16–17, 62.

92. Flint, "National Character of the Western People," 134–35.

93. Flint, *Recollections of the Last Ten Years,* 128–29. For a scholarly examination of the sharp difference between expectations and reality, see Bushman, *The Refinement of America,* 383–90.

94. For a look at the communal nature of frontier settlement, see Ferrall, *A Ramble of Six Thousand Miles,* 67. On the communal nature of agriculture, see Merrill, "Cash Is Good to Eat"; and Henretta, "Families and Farms." Henretta argues that the family remained the center of western life long after markets began to replace the family as the center of the western economy.

95. The human relationship with the land is discussed in Gates, *The Farmer's Age.* Also see Atack and Bateman, *To Their Own Soil.*

96. *Congressional Globe,* 24th Cong., 2nd sess., 4: appendix, 289, 291. My italics.

97. Ibid., 291.

98. *Congressional Globe,* 25th Cong., 2nd sess., 6: 143.

99. *Congressional Globe,* 24th Cong., 2nd sess., 4: appendix, 289, 291.

100. Tipton gave this speech on the Senate floor on January 24, 1837. A copy of the speech may be found in Riker and Robertson, *The John Tipton Papers,* 349–53.

101. Miller, "Thomas Ewing, Last of the Whigs."

102. Sheraton, *Robert John Walker,* 136.

103. *Congressional Globe,* 25th Cong., 2nd sess., 6: 136

104. Ibid., 436. Congress passed a preemption act in 1838. See *An Act to Grant Pre-emption to the Settlers on the Public Lands,* 4 STAT 251. The measure was retroactive, like its predecessors.

105. Ball, *Lake County, Indiana,* 64–65.

106. Ibid; and Goodspeed and Blanchard, *Counties of Porter and Lake, Indiana,* 405–12. A copy of the Lake County Squatters' Union constitution can be found in Keller, *Solon Robinson,* 1: 68–76.

107. Ibid., 1: 5–7.

108. Much of the information on Robinson's background can be found in Herbert Keller's illuminating biographical introduction to Robinson's papers. See ibid., 1: 5–41.

109. *Madison (Ind.) Republican and Banner,* May 5, 1831.

110. Ibid., October 25, 1831.

111. Ibid., November 21 and November 28, 1833.

112. Ibid., February 13, 1834.

113. Robinson described his move in two articles. See ibid., January 12 and April 30, 1835.

114. Keller, *Solon Robinson*, 1: 51–64.

115. Ibid., 66–70.

116. Ball, *Lake County, Indiana*, 37; and Keller, *Solon Robinson*, 1: 18–20.

117. Before the auction, the Lake County squatters, like many of those who came before them, petitioned Congress for preemption rights. They argued that "all the land that had been offered for sale by the General Government had been taken up by speculators and land jobbers." Robinson was not one of the signers. *Senate Journal*, 25th Cong., 3rd sess., February 23, 1839, 256.

118. Ball, *Lake County, Indiana*, 37.

119. *ASPPL*, 7: 701.

120. Records of the General Land Office, Records of Local Land Offices, 1831–36, Quincy, Illinois, Registers Cash Certificates: 1–9223, Record Group 49, NARA, Great Lakes Region, Chicago.

121. Burr, *The Life and Times of William Henry Harrison*, 15–34, 70–71.

122. Cushing, *Outlines of the Life and Public Services*, 17–24.

123. Jackson, *The Life of William Henry Harrison*, 19–24. Also, see the *Log Cabin Almanac, 1841.*

124. Gunderson, *The Log-Cabin Campaign.*

125. *Indianapolis Semi-Weekly Journal*, April 7, 1840.

126. *Lafayette Free Press*, May 5, 1840.

127. Van Tassel, *Story of Fort Meigs and Other Original Documents*, 31–33.

128. Packard, *History of La Porte County, Indiana*, 210.

129. "A Hint to Travelers," *Indiana Republican*, October 25, 1832.

130. Keppler, *Solon Robinson*, intro.

131. Van Rensselaer, *Funeral Sermon*, 22.

132. Frelinghuysen, "Oration," in *Report of the Committee of Arrangements*, 98; and Haddock, *A Discourse Delivered at Hanover, N.H., May 7, 1841*, 17.

133. *Celebration of the Fifty-seventh Anniversary of the Settlement of Ohio*, 9–10.

CHAPTER 3. "THE LONG LOOKED FOR STORM"

1. Many historians who study American Indian removal tend to either ignore the entire Great Lakes region or underplay the agency of Native peoples in the period leading up to removal by focusing on the "voluntary removal" of Great Lakes Indians. Moreover, scholars often portray Native communities as mere victims of white land lust as they chronicle the details of the Indian removal process; see Wallace, *The Long, Bitter Trail*; Heidler and Heidler, *Indian Removal*, esp. 30–34; Satz, *American Indian Policy in the Jacksonian Era*.

2. White, *The Middle Ground*, 523.

3. Gardiner to Lewis Cass, October 26, 1831, Letters Received by the Office of Indian Affairs, 1824–81, Ohio Agency Emigration, 1831–39; and Gardiner to Cass, January 4, 1832, NARA Microfilm Publications, microcopy, 234: reel 603.

4. Gardiner to Cass, January 4, 1832; Gardiner to Col. Elbert Herring, January 4, 1832; copy of "The Chiefs of the Wyandotte Tribe Whose Names Are Undersigned," enclosed with Gardiner to Lewis Cass, October 26, 1831; and Gardiner to Samuel Hamilton, September 16, 1831, ibid.

5. Gardiner to Cass, January 5, 1832, ibid. Gardiner, desperate to avert failure, proposed that he forge a removal treaty with part of the tribe "willing to treat." Ultimately, he abandoned the idea.

6. Gardiner to Cass, January 4, 1832; and Report of the Wyandot Exploring Delegation, Jan. 28, 1832, ibid. Historians have examined the Wyandot since their dispossession occurred late in the era of Indian removal (1843), but most scholars simply recognize Walker as a "mixed-blood" chief who opposed removal. Historian John Bowes's recent assessment of Great Lakes Indian removal does more to examine Walker's "importance to both Indian and white communities" than previous works, but he focuses primarily on Walker's rise to power following Wyandot emigration westward. Bowes, *Exiles and Pioneers*, 164, 184. Early histories of removal include short examinations of the Wyandot. See Foreman, *The Last Trek of the Indians*. Foreman discusses Walker but at times confuses the son with the father. The *Northwest Ohio Quarterly* recently published an entire issue devoted to the Wyandot in Ohio, but here, too, each article details a different aspect of Wyandot life, Methodist missions, and removal. See *Northwest Ohio Quarterly* 75, no. 2 (2004). Carl Grover Klopfenstein's doctoral dissertation still serves as the authoritative study of the Wyandot in Ohio. While he provides a detailed account of Wyandot removal, Klopfenstein is several generations removed from the current literature on American Indian Studies, and his study contains many instances of antiquated and racist assumptions about Native peoples. See Klopfenstein, "The Removal of the Indians from Ohio."

7. *APSIA*, 1: 575, 580.

8. "Narrative of a Journey to Sandusky, Ohio," 292–95, 321–25, 326. For information on the Presbyterian mission, see Smith, "The Clash of Leadership at the Grand Reserve," 182; and Conover, *Recollections of 60 Years on the Ohio Frontier*, 59.

9. "Narrative of a Journey to Sandusky, Ohio," 326–27.

10. Finley, *History of the Wyandott Mission*, 375–77; and Powell, "Wyandot Government."

11. Lisa Brooks demonstrates how Algonquian tribes of the Great Lakes "conceptualized Native space as a network of villages connected by rivers and relations." This may help explain the perceived disorder by the Quaker missionaries. See Brooks, *The Common Pot*, esp. 106–62.

12. Historian Thelma Marsh spent thirty years conducting an extensive genealogical study of the Wyandot nation. Her work demonstrates the complex web of marriages, intermarriages, and captivities that helped color the Wyandot nation by the early nineteenth century—the Armstrong, Walker, Hicks, Zane, Brown, and Vanmetre families could be traced to late eighteenth-century captivity stories and Henry Jacques and the Williams family to French traders. Methodist missionary James Finley, who served on the Wyandot Reserve in the 1820s, suspected that nearly three-fourths of the Wyandot could trace their lineages to Euro-American ancestors. Finley to Cass, December 15, 1825, Finley Collection (microfilm collection at the Hayes Presidential Library), original copies at OWU. Chiefs Council Resolution, May 2, 1825, quoted in Finley, *Life among the Indians*, 371. Nearly seven hundred note cards containing genealogical information on the Wyandot can be found in the Thelma Marsh Collection, Upper Sandusky County Library, Upper Sandusky, Ohio. A copy of the cards also can be found on microfilm at the Center for Archival Collections, Bowling Green State University Library, Bowling Green, Ohio.

13. Cave, *Prophets of the Great Spirit*, 87, 107; Cave, "The Failure of the Shawnee Prophet's Witch-Hunt," 460–62; and Edmunds, *The Shawnee Prophet*, 46–47.

14. Finley, *History of the Wyandott Mission*, 101–103, 351; Walsh, "The 'Heathen Party'"; and Wallace, *The Death and Rebirth of the Seneca*, 297–98. For an overview of Handsome Lake's message, see Wallace, 303–37.

15. At least one source indicates that Walker attended a mission school in Worthington, south of Lower Sandusky (near modern Sandusky). See Hanacks, *The Emigrant Tribes*, 65.

16. *ASPIA*, 1: 834.

17. Finley, *Life among the Indians*, 239. A similar version, although differently worded, appears in Elliott, *Indian Missionary Reminiscences*, 17. "When Johnston ascertained his errand, he endeavored to dissuade him from undertaking, telling that many wise and learned men had already, to no purpose, preached to the Indians." On the racist attitudes of white outsiders toward Pointer, see Mitchell, *The Missionary Pioneer*, 31; and Finley, *Life among the Indians*, 315–16. Methodist missionary James Finley recollected that Stewart had told him that his parents "claimed to be mixed with Indian blood." See Finley, 234.

18. Finley, *Life among the Indians*, 240–41. Visitors to the Wyandot Grand Reserve in the 1820s recalled older Wyandot who wore silver crosses under their shirts; they also believed that words in the Wyandot language could be traced to Latin roots (evidence of the influence of the Jesuits). See Johnston to Caleb Atwater, October 2, 1843, in Johnston, *Sixty Years*, 58.

19. Finley, *Life among the Indians*, 240–41.

20. Finley, *History of the Wyandott Mission*, 257.

21. Mitchell, *The Missionary Pioneer*, 31.

22. Finley, *Life among the Indians*, 245.

23. Ibid., 257.

24. Ibid., 315–16.

25. Elliott, *Indian Missionary Reminiscences*, 24–25.

26. *ASPIA*, 2: 131–34. The list of individuals who were granted individual reserves included Elizabeth Whitaker, Robert Armstrong, John Vanmeter, the children of William M'Collock, Sarah Williams, Joseph Williams, Rachel Nugent, Catharine Walker, John Walker, and Cherokee Boy.

27. Senators refused to approve stipulations of the treaty that ceded individual plots of land, so another treaty needed to be negotiated the following September along the St. Mary's River in Ohio. Tanner, *Atlas of Great Lakes Indian History*, 159. Also, *ASPIA*, 2: 166.

28. Smith, "The Clash of Leadership on the Grand Reserve," 184.

29. Finley, *Life among the Indians*, 263, 233.

30. Historian Gregory Dowd's work on spiritual resistance in the period immediately preceding 1816 reminds us that Native spiritual movements often included political and social agendas. Additionally, historian Robert F. Berkhofer has argued that missionaries did not separate their spiritual mission from the government-sponsored civilization campaigns that often accompanied missionaries onto Indian lands; neither did Indians. Religion, cultural practices, politics, and economic interests blended together in a symbiotic representation of the larger culture. Berkhofer, *Salvation and the Savage*.

31. Westrick, "The Race to Assimilate."

32. Wallace, *The Death and Rebirth of the Seneca*, 297.

33. Ibid., 277–84, 297–98.

34. Mitchell, *The Missionary Pioneer*, 52–53; and Finley, *Life among the Indians*, 259.

35. Finley, *History of the Wyandott Mission*, 45–46.

36. Ibid., 98. Stewart had not been the first evangelist to draw the confidence of Between-the-Logs. Before the War of 1812, he had followed the message of the Shawnee Prophet, seeing it as an opportunity for personal redemption and a path toward Native revivalism that would rid Great Lakes Indians of the destructive influence of white traders, including alcohol. But he felt betrayed by the failure of the Prophet's spiritual movement in ridding the region of the harmful influence of white traders, and accused the Prophet of failing to follow his own preaching. In fact, he admitted that he first opposed Stewart's attempts at conversion because he thought the black missionary would "be like the others." Ibid., 102–105.

37. Finley, *Life among the Indians*, 236–39; and Elliott, *Indian Missionary Reminiscences*, 21–25, 30.

38. "To the Chiefs the Speakers . . . ," August 16, 1820, James B. Finley Papers, Hayes.

39. Finley, *Life among the Indians,* 324. Historian Daniel Richter demonstrates how the expectations of religious missionaries often shaped their views of the Native peoples they encountered in the early nineteenth century and made it impossible for them to accept the realities that they witnessed once they traveled to indigenous communities. See Richter, "'Believing That Many of the Red People Suffer,'" 601–28.

40. William Walker, Sr., took credit for helping introduce the Wyandots to the Christian Bible. In his preface to *The Missionary Pioneer,* Joseph Mitchell claims that Walker examined John Stewart's Bible and verified to the head chiefs that it was the word of God. According to the preface, the contents for Mitchell's *Missionary Pioneer* were "collected and arranged" by Walker himself. Although Walker chronicled little of his thoughts on Methodism, race, or removal in print during the early nineteenth century (most of his life in Ohio is chronicled in late-life reminiscences or a handful of private correspondence), his fingerprints appear throughout the historical record. Walker was everywhere at the Wyandot Mission; he served a long career as interpreter for the federal government and the local missionaries, he befriended the head missionary at the Reserve and became a close confidant, he served as Lewis Cass's private secretary in the 1810s, he occupied the office of postmaster for nearly a decade and a half, he taught at the missionary school, he ran the mission store, and he attended both the Chiefs Councils and an occasional Methodist Annual Conference.

41. Journal entry, November 15, 1822, in Elliott, *Indian Missionary Reminiscences,* 83. Finley's article is quoted in Cole, *Lion of the Forest,* 48.

42. Johnston to Finley, September 10, 1825; Johnston to Finley, November 5, 1825; and Johnston to Finley, November 30, 1825, OWU. Indian agent John Johnston pushed Finley to remove Indian children from the larger Wyandot community and place them in white homes. He became convinced that unless the Indian scholars were "scattered a *part* of the year in white families," Finley's "labour and expense" would be lost. Johnston led by example: he financed the education of an Indian boy, whom he had named after himself. See Johnston to Finley, December 5, 1825, OWU; and Cole, *Lion of the Forest,* 51. Gardiner accused Johnston of trying to delay the removal of the Shawnee in 1831. See Gardiner to Cass, December 1, 1831, NARA, roll 603.

43. Finley to Martin Ruter, December 19, 1825, Finley Papers, Cincinnati Historical Society. Photocopies of these letters also can be found in the James Finley Papers at the Rutherford B. Hayes Presidential Library, Fremont, Ohio.

44. Lewis Cass to Finley, March 25, 1825, Hayes.

45. McKenney to Finley, September 10, 1825, quoted in Finley, *History of the Wyandott Mission,* 304. Government agents and officials fed confusing and often contradictory information to Finley about Indian removal. John Johnston, who later would push for removal, tried to convince Finley that, despite Cass's assurances, Michigan's territorial governor truly believed that removal was the only

answer. Johnston informed Finley that Cass planned a council at Wapakoneta "on the subject of removing to the west." Johnston to Finley, May 16, 1825, OWU. Circulating rumors about an impending removal caused the managers of the Mission Society to withhold money due to "the uncertain state of things." Thomas Jackson to Finley, April 27, 1825, Hayes.

46. Cass to Finley, February 6, 1826, Hayes; Cass to Finley, February 26, 1826, OWU; and Johnston to Finley, November 30, 1825, OWU.

47. Finley to Ruter, December 19, 1825, Cincinnati Historical Society.

48. Finley to Lewis Cass, December 15, 1825, OWU.

49. Finley, *History of the Wyandott Mission*, 375–77; and Powell, "Wyandot Government."

50. Finley, *History of the Wyandott Mission*, 376–78; and Bowes, *Exiles and Pioneers*, 162–64.

51. Finley, *History of the Wyandott Mission*, 110–11; Chiefs Council, May 2, 1825, and "Chiefs Certificate," January 31, 1826, Hayes.

52. Walker to Finley, May 17, 1824, Hayes. Their friendship may have gone beyond mere formality. Finley believed that he had saved Walker's wife during a particularly difficult childbirth. See Finley to Martin Ruter, February 15, 1825, Cincinnati Historical Society. Letters from Finley to Walker are scarce, but the tone of letters sent to Walker by the Reverend can be understood via Walker's responses. See Walker to Finley, May 21, 1831, Hayes; Walker to Finley, March 15, 1837, OWU.

53. Walker to Finley, May 21, 1831, Hayes.

54. Johnston wrote Finley at the beginning of the year, warning, "The Indians must all leave this country sooner or later this is a position which every reflecting man must assent to." See Johnston to Finley, January 10, 1826, OWU.

55. Walker to Finley, July 15, 1826, OWU.

56. Cass to Finley, March 22, 1826, Hayes. Walker would have been particularly aware of Cass's attitudes on the issue, as he had served as a secretary and aide for Cass around the War of 1812.

57. Chiefs Certificate, January 31, 1826, and Walker to Finley, May 21, 1831, Hayes.

58. Satz, *American Indian Policy in the Jacksonian Era*, 54; Brown, "Lewis Cass and the American Indian," 286–98; Tanner, *Atlas of Great Lakes Indian History*, 136; *General and Local Laws and Joint Resolutions Passed by the General Assembly of Ohio*, 32: 434.

59. Journal of the Proceedings, August and September, 1834; and Robert Lucas to Lewis Cass, March 1835, in Smith, "An Unsuccessful Negotiation for Removal of the Wyandot Indians from Ohio, 1834." See also Lucas to Cass, August 19, 1834; and John McElvain to Lucas, August 27, 1834, in ibid.

60. The Methodist missionary in charge of overseeing the Wyandot mission reported low yields and depleting stores of grain and livestock in his 1835 report.

See Thomas Thompson to the Bishops and Members of the Ohio Annual Conference, August 1835, Hayes. Historian Carl G. Klopfenstein posits a similar argument in "The Removal of the Wyandots from Ohio," 124.

61. Walker to Finley, March 15, 1837, OWU.

62. Walker to Finley, August 8, 1837, OWU.

63. Robert E. Smith, "The Wyandot Exploring Expedition of 1839," 285; petition of William Walker, March 3, 1838, 25th Cong., 2nd sess., HR report 632; Hunter to Crawford, November 6, 1838, NARA, roll 601. Hunter completely misread Walker's intentions as he declared to superiors that Walker worked to oust the non-Christian chiefs and stop removal in order to "remain in the enjoyment of a valuable property."

64. Smith, "The Wyandot Exploring Expedition of 1839," 286; Hunter to Crawford, November 28, 1839, and Articles of a Treaty with the Shawnees, December 18, 1839, NARA, roll 602. For an account of the failed treaty, see Smith, "The Wyandot Exploring Party of 1839." For the removal treaty, see Kappler, *Indian Affairs*, 2: 534–37.

65. Finley, *Life among the Indians*, 325, 405–406.

CHAPTER 4. "LED BY A TOUCH OF ROMANTIC FEELING"

1. George Winter's early life is chronicled in his own words in Thornbrough, *The Journals and Indian Paintings of George Winter*, 17–37.

2. Feest, "G. Winter: Artist"; "Biographical Sketch," in Thornbrough, *The Journals and Indian Paintings of George Winter*, 37–39.

3. Journal, GWMSS, box 1, folder 2, page 1. Subsequent references to boxes, folders, and pages will use this format: 1–2 [1].

4. Winter's journal has been published partially in both Thornbrough, *The Journals and Indian Paintings of George Winter* and *Indians and a Changing Frontier*, but the archivist of the Tippecanoe County Historical Society believes that the published transcriptions were taken as "loose interpretations" of the original journal and "liberties had been taken" with the language. A quick perusal of the journal in the Historical Society's possession reveals these discrepancies. Environmental historian John Hausdoerffer demonstrates how farther west George Catlin similarly "set out to address the ethical conundrum of his times but enacted the very narratives that limited the possibility of ethics." Hausdoerffer, *Catlin's Lament*, 159.

5. Edmunds, "George Winter: Mirror of Acculturation," 23; Sleeper-Smith, *Indian Women and French Men*, 128.

6. For some recent works that explore the removal of Indians in literature and the popular imagination, see Scheckel, *The Insistence of the Indian*; Dippie, *The Vanishing American*; and Maddox, *Removals*.

7. On man's attempt to control nature in the early nineteenth century, see Rose, *Voices of the Marketplace*, esp. 62–72. The *Logansport Telegraph* cited census

numbers on April 16, 1836, that indicated that 3,000 Potawatomis and 1,100 Miamis remained in Indiana.

8. S.J.B., "The Indian," *CCT*, November 16, 1831. The poem was reprinted from the *Daily National Republican* (New York).

9. *LT*, August 30, 1834.

10. *CCT*, February 21, 1833.

11. Tanner, *Atlas of Great Lakes*, 136–37.

12. Winter, letter to editor, *LT*, November 8, 1834. Local citizens also charged agents with corruption and conspiracy to fleece the Indians of their annuity payments. In fact, Winter's first journey into the world of American-Indian affairs centered on an investigation into an Indian payment conspiracy. *LT*, October 15, 22, and 29, 1836, and November 5, 1836.

13. *CCT*, June 2 and 9, 1832.

14. *CCT*, July 14, 1832.

15. *LT*, February 1, 1834. The Winnebago chief Red Bird led a similar resistance movement before being crushed by the American military in 1827. For violence caused by the forced removal of Sac and Fox Indians, see Thomas J. Lappas, "'A Perfect Apollo'"; Josephy, *The Patriot Chiefs*, 213; and Nichols, *Black Hawk and the Warrior's Path*.

16. H. Lasselle, "The Frontier Call," *CCT*, June 9, 1832.

17. Editorial, *CCT*, June 23, 1832, and November 14, 1833. Some westerners took advantage of the tenuous hold of Indians on their lands and tried to purchase reserves directly from local indigenous leaders. See Letters from Ethan A. Brown (General Land Office) to A. C. Pepper, December 18, 1835, Letter Received by the Office of Indian Affairs, 1824–81, NARA Microfilm Publications, M-234; reel 361.

18. For reaction to Miami cession, see *LT*, November 1 and 8, 1834.

19. Census figures were reported in *LT*, April 16, 1836. A third category for western Indians existed: "Number of Indians of the Indigenot [*sic*] Tribes within Striking Distance of the Frontier."

20. "Editorial," *Pottawatomie and Miami Times*, October 10, 1829.

21. "Some May Be Surprised," *Pottawatomie and Miami Times*, October 10, 1829.

22. *LT*, July 18, 1835.

23. *LT*, January 14, 1837.

24. From George Winter's journal found in GWMSS, 1–2. Winter's reactions were not unique; Sleeper-Smith has demonstrated the surprise of federal officials who encountered the unexpectedly large Indian populations of Indiana. See Sleeper-Smith, *Indian Women and French Men*, 96–115. But the artist was not an impartial witness, and evidence Winter left behind should be read cautiously. Many of his self-titled journals were compiled years, even decades, after his arrival in Logansport. More troubling are the lavishly colored oil paintings that

have been used by ethnographers to document specifics about indigenous clothing and jewelry: many of these also were completed decades later from crude
pencil sketches. Winter's work no doubt contributes significantly to our understanding of how westerners attempted to "cleanse," or clear, Indians from the
middle ground, but the evidence is hardly immediate or transparent.

25. Journal, GWMSS, 1–2 [entire].

26. "Face of the Country," *LT*, November 4, 1837.

27. Conn, *History's Shadow*, 56.

28. Many of Catlin's pieces were reproduced in western papers, and Winter
would have been aware of their existence. Catlin began writing articles for the
New York Commercial Advertiser on July 24, 1832. For an overview of Catlin's early
career, see Reddin, *Wild West Shows*, 8–11; and Hausdoerffer, *Catlin's Lament*,
21–49. The rise in western newspaper publication brought along by advances
in publishing technology gave Winter a different outlet for printing his pieces.
While Catlin produced articles for eastern newspapers whose stories were re-
cycled by other periodicals, Winter used his personal connections with local editors to print articles in Indiana, permitting eastern papers to reprint the pieces.
For an overview of the rise of newspaper production in the early nineteenth century, see Humphrey, *The Press of the Young Republic*, 133–54. For additional sources
that examine Catlin's career, see Anderson, "'Curious Historical Artistic Data'";
Truettner, *The Natural Man Observed*, 61–80; and Viola, Crothers, and Hannan,
"The American Indian Genre Paintings of Catlin, Stanley, Wimar, Eastman, and
Miller."

29. *LT*, September 11 and November 4, 1837.

30. *LT*, September 20, 1834.

31. Winter to Pepper, April 10, 1838, GWMSS, 1–4 [4]. Winter also tried unsuccessfully to have his work purchased by the Wisconsin Historical Society and
the congressional committee assigned to decorate the federal capitol. Winter to
Lyman Draper, January 14, 1858, GWMSS, 1–15 [15]; and Winter to Judge W.
Pettit, January 8, 1858, GWMSS, 1–15 [13].

32. For the government market for western art, see Dippie, *Catlin and His
Contemporaries*, 10–46; Reddin, *Wild West Shows*, 6–8; and Sandweiss, "The Pub-
lic Life of Western Art." For Catlin's efforts, see Dippie, "Green Fields and Red
Men" ; and Conn, *History's Shadow*, 55. Catlin had turned down an early offer by
Thomas McKenney and James Hall to join their "Indian Gallery." See Conn, *His-
tory's Shadow*, 54.

33. Cottman, "George Winter, Artist," 111.

34. Edmunds, *The Potawatomis*, 265–69; and Clifton, *The Prairie People*,
298–300.

35. GWMSS 2–33 [1]. Also see GWMSS, 2–33 [5].

36. "Lake Man-i-tou," *LT*, July 21, 1838. For an account of the town meeting,
see GWMSS 2–33 [1].

37. *LT*, July 21, 1838.

38. Trowbridge, "Shawnee Traditions," 60–65; and Trowbridge, "Meēārmeear Traditions," 72–76.

39. Trowbridge, "Meēārmeear Traditions," 58.

40. Joseph Allen Survey Book, 1819, Indiana Historical Society, Indianapolis, Indiana.

41. Saunt, "Telling Stories," 675.

42. *LT*, July 21, 1838. Also see *LT*, August 11 and September 15, 1838.

43. "The Monster," *LT*, July 28, 1838.

44. Brown, "A Natural History of the Gloucester Sea Serpent," 402–36.

45. *LT*, June 10, 1837.

46. Phrenologists used the same system of classification endorsed by the Linnaean Society, who sought to capture the Gloucester sea serpent. Dain, *A Hideous Monster of the Mind*, 9–14, 26–30, 72–75; Regis, *Describing America*, 9–25; Bieder, *Science Encounters the Indian*, 64–83. For phrenology, see Morton, *Crania Americana*. For the connection between Morton and thoughts on Native Americans, see Conn, *History's Shadow*, 168–73. The 1837 western phrenology tour was in anticipation of famed English craniologist George Combe's tour of the United States. See Combe, *Notes on the United States of North America*, esp. vol. 2. Anthropologist Stephen Jay Gould called the observational study of human skulls a "leading science of biological determinism." He demonstrated how both Combe's and Morton's data manipulated their evidence to reinforce preconceived notions about Indians; nineteenth-century American scientists searched for ways to connect the success of the young republic to the superiority of the Anglo-Saxon race. Gould demonstrated that Morton's samples were not equally weighted based on the populations of each subset; instead, the dataset for Native Americans included a disproportional number of smaller South American skulls, while datasets for Euro-Americans included a disproportional selection of abnormally large skulls. In fact, Gould argued that an examination of the subcategories shows that the average Native American skull far exceeded the average white American. A modern manipulation of the data, for example, could demonstrate that indigenous persons had exceedingly large craniums compared with whites, especially if the dataset compared Inuit skulls with Euro-American ones. Gould, *The Mismeasure of Man*, 25.

47. *Boston Transcript*, August 13, 1838; *New-York Mirror*, September 1, 1838; and *Cincinnati Daily Evening Post*, August 18, 1838.

48. *Maysville Sentinel*, reprinted in *LT*, September 15, 1838.

49. For the details of the internal debate within Logansport, see Smalley, "The Logansport *Telegraph* and the Monster of the Indiana Lakes."

50. *LT*, August 11, 1838.

51. "To the Northern Monster," *LT*, July 28, 1838.

52. *LT*, September 15, 1838.

53. Lewis, "Truth or Consequences."

54. "To a Decaying Trunk," July 26, 1838, GWMSS 1–4 [6].

55. *LT*, November 4, 1837; and *Delphi Oracle*, November 11, 1837.

56. For example, see works on J.M.W. Turner, especially Bailey, *Standing in the Sun*, 322–46.

57. Journal of a Visit to Lake Kee-wau-nay, GWMSS, 1–4 [1]. Winter's reports of the Council were published in local newspapers. See *LT*, November 11, 18, and 25, 1837, and December 2, 1837. They were also published in the *Delphi Oracle*, November 11 and 23, 1837.

58. Winter to Pepper, January 7, 1839, GWMSS, 1–4 [8]; Feest, "G. Winter: Artist."

59. Winter to Pepper, January 7, 1839, GWMSS, 1–4 [8].

60. My understanding of Bingham's career relies on Shapiro, Groseclose, Johns, Nagel, and Wilmerding, *George Caleb Bingham*; McDermott, *George Caleb Bingham*; Rash, *The Painting and Politics of George Caleb Bingham*; and Nagel, *George Caleb Bingham*.

61. Sale of Delinquent Lands, *LT*, November 30, 1844.

62. Charles Winter to George Winter, March 16 and 23, 1851, GWMSS, 1–13 [7]; "Biographical Sketch," in Thornbrough, *The Journals and Indian Paintings of George Winter*, 77–80. He earlier begged his brother Thomas to sell lottery tickets for some of his paintings. Thomas Winter to George Winter, September 14, 1846, GWMSS, 1–9 [16].

63. Winter to Rev. T. B. Tefft, October 18, 1849, GWMSS, 1–12 [13].

64. Ibid.

65. Professor Tefft to Northern Indiana Conference, *Logansport Democratic Pharaoh*, December 5, 1849.

66. *LDC*, January 7, 1852; George Winter to Reverend and Dear Sir, January 24 and May 17, 1853, Harlow Lindley Collection, IHS, box 2, folder 2.

67. W. Hubbell to George Winter, March 12, 1849, in GWMSS, 1–12 [8].

68. George Winter to C. B. Lapelle, January 1, 1855, Lindley Collection, IHS, box 2, folder 2. Several unsold distribution tickets can be found in this same folder.

69. Western Art Union, *LT*, October 9, 1847. Most of Winter's income came not from his work with Indians, but from portraits and scenic views that he sold to individuals or offered in the distribution venues that appealed to wider audiences. For information on Winter's lotteries and distributions in Lafayette, Indiana, see GWMSS 1–14 [4, 10, 14–15]; 1–15 [6–7, 11, 18–19]; 1–16 [1, 6, 11]; 1–17 [2–3, 11–18]; 1–18 [2, 16]; 1–19 [1, 12–13]; 1–20 [1–3, 15, 17, 19–39]; 1–21 [1–7, 20b, 22]; 1–22 [2–3, 26]; 1–23 [18]; 1–24 [18–19]; 1–25 [2, 14]; 2–1 [1–10a, 12a-68]; 2–2; 2–3; 2–17 [1]; 2–22 [3]; 2–27 [1]; 2–30 [2]; 2–34 [12, 14]. For distributions in other cities, see 1–10 [8, 15]; 1–11 [3, 9, 11, 14]; 1–12 [2, 11, 20]; 1–13 [11–12, 16, 29–30]; 1–14 [3, 8, 13]; 2–12 [17]; 2–1 [3, 12, 15, 19,

19a, 20a, 25–30]; 2–3; 2–4. For the estimates of Winter's pieces, see 2–1 [5]; 2–1 [6]; 2–1 [12]; 2–1 [17]; 2–1 [22]; 2–1 [24]; 2–1 [25]; 2–1 [30]; 2–1 [38]; *LDC*, February 22, 1851; Winter to Lapelle, January 1, 1855, Lindley Collection, HIS, box 2, folder 2. For Bingham, see Nagel, *George Caleb Bingham*, 23, 38–54, 70–76; McDermott, *George Caleb Bingham*, 48–62, 75–76, 79–80.

70. Distribution Announcement, April, 1852, GWMSS, 2–1 [5]; *LDC*, April 6, 1853. Also see collection of press clippings in 2–1 [1].

71. *LDC*, February 20 and 22, 1851; Winter to Lapelle, January 1, 1855, Lindley Collection, IHS; GWMSS, 2–1 [5], 2–1 [6], 2–1 [24], 2–1 [25], 2–1 [30]. Charles Bruce to George Winter, February 1, 1848, GWMSS, 1–10 [10]. Chapman's *The Chief's Daughter* was copied by many popular artists of the nineteenth century. For a study of how artists copied and redistributed the work of others, see Dippie, *Catlin and His Contemporaries*, 10–46; and Sandweiss, "The Public Life of Western Art."

72. Francis Hegan to Winter, February 1, 1848, GWMSS, 1–10 [11].

73. Harriet Groat and Mary Winter to Winter, June 12, 1848, GWMSS, 1–10 [21]; and Groat to Winter, October 9, 1848, GWMSS, 1–11 [10].

74. GWMSS, 2–35 [6] The actual handwritten account of the story in the archives, as I am told by the curator of the archives, is probably that of Winter's son-in-law, who transcribed many of Winter's original notes.

75. Scheckel, *The Insistence of the Indian*, 139. Other scholars have examined America's fascination with the romanticized Indian princess in the nineteenth century. See Faery, *Cartographies of Desire*, esp. chap. 2; and Tilton, *Pocahontas*, 58–93.

76. For the influence of other Indian artists and ethnographers, see Feest, "G. Winter: Artist," 6. Also see GWMSS, 1–18 [10]. The illustrated journal compiling travels throughout Indian country was common in the early nineteenth century. Steven Conn has argued that these large compendiums of lithographs connected textual and visual representations of Indians, but they often gave simple biographies or reprinted popular ideas that circulated about Native peoples. Conn, *History's Shadow*, 52.

77. GWMSS, 1–15 [13].

78. Journal of a Visit to Deaf Man's Village, GWMSS, 2–23 [26].

CHAPTER 5. "THEY FOUND AND LEFT HER AN INDIAN"

1. The use of the phrase Young Bear as the English translation of Maconaquah is problematic, as researchers and biographers over the years have used "Young Bear," "Little Bear," and "Little Bear Woman." Some more recent biographers use "Little Bear" or "Little Bear Woman." I use Young Bear throughout the following pages because it appears earliest and most frequently in the historical record. Twentieth-century Miamis in Indiana have come to refer to Maconaquah

as Frances Slocum. See Stewart Rafert, comp., Oral History Interviews with Miami Indians of Indiana, IHS (especially interviews with Anthony Goodboo conducted by William Kearney in July 1949 and an interview with descendent Eva Bossley conducted by Stewart Rafert in August 1978). Additionally, the spelling of Mo-con-o-quah, Ma-con-a-quah, Ma-con-o-quah, Moconaquah, or Maconaquah varies, as do most of the indigenous names in the sources. I have, rather arbitrarily, chosen Maconaquah for consistency throughout the text. I also have tried to use the name Maconaquah or Young Bear when talking about the Native person who lived most of her life among the Delawares and Miamis and the name Frances Slocum in instances where others talked about the captive girl or white elderly woman.

    2. This story appeared in several publications in the mid-nineteenth century. See Todd, *The Lost Sister*; Miner, *History of Wyoming*; Lossing, *Pictorial Field Book of the Revolution*, 1: 367–70; and Peck, *Wyoming*. The bulk of the narrative re-created at the beginning of this essay comes from Todd's account (the earliest biography) and the documents and journals reprinted in Phelps, *Frances Slocum*. The earliest accounts include references to her being sick, tired, and perhaps wanting to confess. The paragraph that opens this essay represents a compilation of these narratives in order to introduce the scene at the center of most stories about Frances Slocum. For later nineteenth- and twentieth-century accounts, see Meginness, *Biography of Frances Slocum*; Phelps, *Frances Slocum*; Winger, *The Last of the Miamis*, 21–23; Cottman, "Sketch of Frances Slocum," 119–22; and Minturn, *Frances Slocum of Miami Lodge*. The number of Frances Slocum narratives seems to be ever-expanding, but only a few brief scholarly treatments exist; see Anson, *The Miami Indians*, 211–12; Axtell's extremely brief caption in *The Invasion Within*, 313; Rafert, *The Miami Indians of Indiana*, 102–108; and Sleeper-Smith, *Indian Women and French Men*, 123–27; Sleeper-Smith, "Resistance to Removal." For different versions of Ewing's "discovery" of Slocum, see Lossing, *Pictorial Field Book of the Revolution*, 1: 368; Meginness, *Biography of Frances Slocum*, 37–38; Peck, *Wyoming*, 256–73; Phelps, *Frances Slocum*, 33–50; and Todd, *The Lost Sister*, 101–16.

    3. Ewing, quoted in Todd, *The Lost Sister*, 105–106.

    4. An act that places the captivity story into what Richard Slotkin calls an "archetypal drama." See Slotkin, *Regeneration through Violence*, 94.

    5. Namias, *White Captives*, 9.

    6. Wiegman, *American Anatomies*, 11. This essay is not the first to examine the intersection of race and gender in captivity narratives; June Namias has done an incredible job highlighting connections of race and gender in the story of Mary Jemison—a captivity narrative that appeared slightly earlier than Slocum's story. See "Editor's Introduction," in Namias, *A Narrative in the Life of Mrs. Mary Jemison*; and Namias, *White Captives*. Also see essays in Hodes, *Sex, Love, Race*, especially her introduction.

    7. Brown, *Strangers in Blood*; Clifton, *The Prairie People*; Edmunds, *The Potawatomis*; Murphy, *A Gathering of Rivers*; Sleeper-Smith, *Indian Women and French Men*;

Van Kirk, *Many Tender Ties*; and White, *The Middle Ground*. Also see essays in Barr, *The Boundaries between Us*; and Cayton and Teute, *Contact Points*.

8. Sleeper-Smith, *Indian Women and French Men*, 123, 135.

9. This essay does not intend to read the reality of the "Other" by deconstructing Euro-American texts in the way that other scholars have done. For an example, see Sparks, "The Land Inaccurate," 137. Instead, I explain how and why the Slocum narrative has performed as a tool of the colonial project by connecting examinations of race and gender.

10. Edmunds, "George Winter: Mirror of Acculturation," 23.

11. Thornbrough, *The Journals and Indian Paintings of George Winter*, 157, 160, 161. He believed that the "slight and temporary character" of the indigenous homes demonstrated the evil influence of alcohol and the blighted conditions that too often preceded removal.

12. Ibid., 102, 162–63, 171.

13. Ibid., 167. These multicultural villages existed throughout the region. For an earlier example, see Tanner, "The Glaize in 1792."

14. Here I am speaking about the earliest eyewitness accounts contained in Winter's journal, the Phelps journals, contemporaneous newspaper reports, and the Todd biography (based on primary eyewitness accounts). For details, see Phelps, *Frances Slocum*, 55–56. Also see Todd, *The Lost Sister*, 124–25. Some accounts erroneously place Joseph and Isaac's sister Mary at this scene, but Joseph recounts in a letter that she stayed in Peru, "being old and enfeebled by the long course of years which had glided over her head." Quoted in Phelps, 68. Historian Karen Halttunen argues, "Sentimentalists insisted that true women were constitutionally transparent, incapable of disguising their feelings." See Halttunen, *Confidence Men and Painted Women*, 57.

15. Cottman, "Sketch of Frances Slocum."

16. Thornbrough, *The Journals and Indian Paintings of George Winter*, 177. In 1871, the description was reprinted, verbatim, in the *Philadelphia Press*, and in 1905, it was reprinted as "Winter's Description of Francis [*sic*] Slocum." Westerners often had commented on the physical transformation of Frenchmen who intermingled with Native communities. Timothy Flint, a popular Western writer, told his readers, "The French settle among them, learn their language, intermarry, and soon get smoked to the same copper complexion." See Flint, *Recollections of the Last Ten Years*, 159; Thornbrough, *The Journals and Indian Paintings of George Winter*, 17–37. For an examination of Euro-American fashion and the cross-cultural world of Deaf Man's Village, see Sleeper-Smith, *Indian Women and French Men*, 123–27.

17. These accounts and Frances Slocum's words are taken from two published accounts of her interview. See Phelps, *Frances Slocum*, 59–60; and Todd, *The Lost Sister*, 126–37. The questionability of the interview and its origins are discussed later. Joseph had been warned by Ewing, "She is now, by long habit,

an Indian, and her manners and customs precisely like theirs, yet she will doubtless be happy to see any of you." Ewing to Joseph Slocum, Aug. 26, 1837, copy in Phelps, 43.

18. *Peru Gazette* (Indiana), October 5, 1839.

19. Phelps, *Frances Slocum*, 59–61; and Todd, *The Lost Sister*, 127–28. There is no indication that the Slocum family offered gifts or participated in a reciprocity ceremony when they first arrived at Deaf Man's Village.

20. Phelps, *Frances Slocum*, 62; and Todd, *The Lost Sister*, 139–40.

21. Phelps, *Frances Slocum*, 63; and Todd, *The Lost Sister*, 140–42.

22. Joseph Slocum to W. S. Ross, September 24, 1837, copy in Phelps, *Frances Slocum*, 69–70.

23. Scheckel, *The Insistence of the Indian*, 73. Also see Ebersole, *Captured by Texts*, 110–12. David Haberly, writing about captivity literature, suggests that Indian violence and the perceived drudgery faced by captive women provided an opportunity for men to demonstrate their manliness by performing the role of redeemers. See Haberly, "Women and Indians," 431–44.

24. On captivities and adoption, see Lepore, *The Name of War*, 126–36; Richter, *The Ordeal of the Longhouse*, 64–74; and Wallace, *The Death and Rebirth of the Seneca*, 101–107. For Young Bear's insistence that she was a "half-breed Potawattomie [*sic*]," see Thornbrough, *The Journals and Indian Paintings of George Winter*, 177.

25. For scientific thought on race, particularly Indians, in the nineteenth century, see Bieder, "Scientific Attitudes toward Indian Mixed-Bloods in Early Nineteenth-Century America," 17–30.

26. Rebecca Blevins Faery connects justification of Indian removal to elements of the captivity genre; see Faery, *Cartographies of Desire*, 190–98. For the scientific justifications for white expansion and genetic dominance, see Gould, *The Mismeasure of Man*, 1–29, 39–42; Jacobson, *Whiteness of a Different Color*, 31–38; Smedley, *Race in North America*; and Stanton, *The Leopard's Spots*. The popularity of phrenology and ideals of biological determinism in the Jacksonian era can be traced to Combe, *Notes on the United States of North America during a Phrenological Visit*, 2: 14; and Morton, *Crania Americana*.

27. Faery, *Cartographies of Desire*, 195–96. Anne Marie Plane reminds us that marriage between whites and Indians revealed much about the "struggles between colonists and those whom they sought to colonize." Plane, *Colonial Intimacies*, 4.

28. Quoted in Phelps, *Frances Slocum*, 108.

29. For the background of Miami treaties, see Rafert, *The Miami Indians of Indiana*, 95–101. "List of Names Permitted to Remain in Indiana by Joint Resolution of Congress for the Benefit of Frances Slocum and Her Children and GrandChildren," March 3, 1845, Indians-Crawfordsville Collection, HIS.

30. Meginness, *Biography of Frances Slocum*, 96–99. A copy of the 1838 treaty that granted Slocum and her daughters a reserve around Deaf Man's Village

can also be found in Meginness, 85–91. For copies of the petitions and decisions to allow Slocum's Indian family to remain in Indiana, see Meginness, 125–28, 131–32. For the additional correspondence between Slocum's family and members of Congress, see Phelps, *Frances Slocum*, 110–11, 138–44.

31. Todd, *The Lost Sister*, 126.

32. Ibid., 129.

33. Miner, *History of Wyoming*, 251. Miner's biography (1845) was published shortly after Todd's (1842) and probably relied on the older work for its ba sic story. Lossing's short story, included in the *Pictorial History of the Revolution*, mainly focused on Slocum's capture; the remainder of her life story passes in a few paragraphs.

34. Lossing, *Pictorial Field Book of the Revolution*, 368.

35. In an earlier essay I erroneously dated the piece to 1846, as the date printed on the copy of Sigourney's poems at hand (at that time) appeared to indicate a 1846 publication. Instead, the poem first appeared in Sigourney, *Illustrated Poems* (1849). For the error, see Buss, "'They found and left her an Indian,'" 1.

36. Bennett, *Poets in the Public Sphere*, 59. It's interesting to note here that Bennett also misdates Sigourney's "The Lost Lily." She attributes the poem to Sigourney's collection, *The Western Home and Other Poems*.

37. Baym, *Feminism and American Literary History*, 158.

38. Sigourney, *Illustrated Poems*, 391.

39. Ibid., 394.

40. Ibid., 395.

41. Ibid., 397.

42. Ibid., 396.

43. Ibid., 397.

44. Todd, *The Lost Sister*, 157.

45. For an explanation of the "missing" documents, see Phelps, *Frances Slocum*, introduction.

46. Winter's journal indicates that Deaf Man's Village consisted of far more than one family. For the diversity and size of the village, see Sleeper-Smith, *Indian Women and French Men*, 123–27. The 1845 provision that allowed Young Bear's family to remain in Indiana lists many of those who lived at Deaf Man's Village. The following are the list of Frances Slocum's extended family members granted a reserve and permitted to stay in Indiana. Ages, when documented, are in parentheses. Tah-quah-ke-aw (55), Waw-faw-te-taw (32), Me-con-se-quah—Young Bear (78), Ke-ke-na-kush-wa (43), We-sah-she-no-quah (33), Ke-po-ke-na-mo-quah (33) Waw-faw-noe-shi-no-quah (14), Ki-no-sack-quah (10), Ching-shing-quah (6), Peter Soc-a-to-qaw, Sho-quaq-qaw (12), So-che-ton-qe-saw (11), No-ae-co-mo-quah, Co-che-no-quah, Po-con-de-naw, Tah-he-quah, Ke-ki-o-quah, Te-quock-saw, Jr., Soc-o-chee-quah, Pene-o-ty-ma (22), So-eel-en-qe-saw, Jr., Pung-ge-shi-no-quah.

The following names were added later: Pong-ge-shi-no-quah, Sol-la-no-ge-zah, Wah-pon-ce-pon. For this list, see "List of Names Permitted to Remain in Indiana by Joint Resolution of Congress for the Benefit of Frances Slocum and Her Children and Grand-Children."

47. Uday S. Metha has shown how the redefining of racial categories, in an effort to liberalize societies and expand citizenship, results in the marginalization of some groups while empowering others. Mehta, "Liberal Strategies of Exclusion." For the cultural construction of whiteness and the connections between inclusion and exclusion, see Ignatiev, *How the Irish Became White*; Roediger, *The Wages of Whiteness*; Saxton, *The Rise and Fall of the White Republic*; Sale, "Critiques from Within"; Jacobson, *Whiteness of a Different Color*, 31–38; and Smedley, *Race in North America*.

48. For the popularity of captivity narratives, see Pearce, "The Significance of the Captivity Narrative."

49. Ebersole, *Captured by Texts*, 120. On the sentimentalism of the genre, see Burnham, *Captivity and Sentiment*; Tawil, *The Making of Racial Sentiment*, 94–97; and Derounian-Stodola and Levernfer, *The Indian Captivity Narrative*, 168.

50. For a discussion of the difficulties in defining a "typical" captivity narrative and guidelines on identifying commonalities across the genre, see Scheckel, *The Insistence of the Indian*, 79. John Demos examined similar issues involving Eunice Williams in *The Unredeemed Captive*. Moreover, Demos discusses the difficulties in imagining the lives of captives who have left little record of their lives among Indians.

51. Seaver, *A Narrative of the Life of Mrs. Mary Jemison*. Seaver had a heavy hand in penning Jemison's account. His personal reflections are woven throughout the narrative, making it difficult to distinguish Seaver's thoughts from Jemison's personal account. For the trope of the redeemed and "unredeemed" captive, see Demos, *The Unredeemed Captive*.

52. Namias, *White Captives*, 149. Other scholars have made similar arguments about Jemison as the unredeemed captive. See Kolodny, *The Land before Her*, 68–81; and Slotkin, *Regeneration through Violence*, 450. Early historians and their overt focus on the masculine conquest and "winning of the West" have long distorted our understanding of these relationships. Even early attempts to explore interracial relationships involving Indians focused on masculine constructions of popular opinion. See Smits, "'Squaw Men,' 'Half-Breeds,' and Amalgamators," 29–62.

53. Scheckel, *The Insistence of the Indian*, 74.

54. Tawil, *The Making of Racial Sentiment*, 101.

55. In fact, Todd devotes more pages to the discovery story narrated in the opening paragraphs of this article than to Slocum's fifty-plus years living among the Indians. Conversely, the bulk of Mary Jemison's account chronicles her life living among her Native communities.

56. Todd, *The Lost Sister*, 131.

57. Phelps, *Frances Slocum*, 96–102; Todd, *The Lost Sister*, 130–39.

58. In particular, white men eroticized the indigenous female body to justify the separation of whites and Indians and explain the pressing need to rescue white female captives before they lost their innocence and exposed their vulnerability. See Faery, *Cartographies of Desire*, 176–90. For the history of white infatuation with the Indian body, see Brown, "Native Americans and Early Modern Concepts of Race."

59. Hannah and Harriet's journals are reprinted by one of their descendants; see Phelps, *Frances Slocum*. Hannah's diary was published also in Meginness, *Biography of Frances Slocum*, 101–22.

60. Susan Sleeper-Smith has demonstrated how Americans in the late nineteenth century reshaped multicultural worlds into "white pioneer settlement[s]." Sleeper-Smith, "'[A]n Unpleasant Transaction on This Frontier.'"

61. Meginness, *Biography of Frances Slocum*, 2.

62. Strobel, "Gender and Race," 376.

63. Phelps, *Frances Slocum*, 74–75; Tuan, *Space and Place*, 54. These ideas build off the work of cultural geographers who have examined the imaginative ways that humans impart meaning over physical landscapes. Kent C. Ryden calls the imposition of significance to an area he calls the "invisible landscape." Like Tuan, Ryden argues that "space is primarily two-dimensional, a pattern of locations, a system in which the places of human experience have significance primarily as geometrical coordinates or identical dots on a map. . . . A sense of place results gradually and unconsciously from inhabiting a landscape over time, becoming familiar with its physical properties, accruing a history within its confines." See Ryden, *Mapping the Invisible Landscape*, 37–38.

64. Boydston, *Home and Work*, 142. My thoughts on gendered language and domesticity rely heavily on historians of America before Indian removal. Certainly, gender roles changed between the early days of British colonialism and the mid-nineteenth century, but available theoretical models involving Indian-white marriages, widowhood, and female childhood are rare for this later period. For studies that examine female domesticity in the "colonial" period, see Brown, *Good Wives, Nasty Wenches, and Anxious Patriarchs*; Norton, *Liberty's Daughters*; Kerber, *Women of the Republic*; Lewis, *The Pursuits of Happiness*; Ulrich, *Good Wives* and *A Midwife's Tale*. Scholars of nineteenth-century gender relations (especially tied to religious revivalism) include Cott, *Bonds of Womanhood*; and Ryan, *The Cradle of the Middle-Class*. For an overview of this historiographical debate, see Kerber, "Separate Spheres, Female Worlds, Woman's Place."

65. Amy Kaplan argues, "These spatial and gendered configurations [of white, female domesticity] are linked in complex ways that are dependent upon racialized notions of the foreign." Kaplan, "Manifest Domesticity," 583. Also see Lora Romero, "Vanishing Americans."

66. Phelps, *Frances Slocum*, 74–76, 85. Historian Jeanne Boydston has outlined the cultural construction of gender roles in the early nineteenth century and shown how a heightened importance of household work, combined with the activities associated with motherhood, dramatically defined the role of women in this period. Boydston, *Home and Work*, 142–63. Additionally, Nancy Cott has shown how the home acted as a sanctuary from the outside world, making women into symbols of disinterestedness as they represented a home void of competition. Cott, *Bonds of Womanhood*, esp. 63–100. Cott differentiates between Barbara Welter's idea of "cult of true womanhood" and Aileen S. Kraditor's "cult of domesticity." Margaret Strobel has found in her studies of the British colonial experience that "the task of homemaker and mother [two labels stressed in the Frances Slocum case] had even greater implications for preserving 'civilization' when carried out in the outposts of the empire." See Strobel, "Gender and Race," 381. Also see Welter, "The Cult of True Womanhood, 1820–1860," and Kraditor, *Up from the Pedestal*, 3–28. Welter focuses on the perfection and purity of women as ideals for the nation, while Kraditor examines roles of each family member. Cott agrees with Kraditor much more so than Welter. She acknowledges that women played a role in defining gender roles in the early republic, rather than being objects of a masculine society that independently prescribed familial roles within the "cult of domesticity." Furthermore, Cott argues that the discourse of domesticity prescribed roles for women and men. For other works that have examined the role of women in relationship to the discourse of domesticity, see Ryan, *The Cradle of the Middle Class*; and Stansell, *City of Women*.

67. Phelps, *Frances Slocum*, 85, 86.

68. Namias, *Whites Captives*, 46.

69. Phelps, *Frances Slocum*, 146–47. The last sentence in the quote is an adaptation of Psalms 69:3, as cited on the marker. In the mid-1960s, the United States Army Corps of Engineers moved the cemetery where Young Bear was buried. When they dug under the massive monument, the workers could not find the remains of Young Bear. Instead, they discovered a redwood box containing her son-in-law, Captain Brouillette. Had her indigenous families kept her whereabouts secret after her death to protect her from grave robbers? Had they simply mistaken her gravesite in 1900, when they laid the marker? Workers searched the burial yard, and after finding what they identified as Frances Slocum, reburied her remains under the monument that narrated her dual life stories. Oral History Interview with Herman and Wyneeta Bundy conducted by Stewart Rafert, November 24, 1980, in Oral History Interviews with Miami Indians of Indiana, IHS.

70. Phelps, *Frances Slocum*, 120–23.

71. Ibid., 140–41.

72. Slotkin, *Regeneration through Violence*, 94–115, 121–41.

73. David H. Fowler argues, "Among laws making racial distinctions those prohibiting or penalizing marriage of whites with Negroes have constituted the

most wide-spread form of positive discrimination against non-whites." See Fowler, *Northern Attitudes towards Interracial Marriage*, 7, 147–56.

74. Cott, *Public Vows*, 1. Also see Brown, *Good Wives, Nasty Wives, and Anxious Patriarchs*, 88–94, 334–42; Hartog, *Man and Wife in America*; and Smith-Rosenberg, "Sex as Symbol in Victorian Purity."

75. Fowler, *Northern Attitudes towards Interracial Marriage*. Elise Lemire argues that many stories written about indigenous and white race relations were reflections and lessons about black/white separation, see Lemire, *"Miscegenation,"* esp. 35–86.

76. Fowler, *Northern Attitudes towards Interracial Marriage*, 24–25. For general studies of Indian/white families, see Coontz, *The Social Origins of Private Lives*, esp. 41–72; and Shammas, "Anglo-American Household Government in Comparative Perspective." For the incorporation of whites (male and female) into Indian communities, see Axtell, "The White Indians of Colonial America," 55–88; and Turner, *Beyond Geography*, 244.

77. Perdue, *"Mixed Blood" Indians*, 15.

78. On the focus of the intermarriage between Indian women and white men, see Sleeper-Smith, *Indian Women and French Men*; Brown, *Strangers in Blood*; Van Kirk, *Many Tender Ties*; Van Kirk, "From 'Marrying-In' to 'Marrying-Out,'" 1–11; Peterson and Brown, *The New Peoples*; and Faragher, "The Custom of the Country."

79. Jacobs, "The Eastmans and the Luhans," 32. Katherine Ellinghaus examines the same types of relationships in Australia in "Reading the Personal as Political," 23–41. Also see Hartog, *Man and Wife in America*, esp. 93–135.

80. Sleeper-Smith, "'[A]n Unpleasant Transaction on This Frontier,'" esp. 424–31.

81. Todd, *The Lost Sister*, 138; Meginness, *Biography of Frances Slocum*, 66.

82. Phelps, *Frances Slocum*, 100.

83. According to June Namias, by the 1830s "a culture of delicate femininity had so infiltrated much of the ideology of white middle-class womanhood and an ever-present God had become so modified and removed that for some captive women, most of whom were mothers of small children, the loss of a protective husband brought a sense of overwhelming defenselessness and powerlessness." Namias, *White Captives*, 46.

84. Todd, *The Lost Sister*, 138; Meginness, *Biography of Frances Slocum*, 67; and Phelps, *Frances Slocum*, 101.

85. For studies that highlight the history of widowhood in earlier periods, see Carlton, "The Widow's Tale," 118–29. For studies of widowhood in this period, see Grigg, "Toward a Theory of Remarriage"; Keyssar, "Widowhood in Eighteenth-Century Massachusetts," 99–111.

86. Patricia Grimshaw, studying the colonization of New Zealand, points toward the relationships between aboriginal and European partners as a starting

point for investigating colonial power relationships. Grimshaw argues that these intimate relationships are central to "colonizing white societies' management strategies of subject groups." Likewise, the attempt of American authors to hide or dismiss white-indigenous intermarriage in the case of Frances Slocum was used as a "management strategy" for disempowering the Indian men of Deaf Man's Village. Grimshaw, "Interracial Marriages and Colonial Regimes," 12. For the interconnectedness of sexuality and racist ideologies, see Gilman, *Difference and Pathology*.

87. McClurg, *Miami Indian Stories*, 7.

88. Young Bear's actions are not inconsistent with modern studies of Miami women in the period. Stewart Rafert argues, "Miami women's roles [consequent of the loss of Miami men in war and conflict] were more diverse than those of the pioneer women, and their activities often shocked white observers." Rafert, *The Miami Indians of Indiana*, 103.

89. Winter, "Winter's Description of Frances Slocum," 116–17; and Thornbrough, *The Journals and Indian Paintings of George Winter*, 177. For the sequentially whiter versions of Slocum, see Peck, *Wyoming*, 267; Phelps, *Frances Slocum*, frontispiece; Lossing, *Pictorial Field Book of the Revolution*, 369; and Meginness, *Biography of Frances Slocum*, frontispiece. Chief Clarence Godfroy considered Winter's original oil-on-canvas portrait his "favorite picture of his grandmother." McClurg, *Miami Indian Stories*, 95.

90. The Frances Slocum State Park in Luzeme County, Pennsylvania, includes a lake named after her and park grounds that cover nearly 1,035 acres. Perhaps most interesting, in terms of colonial appropriation and Indian disempowerment, is the high school in Indiana—Maconaquah High School—whose mascot is the Braves.

91. Sleeper-Smith, *Indian Women and French Men*; Edmunds, "George Winter: Mirror of Acculturation"; and Rafert, *The Miami Indians of Indiana*.

92. Peck, *Wyoming*, 65.

CHAPTER 6. "WITH STRONG HANDS AND BRAVE HEARTS"

1. Blight, *Race and Reunion*.

2. Historian Robert Wiebe has described this "distended society" of the late nineteenth century and shown how Americans took great pride in their local communities, even as they were becoming more and more connected to larger national economic and political systems. Alan Trachtenberg extends Wiebe's premise in explaining how "new hierarchies of control" came to reshape American culture and society, effectively creating a sense of national culture. See Wiebe, *The Search for Order*; and Trachtenberg, *The Incorporation of America*.

3. Ulysses S. Grant and Congress, "A Centennial Proclamation," joint resolution, May 25, 1876, copy accessed in John Brown Dillon Papers, ISL, box 1.

4. Dillon, "Address to the Public at Indianapolis Centennial Celebration," July 4, 1876, in Dillon Scrapbook, Dillon Papers, ISL, box 2.

5. "The Centennial: Address to the People of Ohio by the State Board of Centennial Managers," 1876, Hayes, T 825 57.

6. *Final Report of the Ohio State Board of Centennial Managers*, 5.

7. Ibid., 65.

8. *Address of Hon. A. P. Edgerton of Fort Wayne*, 17.

9. Ibid., 4.

10. Ibid., 11–17.

11. Ibid.

12. Ibid., 5.

13. *History of Allen County, Indiana*. These organizations reflect the deep pride that Americans took in their local communities, as discussed by Wiebe in *The Search for Order*.

14. Clinton County, Indiana, defined "Old Settlers" as those who came prior to 1826; Defiance County, Ohio, not until 1846; Henry County, Indiana, 1825; Allen County, Indiana, 1840.

15. *An Account of the Celebration of American Independence, at Clay Lick*.

16. Bassett, *Inaugural Address of the Mad River Valley Pioneer and Historical Association*, 1–4.

17. *History of Henry County, Indiana*, 254.

18. Lears, *No Place of Grace*.

19. *History of Clinton County, Indiana*, 283.

20. *Address of Hon. R. C. Parsons*, 6.

21. *Address of W. W. Andrews*, 6.

22. *Twenty-eighth Report of the Indiana State Board of Agriculture, 1878*, 20: 376.

23. Prospective members filed their names and address with the Pioneer Association at the beginning of the meeting. Of the 761 applying for membership, 718 reported their age. See the *Twenty-eighth Report of the Indiana State Board of Agriculture, 1878*, 20: 410–21.

24. C. H. Test, "Opening Address," in ibid., 20: 379, 380. The society met in a permanent exposition hall built for annual fairs, following cities like Cincinnati. See "The Indiana Fair," *Manufacturer and Builder* 5, no. 8 (August 1873): 172.

25. Test, "Opening Address," in ibid., 20: 382–83, 386.

26. Dillon, "Mr. Dillon's Address," in *Twenty-eighth Report of the Indiana State Board of Agriculture*, 20: 397–98.

27. Test, "Opening Address," 382–83.

28. Indiana Historical Society, constitution, quoted in Ruegamer, *A History of the Indiana Historical Society*, 29–30.

29. Ruegamer, *A History of the Indiana Historical Society*, 45–47, 71–73.

30. *Twenty-ninth Report of the Indiana State Board of Agriculture, 1879*, 21: 496.

31. *History of Clinton County, Indiana*, 283. For pioneer and old settler societies,

see Powell, *History of Cass County, Indiana*, 1: 393–402; *History of DeKalb County, Indiana*, 417–21; *History of Grant County, Indiana; History of Henry County, Indiana*, 253–57; *History of Elkhart County, Indiana*, 360; *History of Allen County, Indiana.*

32. *Twenty-ninth Report of the Indiana State Board of Agriculture, 1879*, 21: 500.

33. Circular from Jas. Robinson, N. S. Townsend, and A. A. Graham, February 1885, in Albert Adams Graham Papers, OHS.

34. Circular Sent to Prospective Members from the Ohio State Archaeological and Historical Society, [1885], in ibid.

35. Ibid.

36. "To the School Children," December 1885, Graham Papers, OHS.

37. Circular from Jas. Robinson, N.S. Townsend, and A. A. Graham, February 1885, and Circular Sent to Prospective Members from the Ohio State Archaeological and Historical Society, [1885], Graham Papers, OHS.

38. Mrs. D. L. Nielson to Graham, January 25, 1885; Isaac Smucker to Graham, February 16, 1885; Wells to Graham, March 2, 1885; A. W. Jones to Graham, March 5, 1885; A. W. Munson, March 5, 1885, all in OHS, Director's Office, 1885–1916, OHS, series 4005, box 1, folder 1. Most of these letters were direct responses to the circular distributed by Graham. The circular contained a form for local organization leaders to fill out. The letters above represent extended individual responses, while the folder contains many more respondents who simply filled out the form and returned it. Graham also received support from other state historical societies. The secretary of the Minnesota Historical Society, J. Fletcher, a transplanted Ohioan, wished Graham success and sent him copies of the Minnesota Historical Society's constitution and bylaws on February 16, 1885.

39. *Magazine of Western History* to Graham, March 3, 1885, ibid.

40. The celebration of local history rather than state or national commemorations may have been a reflection of the resistance of rural island communities in the early Gilded Age to accept their incorporation into the larger, market-driven economy and political society. Wiebe, *The Search for Order*, esp. chapter 2.

41. *Ninety-fifth Anniversary of the Settlement of Ohio, at Marietta*, 4, 9.

42. Ibid., 4.

43. *Centennial Souvenir of Marietta, Ohio*, 10.

44. *Oration Delivered by George F. Hoar*, 5.

45. The translation is taken from English, *Conquest of the Country*, 774. Thomas Hallock translates it differently as "a better one has replaced it." Hallock, *From the Fallen Tree*, 10.

46. English, *Conquest of the Country*, 774.

47. Dunn, *Indiana and Indianans*, 376.

48. Ibid., 378–79. Also see Bennett, "Indiana's State Seal," http://www .in.gov/history/2804.htm.

49. "The Memorial Structure at Marietta," 222, 225; and "Proceedings of the Third Annual Meeting held at Marietta, April 5th and 6th, 1888," 332.

50. "Annual Address of President F. C. Sessions," 145, 148; and "Proceedings of the Third Annual Meeting Held at Marietta," 334–35.

51. *Address of General Thomas Ewing at the Centennial Celebration at Marietta*, 2.

52. Glassberg, *American Historical Pageantry*. Also, see Bellah, "Civil Religion in America," 1–21. For worries about progress, see Welter, "The Idea of Progress in America"; and Ekirch, *The Idea of Progress in America*; Lears, *No Place of Grace*.

53. "Remarks of Hon. Samuel F. Hunt," 93.

54. Ruegamer, *A History of the Indiana Historical Society*, 80.

55. Coburn, *Life and Services of John B. Dillon*, 39–62.

56. Duncan, "Old Settlers," 396. The Society published volume 2 of their *Publications* eleven years prior to publishing volume 1. See Ruegamer, *A History of the Indiana Historical Society*, 84–86.

57. Tebbel, *A History of Book Publishing*, 2: 511–20, 532–33.

58. Filby, *A Bibliography of American County Histories*, ix. For an earlier estimate, see Peterson, comp., *Consolidated Bibliography of County Histories in Fifty States*.

59. Van Tassel, *Recording America's Past*, 171–79. *History of Washington County, Ohio*, 9–12 cites Parkman's history of the French experience in New World. For the rise of historical professionalism as a reaction to romanticism, see Conn, *History's Shadow*, 200–229. A historiographical debate exists about the meaning of romanticism, and if historians, as writers, have always been romantics. See White, *Metahistory*; and Berkhofer, *Beyond the Great Story*.

60. *History of Allen County, Indiana*, preface; Powell, *History of Cass County, Indiana*, 1: preface; Blanchard, *Counties of Clay and Owen, Indiana*, preface; Blanchard, *Counties of Howard and Tipton, Indiana*, preface; Goodspeed and Blanchard, *County of Williams, Ohio*, preface; *Counties of LaGrange and Noble, Indiana: Historical and Biographical*, preface; Montgomery, *History of Jay County, Indiana*, x; and Aldrich, *History of Henry and Fulton Counties, Ohio*, preface; Wilson, *History of Dubois County from Its Primitive Days to 1910*.

61. Others cited congressional journals, General Land Office records, and diaries, see *A History and Biographical Cyclopedia of Butler County, Ohio*, 2–4; and Ball, *Lake County, Indiana*, frontispiece; *History of Clinton County, Indiana*, preface; *History of Franklin and Pickaway Counties, Ohio*, 7; *History of Henry County, Indiana*, preface; Beardsley, *History of Hancock County*, 3.

62. *History of Defiance County, Ohio*, preface; *Early Life and Times of Boone County, Indiana*, 5; *History of Grant County, Indiana*, preface; *History of Darke County, Ohio*, preface.

63. Tebbel, *A History of Book Publishing*, 2: 511–33. In 1887, the Lewis Brothers tried to incorporate Inter-State, but they discovered another company had already taken the name. Therefore, after 1887, their company changed names to Lewis Publishing Company. They published as lest twelve county histories in Indiana alone. A history of the Williams brothers can be found in the frontispiece of reprint of *History of Washington County, Ohio*.

64. For examples of the "History of Indiana," see *History of Clinton County*, *History of Elkhart County, Indiana*, and *History of Grant County, Indiana.*

65. Graham, "History of Ohio," 17, 18–19, 127. For examples of the "History of Ohio," see Goodspeed and Blanchard, *County of Williams, Ohio; History of Marion County, Ohio; History of Brown County, Ohio;* and *History of Hardin County, Ohio.* Graham's "History of Ohio" appeared in his self-published Hill, *History of Coshocton County, Ohio;* Hill, *History of Knox County, Ohio;* and Hill, *History of Licking County, Ohio.* Also see *History of Crawford County, Ohio;* Perrin and Battle, *History of Logan County and Ohio; History of Morrow County, Ohio.*

66. *History of Clinton County, Indiana*, 245. For examples of this type of treatment for the pioneer, see *History of Allen County, Indiana*, 46–56; Williams, *History of Ashtabula County, Ohio*, 20–26; *History of Clinton County, Ohio*, 246–47, 278; *History of Crawford County, Ohio*, 205–93; *History of DeKalb County, Indiana*, 267–69; *History of Franklin and Pickaway Counties, Ohio*, 38–174; *History of Geauga and Lake Counties, Ohio*, 20–24; *History of Henry County, Indiana*, 250; Blanchard, *Counties of Howard and Tipton, Indiana*, 11; Banta, *A Historical Sketch of Johnson County, Indiana*, 9; *History of Knox and Daviess Counties, Indiana*, 87–90; *Biographical and Historical Record of Kosciusko County, Indiana*, 630; *History of Ross and Highland Counties, Ohio*, 44, 56; *History of St. Joseph County, Indiana*, 370; *History of Wyandot County, Ohio*, iii, 302–304.

67. Miller, *History of Allen County, Ohio*, 23.

68. *History of Henry County, Indiana*, 252; *History of Darke County, Ohio*, 263; Beardsley, *History of Hancock County, Ohio*, 11; *History of Miami County, Ohio*, 15.

69. Ford and Ford, *History of Hamilton County, Ohio*, 64.

CHAPTER 7. "A MELANCHOLY BUT NECESSARY DUTY"

1. "Joint Resolution Declaring the True Intent and Meaning of the Act Approved May Twenty-eighth, Eighteen Hundred and Eighty-eight," approved July 16, 1888, copy found in SIA, RU 70, Exposition Records of the Smithsonian Institution and the United States National Museum, 1875–1919, box 92.

2. Gardner, comp., *Catalogue of the Exhibit;* R. Edward Earll, "Report upon the Exhibit of the Smithsonian Institution, Including the United States National Museum, as the Centennial Exposition of the Ohio Valley and Central States, Held at Cincinnati, Ohio, in 1888," SIA, RU 70, Exposition Records of the Smithsonian Institution and the United States National Museum, 1875–1919, box 29, 1–3. For the history of fairs in Cincinnati, see Spiess, "Exhibitions and Expositions." Goshorn served as exposition director in 1871 and 1872.

3. "Cincinnati Exposition," *Manufacturer and Builder* 5, no. 11 (November 1873): 242

4. "The Cincinnati Exhibition," *Manufacturer and Builder* 11, no. 11 (November 1879): 260.

5. "Cincinnati Exposition," *Manufacturer and Builder* 20, no. 4 (April 1888): 90.

6. Earll, "Report upon the Exhibit," 2.

7. For the history of fairs in Cincinnati, see Spiess, "Exhibitions and Expositions." Cincinnati, St. Louis, and Chicago competed in the late nineteenth century to become the region's metropolitan center. See Cronon, *Nature's Metropolis*.

8. "Ohio's Centennial Exposition, 1788–1888: Circular No. 1," Hayes Presidential Center Pamphlets, F491.6 O37 1888, no. 2; and Earll, "Report upon the Exhibit," 3–4.

9. "Act Authorizing Participation by the Government Departments and Bureaus," approved May 28, 1888; "Joint Resolution Declaring the True Intent and Meaning of the Act Approved May Twenty-eighth, Eighteen Hundred and Eighty-eight," approved July 16, 1888. An overview of the legislation, including copies of the bills, acts, and resolutions, related to the Centennial Celebration can be found in Earll, "Report upon the Exhibit," 5–17; and Centennial Exposition of the Ohio Valley, April 25, 1888, report to accompany H.R. 9711, United States House of Representatives, 50th Cong., 1st sess., Report 1958, 2, 5, 10, 12.

10. Rydell, *All the World's a Fair*, 25.

11. Giberti, "The Classified Landscape," 1–2.

12. Steven Conn calls this "object-based epistemology." Conn, *Museums and American Intellectual Life*, 4, 5.

13. "Centennial Exposition of the Ohio Valley," April 25, 1888, report to accompany H.R. 9711, United States House of Representatives, 50th Cong., 1st sess., Report 1958, 2, 5, 10, 12; Earll, "Report upon the Exhibit," 71.

14. Earll, "Report upon the Exhibit," 18, 20, 21–22; R. E. Earll, "Report upon the Participation of the Smithsonian Institution in the Ohio Valley and Central State Centennial Exposition," SIA, RU 70, box 29, 1, 3.

15. Gardner, *International Exhibition*, 120, 125–31. When the first train cars arrived on June 28, 1888, Smithsonian officials found the annex where the materials would be displayed unfinished. Workers unloaded the train and stored the crates in the main building. Two days later, the building was completed, and forty-five men, including Earll, Morrill, and the curators, hurriedly unpacked the boxes and began assembling the exhibits. The team of workmen worked from sunrise until late into the night but could not complete the task before the fair began on July 4, 1888. In fact, no department had completely finished their exhibits when the gates of the fair opened; it took nearly a month before the exhibits were finished.

16. Earll, "Report upon the Exhibit," 26–28.

17. Earll, "Report upon the Participation," 5.

18. Earll, "Report upon the Exhibit," 32.

19. Ibid., 33; also see O. T. Mason to W. V. Cox, June 13, 1888, SIA, RU 70, box 28.

20. Earll, "Report upon the Exhibit," 31–32. Also see Thomas Wilson, "Description of Exhibit Made by the Department of Prehistoric Anthropology in the National Museum at the Ohio Valley and Central States Exposition in Cincinnati, Ohio, 1888," in *Proceedings of the United States National Museum*, Volume 11: Appendix.

21. Tyler, *Primitive Culture*, 1: 28

22. "Lamarckianism in America Social Science," in Stocking, *Race, Culture, and Evolution*, 240. On the influence of anthropology and American thoughts about Indians, see Berkhofer, *The White Man's Indian*, 52–55; Conn, *History's Shadow*, 154–97; Conn, *Museums and American Intellectual Life*, 77, 89; Eggan, "Lewis Henry Morgan and the Study of Social Organization" ; Pearce, *Savagism and Civilization*, 130–34; and Trachtenberg, *The Incorporation of America*, 35–37.

23. Earll, "Report upon the Participation," 7; Cosmos Mindeleff to R. E. Earll, September 28 and October 6, 1888, SIA, RU 70, box 28; Earll, "Report upon the Exhibit," 35–36.

24. Earll, "Report upon the Participation," 17.

25. J. Elfreth Watkins, "Contributions of the Development of Transportation and Engineering to the Ohio Valley Centennial Exhibition, 1888," in *Proceedings of the United States National Museum*, Volume 11: Appendix, 1–2, 15.

26. "Cincinnati Exposition," *Manufacturer and Builder* 20, no. 4 (April 1888): 90.

27. Earll, "Report upon the Exhibit," 25–26.

28. Ibid., 28–29.

29. Dillon, *The National Decline of the Miami Indians*, 140–41.

30. Ibid.

31. Ibid., 142.

32. Ibid., 142–43.

33. Ibid., 143.

34. Dillon, *A History of Indiana*; and Coburn, "Life and Services of John B. Dillon."

35. Dillon, *A History of Indiana*, v.

36. Cottman, "John Brown Dillon," 4–8.

37. Trachtenberg, *Shades of Hiawatha*, xxii. For an overview of the Gilded Age that explores these tensions, but places "greater stress on continuities across the period," see Edwards, *New Spirits*. Also see the essays in Calhoun, *The Gilded Age*.

38. *History of Franklin and Pickaway Counties, Ohio*, 8.

39. The quote and story cited here is from "History of Indiana," 111–16. The same version of the "History of Indiana," a common history of the Hoosier state, appeared in numerous county histories in the late nineteenth century, including *History of Clinton County, History of Elkhart County, Indiana*, and *History of Grant County, Indiana*. At least three publishing companies used the standard account: Inter-State Publishing, Charles C. Chapman, and Brant and Fuller. In almost all

of these cases, the "History of Indiana" maintained its original pagination. Subsequent citations simply refer to "History of Indiana," which can be found in any of the above-mentioned county histories.

40. Cave, "The Shawnee Prophet, Tecumseh, and Tippecanoe," 671.

41. "History of Indiana," 126.

42. For the Black Hawk chapter, see ibid., 126–30.

43. Ibid., 131–32.

44. The "History of Indiana" borrowed from many early nineteenth-century sources. For example, the accounts of land sales that followed the section on Potawatomi removal came directly from Stanford Cox's often unreliable accounts of public land auctions in the 1820s. See ibid., 133–34.

45. *History of Wyandot County, Ohio*, 224.

46. Ibid., iii.

47. Ibid., 274.

48. Quotes from *History of Franklin and Pickaway Counties, Ohio*, 9, 207–209. For additional county histories that included similar accounts, see Blanchard, *Counties of Howard and Tipton, Indiana*, 11; Ford and Ford, *History of Hamilton County, Ohio*, 21; Blanchard, *Counties of Clay and Owen, Indiana*, 11–26, 553; *History of Muskingum County, Ohio*, 26; *History of Clermont County, Ohio*, 3. For more examples of the treatment of the Mound Builders, see Williams, *History of Ashtabula County, Ohio*, 16–20; *History of Clark County, Ohio*, 244–46; Hill, *History of Coshocton County, Ohio*, 180–93; *History of Crawford County, Ohio*, 184–88; *History of Hardin County, Ohio*, 215–32; Perrin and Battle, *History of Logan County and Ohio*, 185; *History of Madison County, Ohio*, 215–29; *History of Marion County, Ohio*, 233–34; *History of Muskingum County*, 3, 9–26; *History of Ross and Highland Counties, Ohio*, 20–31; Perrin, *History of Summit County*, 207–11.

49. Harrison, *A Discourse on the Aborigines*, 10.

50. Conn, *History's Shadow*, 121.

51. Thomas, *Report of the Mound Exploration of the Bureau of American Ethnology*.

52. *History of Allen County, Indiana*, 17.

53. The "History of Indiana" could be found in *History of Clinton County, Indiana*; *History of Elkhart County, Indiana*; *History of Grant County, Indiana*; and *History of Henry County, Indiana*.

54. *History of Hardin County, Ohio*, 257.

55. Ibid., 258.

56. Barber, *Early History of Greene County, Indiana*, 1.

57. *History of Brown County, Ohio*, 220

58. Montgomery, *History of Jay County, Indiana*, ix.

59. *History of Champaign County, Ohio*, preface.

60. *History of Henry County, Indiana*, 257.

61. Barber, *Early History of Greene County, Indiana*, 2.

62. Montgomery, *History of Jay County, Indiana*, ix.

63. For the emphasis on these events as turning points, see *History of Allen County, Indiana*, 39–41; Williams, *History of Ashtabula County, Ohio*, 11–12; Blanchard, *Counties of Clay and Owen, Indiana*, 26–27; *History of Clermont County, Ohio*, 36–37; *History of Defiance County, Ohio*, 83; *History of Franklin and Pickaway Counties, Ohio*, 35; Ford and Ford, *History of Hamilton County, Ohio*, 34; *History of Hardin County, Ohio*, 251–53; Blanchard, *Counties of Howard and Tipton, Indiana*, 25–31; *History of Knox and Daviess Counties, Indiana*, 582–86; *History of Ross and Highland Counties, Ohio*, 54; *History of Sandusky County, Ohio*, 87–89; *History of Brown County, Ohio*, 251; Perrin, *History of Summit County*, 225; Beardsley, *History of Hancock County, Ohio*, 9; *History of Champaign County, Ohio*, 230–31.

64. *History of Allen County, Indiana*, 23

65. *History of Morrow County, Ohio*; and Ford and Ford, *History of Hamilton County, Ohio*, 64.

66. Beardsley, *History of Hancock County, Ohio*, 9.

67. *History of Darke County, Ohio*, 225.

68. Ibid., 249.

69. *Historical and Biographical Record of Wood County, Ohio*, 26–27. For additional histories that marked the 1818 St Mary's Treaty as the end of an Indian presence in the region, see *History of Henry County, Indiana*, 3; Barber, *Early History of Greene County, Indiana*, 1–2; *History of Franklin and Pickaway Counties, Ohio*, 30.

70. Perrin, *History of Summit County*, Ohio, 207.

71. Perrin and Battle, *History of Logan County and Ohio*, 193.

72. Caldwell, *History of Belmont and Jefferson Counties, Ohio*, 22.

73. Hill, *History of Ashland County, Ohio*, 7.

74. *History of Clinton County, Indiana*, 277.

75. Hill, *History of Coshocton County, Ohio*, 193; *History of Darke County, Ohio*, 243. N. H. Hill, Jr., made the same predictions in his 1881 *History of Knox County, Ohio*, 178 and *History of Licking County, Ohio*, 198. See also Beardsley, *History of Hancock County, Ohio*, 195; *History of Hardin County, Ohio*, 234; and *History of Marion County, Ohio*, 242–43.

76. *History of Franklin and Pickaway Counties, Ohio*, 8.

77. Roosevelt, *The Winning of the West*, 1: 104.

78. *History of Brown County, Ohio*, 225.

EPILOGUE

1. Randall, *Ohio Centennial Anniversary Celebration at Chillicothe*, viii.

2. Ibid., iv.

3. "An Act to encourage the holding of the Ohio Centennial and Northwest Territory Exposition at the city of Toledo, Ohio," SIA, RU 70, box 93.

4. Notes from Smithsonian Institution Report for 1899, SIA, RU 70, box 92.

5. Randall, *Ohio Centennial Anniversary Celebration at Chillicothe*, viii.

6. Ibid., 29.

7. Ibid., 50.

8. Ibid., 61.

9. Ibid., 71.

10. Ibid., 72.

11. Ibid., 73.

12. Ibid., 90.

13. Ibid., 162.

14. Ibid.

15. Ibid., 212.

16. Ibid., 213.

17. Ibid., 548.

18. "Governor Ralston at Corydon Centennial Celebration," June 2, 1916, SMR Papers, box 6, folder June 1–15, 1916.

19. Orin Walker to Ralston, March 24, 1915, SMR Papers, box 4, folder March 21–31, 1915.

20. "Proposed Fetes for the Centennial," *Indianapolis Star*, March 28, 1915.

21. Ralston to Frank Guthrie, September 16, 1915, SMR Papers, box 5, folder September 11–20, 1915.

22. "A Public Statement by the Governor," August 27, 1915, SMR Papers, box 5, folder August 26–31, 1915.

23. "An Imposture," n.d., William L. Barker Mss., box 3, folder 1.

24. "To the Indiana Historical Commission," September 10, 1915, SMR Papers, box 5, folder September 1–10, 1915.

25. Harlow Lindley to Ralston, SMR Papers, December 9, 1916, box 7, folder December 9–10, 1916.

26. Lindley, *The Indiana Centennial, 1916*, 33.

27. Proclamation, October 13, 1916, SMR Papers, box 7, folder September 26–30, 1916.

28. Lindley, *The Indiana Centennial, 1916*, 34.

29. *Suggestive Plans for a Historical and Educational Celebration in Indiana in 1916*, 9.

30. Ibid., 18.

31. Ibid., 30.

32. Ibid., 30–31. For Woodburn's chronological timetable, also see Woodburn, *The Indiana Centennial*.

33. Quoted in Glassberg, *American Historical Pageantry*, 78. Glassberg states that Langdon used this quote often to describe the role of his pageants. According to Ethel Rockwell, who compiled a bibliography of pageantry in America, Langdon defined it as "a dream of a community in which the place is the hero and history is the plot." Rockwell, "Historical Pageantry," 5.

34. Lindley, *The Indiana Centennial, 1916*, 36.

35. Ibid., 39.

36. Langdon, *The Pageant of Corydon*; and Langdon, *The Pageant of Bloomington and Indiana University*.

37. McReynolds, "The Centennial Pageant for Indiana," 248–49.

38. Ibid., 266–67.

39. Glassberg, *American Historical Pageantry*, 143. This particular quote is in direct reference to the centennial pageant held in Fort Wayne, Indiana.

40. Anderson, *The Owen County Centennial Pageant*.

41. Langdon, *The Pageant of Bloomington*, 7–10.

42. Meek and Miller, *Decatur County Pageant*, 22.

43. Ibid., 34.

44. *Program of the Cass County Celebration of Indiana's Statehood Centennial*.

45. Lindley, *The Indiana Centennial, 1916*, 204.

46. Ibid., 206. For another account of the Miami pageant, see "The March of Pageantry Indiana," 1916, William Barker Mss., box 3, folder 1.

47. Meeting of the Illinois State Centennial Commission, March 1916, Schmidt Papers, folder 3.

48. Minutes of the Illinois Centennial Commission, November 19, 1913, ibid.

49. "Illinois Centennial Celebration," 74.

50. For the visit to Indiana, see minutes of the Centennial Commission, September 21, 1916, and minutes, October 18, 1916, Schmidt Papers, folder 3.

51. Illinois Centennial Commission to the Members of the Senate and House of Representatives, November 30, 1916, ibid.

52. Minutes, July 9, 1917, ibid.; *Centennial Bulletin*, no. 2, November 1917, Rice Papers, folder 162.

53. *Centennial Bulletin*, no. 5, February 1918, Rice Papers, folder 162.

54. *Centennial Bulletin*, no. 9, October 1918, ibid.; Rice, *The Masque of Illinois*.

55. Rice, *Masque of Illinois*, 4–10.

56. Ibid., 11.

57. Ibid., 12–15.

58. *Centennial Bulletin*, no. 2, November 1917, Rice Papers.

59. Minutes, October 24, 1918, Schmidt Papers, folder 4.

60. Report of the Centennial Commission, 1918, ibid.

61. For a larger discussion of this concept of people without histories, see Klein, "In Search of Narrative Mastery."

Bibliography

ARCHIVAL SOURCES

Beinecke Rare Book and Manuscript Library, Yale University, New Haven, Connecticut
    Guy Johnson Papers
    U.S. Office of Indian Affairs. Piqua Agency. Account and Memorandum Book.
Center for Archival Collections, Bowling Green State University Library, Bowling Green, Ohio
    Thelma Marsh Papers (Microfilm Collection)
Chicago Historical Society
    Otto Schmidt Papers
Cincinnati Historical Society, Cincinnati, Ohio
    James B. Finley Papers
Houghton Library, Harvard University, Cambridge, Massachusetts
    Henry Hamilton Collection
Indiana Historical Society, Indianapolis
    Cauthorn-Stout Family Papers
    Harlow Lindley Collection
    Indians-Crawfordsville Collection
    Joseph Allen Survey Book
    John Armstrong Papers
    Miami Indian Oral History Interviews
    Taylor Berry Mss
    William Hayden English Mss
Indiana State Library, Indianapolis
    Allen Hamilton Family Papers
    Francis Godfroy Papers

General Court of Indiana Territory
  John Brown Dillon Papers
  Order Book of the General Court of Indiana Territory, 1801–10
  William Barker Mss
Lilly Library, Indiana University, Bloomington
  Niles Mss
  Samuel Moffitt Ralston Papers
  William Henry Harrison Mss
Michigan State University Archives Historical Collections, East Lansing
  Buzzard Family Papers, Correspondences, 1844–1849
National Archives and Records Administration-Great Lakes Region, Chicago
  Records of the General Land Office. Record Group 49
  Newberry Library, Chicago
  Ayers Collection
  Graff Collection
  Posey and Gibson County Court Records
  Wallace Rice Papers
Ohio Historical Society, Columbus
  Albert Adams Graham Papers
  A. Griswold Family Papers
  Jared Mansfield Papers
  Ohio Historical Society, Director's Office, 1885–1916
  Thomas Worthington Papers
Ohio Wesleyan University, Delaware
  James B. Finley Papers
Rutherford B. Hayes Presidential Library, Fremont, Ohio
  James B. Finley Papers
  Rutherford B. Hayes Collection
Smithsonian Institution Archives, Washington, D.C.
  Exposition Records of the Smithsonian Institution and the United States
    National Museum, 1875–1916. Record Unit 70.
Tippecanoe County Historical Society, Lafayette, Indiana
  George Winter Mss
Upper Sandusky County Library, Upper Sandusky, Ohio
  Thelma Marsh Papers

NEWSPAPERS AND OTHER PERIODICALS

American Pioneer (Cincinnati)
American Republic (Frankfort, Ky.)
Cass County Times (Logansport, Ind.)

Centinel of the Northwest Territory (Cincinnati)
Crockett Almanack (Nashville, Tenn.)
Daily Courier (Lafayette, Ind.)
Daily Evening Post (Cincinnati)
Daily National Republican (New York)
Daily Student (Bloomington, Ind.)
Delphi Oracle (Delphi, Ind.)
Democratic Pharaoh (Logansport, Ind.)
Franklin Repository (Franklin, Ind.)
Harper's New Monthly Magazine (New York)
Independent Chronicle (Boston)
Indiana Gazette (Vincennes, Ind.) [IG]
Indiana Republican (Madison, Ind.)
Indianapolis Semi-Weekly Journal
Indianapolis Star (Indianapolis, Ind.)
Kentucky Gazette (Lexington, Ky.)
Lafayette Free Press (Lafayette, Ind.)
Log Cabin Almanac
Logansport Canal Telegraph (Logansport, Ind.)
Logansport Telegraph (Logansport, Ind.)
Manufacturer and Builder (New York)
Massachusetts Centinel (Boston)
Massachusetts Spy (Worcester)
Missouri Gazette (St. Louis)
New York Commercial Advertiser (New York)
New-York Mirror
Peru Gazette (Peru, Ind.)
Pottawatomie and Miami Times (Delphi, Ind.)
Providence Gazette (Providence, R.I.)
Republican and Banner (Madison, Ind.)
Sentinel (Maysville, Ohio)
Transcript (Boston)
U.S. Gazette
United States Democratic Review (New York)
Western Eagle (Madison, Ind.)
Western Intelligencer (Worthington, Ohio)
Western Monthly Review (Cincinnati)
Western Spectator (Indianapolis)
Western Spy (Cincinnati)
Western Sun (Vincennes, Ind.)

GOVERNMENT DOCUMENTS

Letters Received by the Office of Indian Affairs, 1824–81, Ohio Agency Emigration, 1831–39, National Archives Microfilm Publications, Microcopy 234, reel 603

Letters Received by the Office of Indian Affairs, 1824–1881, National Archives Microfilm Publications, M-234, reel 361.

U. S. Congress. General Land Office, *Letter from the Commissioner of the General Land Office, Transmitting an Estimate of the Number of Acres of Land to Which Preemption Rights Have Been Granted, and a Statement of the Differences in the Amount of Moneys for Lands Sold at Public Auction, and at Private Sale.* Washington, D.C.: William Davis, 1816.

U.S. Congress. House. *Letter from the Chairman of the Committee on Unsettled Balances, to the Comptroller of the Treasury, and the Answer of the Comptroller Thereto, Relative to the Usage of the Treasury upon the Subject of Such Balances Remained Unsettled for Three Years, April 24, 1816.* Washington, D.C.: n.p., 1816.

U.S. Department of State. *Compendium of the Enumeration of the Inhabitants and Statistics of the United States from the Returns of the Sixth Census.* Washington, D.C.: Government Printing Office, 1841.

U.S. Department of Treasury. *Letter from the Secretary of the Treasury, Transmitting Statements of the Sales of Public Lands during the Year 1817, and the Three First Quarters of the Year 1818, December 21, 1818.* Washington, D.C.: E. De Krafft, 1818.

PUBLISHED PRIMARY SOURCES

An Account of the Celebration of American Independence at Clay Lick, by the Licking County Pioneers, Together with an Address, by Dr. Coulter, on Early Times in the Clay Lick Settlements, also, Historical Sketches of the Townships of Licking, Bowling Green, Franklin, and Hopewell by Isaac Smucker. Newark, Ohio: Clark and King, 1869.

Address of General Thomas Ewing at the Centennial Celebration at Marietta, Ohio, July 15th, 1888, of the Settlement of the Northwest Territory. Marietta, Ohio: For the Woman's Centennial Association of Marietta, 1888.

Address of Hon. A. P. Edgerton of Fort Wayne, Ind., at the Annual Meeting of the Williams, Defiance, and Paulding Counties, O., Old Settlers' Association, held at Hicksville, Defiance Co., September 11, 1878. Hicksville, Ohio: Thomas A. Starr Book and Commercial Printer, 1878.

Address of Hon. R. C. Parsons, before the Pioneer Association, at North Solon, Ohio, August 30, 1876. Cleveland: Leader, 1876.

Address of W. W. Andrews, before the Pioneer Association of Cuyahoga County, at North Solon, Ohio, September 5, 1877. Cleveland: DeVeny, 1877.

Aldrich, Lewis Cass, ed. *History of Henry and Fulton Counties, Ohio, with Illustrations and Biographical of Its Prominent Men and Pioneers.* Syracuse, N.Y.: D. Mason, 1888.

Alvord, Clarence Walworth. *The Illinois Country, 1673–1818.* Springfield: Illinois Centennial Commission, 1920.

———, ed. *Kaskaskia Records, 1778–1790.* Springfield: Trustees of the Illinois Historical Library, 1909.

Alvord, Clarence Walworth, et al., eds. *Collections of the Illinois State Historical Library.* 26 vols. Springfield: Illinois Historical Society, 1905–34.

American Society for Promoting the Civilization of the Indian Tribes in the United States. *The First Annual Report.* New Haven, Conn.: Printed for the Society by S. Converse, 1824.

———. *A New Society for the Benefit of Indians: Constitution and Circular.* New Haven, Conn.: n.p., 1822.

Anderson, Carl. *The Owen County Centennial Pageant.* N.p., 1916.

"Annual Address of President F. C. Sessions." *Ohio Archaeological and Historical Quarterly* 2, no. 1 (June 1888): 144–48.

Austin, Frederick, ed. *Personal Narrative of Travels in Virginia, Maryland, Pennsylvania, Ohio, Indiana, Kentucky; and of a Residence in the Illinois Territory, 1817–1818 by Elias Pym Fordham.* Cleveland: Arthur H. Clark, 1906.

Ball, Timothy Horton. *Lake County, Indiana, from 1834 to 1872.* Chicago: J. W. Goodspeed, 1873.

Banta, D. D. *A Historical Sketch of Johnson County, Indiana.* Chicago: J. H. Beers, 1881.

Barber, Uncle Jack. *Early History of Greene County, Indiana, as Taken from the Official Records, and Compiled from Authentic Recollections, by Pioneer Settlers, Embracing All Matters of Interest Connected with the Early Settlement of the County, from 1813 to 1875.* Worthington: N. B. Milleson, 1875.

Bassett, A. H. *Inaugural Address of the Mad River Valley Pioneer and Historical Association: Delivered at Its Organization, May 2, 1870.* Mad River Valley Pioneer and Historical Association, 1870.

Beardsley, D. B. *History of Hancock County, Ohio, from Its Earliest Settlement to the Present Time.* Springfield, Ohio: Republic, 1881.

Biographical and Historical Record of Kosciusko County, Indiana. Chicago: Lewis, 1887.

Blanchard, Charles, ed. *Counties of Clay and Owen, Indiana: Historical and Biographical.* Chicago: F. A. Battey, 1884.

———. *Counties of Howard and Tipton, Indiana: Historical and Biographical.* Chicago: F. A. Battey, 1883.

Burr, S. J. *The Life and Times of William Henry Harrison.* New York: L. W. Ransom, 1840.

Caldwell, J. A. *History of Belmont and Jefferson Counties, Ohio, and Incidentally Historical Collections Pertaining to Border Warfare and the Early Settlement of the Adjacent Portion of the Ohio Valley.* Wheeling, W.Va.: Historical, 1880.

Carter, Clarence Edwin, ed. *The Territorial Papers of the United States.* 28 vols. Washington, D.C.: Government Printing Office, 1934–75.

Celebration of the Fifty-seventh Anniversary of the Settlement of Ohio, April 8, 1844. Cincinnati: E. Morgan, 1844.

Celebration of the Forty-seventh Anniversary of the First Settlement of the State of Ohio, by Native Citizens. Cincinnati: Lodge, L'Hommedieu, 1835.

Centennial Souvenir of Marietta, Ohio: Settled April Seventh, 1788; Celebration, April Seventh, 1888. Marietta: E. R. Alderman & Sons, 1888.

Coburn, John. *Life and Services of John B. Dillon.* Indianapolis: Bowen-Merrill, 1886.

Combe, George. *Lectures on Phrenology.* New York: James P. Giffing, 1841.

———. *Notes on the United States of North America during a Phrenological Visit in 1838–9–40.* 2 vols. Philadelphia: Carey and Hart, 1841.

Combined History of Randolph, Monroe, and Perry Counties, Illinois, with Illustrations Descriptive of Their Scenery and Biographical Sketches of Some of Their Prominent Men and Pioneers. Philadelphia: J. L. McDonough, 1883.

Conklin, Julia S. *The Young People's History of Indiana.* Indianapolis: Bobbs-Merrill, 1899.

Conover, Charlotte Reave, ed. *Recollections of 60 Years on the Ohio Frontier: Including Accounts of Notable Ohio Indians, Examples of the Shawnee and Wyandot Languages, and Manners and Customs of the Tribes.* Dayton, Ohio: John Henry Patterson, 1915.

Cottman, George. "George Winter, Artist: The Catlin of Indiana." *Indiana Quarterly Magazine of History* 1, no. 3 (1905): 111–14.

———. "John Brown Dillon." *Indiana Quarterly Magazine of History* 1, no. 1 (1905): 4–8.

———. "Sketch of Frances Slocum." *Indiana Quarterly Magazine of History* 1, no. 3 (1905): 118–22.

Counties of LaGrange and Noble, Indiana: Historical and Biographical. Chicago: F. A. Battey, 1882.

Cuming, Fortescue. *Sketches of a Tour to the Western Country, through the States of Ohio and Kentucky; A Voyage down the Ohio and Mississippi Rivers.* Pittsburgh: Cramer, Spear, and Eichbaum, 1810.

Cushing, Caleb. *Outlines of the Life and Public Services, Civil and Military, of William Henry Harrison.* Boston: Weeks, Jordan, 1840.

Cutler, Julian Perkins, and William Parker Cutler, eds. *Journals and Correspondence of Rev. Manasseh Cutler.* Cincinnati: Robert Clarke, 1888.

Cutler, Manassah. *An Explanation of the Map Which Delineates That Part of the Federal Lands, Comprehended between Pennsylvania West Line, the Rivers Ohio and Scioto, and Lake Erie; Confirmed to the United States by Sundry Tribes of Indians, in the Treaties of 1784 and 1786, and Now Ready for Settlement.* Salem, Mass.: Dabney and Cushing, 1787.

Dawson, Moses. *Historical Narrative of the Civil and Military Services of Major-General William H. Harrison.* Cincinnati: M. Dawson, 1824.

Dillon, John Brown. *A History of Indiana, from Its Earliest Explorations by Europeans, to the Close of the Territorial Government in 1816.* Indianapolis: William Sheets, 1843.

———. *The National Decline of the Miami Indians.* Indianapolis: Bowen-Merrill, 1897.

Drake, Benjamin. *Life of Tecumseh, and of His Brother the Prophet.* Cincinnati: Anderson, Gates & Wright, 1858.

Drake, Daniel. *Discourse on the History, Character, and Prospects of the West: Delivered to the Union Literary Society of Miami University, Oxford, Ohio, at Their Ninth Anniversary, September 23, 1834.* Cincinnati: Truman and Smith, 1834.

Duncan, Robert. *Old Settlers.* Indiana Historical Society Publications 2, no. 10. Indianapolis: Bowen-Merrill, 1894.

Dunn, Jacob Piatt. *Indiana and Indianans: A History of Aboriginal and Territorial Indiana and the Century of Statehood.* Chicago: American Historical Society, 1919.

Dwight, Timothy. *Recollections of the Last Ten Years, Passed in Occasional Residences and Journeyings in the Valley of the Mississippi.* Boston: Cummings, Hilliard, 1826.

Early Life and Times of Boone County, Indiana, Giving an Account of the Early Settlement of Each Locality, Church Histories, County and Township Officers from the First Down to 1886; Histories of Some of the Pioneer Families of the County. Lebanon, Ind.: Harden and Spahr, 1887.

Elliott, Charles. *Indian Missionary Reminiscences, Principally of the Wyandot Nation: In Which Is Exhibited the Efficacy of the Gospel in Elevating Ignorant and Savage Men.* New York: Mason and Lane, 1837.

English, William Hayden. *Conquest of the Country Northwest of the River Ohio, 1778–1783.* Indianapolis: Bowen-Merrill, 1896.

Esarey, Logan, ed. *Governors Messages and Letters: Messages and Letters of William Henry Harrison.* 2 vols. Indianapolis: Indiana Historical Commission, 1922.

Evans, Estwick. *A Pedestrious Tour, or Four Thousand Miles, through the Western States and Territories, during the Winter and Spring of 1818.* Concord, Mass.: Joseph C. Spear, 1819.

Fearon, Henry Bradshaw. *Sketches of America: A Narrative of a Journey of Five Thousand Miles through the Eastern and Western States of America.* London: Longman, Hurst, Orme, and Brown, 1818.

Ferrall, S. A. *A Ramble of Six Thousand Miles through the United States of America.* London: Effingham Wilson, 1832.

Final Report of the Ohio State Board of Centennial Managers to the General Assembly of the State of Ohio. Columbus, Ohio: Nevins and Myers, 1877.

Finley, James B. *History of the Wyandott Mission.* Cincinnati: J. F. Wright, 1840.

———. *Life among the Indians; or, Personal Reminiscences and Historical Incidents Illustrative of Indian Life and Character.* Cincinnati: Curts and Jennings, 1857.

Fitzpatrick, John C., ed., *The Writings of George Washington.* 39 vols. Washington, D.C.: Government Printing Office, 1938.

Flint, James. *Letters from America, Containing Observations on the Climate and Agriculture of the Western States, the Manners of the People, the Prospects of Emigrants, &c. &c.* Edinburgh: Printed for W. & C. Tait, 1822.

Flint, Timothy. "The National Character of the Western People." *Western Monthly Review,* July 1827, 133–39.

———. *Recollections of the Last Ten Years, Passed in Occasional Residences and Journeyings in the Valley of the Mississippi.* Boston: Cummings, Hilliard, 1826.

Ford, Henry, and Kate Ford, comps. *History of Hamilton County, Ohio, with Illustrations and Biographical Sketches.* Cleveland: L. A. Williams, 1881.

Gardner, Dorsey, ed. *International Exhibition, 1876: Grounds and Buildings of the Centennial Exhibition, Philadelphia.* Washington, D.C.: Government Printing Office, 1880.

Gardner, M., comp. *Catalogue of the Exhibit of the Department of the Interior for the Centennial Exposition of the Ohio Valley and Central States, Cincinnati, Ohio, July 4 to October 27, 1888.* Washington, D.C.: R. Beresford, 1888.

General and Local Laws and Joint Resolutions Passed by the General Assembly of Ohio, vol. 32. Columbus, 1834.

Glascock, Will H. *Young Folks' Indiana: A Story of Triumphant Progress.* Chicago: Scott, Foresman, 1898.

Goodspeed, Weston A., and Charles Blanchard, eds. *Counties of Porter and Lake, Indiana.* Chicago: F. A. Battey, 1884.

———. *County of Williams, Ohio: Historical and Biographical.* Chicago: F. A. Battey, 1882.

Haddock, Charles B. *A Discourse Delivered at Hanover, N.H., May 7, 1841, on the Occasion of the Death of William Henry Harrison.* Windsor, Vt.: Tracy and Severance, 1841.

Hall, James. *Sketches of History, Life, and Manners, in the West.* Philadelphia: H. Hall, 1835.

Hall, James, and Thomas McKenney. *History of the Indian Tribes of North America, with Biographical Sketches and Anecdotes of the Principal Chiefs.* Philadelphia: D. Rice and J. G. Clark, 1842–44.

Harris, Thaddeus Mason. *The Journal of a Tour into the Territory Northwest of the Alleghany Mountains: Made in the Spring of the Year 1803.* Boston: Manning and Loring, 1805.

Harrison, William Henry. *A Discourse on the Aborigines of the Valley of the Ohio.* Cincinnati: Cincinnati Express, 1838.

Harvey, Henry. *History of the Shawnee, from the Year 1681–1854.* Cincinnati: Ephraim Morgan and Sons, 1855.

Heckewelder, John. *History, Manners, and Customs of the Indian Nations, Who Once*

Inhabited Pennsylvania and the Neighboring States. Philadelphia: Publication Fund of the Historical Society of Pennsylvania, 1876.

Hildreth, Samuel P. *Pioneer History: Being an Account of the First Examinations of the Ohio Valley, and the Early Settlement of the Northwest Territory.* Vol. 1. Cincinnati: H. W. Derby, 1848.

Hill, George William. *History of Ashland County, Ohio, with Illustrations and Biographical Sketches.* Cleveland: Williams Brothers, 1880.

Hill, N. H., Jr., comp. *History of Coshocton County, Ohio: Its Past and Present, 1740–1881.* Newark, Ohio: A. A. Graham, 1881.

———. *History of Knox County, Ohio: Its Past and Present.* Mt. Vernon, Ohio: A. A. Graham, 1881.

———. *History of Licking County, Ohio: Its Past and Present.* Newark, Ohio: A. A. Graham, 1881.

Historical and Biographical Record of Wood County, Ohio: Its Past and Present. Chicago: J. H. Beers, 1897.

History and Biographical Cyclopedia of Butler County, Ohio, with Illustrations and Sketches of Its Representative Men and Pioneers. Cincinnati: Western Biographical, 1881.

History of Allen County, Indiana, with Illustrations and Biographical Sketches of Some of Its Prominent Men and Pioneers. Chicago: Kingman Brothers, 1880.

History of Brown County, Ohio, Containing a History of the County; Its Township, Towns, Churches, Schools, Etc.; General and Local Statistics; Portraits of Early Settlers and Prominent Men; History of the Northwest Territory; History of Ohio; Map of Brown County; Constitution of the United States; Miscellaneous Matters, Etc. Chicago: W. H. Beers, 1883.

History of Champaign County, Ohio, Containing a History of the County; Its Cities, Towns, Etc.; General and Local Statistics; Portraits of Early Settlers and Prominent Men; History of the Northwest Territory; History of Ohio; Map of Champaign County; Constitution of the United States, Miscellaneous, Matters, Etc., Etc. Chicago: W. H. Beers, 1881.

History of Clark County, Ohio, Containing a History of the County; Its Cities, Towns, Etc. Chicago: W. H. Beers, 1881.

History of Clermont County, Ohio, with Illustrations and Biographical Sketches of Its Prominent Men and Pioneers. Philadelphia: Louis H. Everts, 1880.

History of Clinton County, Indiana, Together with Sketches of Its Cities, Villages, and Towns, Educational, Religious, Civil, Military, and Political History, Portraits of Prominent Persons, and Biographies of Representative Citizens. Chicago: Inter-State, 1886.

History of Crawford County, Ohio. Chicago: Baskin and Battey, 1881.

History of Darke County, Ohio, Containing a History of the County; Its Cities, Towns, Etc. Chicago: W. H. Beers, 1880.

History of Defiance County, Ohio. Chicago: Warner, Beers, 1883.

History of DeKalb County, Indiana, Together with Sketches of Its Cities, Villages, and Towns, Educational, Religious, Civil, Military, and Political History, Portraits of Prominent Persons, and Biographies of Representative Citizens. Chicago: Inter-State, 1885.

History of Elkhart County, Indiana; Together with Sketches of Its Cities, Villages, and Townships, Educational, Religious, Civil, Military, and Political History; Portraits of Prominent Persons, and Biographies of Representative Citizens. Chicago: Charles C. Chapman, 1881.

History of Franklin and Pickaway Counties, Ohio, with Illustrations and Biographical Sketches, of Some of the Prominent Men and Pioneers. Cleveland: Williams Brothers, 1880.

History of Geauga and Lake Counties, Ohio, with Illustrations and Biographical Sketches of Its Pioneers and Most Prominent Men. Philadelphia: Williams Brothers, 1878.

History of Grant County, Indiana, from the Earliest Time to the Present, with Biographical Sketches, Notes, Etc., Together with an Extended History of the Northwest, the Indiana Territory, and the State of Indiana. Chicago: Brant and Fuller, 1886.

History of Greene and Sullivan Counties, State of Indiana, from Its Earliest Time to the Present; Together with Interesting Biographical Sketches, Reminiscences, Notes, Etc. Chicago: Goodspeed Brothers, 1884.

History of Hardin County, Ohio. Chicago: Warner, Beers, 1883.

History of Henry County, Indiana, Together with Sketches of Its Cities, Villages, and Towns. Chicago: Inter-State, 1884.

History of Knox and Daviess Counties, Indiana: From the Earliest Times to the Present; with Biographical Sketches, Reminiscences, Notes, Etc. Chicago: Goodspeed, 1886.

History of Madison County, Ohio. Chicago: W. H. Beers, 1883.

History of Marion County, Ohio, Containing a History of the County; Its Local Statistics; Military Record; Portraits of Early Settlers and Prominent Men; History of the Northwest Territory; History of Ohio; Miscellaneous Matter, Etc. Chicago: Leggett, Conaway, 1883.

History of Miami County, Ohio, Containing a History of the County. Chicago: W. H. Beers, 1880.

History of Morrow County, Ohio. Chicago: O. L. Baskin, 1880.

History of Muskingum County, Ohio, with Illustrations and Biographical Sketches of Prominent Men and Pioneers. Columbus, Ohio: J. F. Everhart, 1882.

History of Ross and Highland Counties, Ohio, with Illustrations and Biographical Sketches. Cleveland: Williams Brothers, 1880.

History of Sandusky County, Ohio, with Portraits and Biographies of Prominent Citizens and Pioneers. Cleveland: H. Z. Williams and Brothers, 1882.

History of St. Joseph County, Indiana; Together with Sketches of Its Cities, Villages, and Townships, Educational, Religious, Civil, Military, and Political History; Portraits of Prominent Persons, and Biographies of Representative Citizens. Chicago: Charles C. Chapman, 1880.

History of Washington County, Ohio; with Illustrations and Biographical Sketches. 1881; reprint, Knightstown, Ind.: Bookmark, 1976.

History of Wyandot County, Ohio. Chicago: Leggett, Conaway, 1884.

Hooper, Johnson Jones. *Adventures of Captain Simon Suggs, Late of the Tallapoosa Volunteers; Together with "Taking the Census" and Other Alabama Sketches.* With an introduction by Johanna Nicol Shields. Tuscaloosa: University of Alabama Press, 1993.

Hulbert, Archer Butler, ed. *The Records of the Proceedings of the Ohio Company.* Marietta, Ohio: Marietta Historical Commission, 1917.

Hulbert, Archer Butler, and William Nathaniel Schwarze, eds. *David Zeisberger's History of the Northern American Indians.* Columbus: Ohio State Archaeological Society, 1910.

"Illinois Centennial Celebration." *Journal of the Illinois State Historical Society* 9, no. 1 (April 1916): 70–76.

Illinois Constitutional Convention of 1818. Springfield: Illinois State Historical Society, 1894.

Illinois State Historical Society. *Transactions of the Illinois State Historical Society for the Year 1901.* Springfield: By authority of the Board of Trustees of the Illinois State Historical Library, 1901.

Imlay, George. *A Topographical Description of the Western Territory of North America.* London: Printed for J. Debrett, 1792.

Jackson, Isaac R. *The Life of William Henry Harrison, (of Ohio), the People's Candidate for the Presidency.* Philadelphia: Marshall, Williams & Butler, 1840.

Jones, A. D. *Illinois and the West with a Township Map Containing the Latest Survey and Improvements.* Boston: Weeks, Jordan, 1838.

"Journal of an Emigrating Party of Pottawatomie Indians, 1838." *Indiana Magazine of History* 21 (1925): 315–36.

Keller, Herbert Anthony, ed. *Solon Robinson: Pioneer and Agriculturist.* 2 vols. Indianapolis: Indiana Historical Bureau, 1936.

Knopf, Richard C., ed. *Anthony Wayne: A Name in Arms; Soldier, Diplomat, Defender of Expansion Westward of a Nation.* Pittsburgh: University of Pittsburgh Press, 1960.

———, ed. *Campaign into the Wilderness: The Wayne-Knox-Pickering-McHenry Correspondence.* Columbus: Ohio Historical Society, 1955.

Langdon, William Chauncy. *The Pageant of Bloomington and Indiana University: The Educational Development of Indiana as Focused in This Community and Served by the State University.* Bloomington: William Chauncy Langdon, 1916.

———. *The Pageant of Corydon: The Pioneer Capital of Indiana, 1816–1916.* New Albany, Ind.: Baker's Printing House, 1916.

———. *The Pageant of Indiana: The Drama of the Development of the State as a Community from Its Exploration by La Salle to the Centennial of Its Admission to the Union.* Indianapolis: Hollenbeck Press, 1916.

Lindley, Harlow, ed. *Indiana as Seen by Early Travelers: A Collection of Reprints from Books of Travel, Letters, and Diaries prior to 1830.* Indianapolis: Indiana Historical Commission, 1916.

———, ed. *The Indiana Centennial, 1916: A Record of the Celebration of the One Hundredth Anniversary of Indiana's Admission to Statehood.* Indianapolis: Indiana Historical Commission, 1919.

Lossing, Benson J. *Pictorial Field Book of the Revolution.* New York: Harper Brothers, 1850.

Lowrie, Walter, and Matthew St. Clair, eds. *American State Papers, Documents, Legislative, and Executive of the Congress of the United States (1789–1838), Class 2, Indian Affairs.* 2 vols. Washington, D.C.: Gales and Seaton, 1832–34.

———. *American State Papers, Documents, Legislative and Executive of the Congress of the United States (1789–1838). Class 8, Public Lands.* 8 vols. Washington, D.C.: Gales and Seaton, 1834–61.

McCabe, James. *The Illustrated History of the Centennial Exhibition.* Philadelphia: National, 1876.

McKee, Irving, ed. *The Trail of Death: Letters of Benjamin Marie Petit.* Indianapolis: Indiana Historical Society, 1941.

McReynolds, George. "The Centennial Pageant for Indiana: Suggestions for Its Performance." *Indiana Magazine of History* 9, no. 3 (September 1915): 248–71.

Meek, Mrs. Jethro, and Mrs. Oscar Miller. *Decatur County Pageant: A Drama of Development of the County and the State.* N.p., 1916.

Meginness, John F. *Biography of Frances Slocum, the Lost Sister of Wyoming.* Williamsport, Pa.: Heller Brothers' Printing House, 1891.

"The Memorial Structure at Marietta: Report of a Committee of the Ohio Archaeological and Historical Society, Made April 6, 1888." *Ohio Archaeological and Historical Quarterly* 2, no. 1 (June 1888): 221–25.

Miller, Charles C, ed. *History of Allen County, Ohio, and Representative Citizens.* Chicago: Richmond and Arnold, 1906.

Miner, Charles. *History of Wyoming: In a Series of Letters.* Philadelphia: J. Crissy, 1845.

Minturn, Joseph Allen. *Francis Slocum of Miami Lodge: The Dramatic Story of the White Girl That Became an Indian Princess and Her Relation to the Stirring Events through Which the Northwest Territory Was Wrested Away from the British and Indians.* Indianapolis: Globe, 1928.

Mitchell, Joseph. *The Missionary Pioneer; or, A Brief Memoir of the Life, Labours, and Death of John Stewart (Man of Colour), Founder, under God of the Mission among the Wyandotts at Upper Sandusky, Ohio.* New York: J. C. Totten, 1827.

Montgomery, M. W. *History of Jay County, Indiana.* Chicago: Church, Goodman, and Cushing, n.d.

Morton, Samuel George. *Crania Americana; or, A Comparative View of the Skulls of Various Aboriginal Nations of North and South America; to Which Is Affixed an Essay on the Variety of the Human Species.* Philadelphia: J. Pennington, 1839.

————. *Synopsis of the Organic Remains of the Cretaceous Group of the United States.* Philadelphia, 1834.

"Narrative of a Journey to Sandusky, Ohio, to Visit the Wyandot Indians Residing There." *Friends Miscellany* 7, no. 7 (October 1835): 292–326.

The Ninety-fifth Anniversary of the Settlement of Ohio, at Marietta: Historical Address by Hon. George B. Loring and Other Addresses before the Washington County Pioneer Association, Marietta, Ohio, April 7, 1883. Marietta: Washington County Pioneer Association, 1883.

An Oration Delivered at Marietta, July 4, 1788, by the Hon. James M. Varnum, Esq., One of the Judges of the Western Territory; The Speech of Arthur St. Clair, Esq., upon the Proclamation of the Commission Appointing Him Governor of Said Territory, and the Proceedings of the Inhabitants of the City of Marietta. Newport, R.I.: Peter Edes, 1788.

Oration Delivered by George F. Hoar, of Massachusetts, April 7, 1888, at the Centennial of the Founding of the Northwest at Marietta, Ohio. Washington, D.C.: Judd and Detweiler, 1888.

Owens, Robert M. *Mr. Jefferson's Hammer: William Henry Harrison and the Origins of American Indian Policy.* Norman: University of Oklahoma Press, 2007.

Packard, Jasper. *History of La Porte County, Indiana.* La Porte, Ind.: S. E. Taylor, 1876.

Paulding, James Kirke. *The Lion of the West; Retitled The Kentuckian; or, A Trip to New York.* Edited by James N. Tidwell. Stanford: Stanford University Press, 1954.

Peace, Theodore. *Laws of the Northwest Territory.* Springfield: Trustees of the Illinois State Historical Library, 1925.

Peattie, Elia W. *History of Gibson County, Indiana.* Chicago: American Publishing and Engraving, 1897.

Peck, George. *Wyoming: Its History, Stirring Incidents, and Romantic Adventures.* New York: Harper & Brothers, 1858.

Perrin, William Henry, ed. *History of Summit County, with an Outline Sketch of Ohio.* Chicago: Baskin and Battey, 1881.

Perrin, William Henry, and J. H. Battle. *History of Logan County and Ohio.* Chicago: O. L. Baskin, 1880.

Phelps, Martha Bennett. *Frances Slocum: The Lost Sister of Wyoming.* Wilkes-Barre, Pa.: Privately printed, 1916.

Philbrick, Francis, ed. *The Laws of Indiana Territory, 1801–1809.* Springfield: Illinois State Historical Library, 1930.

Pollack, Ervin, ed. *Ohio Unreported Judicial Decisions prior to 1823.* Indianapolis: A. Smith and Comp., 1952.

Powell, Jehu Z. *History of Cass County, Indiana: From Its Earliest Settlement to the Present Time; with Biographical Sketches and Reference to Biographies Previously Compiled.* Chicago: Lewis, 1913.

Powell, John Wesley. *Wyandot Government: A Short Study of Tribal Society.* An Address before the Subsection of Anthropology, American Association for the Advancement of Science: Boston Meeting, August, 1880. Salem: Salem Press, 1881.

Premium List and Rules and Regulations of the Ohio Centennial at Columbus, Opens September 4th, Closes October 19th, 1888. Columbus, Ohio: Gazette Printing House, 1888.

"Proceedings of the Third Annual Meeting Held at Marietta, April 5th and 6th, 1888, in Connection with the Centennial of the Settlement of the Northwest Territory." *Ohio Archaeological and Historical Quarterly* 2, no. 1 (June 1888): 332.

Proceedings of the United States National Museum. 125 vols. Washington, D.C.: Government Printing Office, 1878–1968.

Program of the Cass County Celebration of Indiana's Statehood Centennial. Logansport: Riverview-Spencer Park, 1916.

Randall, E. O., ed. *Ohio Centennial Anniversary Celebration at Chillicothe, May 20–21, 1903.* Columbus: Ohio State Archaeological and Historical Society, 1903.

"Remarks of Hon. Samuel F. Hunt." *Ohio Archaeological and Historical Quarterly* 2, no. 1 (June 1888): 93.

Report of the Committee of Arrangements of the Common Council of the City of New York for the Funeral Obsequies in Memory of William H. Harrison. New York: Bryant and Boggs, n.d.

Reynolds, John. *The Pioneer History of Illinois, Containing the Discovery, in 1673, and the History of the Country to the Year Eighteen Hundred and Eighteen, When the State Government Was Organized.* Belleville, Ill.: N. A. Randall, 1852.

Rice, Wallace. *The Masque of Illinois.* Springfield, Ill.: Jefferson's Printing, 1918.

Richardson, James D., ed. *A Compilation of the Messages and Papers of the Presidents.* New York: Bureau of National Literature, Inc., 1897. 5 vols.

Riker, Dorothy, ed. *Unedited Letters of Jonathon Jennings.* Indianapolis: Indiana Historical Society, 1932.

Riker, Dorothy, and Nellie A. Robertson, eds. *The John Tipton Papers.* 3 vols. Indianapolis: Indiana Historical Bureau, 1942.

Robb, John S. *Streaks of Squatter Life, and Far-West Scenes: A Series of Humorous Sketches Descriptive of Incidents in the South and South-West.* Philadelphia: Carey and Hart, 1845.

Rockwell, Ethel, comp. "Historical Pageantry: A Treatise and a Bibliography." State Historical Society of Wisconsin *Bulletin of Information,* no. 84 (July 1916).

Roosevelt, Theodore. *The Winning of the West.* 6 vols. New York: Current Literature, 1905.

Seaver, James, ed. *A Narrative of the Life of Mrs. Mary Jemison.* New York: Corinth Books, 1961.

Sigourney, Lydia. *Illustrated Poems.* Philadelphia: Carey and Hart, 1849.

———. *The Western Home and Other Poems.* Philadelphia: Parry and McMillan, 1854.

Smith, Dwight L., ed. "A Continuation of the Journal of an Emigrating Party of Potawatomi Indians, 1838, and Ten William Polke Manuscripts." *Indiana Magazine of History* 14 (1948): 393–408.

Smith, Seba. *My Thirty Years Out of the Senate.* New York: Oaksmith, 1959.

Smith, William Henry, ed. *The St. Clair Papers: The Life and Public Services of Arthur St. Clair.* Cincinnati: Robert Clarke, 1882.

Stott, Richard B., ed. *History of My Own Times.* Ithaca: Cornell University Press, 1995.

Suggestive Plans for a Historical and Educational Celebration in Indiana in 1916: Prepared under Direction of the Indiana Centennial Celebration Committee, 1912. Indianapolis: Burford Print, 1912.

Thomas, Cyrus. *Report of the Mound Exploration of the Bureau of American Ethnology.* Washington, D.C.: Smithsonian Institution, 1894.

Thompson, Maurice. *Stories of Indiana.* New York: American, 1898.

Thornbrough, Gayle, ed. *The Journals and Indian Paintings of George Winter, 1837–1839.* Indianapolis: Indiana Historical Society, 1948.

———. *Letter Book of the Indian Agency at Fort Wayne, 1809–1815.* Indianapolis: Indiana Historical Society, 1961.

———. *Outpost on the Wabash, 1787–1791: Letters of Brigadier General Josiah Harmar and Major John Francis Hamtramck and Other Letters and Documents Selected from the Harmar Papers in the William L. Clements Library.* Indianapolis: Indiana Historical Society Publications, 1957.

Thornbrough, Gayle, and Dorothy Riker, eds. *The Correspondence of John Badollet and Albert Gallatin, 1804–1836.* Indianapolis: Indiana Historical Society Publications, 1963.

———. *Journals of the General Assembly of Indiana Territory, 1805–1815.* Indianapolis: Indiana Historical Bureau, 1950.

Todd, John. *The Lost Sister of Wyoming: An Authentic Tale.* Northampton, Mass.: J. H. Butler, 1842.

Twenty-eighth Report of the Indiana State Board of Agriculture, 1878. Indianapolis: Indianapolis Journal, 1879.

Twenty-ninth Report of the Indiana State Board of Agriculture, 1879. Indianapolis: Douglass and Carlon, 1879.

Tyler, Edward B. *Primitive Culture: Researches into the Development of Mythology, Philosophy, Religion, Art, and Custom.* London: John Murray, 1871.

Van Rensselaer, Cortlandt. *Funeral Sermon, Delivered in the Presbyterian Church, in Washington, on the Sabbath after the Decease of William Henry Harrison.* Washington, D.C.: n.p., 1841.

Van Tassel, C. S., ed. *Story of Fort Meigs and Other Original Documents*. Bowling Green, Ohio: Historical Publications Company, n.d.

Volney, C. F. *A View of the Soil and Climate of the United States of America*. Philadelphia: J. Conrad, 1804.

Walker, Charles M., ed. *Ohio Company Settlements in Ohio Country to 1868, and a History and Aid to Genealogical Study for Athens County, Ohio; and Incidentally of the Ohio Land Company and the First Settlement of the State at Marietta*. Cincinnati: Robert Clarke, 1869.

Walker, Joseph E., ed. "Plowshares and Pruning Hooks for the Miami and Potawatomi: The Journal of Gerard T. Hopkins." *Ohio History* 88, no. 4 (Autumn 1979): 361–407.

Welby, Adlard. *A Visit to North America and the Settlements in Illinois, with a Winter Residence in Philadelphia*. London: Baldwin, Cradock, and Joy, 1821.

Williams, William W. *History of Ashtabula County, Ohio, with Illustrations and Biographical Sketches of Its Pioneers and Most Prominent Men*. Philadelphia: Williams Brothers, 1878.

Wilson, George R. *History of Dubois County from Its Primitive Days to 1910*. Jasper, Ind.: George R. Wilson, 1910.

———. "Winter's Description of Frances Slocum." *Indiana Quarterly Magazine of History* 1, no. 3 (1905): 116–17.

Woodburn, James A. *The Indiana Centennial, 1916*. Indianapolis: n.p., 1912.

Woollen, William W., Daniel W. Howe, and Jacob P. Dunn, eds. *Executive Journal of Indiana Territory*. Indianapolis: Indiana Historical Society Publications, 1900.

SECONDARY SOURCES

Adelman, Jeremy, and Stephen Aron. "From Borderlands to Borders: Empires, Nation-States, and the Peoples in Between in North American History." *American Historical Review* 104, no. 3 (June 1999): 814–41.

Alvord, Clarence Wolworth. *The Illinois Country, 1673–1818*. Springfield: Illinois Centennial Commission, 1920.

Anderson, Benedict. *Imagined Communities: Reflections on the Origins and Spread of Nationalism*. London: Verso, 1991.

Anderson, Nancy. "'Curious Historical Artistic Data': Art History and Western American Art." In *Discovered Lands/Invented Pasts*, ed. Jules David Brown et al., 1–36. New Haven: Yale University Press, 1992.

Anson, Bert. *The Miami Indians*. Norman: University of Oklahoma Press, 1970.

Aron, Stephen. *American Confluence: The Missouri Frontier from Borderland to Border State*. Bloomington: Indiana University Press, 2006.

———. "Lessons in Conquest: Towards a New Western History." *Pacific Historical Review* 63 (May 1994): 125–47.

Atack, Jeremy, and Fred Bateman. *To Their Own Soil: Agriculture in the Antebellum North*. Ames: Iowa State University Press, 1987.

Axtell, James. *The Invasion Within: The Contest of Cultures in Colonial North America*. New York: Oxford University Press, 1985.

———. "The White Indians of Colonial America." *William and Mary Quarterly* 32, no. 1 (1975): 55–88.

———, ed. *After Columbus: Essays in the Ethnohistory of Colonial North America*. New York, Oxford University Press, 1988.

Bailey, Anthony. *Standing in the Sun: A Life of J. M. W. Turner*. New York: Harper Collins, 1998.

Barce, Elmore. *The Land of the Miamis: An Account of the Struggle to Secure Possession of the North-West from the End of the Revolution until 1812*. Fowler, Ind.: Benton Review Shop, 1922.

Barnhart, John. *Valley of Democracy: The Frontier versus Plantation in the Ohio Valley, 1775–1818*. Bloomington: Indiana University Press, 1934.

Barr, Daniel P., ed. *The Boundaries between Us: Natives and Newcomers along the Frontier of the Old Northwest Territory, 1750–1850*. Kent, Ohio: Kent State University Press, 2006.

Basso, Keith H. *Wisdom Sits in Places: Landscape and Language among the Western Apache*. Albuquerque: University of New Mexico Press, 1996.

Basso, Keith H., and Steven Feld, eds. *Senses of Place*. Santa Fe, N.M.: School of American Research Press, 1996.

Bataille, Gretchen M., ed. *Native American Representations: First Encounters, Distorted Images, and Literary Appropriations*. Lincoln: University of Nebraska Press, 2001.

Baym, Nina. *Feminism and American Literary History: Essays*. Princeton: Princeton University Press, 1992.

Beauchamp, William M. "Wampum Used in Council and as Currency." *American Antiquarian and Oriental Journal* 20 (1898): 1–13.

Bellah, Robert N. "Civil Religion in America." *Daedalus: Journal of the American Academy of Arts and Sciences* 96, no. 1 (Winter 1967): 1–21.

Bennett, Paula Bernat. *Poets in the Public Sphere: The Emancipatory Project of American Women's Poetry, 1800–1900*. Princeton: Princeton University Press, 2003.

Berkhofer, Robert F., Jr. *Beyond the Great Story: History as Text and Discourse*. Cambridge, Mass.: Belknap Press of Harvard University Press, 1995.

———. *Salvation and the Savage: An Analysis of Protestant Missions and the American Indian Response, 1787–1862*. Lexington: University of Kentucky Press, 1965.

———. *The White Man's Indian: Images of the American Indian from Columbus to the Present*. New York: Alfred Knopf, 1978.

Bhabha, Homi. *The Location of Culture*. New York: Routledge, 1994.

———, ed. *Nation and Narration*. New York: Routledge, 1990.

Bieder, Robert E. *Science Encounters the Indian, 1820–1880: The Early Years of American Ethnology*. Norman: University of Oklahoma Press, 1986.

————. "Scientific Attitudes toward Indian Mixed-Bloods in Early-Nineteenth-Century America." *Journal of Ethnic Studies* 8, no. 2 (Summer 1980): 17–30.

Billington, Ray Allen. *America's Frontier Heritage*. Albuquerque: University of New Mexico Press, 1974.

Blackhawk, Ned. *Violence over the Land: Indians and Empires in the Early American West*. Cambridge, Mass.: Harvard University Press, 2006.

Blight, David. *Race and Reunion: The Civil War in American Memory*. Cambridge, Mass.: Harvard University Press, 2001.

Bodnar, John. *Remaking America: Public Memory, Commemoration, and Patriotism in the Twentieth Century*. Princeton: Princeton University Press, 1992.

Bogue, Allan G. "The Iowa Claim Clubs: Symbol and Substance." *Mississippi Valley Historical Review* 45, no. 2 (September 1958): 231–53.

Bond, Beverly, Jr. *The Civilization of the Old Northwest: A Study of Political, Social, and Economic Development, 1788–1812*. New York: Macmillan, 1934.

Bowes, John P. *Exiles and Pioneers: Eastern Indians in the Trans-Mississippi West*. New York: Cambridge University Press, 2007.

Boydston, Jeanne. *Home and Work: Housework, Wages, and the Ideology of Labor in the Early Republic*. New York: Oxford University Press, 1990.

Brooks, Lisa. *The Common Pot: The Recovery of Native Space in the Northeast*. Minneapolis: University of Minnesota Press, 2008.

Brown, Chandos Michael. "A Natural History of the Gloucester Sea Serpent: Knowledge, Power, and the Culture of Science in Antebellum America." *American Quarterly* 42, no. 3 (September 1990): 402–36.

Brown, Elizabeth Gaspar. "Lewis Cass and the American Indian." *Michigan History* 37 (September 1953): 286–98.

Brown, Jennifer S. H. *Strangers in Blood: Fur Trade Company Families in Indian Country*. Vancouver: University of British Columbia Press, 1980.

Brown, Kathleen. *Good Wives, Nasty Wenches, and Anxious Patriarchs: Gender, Race, and Power in Colonial Virginia*. Chapel Hill: University of North Carolina Press, 1996.

————. "Native Americans and Early Modern Concepts of Race." In *Empire and Others*, ed. Martin Daunton and Rick Halpern. Philadelphia: University of Pennsylvania Press, 1999.

Buley, R. Carlyle. *The Old Northwest Pioneer Period, 1815–1840*. Bloomington: Indiana University Press, 1951.

Burnham, Michelle. *Captivity and Sentiment: Cultural Exchange in American Literature, 1682–1861*. Hanover: University Press of New England, 1997.

Bushman, Richard L. *The Refinement of America: Persons, Houses, Cities*. New York: Vintage, 1993.

Buss, Jim J. "'They found and left her an Indian': Gender, Race, and the Whitening of Young Bear." *Frontiers: A Journal of Women Studies* 29, nos. 2–3 (2008): 1–35.

Calcott, George H. *History in the United States, 1800–1860*. Baltimore: Johns Hopkins University Press, 1970.

Calhoun, Charles W., ed. *The Gilded Age: Essays on the Origins of Modern America*. New York: S. R. Books, 1996.

Carlton, Charles. "The Widow's Tale: Male Myths and Female Reality in Sixteenth-Century England." *Albion* 10 (1978): 118–29.

Carmony, Donald F. *Indiana: The Pioneer Era, 1816–1850*. Indianapolis: Indiana Historical Society, 1998.

Carter, Harvey Lewis. "A Frontier Tragedy: Little Turtle and William Wells." *Old Northwest: A Journal of Regional Life and Letters* 6, no. 1 (Spring 1980): 3–18.

———. *The Life and Times of Little Turtle: First Sagamore of the Wabash*. Urbana: University of Illinois Press, 1987.

Caughey, John. "The Insignificance of the Frontier in American History; or, 'Once Upon a Time There Was an American West.'" *Western Historical Quarterly* 5 (January 1974): 5–16.

Cave, Alfred A. "The Failure of the Shawnee Prophet's Witch-Hunt." *Ethnohistory* 42, no. 3 (Summer 1995): 445–75.

———. *Prophets of the Great Spirit: Native American Revitalization Movements in Eastern North America*. Lincoln: University of Nebraska Press, 2006.

———. "The Shawnee Prophet, Tecumseh, and Tippecanoe: A Case Study of Historical Myth-Making." *Journal of the Early Republic* 22, no. 4 (Winter 2002): 637–73.

Cayton, Andrew R. L. *The Frontier Republic: Ideology and Politics in the Ohio Country, 1780–1825*. Kent: Kent State University Press, 1986.

———. "Land, Power, and Reputation: The Cultural Dimensions of Politics in the Ohio Country." *William and Mary Quarterly* 47, no. 2 (April 1990): 266–86.

———. "'Noble Actors' upon 'the Theatre of Honour.'" In *Contact Points*, ed. Cayton and Fredrika J. Teute. Chapel Hill: University of North Carolina Press, 1998.

———. "The Northwest Ordinance from the Perspective of the Frontier." In *The Northwest Ordinance, 1787*, ed. Robert M. Taylor, Jr. Indianapolis: Indiana Historical Society, 1987.

———. *Ohio: A History of a People*. Columbus: Ohio State University Press, 2002.

———. "'A Quiet Independence': The Western Vision of the Ohio Company." *Ohio History* 90 (1981): 5–32.

Cayton, Andrew R. L., and Susan E. Gray, eds. *The Identity of the American Midwest: Essays on Regional History*. Bloomington: Indiana University Press, 2001.

Cayton, Andrew R. L., and Peter Onuf. *The Midwest and the Nation: Rethinking the History of an American Region*. Bloomington: Indiana University Press, 1990.

Cayton, Andrew R. L., and Fredrika J. Teute, eds. *Contact Points: American Frontiers from the Mohawk Valley to the Mississippi, 1750–1830*. Chapel Hill: University of North Carolina Press, 1998.

Ceci, Lynn. "The Value of Wampum among the New York Iroquois: A Case Study in Artifact Analysis." *Journal of Anthropological Research* 38 (Spring 1982): 97–107.

Chang, David A. *The Color of the Land: Race, Nation, and the Politics of Landownership in Oklahoma, 1832–1929.* Chapel Hill: University of North Carolina Press, 2010.

Clifton, James A. *The Prairie People: Continuity and Change in Potawatomi Indian Culture, 1665–1965.* Iowa City: University of Iowa Press, 1998.

———. *The Predicament of Culture: Twentieth-Century Ethnography, Literature, and Art.* Cambridge, Mass.: Harvard University Press, 1988.

Cockrum, William M. *Pioneer History of Indiana, Including Stories, Incidents, and Customs of the Early Settlers.* Oakland City, Ind.: Press of Oakland City Journal, 1907.

Codrescu, Andrei. "The Future Is Now . . . and Then." *Poet on Call, All Things Considered.* National Public Radio, December 11, 2009.

Cohen, Felix. *Handbook on Federal Indian Law.* Charlottesville: University of Virginia Press, 1982.

Cole, Charles C., Jr. *Lion of the Forest: James B. Finley, Frontier Reformer.* Lexington: University Press of Kentucky, 1994.

Collier, Christopher. "The American People as Christian White Men of Property." In *Voting and the Spirit of American Democracy,* ed. Donald W. Rogers, 19–30. Urbana: University of Illinois Press, 1992.

Conn, Steven. *History's Shadow: Native Americans and Historical Consciousness in the Nineteenth Century.* Chicago: University of Chicago Press, 2004.

———. *Museums and American Intellectual Life, 1876–1926.* Chicago: University of Chicago Press, 1998.

Conover, Charlotte Reave. *Concerning the Forefathers: Being a Memoir, with Personal Narrative and Letters of Two Pioneers, Col. Robert Patterson and Col. John Johnston.* Dayton, Ohio: National Cash Register, 1902.

Coontz, Stephanie. *The Social Origins of Private Lives.* New York: Verso, 1988.

Coser, Lewis, ed. *Maurice Halbwachs: On Collective Memory.* Chicago: University of Chicago Press, 1992.

Cott, Nancy. *The Bonds of Womanhood: Women's Sphere in New England, 1780–1835.* New Haven: Yale University Press, 1977.

———. *Public Vows: A History of Marriage and the Nation.* Cambridge, Mass.: Harvard University Press, 2000.

Coward, John M. *The Newspaper Indian: Native Identity in the Press, 1820–1890.* Urbana: University of Illinois Press, 1999.

Cronon, William. *Nature's Metropolis: Chicago and the Great West.* New York: W. W. Norton, 1991.

Cronon, William, George Miles, and Jay Gitlin. "Becoming West: Toward a New Meaning for Western History." In *Under an Open Sky,* ed. Cronon, Miles, and Gitlin. 3–27.

————, eds. *Under an Open Sky: Rethinking America's Western Past.* New York: W. W. Norton, 1992.

Dain, Bruce. *A Hideous Monster of the Mind: American Race Theory in the Early Republic.* Cambridge, Mass.: Harvard University Press, 2002.

Daunton, Martin, and Rick Halpern, eds. *Empire and Others: British Encounters with Indigenous Peoples, 1600–1850.* Philadelphia: University of Pennsylvania Press, 1999.

Davis, Fred. *Yearning for Yesterday: A Sociology of Nostalgia.* New York: Free Press, 1979.

Deloria, Philip. *Indians in Unexpected Places.* Lawrence: University Press of Kansas, 2004.

————. *Playing Indian.* New Haven: Yale University Press, 1998.

Demos, John. *The Unredeemed Captive: A Family Story from Early America.* New York: Alfred Knopf, 1994.

Derounian-Stodola, Kathryn Zabelle, and James Arthur Levernfer. *The Indian Captivity Narrative, 1550–1900.* New York: Twayne, 1993.

Dippie, Brian W. *Catlin and His Contemporaries: The Politics of Patronage.* Lincoln: University of Nebraska Press, 1990.

————. "Green Fields and Red Men." In *George Catlin and His Indian Gallery,* ed. George Gurney and Therese Thau Heyman, 27–62. New York: Published for the Smithsonian American Art Museum by W. W. Norton, 2002.

————. *The Vanishing American: White Attitudes and U.S. Indian Policy.* Middletown, Conn.: Wesleyan University Press, 1982.

Dowd, Gregory Evans. "Little Turtle and the Origins of a Great Native Debate." *Northwest Ohio Quarterly* 74, no. 1 (Winter 2002): 5–21.

————. *A Spirited Resistance: The North American Indian Struggle for Unity, 1745–1815.* Baltimore: Johns Hopkins University Press, 1992.

Drinnon, Richard. *Facing West: The Metaphysics of Indian Hating and Empire Building.* New York: New American Library, 1980.

Eagleton, Terry. *The Ideology of the Aesthetic.* Cambridge, Mass.: Basil Blackwell, 1990.

Ebersole, Gary L. *Captured by Texts: Puritan to Post-Modern Images of Indian Captivity.* Charlottesville: University of Virginia Press, 1995.

Edmunds, R. David. "George Winter: Mirror of Acculturation." In *Indians and a Changing Frontier,* ed. Sarah E. Cooke and Rachel B. Ramadhyani. Indianapolis: Published by the Indiana Historical Society in Cooperation with the Tippecanoe County Historical Society, 1993.

————. *The Potawatomis: Keepers of the Fire.* Norman: University of Oklahoma Press, 1978.

————. *The Shawnee Prophet.* Lincoln: University of Nebraska Press, 1985.

————. *Tecumseh and the Quest for Indian Leadership.* New York: Longman, 1984.

Edwards, Rebecca. *New Spirits: Americans in the Gilded Age, 1865–1905.* New York: Oxford University Press, 2006.

Eggan, Fred. "Lewis Henry Morgan and the Study of Social Organization." In *The American Indian: Perspectives for the Study of Social Change*, ed. Fred Eggan, 1–16. Chicago: Aldine, 1996.

Ekirch, Arthur Alphonse. *The Idea of Progress in America, 1815–1860.* New York: Columbia University Press, 1944.

Elkins, Stanley, and Eric McKitrick. "A Meaning for Turner's Frontier (Part One): Democracy in the Old Northwest." *Political Science Quarterly* 69, no. 3 (1954): 321–53.

Ellinghaus, Katherine. "Reading the Personal as Political: The Assimilationist Views of a White Woman Married to a Native American Man, 1880s–1940s." *Australasian Journal of American Studies* 18, no. 2 (1999): 23–41.

Etcheson, Nicole. *The Emerging Midwest: Upland Southerners and the Political Culture of the Old Northwest, 1787–1861.* Bloomington: Indiana University Press, 1996.

Ethridge, Robbie, and Sheri M. Shuck-Hall, eds. *Mapping the Mississippian Shatter Zone: The Colonial Indian Slave Trade and Regional Instability in the American South.* Lincoln: University of Nebraska Press, 2009.

Faery, Rebecca Blevins. *Cartographies of Desire: Captivity, Race, and Sex in the Shaping of an American Nation.* Norman: University of Oklahoma Press, 1999.

Faragher, John Mack. "The Custom of the Country." In *Western Women: Their Land, Their Lives*, ed. Janice Monk et al. Albuquerque: University of New Mexico Press, 1972.

———. *Rereading Frederick Jackson Turner: The Significance of the Frontier in American History and Other Essays.* New York: Oxford University Press, 1994.

———. *Women and Men on the Overland Trail.* New Haven: Yale University Press, 1979.

Feest, Christian F. "G. Winter: Artist." In *Indians and a Changing Frontier*, ed. Sarah E. Cooke and Rachel B. Ramadhyani, 1–22. Indianapolis: Published by the Indiana Historical Society in Cooperation with the Tippecanoe County Historical Society, 1993.

Fenton, William N. "Northern Iroquoian Culture Patterns." In *Handbook of North American Indians*, ed. Brice G. Trigger, 15: 296–321. Washington, D.C.: Smithsonian Institute Press, 1978.

Fielder, Leslie. *The Return of the Vanishing American.* New York: Stein and Day, 1968.

Filby, P. William, comp. *A Bibliography of American County Histories.* Baltimore: Genealogical, 1985.

Foreman, Grant. *The Last Trek of the Indians.* Chicago: University of Chicago Press, 1946.

Foss, Sonja K., Karen A. Foss, and Robert Trapp. *Contemporary Perspectives on Rhetoric.* Long Grove, Ill.: Waveland Press, 2001.

Foster, Michael K. "Another Look at the Function of Wampum in Iroquois-White Councils." In *The History and Culture of Iroquois Diplomacy: An Interdisciplinary*

Guide to the Treaties of the Six Nations and Their League, ed. Francis Jennings et al., 99–114. Syracuse: Syracuse University Press, 1985.

Foucault, Michel. *The Archaeology of Knowledge and the Discourse on Language.* London: Travistock, 1972.

———. *The Order of Things: An Archaeology of the Human Sciences.* New York: Random House, 1970.

———. *Power/Knowledge: Selected Interviews and Other Writings, 1972–1977.* New York: Oxford University Press, 1980.

Fowler, David H. *Northern Attitudes towards Interracial Marriage: Legislation and Public Opinion in the Middle Atlantic and the States of the Old Northwest, 1780–1930.* New York: Garland, 1987.

Friend, Craig Thompson. "Liberty Is Pioneering: An American Birthright." Organization of American Historians *Magazine of History* 19, no. 3 (May 2005): 16–20.

Galloway, William Albert. *Old Chillicothe: Shawnee and Pioneer History.* Xenia, Ohio: Buckeye Press, 1934.

Gates, Paul W. *The Farmer's Age: Agriculture, 1815–1860.* New York: Holt, Rinehart, and Winston, 1960.

Giberti, Bruno. "The Classified Landscape: Consumption, Commodity Order, and the 1876 Centennial Exhibition at Philadelphia." Ph.D. diss., University of California at Berkeley, 1994.

———. *Designing the Centennial: A History of the 1876 International Exhibition in Philadelphia.* Lexington: University Press of Kentucky, 2002.

Gilman, Sander. *Difference and Pathology: Stereotypes of Sexuality, Race, and Madness.* Ithaca: Cornell University Press, 1985.

Glassberg, David. *American Historical Pageantry: The Uses of Tradition in the Early Twentieth Century.* Chapel Hill: University of North Carolina Press, 1990.

Gould, Stephen Jay. *The Mismeasure of Man.* New York: W. W. Norton, 1981.

Grigg, Susan. "Toward a Theory of Remarriage: A Case Study of Newburyport at the Beginning of the Nineteenth Century." *Journal of Interdisciplinary History* 8 (1977): 183–220.

Grimshaw, Patricia. "Interracial Marriages and Colonial Regimes in Victoria and Aotearoa/New Zealand." *Frontiers: The Journal of Women Studies* 23, no. 3 (2002): 12–28.

Gunderson, Robert Gray. *The Log-Cabin Campaign.* Lexington: University of Kentucky Press, 1957.

Haberly, David T. "Women and Indians: The Last of the Mohicans and the Captivity Tradition." *American Quarterly* 28, no. 4 (Autumn 1976): 431–44.

Halbwachs, Maurice. *The Collective Memory.* Trans. Francis J. Ditter, Jr., and Vida Yazdi Ditter. New York: Harper Colophon Books, 1980.

Hallock, Thomas. *From the Fallen Tree: Frontier Narratives, Environmental Politics, and the Roots of a National Pastoral, 1749–1826.* Chapel Hill: University of North Carolina Press, 2003.

Halttunen, Karen. *Confidence Men and Painted Women: A Study of Middle-Class Culture in American, 1830–1870.* New Haven: Yale University Press, 1982.

Hanacks, Larry K. *The Emigrant Tribes: Wyandot, Delaware, and Shawnee.* Kansas City, Kans.: n.p., 1998.

Hartog, Hendrick. *Man and Wife in America: A History.* Cambridge, Mass.: Harvard University Press, 2002.

Hausdoerffer, John. *Catlin's Lament: Indians, Manifest Destiny, and the Ethics of Nature.* Lawrence: University of Kansas Press, 2009.

Heale, M. J. "The Role of the Frontier in Jacksonian Politics: David Crockett and the Myth of the Self-Made Man." *Western Historical Quarterly* 4, no. 4 (October 1973): 405–23.

Heidler, David S., and Jeanne T. Heidler. *Indian Removal: A Norton Casebook.* New York: W. W. Norton, 2007.

Henretta, James. "Families and Farms: *Mentalité* in Pre-Industrial America." *William and Mary Quarterly* 35, no. 1 (January 1978): 3–32.

Hill, Leonard U. *John Johnston and the Indians in the Land of the Three Miamis.* Columbus, Ohio: Stoneman Press, 1957.

Hinderaker, Erik. *Elusive Empires: Constructing Colonialism in the Ohio Valley, 1673–1800.* Cambridge: Cambridge University Press, 1997.

Hodes, Martha, ed. *Sex, Love, Race: Crossing Bodies in North American History.* New York: Oxford University Press, 1989.

Horsman, Reginald. "American Indian Policy in the Old Northwest, 1783–1812." *William and Mary Quarterly* 18 (1961): 35–53.

———. *Expansion and American Indian Policy, 1783–1812.* East Lansing: Michigan State University Press, 1967.

———. *The Origins of Indian Removal, 1815–1824.* East Lansing: Published by the Michigan State University Press for the Historical Society of Michigan, 1970.

Howard, James H. *Shawnee! The Ceremonialism of a Native Indian Tribe and Its Cultural Background.* Athens: Ohio University Press, 1981.

Howe, Daniel Walker. *What Hath God Wrought: The Transformation of America, 1815–1848.* New York: Oxford University Press, 2008.

Huber, John Parker. "General Josiah Harmar's Command: Military Policy in the Old Northwest." Ph.D. diss., University of Michigan, 1968.

Humphrey, Carol Sue. *The Press of the Young Republic, 1783–1833.* Westport, Conn.: Greenwood Press, 1996.

Hurt, R. Douglas. *The Indian Frontier, 1763–1846.* Albuquerque: University of New Mexico Press, 2002.

Husch, Gail E. "'Poor White Folks' and 'Western Squatters': James Henry Beard's Images of Emigration." *American Art* 7, no. 3 (Summer 1993): 14–39.

Hutton, Paul Andrew, ed. *A Narrative of the Life of David Crockett, by Himself.* Lincoln: University of Nebraska Press, 1987.

Ignatiev, Noel. *How the Irish Became White.* New York: Routledge, 1995.

Jacobs, Margaret D. "The Eastmans and the Luhans: Interracial Marriage between White Women and Native American Men, 1875–1935." *Frontiers: A Journal of Women Studies* 23, no. 3 (2002): 29–54.

Jacobs, Wilbur R. "Wampum, the Protocol of Indian Diplomacy." *William and Mary Quarterly* 6 (1949): 596–604.

Jacobson, Matthew Frye. *Whiteness of a Different Color: European Immigrants and the Alchemy of Race.* Cambridge, Mass.: Harvard University Press, 1998.

Jeffrey, Julie Roy. *Frontier Women.* New York: Hill and Wang 1979.

Jennings, Francis. *The Invasion of America: Indians, Colonialism, and the Cant of Conquest.* New York: W. W. Norton, 1976.

Johns, Elizabeth. *American Genre Painting: The Politics of Everyday Life.* New Haven: Yale University Press, 1991.

Johnson, Paul E. *A Shopkeeper's Millennium: Society and Revivals in Rochester, New York, 1815–1837.* New York: Hill and Wang, 1978.

Jones, Dorothy V. *License for Empire: Colonialism by Treaty in Early America.* Chicago: University of Chicago Press, 1982.

Josephy, Alvin. *The Patriot Chiefs: A Chronicle of American Indian Resistance.* New York: Penguin, 1993.

Kann, Mark. *A Republic of Men: The American Founders, Gendered Language, and Patriarchal Politics.* New York: Oxford University Press, 1998.

Kaplan, Amy. "Manifest Domesticity." *American Literature* 70, no. 3 (September 1998): 581–606.

Kerber, Linda. "The Republican Ideology of the Revolutionary Generation." *American Quarterly* 37, no. 4 (Autumn 1985): 474–95.

———. "Separate Spheres, Female Worlds, Woman's Place: The Rhetoric of Women's History." *Journal of American History* 75, no. 1 (June 1988): 9–39.

———. *Women of the Republic: Intellect and Ideology in Revolutionary America.* Chapel Hill: University of North Carolina Press, 1980.

Kessler, Albert. *The Indian in American Literature.* New York: Oxford University Press, 1933.

Kettleborough, Charles, ed. *Constitution Making in Indiana.* Indianapolis: Indiana Historical Commission, 1916.

Kettner, James H. *The Development of American Citizenship, 1608–1870.* Chapel Hill: University of North Carolina Press, 1978.

Keyssar, Alexander. *The Right to Vote: The Contested History of Democracy in the United States.* New York: Basic Books, 2000.

———. "Widowhood in Eighteenth-Century Massachusetts: A Problem in the History of the Family." *Perspectives in American History* 8 (1974): 99–111.

Klein, Kerwin Lee. "In Search of Narrative Mastery: Postmodernism and the People without History." *History and Theory* 34, no. 4 (1995): 275–98.

———. "Reclaiming the 'F' Word, or Being and Becoming Postwestern." *Pacific Historical Review* 65 (May 1996): 179–215.

Klopfenstein, Carl Grover. "The Removal of the Indians from Ohio, 1820–1843." Ph.D. diss., Case Western University, 1955.

———. "The Removal of the Wyandots from Ohio." *Ohio Historical Quarterly* 66, no. 2 (April 1957): 119–36.

Koerner, Lisbet. *Linnaeus: Nature and Nation.* Cambridge, Mass.: Harvard University Press, 1999.

Kohl, Lawrence Frederick. *The Politics of Individualism: Parties and the American Character in the Jacksonian Era.* New York: Oxford University Press, 1989.

Kolodny, Annette. *The Land before Her: Fantasy and Experience of the American Frontier, 1630–1860.* Chapel Hill: University of North Carolina Press, 1984.

———. *The Lay of the Land: Metaphor as Experience and History in American Life and Letters.* Chapel Hill: University of North Carolina Press, 1975.

———. "Turning the Lens on 'The Panther Captivity': A Feminist Exercise in Practical Criticism." *Critical Inquiry* 8 (1981): 329–45.

Konkle, Maureen. *Writing Indian Nations: Native Intellectuals and the Politics of Historiography, 1827–1863.* Chapel Hill: University of North Carolina Press, 2004.

Kraditor, Aileen S., ed. *Up from the Pedestal: Selected Writings in the History of American Feminism.* Chicago: Quadrangle, 1970.

Kruman, Marc. *State Constitution Making in Revolutionary America.* Chapel Hill: University of North Carolina Press, 1997.

Lappas, Thomas J. "'A Perfect Apollo: Keokuk and Sac Leadership during the Removal Era." In *The Boundaries between Us,* ed. Daniel P. Barr, 219–35. Kent, Ohio: Kent State University Press, 2006.

Lears, T. J. Jackson. *No Place of Grace: Antimodernism and the Transformation of American Culture, 1880–1920.* New York: Pantheon Books, 1981.

Lee, R. Alton. "Indian Citizenship and the Fourteenth Amendment." *South Dakota History* 4 (Spring 1974): 199–206.

Lemire, Elise. *"Miscegenation:" Making Race in America.* Philadelphia: University of Pennsylvania Press, 2002.

Lepore, Jill. "Dead Men Tell No Tales: John Sassamon and the Fatal Consequences of Literacy." *American Quarterly* 46 (1994): 479–512.

———. *The Name of War: King Philip's War and the Origins of American Identity.* New York: Alfred Knopf, 1998.

Lewis, Jan. *The Pursuits of Happiness: Family and Values in Jefferson's Virginia.* New York: Cambridge University Press, 1983.

Lewis, Nathaniel. "Truth or Consequences: Projecting Authenticity in the 1830s." In *True West: Authenticity and the American West,* ed. William R. Handely and Nathaniel Lewis, 21–37. Lincoln: University of Nebraska Press, 2004.

Limerick, Patricia Nelson. *The Legacy of Conquest: The Unbroken History of the American West.* New York: W. W. Norton, 1987.

———. "Making the Most of Words." In *Under an Open Sky,* ed. Cronon, Miles, and Gitlin, 167–84.

Livermore, Shaw. *Early American Land Companies: Their Influence on Corporate Development.* New York: Commonwealth Fund, 1939.

Lowenthal, David. *The Past Is a Foreign Country.* Cambridge: Cambridge University Press, 1985.

Lutz, Donald S. *Popular Consent and Popular Control: Whig Political Theory in the Early State Constitutions.* Baton Rouge: Louisiana University Press, 1980.

MacLean, J. P. "Shaker Mission to the Shawnee Indians." *Ohio Archaeological and Historical Publications* 11 (1963): 215–29.

Maddox, Lucy. *Removals: Nineteenth-Century American Literature and the Politics of Indian Affairs.* New York: Oxford University Press, 1991.

Maga, Timothy P., and Diana L. Ahmad-Maga. "Forgotten Scourge: Gray Squirrels on the American Frontier." *Old Northwest: A Journal of Regional Life and Letters* 13 (Spring 1987): 67–78.

Mahoney, Timothy, and Wendy Katz, eds. *Regionalism and the Humanities.* Lincoln: University of Nebraska Press, 2008.

Marx, Leo. *The Machine in the Garden: Technology and the Pastoral Ideal in America.* London: Oxford University Press, 1964.

McClurg, Martha Una, ed. and comp. *Miami Indian Stories, Told by Chief Clarence Godfroy.* Winona Lake, Ind.: Light and Life Press, 1961.

McCormick, Richard. "Ethno-Cultural Interpretations of Nineteenth-Century Voting Behavior." *Political Science Quarterly* 89 (June 1974): 351–77.

McDermott, John Francis. *George Caleb Bingham: River Portraitist.* Norman: University of Oklahoma Press, 1959.

Meek, Ronald L. *Social Science and the Ignoble Savage.* Cambridge: Cambridge University Press, 1976.

Mehta, Uday S. "Liberal Strategies of Exclusion." In *Tensions of Empire: Colonial Cultures in a Bourgeois World,* ed. Ann Laura Stoler and Frederick Cooper, 59–86. Berkeley: University of California Press, 1997.

Merrell, James. *Into the American Woods: Negotiators on the Pennsylvania Frontier.* New York: W. W. Norton, 1999.

Merrill, Michael. "Cash Is Good to Eat: Self-Sufficiency and Exchange in the Rural Economy of the United States." *Radical History Review* 4 (Winter 1977): 42–71.

Merritt, Jane. *At the Crossroads: Indians and Empires on a Mid-Atlantic Frontier, 1700–1763.* Chapel Hill: University of North Carolina Press, 2003.

Miller, Christopher L., and George R. Hamill. "A New Perspective on Indian-White Contact: Cultural Symbols and Colonial Trade." *Journal of American History* 73 (1986): 311–28.

Miller, Jay. "The 1806 Purge among the Indiana Delaware: Sorcery, Gender, Boundaries, and Legitimacy." *Ethnohistory* 41, no. 2 (Spring 1994): 245–56.

Miller, Paul. "Thomas Ewing, Last of the Whigs." Ph.D. diss., Ohio State University, 1933.

Minturn, Joseph Allen. *Frances Slocum of Miami Lodge: The Dramatic Story of the White Girl That Became an Indian Princess and Her Relation to the Stirring Events through Which the Northwest Territory Was Wrested Away from the British and Indians.* Indianapolis: Globe, 1928.

Murphy, Lucy Eldersveld. *A Gathering of Rivers: Indians, Metis, and Mining in the Western Great Lakes, 1737–1832.* Lincoln: University of Nebraska Press, 2000.

Murray, David. *Forked Tongues: Speech, Writing, and Representation in North American Indian Texts.* Bloomington: Indiana University Press, 1991.

Nagel, Paul C. *George Caleb Bingham: Missouri's Famed Painter and Forgotten Politician.* Columbia: University of Missouri Press, 2005.

Namias, June. *White Captives: Gender and Ethnicity on the American Frontier.* Chapel Hill: University of North Carolina Press, 1993.

————, ed. *A Narrative of the Life of Mrs. Mary Jemison.* Norman: University of Oklahoma Press, 1992.

Nichols, David Andrew. *Red Gentleman and White Savages: Indians, Federalists, and the Search for Order on the American Frontier.* Charlottesville: University of Virginia Press, 2008.

Nichols, Roger. *Black Hawk and the Warrior's Path.* Arlington Heights, Ill.: Harlan Davidson, 1992.

Nicholson, Meredith. "Author Finds Inspiration for Young and Old in Historical Spectacle at Riverside Park." *Indianapolis Star,* October 5, 1916.

Norton, Mary Beth. *Liberty's Daughters: The Revolutionary Experience of American Women, 1750–1800.* Boston: Little, Brown, 1980.

O'Brien, Jean M. *Dispossession by Degrees: Indian Land and Identity in Natick, Massachusetts, 1650–1790.* New York: Cambridge University Press, 1997.

————. *Firsting and Lasting: Writing Indians Out of Existence in New England.* Minneapolis: University of Minnesota Press, 2010.

Onuf, Peter. "From Constitution to Higher Law: The Reinterpretation of the Northwest Ordinance." *Ohio History* 94 (Winter–Spring 1985): 5–33.

————. *Jefferson's Empire: The Language of American Nationalism.* Charlottesville: University of Virginia Press, 2000.

————. *Origins of the Federal Republic: Jurisdictional Controversies in the United States, 1775–1787.* Philadelphia: University of Pennsylvania Press, 1983.

————. *Statehood and Union: A History of the Northwest Ordinance.* Bloomington: Indiana University Press, 1987.

————. "'We shall all be Americans': Thomas Jefferson and the Indians." *Indiana Magazine of History* (June 1999): 103–41.

Onuf, Peter, and Leonard J. Sadosky. *Jeffersonian America.* Malden, Mass.: Blackwell, 2002.

Owens, Robert M. "Jeffersonian Benevolence on the Ground: The Indian Land Cession Treaties of William Henry Harrison." *Journal of the Early Republic* 22 (Fall 2002): 405–35.

————. *Mr. Jefferson's Hammer: William Henry Harrison and the Origins of American Indian Policy.* Norman: University of Oklahoma Press, 2007.

Pagden, Anthony. *The Fall of Natural Man: The American Indian and the Origins of Comparative Ethnology.* Cambridge: Cambridge University Press, 1982.

Parmenter, Jon William. "Pontiac's War: Forging New Links in the Anglo-Iroquois Covenant Chain, 1758–1776." *Ethnohistory* 44, no. 4 (1997): 618–38.

Pascoe, Peggy. "Race, Gender, and Intercultural Relations: The Case of Interracial Marriage." *Frontiers: A Journal of Women Studies* 12, no. 1 (1991): 5–18.

Pearce, Roy Harvey. *The Savages of America: A Study of the Indian in the Idea of Civilization.* Baltimore: Johns Hopkins University Press, 1953.

————. *Savagism and Civilization: A Study of the Indian and the American Mind.* Berkeley: University of California Press, 1988.

————. "The Significance of the Captivity Narrative." *American Literature* 19 (1947–48): 1–20.

Perdue, Theda. *"Mixed Blood" Indians: Racial Construction in the Early South.* Athens: University of Georgia Press, 2003.

Peterson, Clarence S., comp. *Consolidated Bibliography of County Histories in Fifty States.* Baltimore: Genealogical, 1961.

Peterson, Jacqueline, and Jennifer Brown, eds. *The New Peoples: Being and Becoming Metis in North America.* Lincoln: University of Nebraska Press, 1985.

Plane, Ann Marie. *Colonial Intimacies: Indian Marriage in Early New England.* Ithaca: Cornell University Press, 2000.

Power, Richard Lyle. *Planting Corn Belt Culture: The Impress of the Upland Southerner and Yankee in the Old Northwest.* Indianapolis: Indiana Historical Society, 1953.

Pratt, Mary Louise. *Imperial Eyes: Travel Writing and Transculturation.* London: Routledge, 1992.

Prucha, Francis Paul. *The Great Father: The United States Government and the American Indians.* Chapel Hill: University of North Carolina Press, 1973.

Rafert, Stewart. *The Miami Indians of Indiana: A Persistent People, 1654–1994.* Indianapolis: Indiana Historical Society, 1996.

Rash, Nancy. *The Painting and Politics of George Caleb Bingham.* New Haven: Yale University Press, 1991.

Ray, John W. "A Recollection of Dennis Pennington." *Indiana Magazine of History* 3 (1907): 26–28.

Reddin, Paul. *Wild West Shows.* Urbana: University of Illinois Press, 1999.

Regis, Pamela. *Describing America: Bartram, Jefferson, Crèvecoeur, and the Rhetoric of Natural History.* Philadelphia: University of Pennsylvania Press, 1992.

Richter, Daniel. "'Believing That Many of the Red People Suffer Much for Want of Food': Hunting, Agriculture, and a Quaker Construction of Indianness in the Early Republic." *Journal of the Early Republic* 19 (Winter 1999): 601–28.

————. *Facing East from Indian Country: A Native History of Early America.* Cambridge, Mass.: Harvard University Press, 2001.

———. *The Ordeal of the Longhouse: The People of the Iroquois League in the Era of European Colonization.* Chapel Hill: University of North Carolina Press, 1992.

Robertson, Lindsay G. *Conquest by Law: How the Discovery of America Dispossessed Indigenous Peoples of Their Land.* New York: Oxford University Press, 2005.

Roediger, David. *The Wages of Whiteness: Race and the Making of the American Working Class.* Rev. ed. New York: Verso, 1999.

Rohrbough, Malcolm J. *The Land Office Business.* New York: Oxford University Press, 1968.

———. *The Trans-Appalachian Frontier: People, Societies, and Institutions, 1775–1850.* New York: Oxford University Press, 1978.

Romero, Lora. "Vanishing Americans." In *The Culture of Sentiment,* ed. Shirley Samuels, 115–27.

Rosberg, Gerald M. "Aliens and Equal Protection: Why Not the Right to Vote?" *Michigan Law Review* 75 (April–May 1977): 1096–97.

Rose, Anne. *Voices of the Marketplace: American Thought and Culture, 1830–1860.* New York: Rowman and Littlefield, 1995.

Rosenzweig, Roy, and David Thelen. *The Presence of the Past: Popular Uses of History in American Life.* New York: Columbia University Press, 1998.

Ruegamer, Lara. *A History of the Indiana Historical Society, 1830–1980.* Indianapolis: Indiana Historical Society, 1980.

Ryan, Mary P. *The Cradle of the Middle Class: The Family in Oneida County, New York, 1790–1865.* New York: Cambridge University Press, 1981.

Rydell, Robert W. *All the World's a Fair: Visions of Empire at American International Expositions, 1876–1916.* Chicago: University of Chicago Press, 1984.

Ryden, Kent C. *Mapping the Invisible Landscape: Folklore, Writing, and the Sense of Place.* Iowa City: University of Iowa Press, 1993.

Sale, Maggie. "Critiques from Within: Antebellum Projects of Resistance." *American Literature* 64 (1992): 695–718.

Salisbury, Neal. *Manitou and Providence: Indians, Europeans, and the Making of New England, 1500–1643.* New York: Oxford University Press, 1982.

Samuels, Shirley. *The Culture of Sentiment: Race, Gender, and Sentimentality in Nineteenth-Century America.* New York: Oxford University Press, 1992.

Sandweiss, Martha. "The Public Life of Western Art." In *Discovered Lands/Invented Pasts,* ed. Jules David Brown et al., 117–34. New Haven: Yale University Press, 1992.

Satz, Ronald N. *American Indian Policy in the Jacksonian Era.* Norman: University of Oklahoma Press, 1975.

Saunt, Claudio. "Telling Stories: The Political Uses of Myth and History in the Cherokee and Creek Nations." *Journal of American History* 93, no. 3 (December 2006): 673–97.

Saxton, Alexander. *The Rise and Fall of the White Republic: Class, Politics, and Mass Culture in Nineteenth-Century America.* New York: Verso, 1990.

Scheckel, Susan. *The Insistence of the Indian: Race and Nationalism in Nineteenth-Century American Culture.* Princeton: Princeton University Press, 1998.

Schlesinger, Arthur, Jr. *The Age of Jackson.* Boston: Little, Brown, 1945.

Scott, Joan W. "Gender: A Useful Category of Historical Analysis." *American Historical Review* 91, no. 5 (December 1986): 1053–75.

Sellers, Charles. *The Market Revolution: Jacksonian America, 1815–1846.* Oxford: Oxford University Press, 1991.

Shackford, James A., and Stanley J. Folmsby, eds. *A Narrative of the Life of David Crockett of the State of Tennessee.* Knoxville: University of Tennessee Press, 1973.

Shammas, Carole. "Anglo-American Household Government in Comparative Perspective." *William and Mary Quarterly* 52, no. 1 (1995): 104–44.

Shannon, Timothy J. "The Ohio Company and the Meaning of Opportunity in the American West, 1786–1795." *New England Quarterly* 64 (September 1991): 393–413.

Shapiro, Michael Edward, Barbara Groseclose, Elizabeth Johns, Paul C. Nagel, and John Wilmerding. *George Caleb Bingham.* New York: Saint Louis Art Museum in Association with Harry N. Abrams, 1990.

Sheehan, Bernard. *Seeds of Extinction: Jeffersonian Philanthropy and the American Indian.* New York: W. W. Norton, 1974.

Sheraton, James P. *Robert John Walker: Politician from Jackson to Lincoln.* New York: Columbia University Press, 1961.

Shoemaker, Nancy, ed. *Clearing a Path: Theorizing the Past in Native American Studies.* New York: Routledge, 2002.

———. *Negotiators of Change: Historical Perspectives on Native American Women.* New York: Routledge, 1995.

Sleeper-Smith, Susan. *Indian Women and French Men: Rethinking Cultural Encounter in the Western Great Lakes.* Amherst: University of Massachusetts Press, 2001.

———. "Resistance to Removal: The 'White Indian,' Frances Slocum." In *Enduring Nations: Native Americans in the Midwest,* ed. R. David Edmunds, 109–23. Urbana: University of Illinois Press, 2008.

———. "'[A]n Unpleasant Transaction on This Frontier': Challenging Female Autonomy and Authority at Michilimackinac." *Journal of the Early Republic* 25 (Fall 2005): 417–43.

———, ed. *Rethinking the Fur Trade: Cultures of Exchange in an Atlantic World.* Lincoln: University of Nebraska Press, 2009.

Slocum, Charles Elihu. *History of Frances Slocum.* Defiance, Ohio: privately published, 1908.

Slotkin, Richard. *Regeneration through Violence: The Mythology of the American Frontier, 1600–1860.* Middletown, Conn.: Wesleyan University Press, 1973.

Smalley, Donald. "The Logansport *Telegraph* and the Monster of the Indiana Lakes." *Indiana Magazine of History* 42 (1946): 249–67.

Smedley, Audrey. *Race in North America: Origins and Evolution of a Worldview.* Boulder: Westview, 1993.

Smith, Andrea. *Conquest: Sexual Violence and American Indian Genocide.* Cambridge, Mass.: South End Press, 2005.

Smith, Dwight L., ed. "The Attempted Potawatomi Emigration of 1839." *Indiana Magazine of History* 45 (1949): 51–80.

———. "An Unsuccessful Negotiation for Removal of the Wyandot Indians from Ohio, 1834." *Ohio Archaeological and Historical Quarterly* 58 (1949): 305–31.

Smith, Henry Nash. *Virgin Land: The American West as Symbol and Myth.* Cambridge, Mass.: Harvard University Press, 1950.

Smith, Robert E. "The Clash of Leadership at the Grand Reserve: The Wyandot Subagency and the Methodist Mission, 1820–1824." *Ohio History* 89, no. 2 (Spring 1980): 181–205.

———. "The Wyandot Exploring Expedition of 1839." *Chronicles of Oklahoma,* Fall 1977, 282–92.

Smith-Rosenberg, Carroll. "Davey Crockett as Trickster: Pornography, Liminality, and Symbolic Inversion in Victorian America." *Journal of Contemporary History* 17, no. 2 (April 1982): 325–50.

———. "Sex as Symbol in Victorian Purity: Ethnohistorical Analysis of Jacksonian America." *American Journal of Sociology* 84: Supplement (1984): 212–47.

Smits, David D. "'Squaw Men,' 'Half-Breeds,' and Amalgamators: Late Nineteenth-Century Anglo-American Attitudes toward Indian-White Race-Mixing." *American Indian Culture and Research Journal* 15, no. 3 (1991): 29–62.

Snyderman, George S. "The Function of Wampum." *Proceedings of the American Philosophical Society* 97 (1954): 469–94.

Sparks, Carol Douglas. "The Land Inaccurate: Navajo Women and the Dialogue of Colonialism, 1821–1870." In *Negotiators of Change,* ed. Nancy Shoemaker. New York: Routledge, 1995.

Speck, Frank G. "The Functions of Wampum among the Eastern Algonkian." *Memoirs of the American Anthropological Association* 6 (1919): 3–74.

Spiess, Philip, II. "Exhibitions and Expositions in 19th-Century Cincinnati." *Cincinnati Historical Society Bulletin* 28 (1970): 171–92.

Snyderman, George S. "The Function of Wampum." *Proceedings of the American Philosophical Society* 97 (1954): 469–94.

Stansell, Christine. *City of Women: Sex and Class in New York, 1789–1865.* New York: Knopf, 1986.

Stanton, William S. *The Leopard's Spots: Scientific Attitudes toward Race in America, 1815–1859.* Chicago: University of Chicago Press, 1960.

Steinfeld, Robert J. "Property and Suffrage in the Early American Republic." *Stanford Law Review* 41 (January 1989): 335–72.

Stocking, George W., Jr. *Race, Culture, and Evolution: Essays in the History of Anthropology.* Chicago: University of Chicago Press, 1968.

Stoler, Ann Laura. *Along the Archival Grain: Epistemic Anxieties and Colonial Common Sense*. Princeton: Princeton University Press, 2009.

——. *Carnal Knowledge and Imperial Power: Race and the Intimate in Colonial Rule*. Berkeley: University of California Press, 2002.

——. *Race and the Education of Desire: Foucault's* History of Sexuality *and* The Colonial Order of Things. Durham: Duke University Press, 1997.

——, ed. *Haunted by Empire: Geographies of Intimacy in North American History*. Durham: Duke University Press, 2006.

Strobel, Margaret. "Gender and Race in the Nineteenth- and Twentieth-Century British Empire." In *Becoming Visible: Women in European History*, 2nd ed., ed. Renate Bridenthal, Claudia Koonz, and Susan M. Stuard, 375–96. Boston: Houghton Mifflin, 1987.

Sugden, John. *Blue Jacket: Warrior of the Shawnees*. Lincoln: University of Nebraska Press, 2000.

——. *Tecumseh: A Life*. New York: Henry Holt, 1997.

Summers, Mark Wahlgren. *The Gilded Age; or, The Hazards of New Functions*. New York: Prentice Hall, 1997.

Tanner, Helen Hornbeck. "The Glaize in 1792: A Composite Indian Community." *Ethnohistory* 25, no. 1 (Winter 1978): 15–39.

——, ed. *Atlas of Great Lakes Indian History*. Norman: Oklahoma University Press, 1987.

Tatter, Henry W. *The Preferential Treatment of the Actual Settler in the Primary Disposition of the Vacant Lands in the United States to 1841*. New York: Arno Press, 1979.

Tawil, Ezra. *The Making of Racial Sentiment: Slavery and the Birth of the Frontier Romance*. New York: Cambridge University Press, 2006.

Taylor, Alan. *Liberty Men and Great Proprietors: The Revolutionary Settlement on the Maine Frontier, 1760–1820*. Chapel Hill: University of North Carolina Press, 1990.

——. *William Cooper's Town: Power and Persuasion on the Frontier of the Early American Republic*. New York: Vintage, 1995.

Taylor, George Rogers, ed. *The Turner Thesis: Concerning the Role of the Frontier in American History*. Boston: D. C. Heath, 1956.

Taylor, Robert M., Jr., ed. *The Northwest Ordinance, 1787: A Bicentennial Handbook*. Indianapolis: Indiana Historical Society, 1987.

Tebbel, John. *A History of Book Publishing in the United States: The Expansion of an Industry, 1865–1919*. 4 vols. New York: R. R. Bowker, 1975.

Thomas, Keith. *Man and the Natural World: A History of the Modern Sensibility*. New York: Pantheon Books, 1983.

Thomas, Nicholas. *Colonialism's Culture: Anthropology, Travel, and Government*. Princeton: Princeton University Press, 1994.

Thrush, Coll. *Native Seattle: Histories from the Crossing-Over Place*. Seattle: University of Washington Press, 2007.

Tilton, Robert. *Pocahontas: The Evolution of an American Narrative*. Cambridge: Cambridge University Press, 1994.

Tobin, Beth Fowkes. "Native Land and Foreign Desire: William Penn's Treaty with the Indians." *American Indian Culture and Research Journal* 19, no. 3 (1995): 87–120.

Trachtenberg, Alan. *The Incorporation of America: Culture and Society in the Gilded Age*. New York: Hill and Wang, 1982.

———. *Shades of Hiawatha: Staging Indians, Making Americans, 1880–1930*. New York: Hill and Wang, 2004.

Trask, Kerry A. *Black Hawk: The Battle for the Heart of America*. New York: Henry Holt, 2007.

Treat, Payson Jackson. *The National Land System, 1785–1820*. New York: E. B. Treat, 1910.

Trowbridge, C. C. "Meeārmeear Traditions." In *Occasional Contributions from the Museum of Anthropology of the University of Michigan, no. 7*. Ann Arbor: University of Michigan Press, 1938.

———. "Shawnee Traditions." In *Occasional Contributions from the Museum of Anthropology of the University of Michigan, no. 9*. Ann Arbor: University of Michigan Press, 1939.

Truettner, William H. *The Natural Man Observed: A Study of Catlin's Indian Gallery*. Washington, D.C.: Smithsonian Institution Press in Cooperation with the Amon Carter Museum of Western Art and the National Collection of Fine Arts, 1979.

Tuan, Yi-Fu. *Space and Place: The Perspective of Experience*. Minneapolis: University of Minnesota Press, 1977.

Turner, Frederick. *Beyond Geography: The Western Spirit against the Wilderness*. New York: Viking Press, 1980.

Ulrich, Laura Thatcher. *Good Wives: Image and Reality in the Lives of Women in Northern New England, 1650–1750*. New York: Knopf, 1982.

———. *A Midwife's Tale: The Life of Martha Ballard, Based on Her Diary, 1785–1812*. New York: Vintage, 1991.

Valenčius, Conevery Bolton. *The Health of the Country: How American Settlers Understood Themselves and Their Land*. New York: Basic Books, 2002.

VanDerBeets, Richard. *The Indian Captivity Narrative: An American Genre*. New York: University Press of America, 1984.

Van Kirk, Sylvia. "From 'Marrying-In' to 'Marrying-Out': Changing Patterns of Aboriginal/Non-Aboriginal Marriage in Colonial Canada." *Frontiers: A Journal of Women Studies* 23, no. 3 (2002): 1–11.

———. *Many Tender Ties: Women in Fur-Trade Society, 1670–1870*. Norman: University of Oklahoma Press, 1980.

Van Tassel, David. *Recording America's Past: An Interpretation of the Development of Historical Studies in America, 1607–1884*. Chicago: University of Chicago Press, 1960.

Viola, Herman J. *Thomas L. McKenney: Architect of America's Early Indian Policy, 1816–1830.* Chicago: Swallow Press, 1974.

Viola, Herman J., H. B. Crothers, and Maureen Hannan. "The American Indian Genre Paintings of Catlin, Stanley, Wimar, Eastman, and Miller." In *American Frontier Life: Early Western Paintings and Prints,* ed. Ron Tyler et al., 131–66. New York: Abbeville Press, 1987.

Wallace, Anthony F. C. *The Death and Rebirth of the Seneca.* New York: Alfred Knopf, 1970.

———. *Jefferson and the Indians: The Tragic Fate of the First Americans.* Cambridge: Cambridge University Press, 1999.

———. *The Long, Bitter Trail: Andrew Jackson and the Indians.* New York: Hill and Wang, 1993.

Walsh, Martin W. "The 'Heathen Party': Methodist Observation of the Ohio Wyandot." *American Indian Quarterly* 16, no. 2 (Spring 1992): 189–202.

Warren, Stephen. *The Shawnee and Their Neighbors, 1795–1870.* Urbana: University of Illinois Press, 2005.

Welter, Barbara. "The Cult of True Womanhood, 1820–1860." *American Quarterly* 18 (1963): 151–74.

Welter, Rush. "The Idea of Progress in America: An Essay in Ideas and Method." *Journal of the History of Ideas* 16, no. 3 (June 1955): 401–15.

Weslager, C. A. *The Delaware Indians: A History.* New Brunswick, N.J.: Rutgers University Press, 1972.

Westrick, Paul. "The Race to Assimilate: The Wyandot Indians in White Ohio." *Northwest Ohio History* 75, no. 2 (2004): 123–48.

White, Hayden. *Metahistory: The Historical Imagination in Nineteenth-Century Europe.* Baltimore: Johns Hopkins University Press, 1973.

White, Richard. "The Fictions of Patriarchy: Indians and Whites in the Early Republic." In *Native Americans,* ed. Frederick Hoxie, Ronald Hoffman, and Peter J. Albert. Charlottesville: Published for the United States Capitol Historical Society by the University Press of Virginia, 1999.

———. *Land Use, Environment, and Social Change: The Shaping of Island County Washington.* Seattle: University of Washington Press, 1980.

———. *The Middle Ground: Indians, Empires, and Republics in the Great Lakes Region, 1650–1815.* Cambridge: Cambridge University Press, 1991.

———. "Mutual Misunderstandings and New Understandings." In *Rethinking the Fur Trade: Cultures of Exchange in an Atlantic World,* ed. Susan Sleeper-Smith. Lincoln: University of Nebraska Press, 2009.

———. *The Roots of Dependency: Subsistence, Environment, and Social Change among the Choctaws, Pawnees, and Navajos.* Lincoln: University of Nebraska Press, 1983.

Wiebe, Robert H. *The Search for Order, 1877–1920.* New York: Hill and Wang, 1967.

314 BIBLIOGRAPHY

Wiegman, Robyn. *American Anatomies: Theorizing Race and Gender.* Durham: Duke University Press, 1995.

Wilentz, Sean. "Property and Power: Suffrage Reform in the United States, 1787–1860." In *Voting and the Spirit of American Democracy,* ed. Donald W. Rogers, 31–42. Urbana: University of Illinois Press, 1992.

———. *The Rise of American Democracy: Jefferson to Lincoln.* New York: W. W. Norton, 2005.

Wilkins, David E., and K. Tsianina Lomawaima. *Uneven Ground: American Indian Sovereignty and Federal Law.* Norman: University of Oklahoma Press, 2001.

Williams, Hermann Warner, Jr. *Mirror to the American Past: A Survey of American Genre Painting, 1750–1900.* Greenwich, Conn.: New York Graphic Society, 1973.

Williams, Robert A., Jr. *Linking Arms Together: American Treaty Visions of Law and Peace, 1600–1800.* Oxford: Oxford University Press, 1997.

Williamson, Chilton. "American Suffrage and Sir William Blackstone." *Political Science Quarterly* 68, no. 4 (December 1953): 552–57.

Wilson, Denise Marie. "Vincennes: From French Colonial Village to American Frontier Town, 1730–1820." Ph.D. diss., West Virginia University, 1997.

Wilson, Frazer E. *Around the Council Fire: Proceedings at Fort Green Ville in 1795.* Greenville, Ohio: Privately printed, 1945.

———. *The Peace of Mad Anthony: An Account of the Subjugation of the North-Western Indian Tribes and the Treaty of Greenville.* Greenville, Ohio: Charles R. Kemble Book and Job Printer, 1907.

Winger, Otho. *The Last of the Miamis.* North Manchester, Ind.: privately printed, 1935.

Wolfley, Jeanette. "Jim Crow, Indian Style: The Disfranchisement of Native Americans." *American Indian Law Review* 16 (1991): 167–202.

Worster, Donald. *Rivers of Empire: Water, Aridity, and the Growth of the American West.* New York: Pantheon, 1985.

Yagelski, Robert. "A Rhetoric of Contact: Tecumseh and the Native American Confederacy." *Rhetoric Review* 14, no. 1 (Autumn 1995): 64–77.

Year Book of the Society of Indiana Pioneers, 1937. Indianapolis: Printed by Order of the Board of Governors, 1937.

Young, Alfred F., ed. *Beyond the American Revolution: Explorations in the History of American Radicalism.* DeKalb: Northern Illinois University Press, 1993.

Acknowledgments

The ideas for *Winning the West with Words* began many years ago at Bowling Green State University, where Edmund Danziger, Liette Gidlow, and Scott Martin introduced me to the study of history as a profession. Those thoughts matured at Purdue University, where Elliot Gorn, Charles Cutter, Nancy Gabin, Joseph Dorsey, and Donna Akers led seminars that greatly shaped the way I view issues of race, gender, and identity. Although I never took a course from James Farr, he expertly navigated me through a minor field in cultural theory and routinely schooled me on the basketball court. My dissertation committee provided excellent direction in the form of written comments, coffee shop discussions, and hallway conversations. In particular, Frank Lambert and Carrie Janney warrant credit for suggesting that Frances Slocum deserved a space of her own in the final story.

I am amazed how authorship is both a local and global experience. Ideas conceived at a desk in West Lafayette, Indiana, matured at conferences and workshops across the country (and were written and rewritten at desks in Ohio, Indiana, Illinois, the District of Columbia, and Oklahoma). Purdue University's affiliation with the CIC American Indian Studies program and the D'Arcy McNickle Center created opportunities for me to share research with scholars from across the nation. It also allowed me to take a semester-long course with Susan Sleeper-Smith, who acted as a surrogate adviser on American Indian Studies and introduced me to the wonderful collections at the Tippecanoe County Historical Association. In working with the CIC American Indian Studies program, I met a wonderful cadre of scholars who greatly shaped this manuscript and my ideas about Native American history, including Brian Hosmer, Jean O'Brien, Jacki Rand, Ray Fogelson, and Raymond DeMallie. Particular parts of this book owe their insights to the helpful suggestions of individuals at conferences, brown-bag discussions, and seminar workshops. At a graduate conference hosted by the University of North Carolina at Charlotte, Dan Dupre asked valuable questions about the premise behind chapter 1 and encouraged me to focus on the use of historical memory as a tool of colonialism. I presented my initial thoughts on George Winter as part of a workshop at the McNeil Center for Early American Studies, where Daniel Richter kindly suggested that all of my initial conclusions about Winter were wrong. Additional research and reflection proved him right, and the chapter on Winter's work is greatly improved because of his advice. At that same workshop, Sarah Rivett asked tough questions about my methodology and attempts to employ literary criticism. Brian Luskey took copious notes and kindly shared them with me afterward; they served as the basis for revising the chapter on the artist. At a meeting of the American Society for Ethnohistory, both Nancy Shoemaker and Alyssa Mt. Pleasant helped me think more seriously about Winter's story of the Lake Monster. Philip Deloria commented on a paper about William Walker at the Western History Association and convinced me that chapter 3, which was not in the dissertation, was worth adding to the manuscript. I reworked those ideas and presented them at a meeting of the Society for Historians of the Early American Republic where Sarah Miller provided additional, valuable suggestions. At the 2009 meeting of the American Society for Ethnohistory, Coll Thrush generously provided encouragement during a brief conversation about how his work had influenced my own.

Alfred Cave generously read the dissertation after its completion, and Andrew Cayton undertook the unenviable task of reading the manuscript multiple times before its final publication. In the end, they both provided important critiques that guided the revisions from dissertation to book manuscript. Brittany Bayless read the chapter on Frances Slocum before it appeared in *Frontiers: A Journal of Women Studies*; her friendly critique has made me a better writer and greatly contributed to both the style and the prose of this book. Ruth Herndon read chapters 5, 6, and 7 and provided advice and much-needed support, while Steven

Ortiz read an early version of chapter 3 and helped guide my thoughts on late-nineteenth-century veterans' organizations. Robert Owens read the entire manuscript and caught some potentially embarrassing errors; he also suggested important historiographical connections that have enhanced the final product.

Two individuals deserve special recognition. Cathleen Cahill (perhaps unknowingly) read more than her fair share of this book, as she commented on papers at numerous conferences. Additionally, she provided essential suggestions as guest editor for the version of chapter 5 that appeared in a special issue of *Frontiers*. The University of Nebraska Press graciously allowed me to reprint a version of "'They found and left her an Indian': Gender, Race, and the Whitening of Young Bear" from *Frontiers* as the chapter on Frances Slocum. C. Joseph Genetin-Pilawa has provided feedback on literally every page of this book. Nearly a decade and a half ago we met as undergraduates who shared an interest in studying the past. Defying all logic and ignoring family and friends who questioned the practicality of a college degree in history, we both became history professors.

The process of writing one's first book is fraught with challenges and feelings of inadequacy. I feel fortunate to have undertaken this process with the expert staff at the University of Oklahoma Press, especially Alessandra Jacobi Tamulevich and Steven Baker. They both have been wonderful in providing assistance and much-needed encouragement. Elaine Otto's astute eye for detail proved crucial in the copyediting stage. At Oklahoma City University, student Robert Oxford helped with the challenging task of compiling the index.

Historical manuscripts cannot be written without the aid of talented librarians and archivists. Scott Forsyth at the Great Lakes branch of the National Archives and Records Administration introduced me to the dusty, brittle register books of the General Land Office and unknowingly witnessed the genesis of this entire project. Nan Card of the Rutherford B. Hayes Presidential Library led me to President Hayes's personal collection of early-nineteenth-century travel journals and books on midwestern history—a collection well known to Gilded Age historians but often neglected by scholars of early America. Paul Schueler, formerly of the Tippecanoe County Historical Association, guided me (sometimes item by item) through the George Winter Papers and helped decipher the collection's cryptic cataloging system. Kathy Atwell, the current executive director of the TCHA, helped track down images and gain permissions for much of George Winter's artwork reproduced in the book. Mark Vopelak and Brent Abercrombie helped find invaluable collections at the Indiana State Library's manuscript division. Mark and Brent tracked down and scanned images for the manuscript and made the many months in the manuscript reading room enjoyable. Pam Bennett of the Indiana Historical Bureau shared her knowledge of the history of the organization and plans for the state's upcoming bicentennial. Steve Charter at the Center for Archival Collections at Bowling Green State University proved extremely helpful in introducing me to the center's impressive collection on Ohio and Wyandot history.

In addition, the staffs at the Beinecke Library at Yale, Houghton Library at Harvard, Newberry Library in Chicago, Indiana Historical Society, Lily Library at Indiana University, Ohio Historical Society, Syracuse University Special Collections, Smithsonian Institution archives, Chicago Historical Society, Michigan State University Special Collections, and Purdue University Interlibrary Loan Office (who probably were relieved when I finished ordering rolls of midwestern newspapers on microfilm) all proved instrumental in completing research for the book.

This book also could not have been completed without the financial support of numerous institutions. The Purdue Research Foundation provided two years of nonservice funding at the dissertation research phase, allowing me to glean countless collections without the pressures of teaching. Additionally, the Department of History at Purdue University provided a Woodman travel grant to conduct research at the Newberry Library. The CIC American Indian Studies consortium helped pay for research in archives across the Midwest and provided me a scholarly home at the Newberry Library. The Bowling Green State University Department of History funded travel to conferences and archives while I served as a visiting instructor. In the final stages of research and drafting, the Oklahoma Humanities Council provided a short-term grant that enabled me to spend three weeks in Indianapolis tying up loose ends. Oklahoma City University's Faculty Scholarship Committee provided additional funding for conferences and archival work in the final months of research and revising, while the Office of Academic Affairs supplied funding for many of the images that appear in the book.

More than any other individual, John Larson has shaped the book in your hands. He has served as an able academic adviser, gentle critic, and deft editor. Nearly a decade ago he cornered me at a graduate conference and persuaded me to enter this profession. Since then, he has guided me through a graduate program and commented more times than any human should on this book. I am proud to call him a mentor and friend.

I also have been extremely lucky to have been surrounded by an amazing group of friends and colleagues who have shaped my scholarship and academic training over the years, including Ryan Anderson, Megan Birk, Amy Bosworth, Andrew Busch, Cullen Chandler, Blue Clark, Larry Cousineau, Pierre Cyr, Mohamed Daadaoui, Doug and Amy Dean, David R. Haus, Chris and Sheila Johnston, Dennis Jowaisas, Michelle Patterson, Scott Randolph, Jeremy and Elizabeth Schneider, Renee Searfoss, Adam Stanley, Tina Thomas, Dave Welky, and DeeDee Wentland.

Ultimately this book could not have been completed without the unwavering support of family and friends. I want especially to thank Ken and Sandy Buss, Kevin Buss, Charles and Tonya Buss, Jonah Buss, and Robert and JoAnn Brinkman.

Index

Chapman, John Gadsby, 129
Chillicothe (Ohio), 212–13, 215
Cincinnati, 65, 98, 124, 126;
    Centennial Exposition, 190–192;
    industrial fairs, 189–91; statements
    by Indian chiefs in local newspapers,
    35–36
Cincinnati Board of Trade, 189–90
Clark, George Rogers, 2, 53;
    remembered, 218
Clemens, Samuel (Mark Twain), 201
Coburn, Gen. John, 183
Conklin, Julia, 200–201
Conn, Steven, 107, 205
Conner, John, 28, 34
Corydon, Ind., 53
Cott, Nancy, 156
Cottman, George, 109; and *Indiana
    Quarterly Magazine of History*, 183
County histories, 183–188, 202–209;
    Brown County (Ohio), 206; Darke
    County (Ohio), 208; Defiance
    (Ohio), 186; Hardin County
    (Ohio), 206; *History of Allen County*
    (Ind.), 205–206; *History of Franklin
    and Pickaway Counties* (Ohio), 202;
    History of Logan County (Ohio), 209;
    romanticism, 187–88
County history publishers: Appleton
    Company, 186; Charles C. Chapman
    and Company, 186; Inter-State
    Publishing, 186–87; J. P. Lippincott,
    186; Lewis Publishing Company,
    187; Williams Brothers Publishing,
    186
Cowen, Benjamin Rush, 215
Crockett, Davy, 59–60
Cuming, Fortescue (travel writer), 43
Cutler, Manasseh (Ohio Company),
    45, 178

Deaf Man (Che-por-on-wah), 153,
    156–58
Deaf Man's Village, 134–36, 138–43,
    145, 147, 151–54, 158, 263n46

Dearborn, Henry, 27
Delaware Indians: capture of
    Frances Slocum, 154; dispute of
    1804 Treaty of Vincennes, 26–27;
    fictive relationship with Shawnee,
    22; Treaty of Fort Wayne, 33–34;
    turning over criminals, 30–31; use
    of oratory, 22
Depauw, John, 52, 243n49
Deunquot (Wyandot chief), 88
Devil's Lake, 110, 115–16, 119
Dillon, John Brown, 105, 108, 110,
    166, 183, 200, 210; definition of
    "pioneering," 173; death, 174;
    "father of Indiana history," 200;
    influence on other writers, 200–
    201; and Lake Monster, 110; and
    Pioneer Association of Indiana,
    171–74; "The National Decline of
    the Miami Indians," 198–99
D-Mouche-kee-kee-awh (Miami
    woman), 99
Doughty, John, 43
Downing, Major Jack, 59–60
Ducoigne (Kaskaskia chief), 28
Duncan, Robert, 183
Dunn, Jacob Piatt, 183; and history of
    Indiana State Seal, 179–80

Earll, R. Edward, 194
Edgar, John, 54–56
Edgerton, Alfred, 167–69, 186
Edmunds, R. David, 99, 137, 161
Eel River Indians, Treaty of Fort
    Wayne, 33–34; villages destroyed by
    Americans, 40–41
Elliott, Reverend Charles, 85, 89
English, Elizabeth (Mrs. Dennis
    Pennington), 53
English, William Hayden, 179,
    182–83
Evans, Mariah (Mrs. Solon
    Robinson), 65
Ewing, George, 134–35
Ewing, Thomas, 61–62, 180–82